W9-BVR-352

Discovery and Exploration

Doubleday & Company, Inc. Garden City, New York

Discovery and Exploration

an Atlas-History of Man's Wanderings

Frank Debenham

introduction by Edward Shackleton

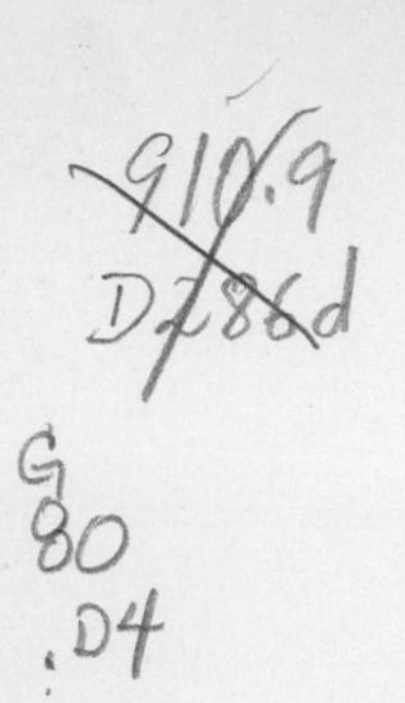

Contents

Wolfgang Foges EDITOR-IN-CHIEF
Roy A. Gallant EDITORIAL ADVISER
Harriet Cole ART DIRECTOR
Shirley Carpenter GEOGRAPHICAL DIRECTOR
Dorothy Woodman RESEARCH

Library of Congress Catalog Card Number 60-13382

Printed in Germany by Chr. Belser, Stuttgart

About this book

Discovery and Exploration is a sweeping statement in words and images about man's sometimes haphazard but more often deliberate discovery of his planet. Our story begins about 50,000 years ago, when men became fairly skilled tool makers, and progresses systematically to present-day efforts at space exploration.

Maps of several different kinds appear throughout this book. Beginning with the front endpaper and concluding with the back endpaper are five large summary maps showing by means of relief coloring those parts of the world which were known up to A.D. 150, 1420, and 1550. The unknown regions are always shown in indigo, hence it is fitting that the front endpaper is entirely indigo, for our story begins in the dark past of prehistory. Although the back endpaper is in full relief coloring, showing the present world fully explored, this is not entirely true. There are still a few regions of our planet that have never been penetrated by man, although they have been photographed from the air—for example, regions of Antarctica, the central mountains of New Guinea, parts of the Amazon and African jungles, the Greenland icecap, and northwest Siberia. These are remote, inaccessible areas still to be examined at close hand by man.

Another group of color maps, one appearing at the end of each major section of the book, shows the successive stages of penetration of each continent. There are also sixteen route maps tracing the voyages and journeys of famous explorers; and six globes show migration routes of peoples from earliest times. Eight other maps show areas of special interest, regions such as Tibet, the Andes, and the Amazon Basin, where the physical characteristics of the land have made exploration exceptionally difficult.

Although our story of exploration ends with the section describing I.G.Y. activities in the Antarctic, the reader will find a substantial appendix which will add to the usefulness and enjoyment of this book. The section beginning on page 214 presents capsule biographical material about each explorer mentioned in the text, together with small route maps which show the life travels of each man. Only the routes of those explorers whose travels are shown on the large route maps in the book proper are omitted from the appendix. Two other special sections—one on ships and navigation, the other on space exploration—also appear in the appendix.

A final note: the Gall projection used for the five summary maps produces increasing distortion in directions away from the Equator, hence the Antarctic Continent appears much larger than it actually is, larger even than Asia; in reality it is only about the size of Africa north of the Equator.

Why man explores

The main Eskimo settlement in northwest Greenland, Thule, the headquarters of a small tribe of Eskimos who once helped me in a journey to Ellesmere Island, is today a major airbase. If you land from an aircraft you are met by a jeep or taxi, and the routes over which we once struggled with sledges, taking about three weeks to cover 500 miles, are frequently being flown by American and Canadian aircraft in little more than an hour.

The same is true of Borneo. Lands that we looked longingly at from mountain peaks have now been successfully worked by scientists with the aid of aircraft.

But discovery and exploration are not simply a matter of flying over a bit of unexplored territory. Nor, indeed, were some of those huge blank areas, or fanciful lands, on early maps unknown to all men. Great areas of the world were, in fact, discovered and explored long before explorers from civilized lands, out to discover new worlds, ever visited them. It is only in the great desert regions of the world that civilized explorers have sometimes been the first men to set foot, and this is true particularly in the polar regions of the great Antarctic and Greenland icecaps.

The earliest travelers and explorers were primitive men spreading out across the earth they were to inherit. Man has always been inquisitive. Sometimes he has crept, and sometimes he has marched boldly to the limit of his known environment; then some have been courageous enough to risk going beyond. Others, on different occasions, have been driven by hostile tribes into unexplored and even uninhabited country, and so, age by age, man has advanced and populated the earth.

Early man had little to guide him and little to help him. The discovery and settlement of New Zealand were achieved in simple canoes by a people traveling without aid of compass and with only the stars to guide them across great oceans. Some settlements may even have resulted from lost and drifting travelers, like the lone Eskimo who once reached the north of Scotland in his kayak.

The real story of discovery and exploration begins with those early travelers who went in search of trade, who felt compelled to disseminate religious ideas, and who wanted to claim new lands for the glory of their country. Yet many explorers have set out without such apparent motives, and if we ask *why* these particular men went traveling, we might just as well ask why man undertakes anything. Sometimes they went out of simple curiosity, which is the basis of sientific exploration today. Certainly some of the very early travelers were men of curiosity who were seeking knowledge for its own sake. It is this striving to know, this inquisitiveness that lies deep in man's nature that has been a mainspring of discovery and exploration.

Although the methods of exploration have changed a great deal over the years, their change has not always been so startling as one might expect. Aircraft and Sno-Cats have not yet taken the place of the age-old dog team of the Eskimo, nor has the camel been entirely displaced by the land rover, the jeep, or tractor. Much travel in tropical regions, and indeed in many other parts of the world, is still done on foot.

In the last resort, the scientific work which today is the main excuse and justification for exploration has to be done not in rapid movement but in slow stages—men browsing along, picking up essential knowledge, hitting the rocks with hammers to find out the kind of history hidden in that particular part of the earth's surface, observing the flora and fauna, collecting and comparing specimens found in different areas, and gradually forming a picture of life on earth, past and present. Of course, too, the map makers are key figures in exploration today. The twentieth-century surveyor with his theodolite and his chronometers is aided by wireless sets which give him accurate time and thus enable him to measure longitude more easily than his predecessors with clumsier instruments could.

The new techniques of exploration depend more on the group than on the individual, but not necessarily the big group. The Antarctic expeditions with icebreakers, aircraft, and every other type of modern equipment are not *typical* of the modern approach to discovery and exploration. There is still the small party, even the one-man expedition, the man who must go off and do survey work and finds himself amid the glaciers of South Georgia. The university expeditions that every year go out to fill in a little more detail of the earth's surface add usefully to our scientific knowledge.

While explorers have been diverse people on a national level, they have also differed widely as individuals: men from secure homes, men from very insecure backgrounds, and sometimes those who just found themselves for no reason at all along for the trip, and others caught up and fired by a sudden flash of imagination which has rescued them from a humdrum background.

In the last hundred and fifty years particularly, many explorers have carried the flags of their countries, seeking to claim the territory they discovered. This was true of the Antarctic, but today national sovereignty seems to be weakening. Let us hope that a "sovereignty of mankind" may one day replace the jealousies and politics underlying national sovereignty. The urges to find new lands for one's country, and claim them, are no longer likely to play the part that they have in the past.

Exploration of our planet grows stronger rather than weaker, for more people than ever before are examining more bits of it and there is still much more to be explored in detail. The great ocean depths have hardly been touched; the science of oceanography is much newer than the science of geography, of which it is just a part. The oceans may yield remarkable knowledge, and explorers will, sooner or later, be as at home on the sea floor as they are on the Antarctic plateau. The same can be said of discovery outside our planet. Already the first movement of mankind into space is being planned, and man's instruments are hurtling in the depths of what hitherto has been forbidden territory. The techniques of travel on the moon may not be so very different from the techniques evolved in the Antarctic—Sno-Cats creeping over the surface, observing as they go along.

All of this adds up to a tremendous and comprehensive story of one aspect of human activity, and it has its own message. The message is that while man today has the same urges that he has had throughout his history, he will continue to discover and to explore, possibly even to the farthest galaxies thousands of millions of light-years away, for as a species man has thousands of millions of years, unless he destroys himself, in which to develop and to move and to discover and to explore.

Shackleton

Man learns to explore

Our common ancestor, from whom man and the primates sprang, was a creature of the trees. We know little of his habits, but we may suppose that at some moment in the remote past he left the forest and ventured onto the open plains. When he took this step, the most significant in human history, he made the first move toward his ultimate destiny, that of becoming man.

In appearance he resembled the great apes and the smaller lemurs. He could stand upright and walk, after a fashion, on two legs. His eyes looked straight ahead, and since he was no longer compelled to use his upper limbs as feet, he put them to other uses. Gradually they assumed a shape which was to become the most remarkable of all tools—the hand of modern man.

No evidence remains to tell us of his earliest struggles. When did he learn to reflect on his experience and so develop foresight? With nothing but his bare hands, a stick, or a stone, he learned to hunt the animals of the plains and so was able to add flesh to his main diet of nuts, fruits, seeds, and roots, which had served him in his forest days and which serve him to this day. Unlike many of the animals around him, man learned to be carnivorous.

In search of this exciting new food he moved in small groups from hunting ground to hunting ground. His skills were few. In common with apes and monkeys he knew that a nut too hard for his teeth could be cracked with a stone, but thousands of years passed before he began to shape the stone into a more serviceable tool. Throughout that long unrecorded period he had wandered far from his original homes.

At one time it was thought that man originated in central Asia, and this might still prove to be true, but at different periods he may also have evolved elsewhere. There is evidence that subhuman man existed in Europe, China, Java, India, and Africa; and by the time he had reached a fairly well advanced tool-making stage, some fifty thousand years ago, Stone Age man had appeared on all continents except Antarctica and possibly the Americas.

But at the time of his first emergence from the forests he was, to a large extent, as much tied to a particular district and climate as were the animals around him. But about a million years ago he made two momentous discoveries which were to lift him far above all other creatures. He learned how to use the sharp cutting edge of a stone or animal bone as a knife or weapon. He also learned how to use fire. With these two skills he began to shape his own future and climb the long, slow ascent to civilization.

He endured devastating changes of climate and wandered over wide areas of the globe, meeting friend and foe in other groups of his kind. Defenseless, he had to flee from animals of great size—mammoth, lion, and saber-toothed tiger. And to these terrors were added the dangers of the increasing cold, as ice from the mountains began to descend and the great icecap crept foot by foot from the polar regions of the north to cover the greater part of northern Europe, northwest Asia, and the northern part of North America. Before it primitive man had to retreat. Without the skill of building, he was forced to find shelter in caves, where he and his descendants remained for thousands of years.

At this stage he knew that stone could cut wood, that friction could make fire, and that a hollow log was more buoyant than a solid one. He could hunt; he could cook food. As a protection against the cold he wore animal skins fashioned into clothing. He is known to us as Early Stone Age man.

Map shows the probable maximum extent of glaciation during the Quaternary period in the Northern Hemisphere. As the great ice sheets advanced, man was forced to retreat before them.

Within a period of less than a million years the ice advanced and retreated four times. Human bones found in rocks which were ice covered during the first three advances have been found, but of what manner of man, no one knows. It was not until about the last warm interval, not less than 50,000 years ago, that man developed refined stone tools, superior to those developed by his ancestors 500,000 years ago. Paleolithic man, in northern Europe especially, was far enough advanced to observe the qualities of different kinds of stone. He discovered that some hard stones would not splinter but would chip or split softer ones, which in turn could be fashioned into hand axes. No longer did he have to rely on the sharp edge of an accidentally splintered stone; he could make and repair his own. But this craftsmanship required many generations to evolve, and during all that time man wandered, drifting through Africa, into Europe, and across Asia.

Tools of the Middle Stone Age included implements which could do the work of chisels, hammers, drills, polishers, and scrapers. To these man added small arrowheads and knives made from the chips flaked from his larger tools. From splintered bone or ivory he made points for his spears and needles to sew animal skins. He made a throwing stick to send his spear farther than it would go with the aid of his arm alone, and he invented the bow and arrow. With the dawning power of invention he leapt ahead of all other living things.

The invention of tools requires imagination, and with this slow awakening of the mind, primitive man made some astonishing advances. He became articulate, inventing sounds which had a meaning, and he made a house-place of his cave to which he could return. From scratching marks in the ground, on rocks, or on trees to show him the way home or to some good hunting ground, his hand began to record what his eye saw. Throughout these long periods man continued to wander. Repeated over centuries, his journeys widened his horizon and altered his way of living by exposing him to different environments. As his inventive skills improved, he was able to go farther afield to explore the miles of land or water that lay around him. Exploration has depended always on the tools man has been able to invent. Indeed, it is man's development as an artificer that forms the background of his discovery of the world.

Asia is regarded as the heartland of the world. All other continents radiate from it—Europe and Africa as peninsulas and the Americas and Australia as near peninsulas, perhaps even once true peninsulas if theories of land bridges are accepted. Excluding Antarctica, modern man has not yet discovered any large tract of land without finding that primitive man had already been there.

In that sense the world was discovered long before the great expeditions with which this book is mainly concerned. Properly speaking, it should be entitled *Rediscovery and Re-exploration*, for who knows how often man in his wanderings has thought he has found new territory for the first time? No one will ever know, for no records have been found.

At this stage in our story we might do well to pause for a moment and attempt to put the terms Paleolithic and Neolithic man in their proper order. The "Age of Stone," the first cultural stage in man's progress, overlapped with the great Ice Age and lasted in some places for nearly a hundred thousand years. It can be roughly divided into three phases, each representing a distinct stage in the development and achievement of early man. The Early and Middle Stone Ages are described as belonging to Paleolithic times. Neolithic is the name given to the Late Stone Age; in some places—the Eastern Mediterranean, for example—this is thought to have lasted from about 5000 B.C. to about 3000 B.C.

Generally speaking, when we talk of Stone Age man we are apt to describe Paleolithic or Neolithic man as he appeared in Europe. This is because more archeological evidence of his emergence has come to light in that part of the world than in any other. That man has lived through a Stone Age at different times in different places is beyond doubt. Until this century some isolated groups of men were still living in Stone Age conditions. North American Indians, for example, were, until instructed by the European invader, making fire by friction. The aborigine of Australia, even today, is near to the Stone Age man of Neolithic times.

The reasons for early man's journeying and his dispersal over great distances may be summed up in two words, "food" and "fear." Living entirely, as he did, on the natural roots and fruits of the earth and on what other animals he could kill, he had to go where such food was to be found, and farther still as his numbers increased and his needs multiplied, or as changes of climate affected his food supplies. The slow advancing and retreating of the ice and the resulting climatic changes altered the distribution of vegetation and the animal life associated with it, so that the search for food often took man farther and farther from his early centers of origin. In times of great scarcity the strongest groups alone can have survived. Only man's imaginative powers and inventive skills, which enabled him to outwit hostile environments, prevented his total extinction.

In the long run, perhaps, it was fear more than the search for food which was the chief motive for man's moving on to the farthest limits that he could reach. In prehistory, as in history, man's greatest enemy has been man himself. It seems certain that most of early man's travels—his dispersal, in fact—were due to pressure from behind: natural catastrophes and persecution of the weaker by the stronger, fears leading to flight.

Before man knew that other groups of men existed, and before the need to defend his tribe from other tribes had become part of the pattern of primitive man's life, he had become a thinking creature, and with thought came curiosity. But not an idle, animal curiosity; it was curiosity with a motive, a desire to expand his knowledge and so make his life

Men of the Old Stone Age relied on simple tools such as this hand axe, found in Swanscombe, Kent.

Lascaux cave drawing of a wounded bison, intended to bring Stone Age hunters good luck.

a better one. As his intelligence developed, early man's desire for knowledge acted as a spur to send him forth to discover the world, but a world so vast that his uninformed imagination could not give him a glimmer of the wonders that lay beyond the slow horizon.

With what feelings did early man take his first cautious steps into lands he did not know? When he stood on the threshold of the exploration of the land or sat in his hollowed-out log and paddled out to sea, were his hopes and fears those we in the twentieth century feel as we take our first cautious steps into space? Not really. There is a fundamental difference. Today man explores not as a solitary individual but as a member of an expedition of specialists. David G. Simons, the American Air Force officer who rose to 102,000 feet in the sealed cabin of a balloon, has no counterpart in Stone Age man. Without dozens of specialists in the fields of metallurgy, physiology, chemistry, and engineering the courageous Simons could never have made his flight. The statistical assurance of his success was lacking in Stone Age man's exploration.

If we met Stone Age man today we would hardly recognize him as "man" at all; to us he would be more like an ape who had somehow learned to fashion rough weapons. Yet he was man, and a man whose imagination taught him not only how to communicate information to others by speech or picture, but to venture forth into a vast and unknown world. But primitive man did not have a record of past experience to help him. His knowledge of the world beyond his immediate environment was more terrifying than is ours of the space beyond our planet.

In the main, Paleolithic man was a hunter-collector, and as such still very much of a wanderer, although the people of later Paleolithic times often dwelt in caves, generally in hilly districts, to which they repeatedly returned, and in which collections of animal bones and shells show signs of long occupation.

Stone tools at much the same stage of development have been found in many parts of Europe, in Palestine, on the high grasslands of Central Africa and in southwest Asia. This may, of course, suggest parallel development, but it does not rule out the possibility of there having been some contact between various Stone Age groups, particularly during the Ice Ages, when at the peak periods of the ice advance the old and the new worlds were very nearly a single continent, sea level having been lowered by hundreds of feet by the extraction of water. The Mediterranean was then not the long arm of ocean that it now is but one, or possibly two, large lakes, the eastern one of fresh water overflowing into the western. For the same reasons, the nearer islands of the East Indies may have been part of the Asiatic continent, and northeast Asia and Alaska may have been much closer in the past.

Gray tone over sea represents land above sea level during the end of the last ice age. These "land bridges" enabled peoples to migrate from one region to another.

Our picture of Paleolithic man can be drawn only from slender evidence, mostly from things dropped in the rubbish heaps of his camps or caves—stone tools, carvings on bone and ivory, drawings on cave walls, and debris from his fires. It would seem that about 50,000 years ago part of the world was inhabited very thinly by groups of this subhuman species of man. He was a hardy hunter and a great wanderer, traveling in families or small bands wherever his quarry led him and, with no competition as a spur, improving his inventions very slowly indeed. In Europe and Asia the hard conditions under which he lived saved him from invasion until the end of the Ice Age when, with the coming of a warmer climate, in southern Europe at any rate, new peoples arrived, probably traveling from eastern Mediterranean lands across the narrow gaps or land bridges then at Gibraltar and Sicily.

A woman gathering honey, (cave art from the Middle Stone Age in Spain).

These newcomers were certainly human by our standards. They were far superior in numbers, in size, and in their techniques, and culturally they had probably already reached the New Stone Age. Their strength was supreme, and they exterminated or drove out or totally absorbed the subhumans, of whom we have no further trace.

This invasion was migration on a small scale, and it was followed by others—several types of peoples successively occupying what is now France and Spain, some coming overland from eastern Europe and beyond, and each with a slightly different way of life. They were still hunters, but they were also fishermen. The workmanship of these later comers was so superior to that of Paleolithic man that it is usual to classify this period as Neolithic (New Stone Age), which in Europe can roughly be dated as having begun about 3000 B.C. and having lasted for some 2000 years or more.

With their superior culture and technology the new peoples from the east and the south replaced earlier peoples: they had better stone weapons, usually polished and with handles, and they were skilled in pottery-making and generally made better use of fire. But their real superiority lay in the fact that they had begun to domesticate wild animals. As these tribes had become more settled, certain kinds of animals crept nearer to man's habitations, perhaps to share the warmth of their fires. Jackals, always scavengers, came to gnaw the bones left in man's rubbish heaps, and as they grew familiar they slept by the embers, to become at long last the animal we now call dog. Sheep, goats, and cattle, too, attached themselves to men and gradually became domesticated. But no animal was used as a beast of burden; the thousands of horses which existed at that time were used only for food. These invaders, whom we now call Neolithic man, also brought with them the beginning of husbandry, perhaps even of cultivation.

Food-storage jar from Jericho.

Their arrival was helped by recession of the ice. Over many centuries the retreating glaciers had kept the rivers full and linked areas by waterways along which Neolithic explorers could move through inner Asia to the northeast of the continent. Many traces of this New Stone Age man have been found in Africa, Europe, and Asia. Even in Siberia, stone tools, harpoons of reindeer horn, and objects of bone and ivory have been found.

Possibly some of the early drifts of man over to America took place around this time through the extreme northeast of Asia and across the narrow seas to what is now Alaska, but these journeys may have been made even earlier, in late Paleolithic times. However it was probably Neolithic man who first discovered and explored the Americas. When he began his long wanderings over these vast continents, it was indeed the beginning of a new world, for he had to work out his own pattern of cultural development without any help from the old world other than a few dim memories of his unrecorded past.

These primitive explorers would have found a vast continent of grassy plains, forests, and mountains inhabited by the beasts they had hunted for centuries elsewhere—the mammoth and mastodon, wild horse and camel, great herds of elk and bison. Animal remains have been found in Alaska, near cutting tools and chipped stone spearheads of the same type as those found in the Gobi Desert.

These first wandering hunters from Asia started a great migration; wave after wave of nomads crossed into this new continent and gradually worked their way southward. Their traces have been found in Alaska, Colorado, New Mexico, and in southern Chile where, in certain caves, evidence has been found of five successive hunting cultures extending over a period of some thousands of years.

The later immigrants from Asia, perhaps the last before the melting of the ice raised the sea level and cut off land bridges linking the old world, introduced a new way of life. They were still hunters, but they were more inclined to settle and to hunt within a limited area; more important still, they had learned how to cook their food. They discovered how to boil water with hot stones—a method of cooking which persisted among North American Indian peoples until our own time. These stone-boilers were without any form of pottery, but they had developed the art of basket-weaving to a very high degree, making cooking pots of bark and fiber so closely woven that they could be filled with water, which could then be boiled by the addition of stones heated in the campfire.

Wood combined with stone made a more serviceable axe than stone alone—this New Stone Age hafted axe was found in Denmark.

These people inhabited a wide area on the Pacific coastlands, from Alaska in the north to southern California, and their staple diet, apart from the game they hunted, was salmon from the great rivers of western Oregon and California. Like early man in other parts of the world they next added to their diet by making use of wild plants, whose seed they gathered and crushed into a kind of meal. Their way of life took no marked forward step until the introduction of maize and corn from the south, probably from Mexico where it had been developed by earlier settlers as the chief food plant. The idea of making pots may have come from the same source—crude unfired pottery used probably for storage rather than for cooking. Such were the ancestors of the simple hunting and farming peoples found by the first voyagers from Europe many thousands of years later.

Recent finds in Africa suggest a flourishing Stone Age population in Kenya and Tanganyika which, in its turn, took the art of tool-making and rock-painting far southward over the plateaus of South Africa. On crudely constructed rafts or in boats these people probably drifted southward into East Africa by sea or by following the great waterways of the Nile Basin. In North Africa there has recently been discovered evidence of occupation from very early times—again by people who may

Bone carvings like this one, made on a reindeer antler and found at Lortet, Hautes-Pyrénées, were made by Stone Age food gatherers.

have emerged originally from the region now called the Middle East, which appears to have been the true cradle of civilization.

It was in this fertile region—which included, in the east, the great fertile stretches of the Indus Valley, the river system of the Tigris and Euphrates; and in the west, the Nile Basin—that the next great step forward in the development of human society seems to have taken place. This was the discovery of bread wheats of wheat and barley which, growing wild on the watered lands somewhere between Mesopotamia and the Caucasus, gave tremendous impetus to the development of agriculture. Some grains were already known and cultivated to a limited extent—millet, in Asia, for example; while in the lake villages of Switzerland there is evidence that the lake dwellers knew that the seeds of wild grasses could be crushed between stones, mixed with water, and baked.

At some time it occurred to these people that fallen grains produced more grains. Once this observation was made, the idea of planting at regular intervals must have occurred to them. Planting meant a controlled and reliable food supply, but it meant something even more important: No longer need they wander; they had become farmers, tied to and living from the soil. Cultivation marked the beginning of pastoral village life.

Such a life did not suit all men. Some preferred the adventure and exploration that result from travel. Others preferred to follow their herds across the plains. Such men were the nomad hunters. Roughly speaking, the nomads took possession of the grassy steppes from the Danube to far across Asia; the farmers stayed in the more fertile valleys to the south, and in comparison with Paleolithic man they lived a civilized life. One

Because early houses were made of perishable materials, archeological records of them are rare. This Paleolithic painting on rock is interpreted as a hutlike structure.

An early Bronze Age plowing scene modeled in clay.

mark of civilized living was the division of labor which an agrarian society could encourage. Planned agriculture meant enough food for all, even a surplus. In turn this meant that certain individuals were freed from food-producing chores; they could develop their natural skills as craftsmen.

Houses of wattle and daub served these villagers until man discovered how to make bricks of mud and straw. Brick houses were fairly strong, but rain eventually reduced them to their original mud. As they were washed away, new ones were built on the old sites, so the fallen houses formed ever increasing mounds. Some buildings stored a seasonal supply of food; here were the foundation stones of fixed communities.

Traces of the earliest known European buildings have been found in Switzerland. There New Stone Age man knew how to fell trees and notch them together to build sturdy wooden houses. These people must have discovered that a finer edge could be put on their tools by grinding them against harder stone; this method replaced the chipping of Paleolithic man. With good tools, regular crops, specialization of labor, and domesticated animals, the life of pastoral man had settled into a pattern which was far removed from the first step taken by his apelike ancestor. His chief enemy was now the nomad hunter, who at times descended on the settlements in organized raids—a habit which was to become one of the most important factors in the story of discovery and exploration.

By the end of the Late Stone Age in the Middle East, civilization was beginning to reach a proud new level. Man had harnessed animals to sledges; plows were commonplace; a simple form of irrigation had been devised; and ships with sails were traveling the eastern Mediterranean and Arabian seas. Objects made of beaten copper, gold, and other metals were in common use as ornaments. Even cosmetics seem to have appeared around this time. Quite likely Egyptian women were using the copper mineral malachite to produce a delicate blue-green eye shadow.

A Mesopotamian stone carving showing a woman spinning. Some textiles are as old as the oldest known basketry.

Along the shores of the Mediterranean, people of settled communities were able to visit each other in boats or rafts on the rivers or by sea; their lives were similar, their development parallel. It must have been a revelation to them when the first "foreign" traders landed on their shores and showed them objects made of metal, a material which they had never seen. They listened to stories of inventions which, said the traders, came from lands far to the east—of ships with sails, and of ornaments that glistened by firelight. This knowledge of the existence of metal was brought to southern Europe about 5000 years ago. But it took a thousand years for the knowledge to spread as far as western and northern Europe. Then, perhaps by accident, some early metallurgist fused the soft metals of copper and tin and produced the heavy strong metal the oriental traders had brought—bronze.

Metals undergo a change when they are dropped into fire. Today this is common knowledge; but what an important discovery it was when some Stone Age man banked his campfire with rocks containing copper. In the morning, when the fire was out, he discovered hard, shining, beadlike objects in the ashes. Who that man was and where and when he made the discovery we will never know. He may have picked up the beads to examine them and dropped them again as useless, or he may have beaten them into shapes, cutting the flattened soft metal into thin strips with his stone knife and bending them into useful or decorative shapes.

In the Middle East some eight thousand years ago another man discovered that by fusing copper with tin he could make bronze, a superior metal that held its shape and retained a sharp cutting edge longer than copper would. Later, by trial and error, men learned to pour molten metal into a mold and to cast a metal blade. This was a tremendous advance, but it took a long time for metal to supersede stone. Stone tools, which wore out fairly quickly, could easily be replaced in areas rich with flint, or the hard vitreous rock called obsidian. Metal-working was more difficult than stone-working, but in the end man gradually abandoned the old cutting tools which had served him for so long for the far more efficient, and far more deadly, sharp metal knife. From so simple a beginning man became a metallurgist.

An Egyptian predynastic boat, about 6000 B.C., powered by wind and steered by side oars.

The Late Stone Age gave way to the Bronze Age some time around 3000 B.C.—a very short time ago, considering man's earliest technological efforts of 500,000 years ago. But, again, we should not suppose that all groups of men entered the Bronze Age at the same time. Some were much slower than others, and people who lived in the warm valleys of the Tigris, Euphrates, and the Nile were far more advanced than their contemporaries in the north. While the north people were still living as savages in caves near glaciers, people in the east were constructing buildings of mud brick. Cities—later to become city-states, such as Ur, Akkad, and Babylon—were already well established; the famous walls of Jericho are thought to have been built soon after 7000 B.C. Durable houses probably were appearing in other places as well; in India they existed before 3000 B.C. and probably earlier still in China.

Man became a frequent traveler and expert potter when he invented the most revolutionary piece of equipment in history—the wheel. There are no records to tell us exactly when or where or how the wheel was first produced. All that is known is that fragments of pottery and stone dated at 3500 B.C. prove that the people of Babylon were using wheeled carts for war chariots.

Before the wheel, slaves and beasts of burden, including the ox, ass, and perhaps camels, were employed to carry man and his belongings. But with the appearance of the wheel it must soon have been obvious, especially to traders, that goods could be carried more efficiently in a wheeled cart than on the backs of men and beasts. In addition to revolutionizing transport and communication, the wheel radically changed pottery-making. With a horizontal wheel a potter could, by spinning the wheel, shape a vessel in minutes; to build the same vessel up by hand would take several hours, or days.

This early example of cuneiform writing bears only the name of the Sumerian King Eannadu, governor of Shirpurla.

Quite possibly these two early uses of the wheel—transportation and pottery-making—developed independently, but it seems unlikely. In parts of Asia—in India—the potter's wheel is certainly as old as wheeled carts. In Egypt, however, pottery wheels came earlier than wheeled vehicles. It wasn't until after 500 B.C. that pottery wheels were used north of the Alps in Europe, but carts with wheels had been used about 1500 B.C. To us the thought of life without the wheel is almost impossible. Yet the Mayans and Aztecs in Central America managed to do without it and led, from their point of view, a satisfactory life.

Some five or six thousand years before Christ a people called Sumerians settled at the southern end of Mesopotamia—Babylonia, as it then was. They were different from the local inhabitants, and they may have come in a mass movement from the east—Persia, perhaps, or even India. They were an inventive people with a highly developed culture; their several cities were autonomous and each had its established religion. They invented a form of measurement, using a forearm, a finger, or a foot as a convenient unit. In America and England, although standardized to a measurement of twelve inches, the foot is used to this day. They also invented a form of writing by pressing characters into clay with a wedge-shaped stick. The characters of this cuneiform script were pictures in their original form, but the speed with which the writers pressed the stick into the clay soon led to a condensed ideograph which bore little resemblance to the original. The same kind of thing happened in China, where the speed of the brush strokes modified the forms into the characters we know today. Egypt, on the other hand, where men painted representational hieroglyphs on walls or on the paper they had made from the papyrus reed, went further and translated their pictures into sounds. Here was the first alphabet.

Life in cities of Egypt and Sumer was similar, most people being occupied in farming. At this stage there was no money, so trading was by exchange. The precious metals then known were used only by the

Section from the Babylonian standard of Ur, showing that wheeled war chariots were known as early as 3500 B.C.

Spoked wheels are shown in this African cave painting. Although later than 3500 B.C., actual date is unknown.

rulers; in Sumer these were priests, who, from their massive temples, dominated the life of the community. They were the highest in the land, but in Egypt there was one even higher—the Pharaoh, who was regarded as god-king.

The establishment of more than one center of civilization in the fertile crescent encouraged the spread of new ideas which must have been carried not only by traders but by nomadic tribes who, wandering in their seasonal drifts in search of new pastures, carried with them pots, tools, and simple jewelry. There were also exchanges of ideas as ruthless tribes from the mountain and desert areas attacked the peaceful groups of people living in the fertile settled districts near the rivers. These raids, early examples of organized warfare, changed in character as populations increased. So far as the marauding nomadic tribes were concerned, the grain and cattle plundered during a raid on a peasant community were just as good as that cultivated or raised by the nomads themselves. Eventually the settled farmers learned to expect organized raids; they must also have learned to protect themselves by some kind of organized defense, for preservation of crops and domestic animals was an economic necessity.

The foundation of the cities of Sumer stemmed from the small villages and farms which were the first signs of a settled state. Simple houses of reeds or mud brick were adequate until the needs of an expanding population called for something more elaborate. Although the people were not short of food, there was little in the way of raw materials for growing communities, so the Sumerians were forced to look abroad for those things which were necessary for the development of their civilization. It was of no use to look to Egypt to supply their wants for, although there was flint in the cliffs of the Nile, there was no timber and little free stone or ores, and in neither country could building begin on any architecturally sound basis until these needs were met.

In each of the numerous villages small farmers tilled their soil, baked their bread, and made their own tools. They were self-sufficient, and had their numbers not increased they might have remained so. But with a rise in population came also a rise in trade, and with the widening of horizons and the importation of foreign ideas came ambition. Men were

Clay model of a New Stone Age Czechoslovakian house.

sent to Armenia to get obsidian in exchange for Sumerian tools. Copper came from Oman, silver and lead from the Taurus Mountains, timber from the rainy side of any mountain range. In search of these materials the Mesopotamian people met the peoples from the Indus, whose shortages were similar.

Articles which were made for exchange on an organized trade level had to be made by craftsmen-specialists and then taken to the buyers who would be willing to trade. Trade, then, provided an added stimulus to specialization of labor. Men capable of working metals, or making pottery or glaze beads, had to be trained, and other men had to carry the finished goods to foreign markets. Gradually more and more men were, by necessity, abandoning the plow for tool-making and for acquiring skill in the mechanics of trade. An industrial revolution was in the making.

By 3000 B.C. the Sumerians were no longer a conglomeration of village farmers producing their own food only. They now had to support craftsmen, merchants, transport workers, soldiers to guard the caravans, and scribes to keep the records. The villages had given way to cities with organized governments. The wizards and magicians of earlier days were replaced by priests and kings. Temples began to appear, the earliest of which were built on artificial hills rising in pyramidal terraces to a square summit. These monumental edifices were called ziggurats.

The movements of armies and traders imply a ceaseless activity in this period, but at this stage in our story we do not have the names of the individual generals, traders, or explorers who penetrated new lands. The fight for supremacy, which seems a characteristic human endeavor, was the mainspring of man's spread from the valleys of the Nile to the Indus.

Sumerian sailing ships rode the waters of the Persian Gulf and most likely followed the south Asian coast to the Indus. References to south Asian trading in metals, textiles and timber, as well as to the deeds of kings, were recorded on clay tablets impressed with cuneiform script. These records, intended to be permanent, were baked in ovens or in the hot sun. So enduring were they that when they were found after four thousand years of burial they were still readable and could be translated.

Detail from a stone carving shows a river trading boat used by Mesopotamians around 4000 B.C.

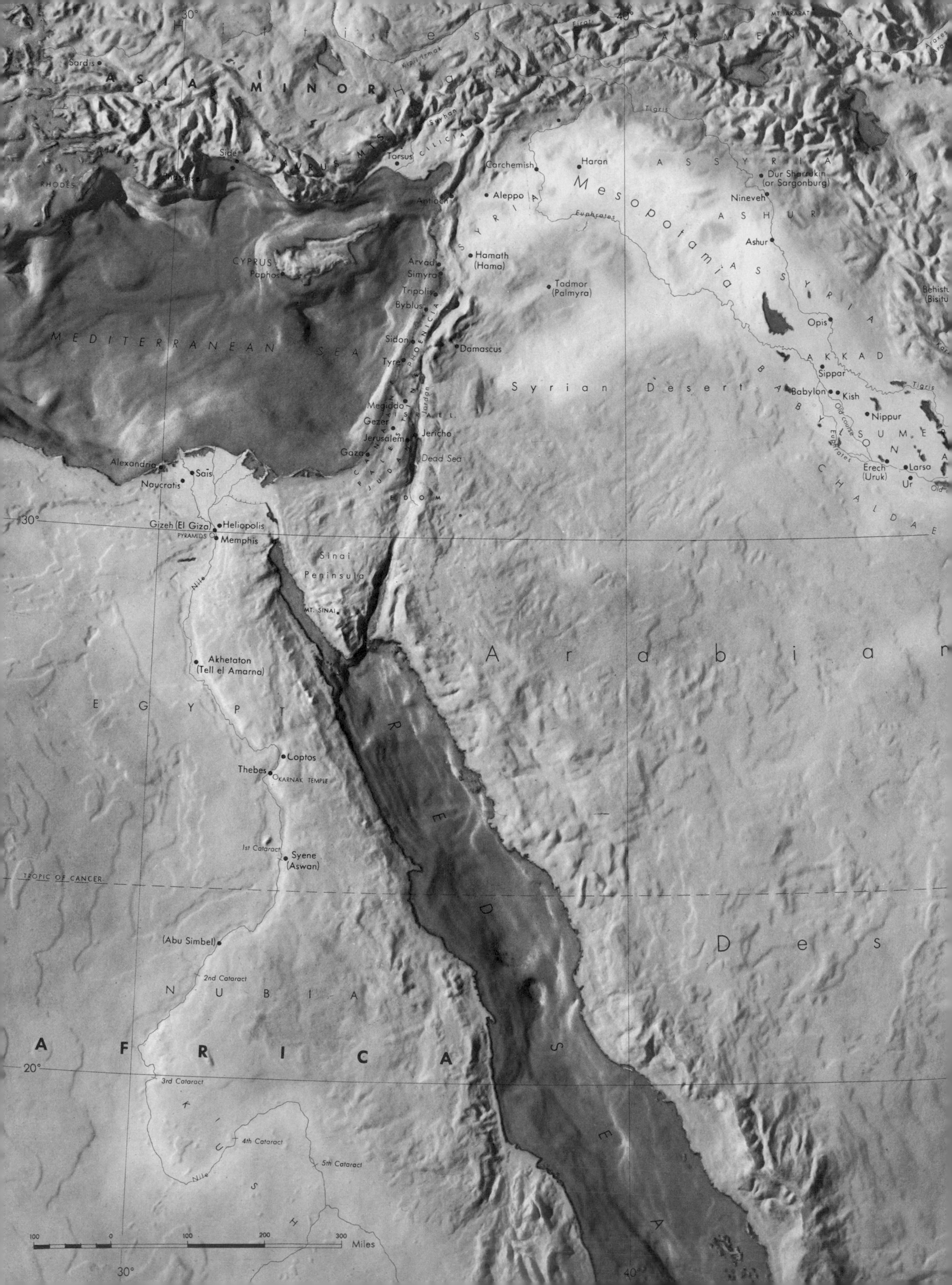

ASIA MINOR
Sardis
Side
RHODES
TAURUS MTS.
Tarsus
CILICIA
Carchemish
Haran
ASSYRIA
Mesopotamia
Dur Sharrukin (or Sargonburg)
Nineveh
ASHUR
Ashur
Aleppo
Antioch
Euphrates
Tigris
SYRIA
CYPRUS
Paphos
Arvad
Simyra
Hamath (Hama)
Tripolis
Byblus
Tadmor (Palmyra)
PHOENICIA
MEDITERRANEAN SEA
Sidon
Damascus
Tyre
Opis
AKKAD
Sippar
Syrian Desert
BABYLONIA
Babylon
Kish
Megiddo
ISRAEL
Jordan
Gezer
Jericho
Jerusalem
Nippur
SUMER
Gaza
Dead Sea
CANAAN
JUDAH
EDOM
Erech (Uruk)
Larsa
Ur
CHALDAEA
Alexandria
Sais
Naucratis
30°
Gizeh (El Giza)
Heliopolis
PYRAMIDS
Memphis
Sinai Peninsula
Nile
MT. SINAI
Arabian Desert
Akhetaton (Tell el Amarna)
EGYPT
RED SEA
Coptos
Thebes
KARNAK TEMPLE
1st Cataract
Syene (Aswan)
TROPIC OF CANCER
(Abu Simbel)
2nd Cataract
NUBIA
AFRICA
20°
3rd Cataract
KUSH
4th Cataract
5th Cataract
100 0 100 200 300 Miles
30°
40°

Gradually villages grew into cities, which in turn grew into city-states, each with a highly organized army. In search of metal and stone, or to acquire the wealth of a neighboring state, or out of sheer pugnacity, men marched in mass formation over the face of the land. But in the wars of conquest the Sumerians seem to have been among the first to suffer, falling before a Semitic nation from Akkad in Syria. Sargon, the great Akkadian ruler, built the small town of Babylon into a city-state and founded the first Babylonian Empire, and from it he sent armies as far away as Palestine and Asia Minor. The Akkadians held their empire for about 200 years, then fell before the Elamites and the Amorites, who in turn were vanquished by the Assyrians who ruled for a thousand years.

Before the height of the Assyrian Empire, the culture of the Assyrians was different from that of the Sumerians, although both were still rooted in the Bronze Age. Geographically the Assyrians were better off, enjoying comfortable highlands as opposed to the sweltering heat of the Babylonian Plains. Their buildings were made of stone and good crops grew in their rich valleys, which also supported fat flocks; but the Assyrians did not trade much nor did they abandon farming to become artisans. They were, however, compelled to support an army. At this time the Sumerians regarded Ashur more or less as a vassal state. The two cultures were in fairly close contact; gradually Sumerian writing and their invention of a calendar were adopted by the men of Ashur.

During this time perpetual warfare raged. The jealousies of Babylon and Assyria were aggravated by their separate political ambitions: Assyria was an inland state whose hopes of gaining supremacy over western Asia could not be realized without access to the Mediterranean, which was then held by a string of Phoenician cities, Tyre and Sidon among them. The Assyrians were also beset by other enemies—Armenians, Hebrews, Hittites, and the powerful kingdom of Damascus. Toughened by the experience of war, the Assyrians eventually displaced the neighboring Sumerians as rulers and the two cultures merged into one.

Stone carving shows Sumerian warriors going into battle.

Map shows Fertile Crescent and the names indicate where the ancient civilizations were centered about the first century A. D.

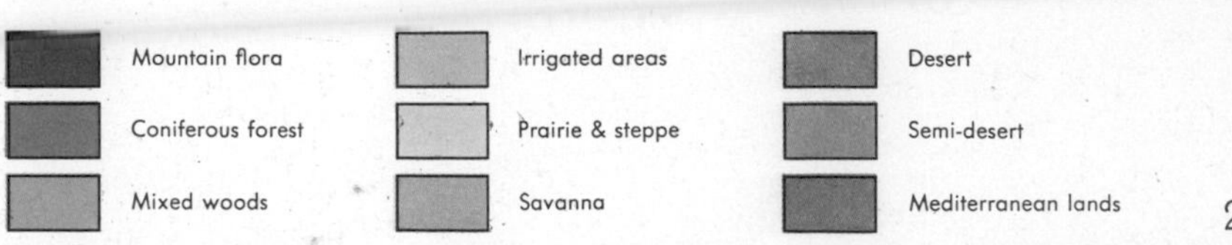

During all this period wars raged between the people of Mesopotamia and the Nile. The Egyptians, who also had succumbed to the rough Semites, whom they ironically described as the Shepherd Kings, rose in rebellion in 1600 B.C., and with a renewed spirit of nationalism their god-kings, the Pharaohs, became aggressive warriors. Egyptian frontiers advanced and receded as military fortunes waxed and waned; but Egypt's days of glory were fading. The Assyrians were destined to become the greatest military nation of that time.

Frontiers elsewhere were also constantly changing. Small Semitic states, Hittite and Syrian, joined with or fought against the two great rivals—the Assyrians and the Egyptians. Whole armies with their goods and chattels, and most likely with their wives and children, moved from place to place, sometimes settling and introducing their own culture to people of foreign lands. Parallels in modern times occurred during the last war when troops from the West occupied areas such as Japan, Burma and New Guinea.

As history shows us, no nation can rule supreme endlessly; and Assyria was no exception. After a thousand years of rule the Assyrian Empire crumbled when still more Semitic people from the desert southeast of Mesopotamia, the Chaldeans, along with the Medes and the Persians, attacked. The Assyrians found themselves helpless in meeting so formidable an enemy. For years they had plundered and scorched their way to conquest, replenishing their armies by taking first their own peasants from the land, and then those of their conquered enemies. Food supplies were devoured, irrigation channels became choked. With mercenaries unable to do anything but fight, there were too few people to till the soil and the land lost heart. The fall of Assyria was complete.

Egyptian wall painting from a tomb at Thebes shows: (above) cultivation of corn, (below) a servant carrying hares, XVIII Dynasty.

The Chaldeans, who are thought to have come originally from Arabia and to have been a Semitic people, had marched along the coast of the Persian Gulf and settled at Ur. A series of small encroachments set the pattern which later helped them to establish their supremacy as a military nation. Under their general, Nabopolassan, they conquered Babylon, partly by war and partly by the time-honored device of infiltration. With dramatic swiftness the son of this general, Nebuchadnezzar, was to found yet another Babylonian Empire.

The Egyptians of the period between 3000 B.C. and 2000 B.C. regarded the Babylonians—whether Sumerian, Akkadian, Assyrian, or Chaldean—as formidable rivals and a threat to their way of life. These people of ancient and cultured Egypt were working in bronze, iron, gold, and silver and were building magnificent cities while western Europe was still in the Stone Age. By any standards the Egyptians of this period had a high level of civilization. Their caravans of donkeys traveled south along the banks of the Nile into the Sudan to trade Egyptian wares for exotic ebony, ivory, sweet-smelling resins, and ostrich feathers.

The men who led these caravans were the first organized explorers of the African interior. But for some reason their expeditions do not seem to have satisfied the reigning Pharaoh, possibly because they did not return with enough of the treasured spices; so in 1750 B.C. he sent an expedition led by the Egyptian nobleman Hannu into unknown lands. By this time the ancient caravan routes had become hardened into recognized roads, one of which led from Coptos, north of Thebes and on the opposite bank of the Nile, through the desert to the Red Sea. Hannu's mission was to "conduct ships to the land of Punt," according to a rock inscription which gives us an account of his voyage. Punt is now known as Somaliland. Hannu was supplied with an army of 3000 men to protect

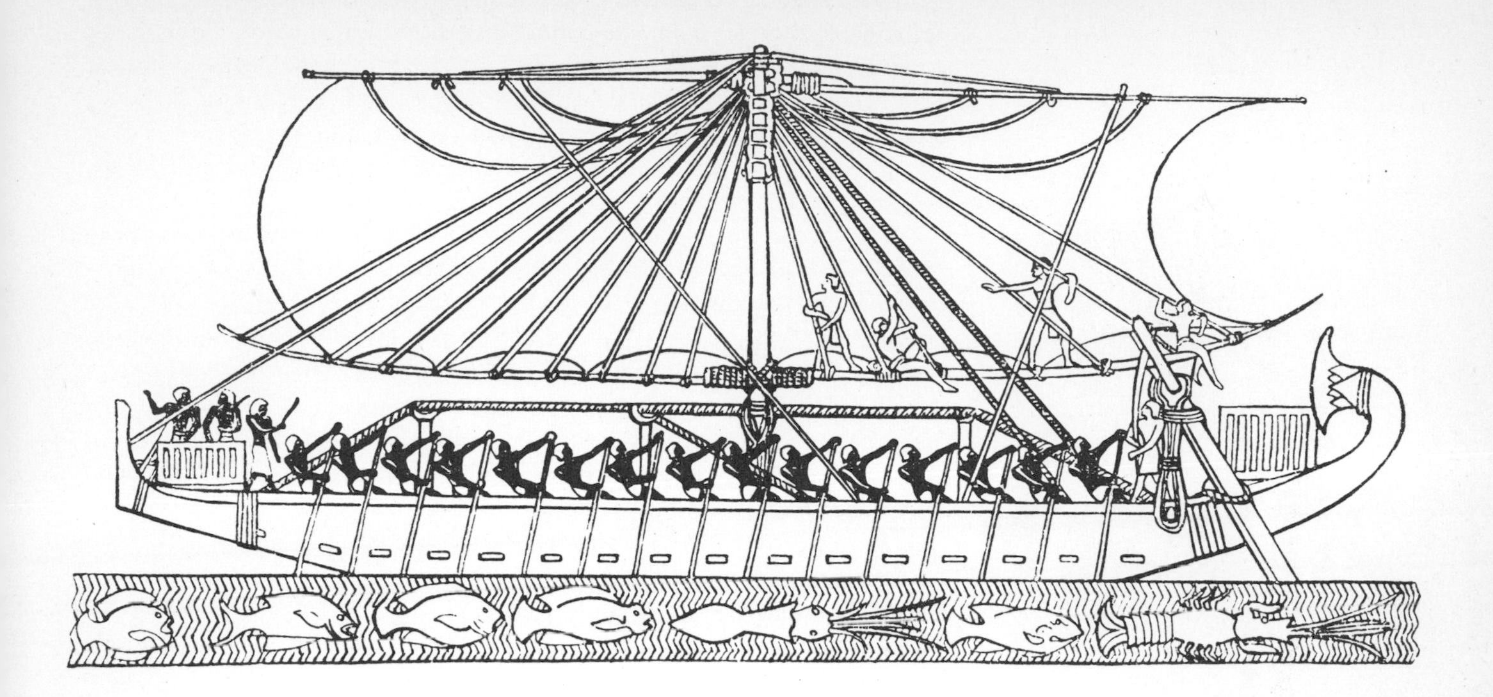

A boat which Queen Hatshepsut sent to Punt on a trading mission. Oarsmen supplemented sail power.

the expedition. In addition his caravan would have been composed of donkeys, their drivers, and servants. He crossed the desert, carrying skins of water, and at intervals he dug reservoirs. When he arrived at Seba on the Red Sea he began building ships to transport the exotic products he hoped to buy.

The Egyptians may not have taken readily to the open sea, but the Nile was alive with their barges, towboats, rafts, and the steeply carved prows of their rigged ships. They were manned by oarsmen and fitted with tackle for loading and unloading cargo, a job done by powered derricks in present-day ships. Royal barges sometimes graced the river as they departed and returned from expeditions. Queen Hatshepsut sent one expedition to the granite quarries at the First Cataract—a distance of 150 miles. The mission of the expedition was to return to Memphis with a 350-ton obelisk. She also sent a fleet of five ships to Punt "to bring back all goodly fragrant woods of God's land [the East], heaps of myrrh resin, with fresh myrrh trees, with ebony and pure ivory, with green gold of Emu, with cinnamon wood, Kheyst wood, with two kinds of incense, eye cosmetic, with apes, monkeys, dogs, and with skins of the southern panther, with natives and their children." Here was trading in the grand manner, an unusual and far-reaching expedition to supplement regular trade.

The ability to fit out such an expedition and the desire for the merchandise it was sent to find reflected the high level of civilization at the time. People wore garments of linen and leather sandals, and their pottery and glass were excellent. Although in the market buying and selling was still by barter, in the palace of the Pharaohs heavy rings of gold or copper representing different weights were exchanged as tokens. They had not yet become "coins," as we know them, but they were to lead to the use of money for trading. Princes and landowners employed freemen and slaves to work their estates. Immense tombs commemorated the illustrious dead. There was luxury for some and toil for others, not unlike the present day; yet for all their magnificence the Egyptians were still living in the Bronze Age.

The mountainous island of Crete, lying between Greece and Egypt, was inhabited by an Iron Age people called the Minoans, whose strange and interesting civilization was dependent on the sea. Ships had been used in the Mediterranean since at least 7000 B.C. and by 3500 B.C., an active trade was in full swing between Crete and Egypt. But the Egyptians were shy of seafaring, so it must have been the Minoans who did most of the fetching and carrying.

Part of the Minoan palace at Knossos, built when Crete ruled the Mediterranean Sea.

Easy access to the many islands of the Aegean encouraged them, mainly in their search for obsidian, to become a maritime nation. They had had, in any case, to cross the sea to reach Crete at all for, although roughly styled Aegeans, like the Phoenicians they may have come originally from the Semitic tribes of Arabia.

The Minoans were ideally situated for trade. The Nile Delta was only 340 miles from Crete and could have been reached in three or four days with a good wind. Athens was only two days away. Their sea lanes extended in all directions, covering most of the ports from Palestine to the shores of north Africa and the southern coast of Europe.

Near the Cretan ports were thriving industries whose products of metal, decorated pottery, and stone were much in demand along the Mediterranean shores. Inland were thriving villages of sun-dried brick. The Minoans were prosperous; their rich valleys were fertile; vines, olives and figs grew on their hillsides; fish enriched the waters round their coasts; quail, partridge, duck and geese inhabited their marshlands. Their civilization was not unlike that of Egypt, from which they freely borrowed ideas. The celebrated palace of King Minos at Knossos, for example, was built along Egyptian lines—a series of rooms around a central court. Daedalus (who also tried to build a flying machine) is said to have designed part of the palace. It was equipped with running water, had bathrooms and other modern devices unknown in any other city at that time. The palace, which was vast, sprawled over most of the city of Knossos. Secure on his island and with a navy to protect him, Minos did not trouble to fortify his palace. For a thousand years Crete had been free of invasion; the Minoan kings were lords of the Mediterranean.

Splendid works of art adorned Knossos. Bullfighting scene is from a palace fresco.

The first King Minos, who gave his name to the people of Crete, deserves some attention. At one time he was thought to be as legendary as the horrible Minotaur, half man and half bull, whose appetite for children had to be satisfied every so often by the unfortunate Athenians who were forced to pay tribute to this powerful maritime nation. Minos was thought to be the son of Zeus, and periodically he retired to a cave to receive instruction from his godly father in the government of the land. From whatever source his inspiration came, he laid down excellent laws, governed wisely, founded a navy, and built himself the remarkable palace which he filled with dazzling works of art.

Recent archeological finds prove that Minoan ships visited Cyprus, Sicily, the Lipari Islands and the Levant. That they went to the south of France and Spain is more than possible, leaving as a legacy a cult which is practiced to this day—the bullfight. The Minotaur was not the only manifestation of the Minoans' interest in the bull. Bullfights, probably regarded as sacred but of appalling ferocity, took place for the edification of the people. In the ring matadors and picadors wore ceremonial clothes resembling those still worn in Spain. Beautiful cups with bull motifs beaten in low relief by a Cretan goldsmith of ancient times are splendid examples of the Minoans' finely observed movements of the bull. Found in Sparta, the cups are exquisite pieces.

The clothes of Minoan women were not unlike those of Victorian England, flounced skirts with a close-fitting bodice and a narrow waist. The Cretan lady wore a tiara on her elaborately curled hair; she was elegant and we can suppose that her house was most adequately staffed.

This faïence statuette, "Goddess of the Serpents," shows typical costume of Minoan women.

Like the Sumerians and the Egyptians, the Minoans used an extremely complex form of writing. The earliest of their three scripts resembles Egyptian hieroglyphics, but around 1800 B.C. this pictorial form of writing was replaced by a syllabic script, which has been named Linear A and which to date has not been deciphered. Roughly three hundred years later Linear A was modified to a form—also syllabic—which scholars have named Linear B. Deciphered in 1952 by Michael Ventris, the Linear B script was revealed as an early form of Greek.

About 2000 clay tablets surviving from Knossos are inventories of goods kept in the palace; although they shed little light on Minoan political history, they do reveal that sometime before 1400 B.C. Knossos had been occupied by the Greeks.

It is from Minoan engraved seals and painted pottery that we know what their ships were like. They carried sail but their chief power came from human muscle. They were large enough to carry grain from Egypt and timber from the mainland of Asia, and they were used as warships during the invasion of Sicily. How their crews navigated is not known, but presumably it was by the sun and the stars; they may even have made use of migratory birds observed during seasonal flights.

Magnificent in their palaces, with a thriving, contented population and dominions overseas, the Minoan kings had little to fear. But their end came with dramatic suddenness in about 1400 B.C. The palace of Knossos was totally destroyed, never to be rebuilt. Recent excavations show traces of fire and plunder, but also of a very destructive earthquake. H. G. Wells suggests that nature may have destroyed Knossos but perhaps the Greeks finished off what the earthquake began. The Greeks certainly had no cause to love the Minoans. Sea trade and piracy often go together, and it is possible that these early mariners, who had explored and become masters of the Mediterranean, raided where they could and traded where they could not.

A Minoan prince with a dagger and staff, taken from relief appearing on a finely worked cup.

The abrupt end to the fortunes of the Minoans presented a golden opportunity to their rivals in Phoenicia. The period between the fall of the one and the rise of the other is that of Homer's much traveled Ulysses, whose adventures one would think would tell us something of the extent of the known world at that time.

But the Greeks were more interested in literature and philosophy than in discovery and trade. They knew the Aegean Sea and had heard of "the burnt-faced men of Ethiopia," who were probably the Nubians of Upper Egypt. They knew, too, of the "misty darkness of Cimmoria" and possibly of the Baltic. But of the great empires of Mesopotamia Homer has hardly a word to say. He does mention tin and amber coming from Spain and Friesland and being traded to the warriors by the Sidonians—that is, the Phoenicians.

The Phoenicians who originally inhabited north Palestine were the Canaanites of the Old Testament. Their important cities of Jerusalem, Jericho, and Gezer, to name only a few, were in existence as far back as 3000 B.C. But in about 1200 B.C. the land of Canaan was conquered by the Israelites, and the refugees left Palestine to settle farther north.

From about 1400 B.C. the Phoenicians became the masters of the Mediterranean for a thousand years, and Carthage, one of the many Mediterranean settlements established by the Phoenicians, was to continue that supremacy until conquered by Rome.

If the Greeks wrote of far more lands than they really knew, the Phoenicians did just the opposite. They were exceedingly secretive about their doings and remained silent about the many discoveries they made. Fearful of competition, the Phoenicians consistently falsified stories of their voyages and the sources of their materials. But secrets are not always kept, and it is known that they were the first to sail through the Pillars of Hercules (Strait of Gibraltar) into the Atlantic. Their ships

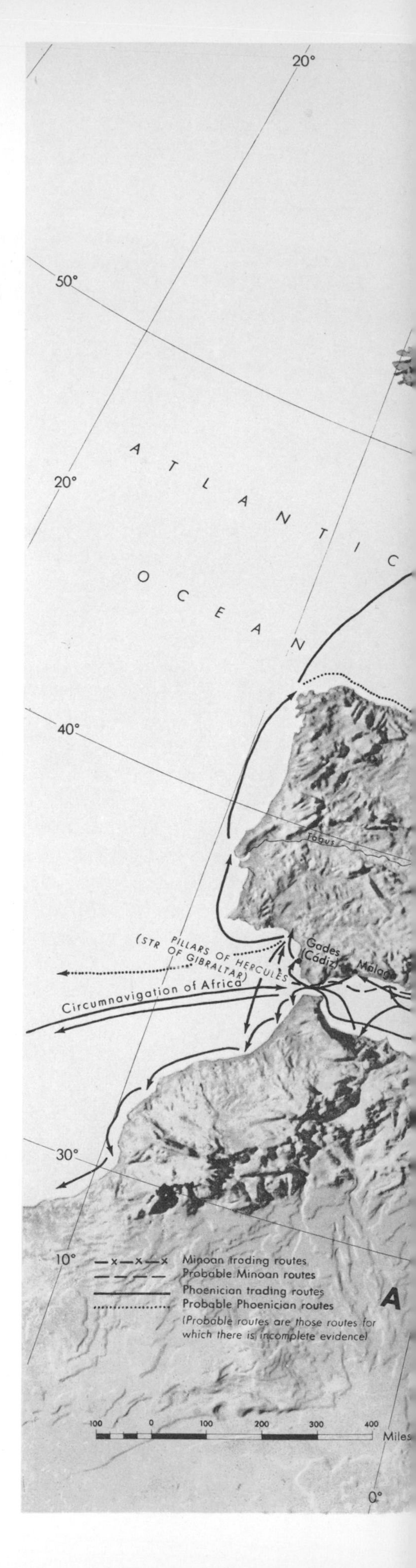

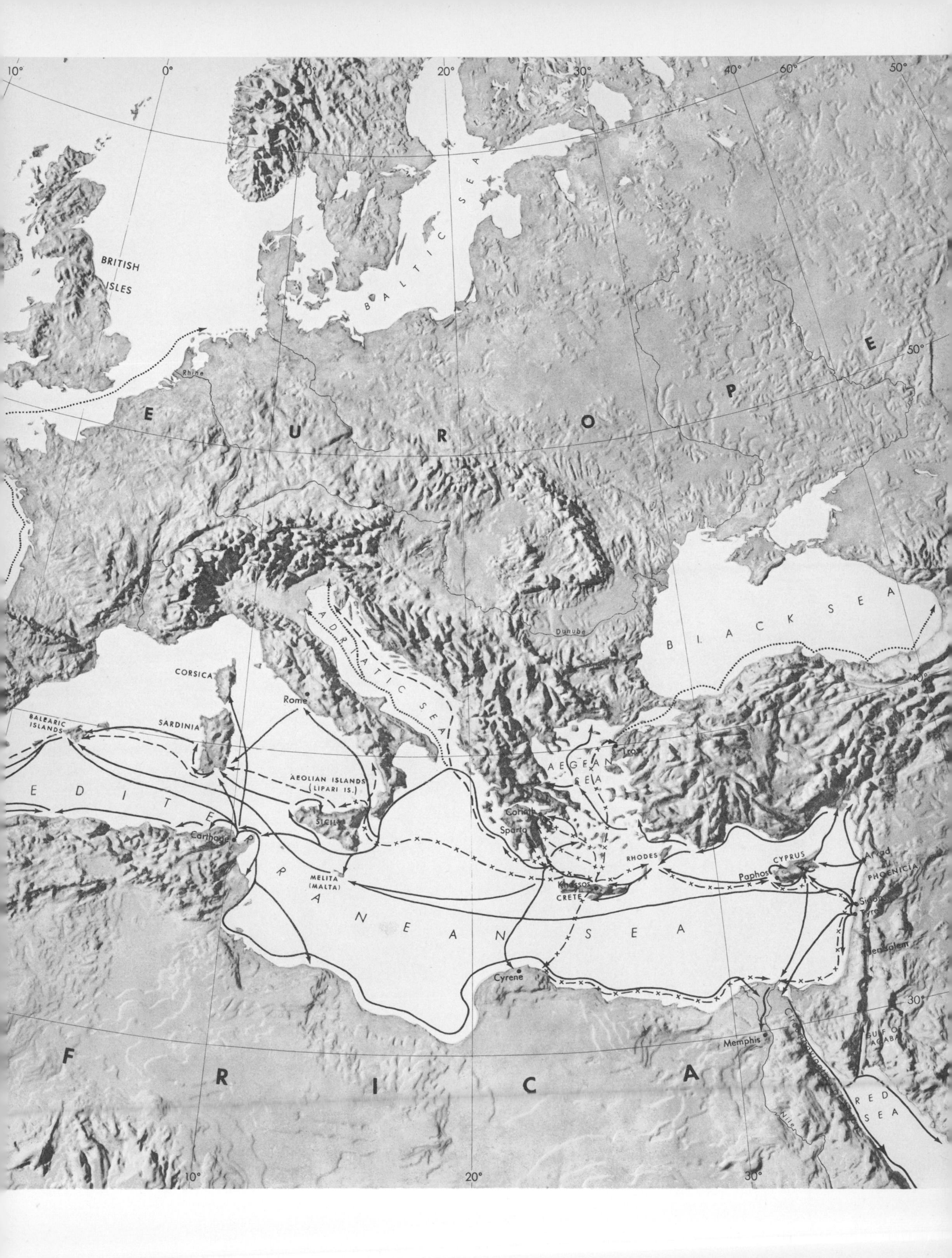

BRITISH ISLES
BALTIC SEA
EUROPE
Rhine
Danube
BLACK SEA
CORSICA
SARDINIA
BALEARIC ISLANDS
Rome
ADRIATIC SEA
AEOLIAN ISLANDS (LIPARI IS.)
Carthage
MEDITERRANEAN SEA
MELITA (MALTA)
Corinth
Sparta
AEGEAN SEA
RHODES
Knossos
CRETE
Paphos
CYPRUS
PHOENICIA
Cyrene
Memphis
Nile
GULF OF AQABA
RED SEA
AFRICA

An armed galley of the Phoenicians, who, around 1400 B. C., ruled the Mediterranean Sea.

also sailed in the Gulf of Aqaba and the Red Sea to trade with Ophir, which, since they went to fetch "gold, silver, peacocks, apes and ivory," may have been that same land of Punt to which Hannu journeyed; its actual position was never disclosed. The voyages must have gone far beyond the Red Sea, since they took three years; also, apes and ivory could have been found in Africa or Asia, but peacocks can have come only from India or Ceylon.

Around 970 B. C., when Solomon was preparing for his days of glory, he sent to Hiram, the king of Tyre, to ask for men and materials to build his palace. He asked for cedarwood and for men "cunning in work of gold, silver, brass, and iron." In return he offered Hiram servants, hewers of wood, 20,000 measures of beaten wheat, the same amount of barley, 20,000 baths of wine and 20,000 baths of oil. The migration of workers from Tyre to Jerusalem was considerable. Solomon counted the strangers in Israel. There were 153,600, among whom where 10,000 bearers, 80,000 hewers, and 600 overseers.

The Phoenicians were the first people in recorded times to sail around the coast of Africa. In 600 B. C. they were sent on this famous expedition by the Egyptian King Necho, whose orders were that the ship was to leave by the Gulf of Aqaba and return through the Pillars of Hercules. That the circumnavigation of Africa would bring them to Gibraltar implies that the shape of the continent was already vaguely known, so the Phoenicians' journey may not have been the first of its kind. Herodotus gives an account of it in his *History*. The ships left Egypt for what is now the Indian Ocean, then "when autumn came, they went ashore, wherever they might happen to be, and having sown a tract of land with corn, waited until the grain was fit to cut. Having reaped it, they again set sail; and thus it came to pass that two whole years went by, and it was not till the third year that they doubled the Pillars of Hercules and made good their voyage home. On their return they declared—I for my part do not believe them, but perhaps others may—that in sailing round Libya [Africa] they had the sun upon their right hand."

Herodotus, who did not know of the great southward extension of Africa, could not accept the idea of the "sun upon the right hand." Had his geography been better, he would have realized that the voyage took the travelers into the Southern Hemisphere, where they saw the sun's path to the north of them.

A century later the Carthaginians tried to round Africa in the opposite direction, but this was far more difficult, since neither winds nor currents were so favorable. The leader of this expedition was a man called Sataspes, who was under sentence of death, but to whom a pardon would be given if he completed the journey. After a few months during his southward journey he met with contrary winds; his ship, he said, "stopped." Disheartened, he returned, reporting that he had seen small black people who kept cattle and who were dressed in palm leaves—probably natives along the Guinea coast. It was the last of Sataspes' adventures, for on failing his mission he was duly executed. The west-to-east rounding of the Cape of Storms (Good Hope) was not achieved until Bartholomew Diaz did it two thousand years later.

About 470 B.C. a different kind of expedition to Africa followed, under the leadership of the Carthaginian Hanno. As explorers these Carthaginians seem to have been a little timid, having landed only a few times. But what they reported on their return to Carthage was quite enough to make up for their timidity. Few people, in fact, believed them. Hanno described great stretches of land ablaze with torrents of fire—probably the grass fires lighted every autumn in many parts of Africa. These grass fires seem to have alarmed the explorers much more than a meeting with what they describe as "savage people whose bodies were covered with hair; these our interpreters called 'Gorillae.' We were unable to catch the men, who defended themselves with stones. We secured three women but these refused to accompany us, scratching and biting us. So we killed them and flayed them and brought their skins to Carthage." This was the first introduction of chimpanzees to Mediterranean civilization.

It can only be a matter of speculation as to how such a large expedition could have been fitted out. Frequent stops must have been made to find fresh water; food was perishable and the feeding of the oarsmen, whose labors must have been terribly difficult, would have been only one of many problems. The explorers did not know what dangers they might have to face. Soldiers may well have formed part of the ship's company, and, since part of the intention was to settle families on the west African coast, furniture and building materials must also have been carried.

Herodotus has something to say about the way in which the Carthaginians traded during their later visits to the western shores of Africa: "They no sooner arrive but forthwith they unlade their wares, and, having disposed them after an orderly fashion along the beach, leave them, and returning aboard their ships, raise a great smoke. The natives, when they see the smoke, come down to the shore, and laying out to view so much gold as they think the worth of the wares, withdraw to a distance. The Carthaginians upon this come ashore and look. If they think the gold enough, they take it and go their way; but if it does not seem to them sufficient, they go aboard ship once more, and wait patiently. Then the others approach and add to their gold, till the Carthaginians are content. Neither party deals unfairly by the other for they themselves never touch the gold till it comes up to the worth of their goods, nor do the natives ever carry off the goods till the gold is taken away."

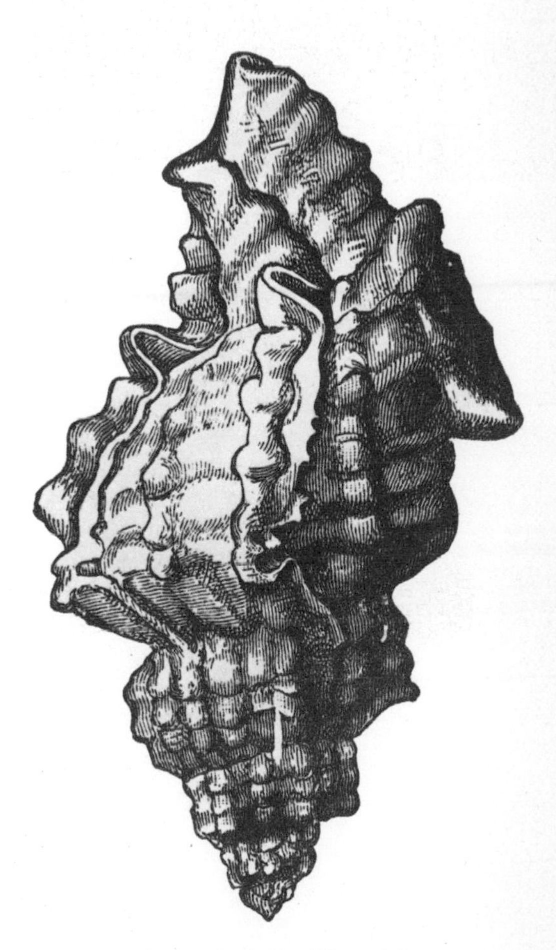

A shell from which the Phoenicians made a successful trade product—their popular dye, Tyrian purple.

Archers of the guard of the King of Persia. Taken from a painted frieze found at Persepolis.

The most interesting people on the fringes of Mesopotamia were the nomads of the plains east of the Caspian Sea and around present Persia. There were many tribes and they had many names—Scythians, Medes, Parthians, Aryans, and others. Together they formed a link between India and southeastern Europe.

About 1700 B.C. these tribes may have come to Babylonia as mercenary soldiers, bringing with them an animal the Babylonians had never seen—the horse. A thousand years later, under the more general name of Persians, they were to overcome the Assyrians, with the destruction of Nineveh, the capital. This period was one of movement, the restless Persians looking for new lands to conquer. Marching armies and trading caravans crossed the wide spaces between Persia and Egypt, and as far north as the Black Sea.

Hardy and well disciplined, the Persians were welded into a strong nation by their great leaders Cyrus and Darius. By 500 B.C., with armies of foot soldiers and mounted cavalry fighting with bronze-tipped arrows, the mighty Persian Empire was the largest the world had yet seen. Cyrus, in his time, subjected the people of Babylon, the Phoenicians, and the Greek cities of Asia Minor to his rule; Cambyses added Egypt; and Darius, the great lawgiver, found himself in supreme command from the Dardanelles to the Indus, from Upper Egypt to Central Asia. But the mastery of Europe was another matter. Neither Greeks, Sicilians, nor the people of the Spanish Phoenician settlements came under Persian rule.

In his determination to make Persia a great sea power, Darius sent an expedition, under one Scylax, to explore the Indian Ocean from Suez to the Indus. He also led his armies into an involuntary voyage of exploration. In 512 B.C., during his wars with the Scythians, he crossed the Bosporus and the Danube and then, under the impression that he was near the Black Sea, he found himself in the steppes of Russia, from which he was forced to return.

Part of a Scythian belt buckle of worked gold shows a hunter running down a boar.

There were other notable marches which led men over new country. One of these is famous in history. Cyrus, in an attempt to overthrow his brother, the king, marched with an army of ten thousand Greek mercenaries across Asia Minor to the Euphrates and down the river almost as far as Babylon. Cyrus was killed, and his soldiers found themselves stranded two thousand miles away from home. They had lost their leaders and their cavalry, and with no support their case seemed hopeless. It was Xenophon, a young volunteer, who led them on a march of two thousand miles to the Black Sea. The way lay through the wilds of Kurdistan, where they were attacked by savage mountain tribes, then through the mountains of Armenia and Georgia. For five months they marched, first reaching Trebizond, then Scutari, where they were incorporated into another army.

The world was beginning to look like a very big place to the Mediterranean peoples. The Greeks, too, were making excursions, but few records were kept and hearsay accounts of these expeditions have been forgotten. Of their sea journeys there was one which stands for all time as the first voyage of discovery with scientific importance. It was made by the Greek, Pytheas. He was born in Marseilles (then a Greek province) and was an astronomer of some repute. About 325 B.C., in search of knowledge for its own sake, he fitted out a ship at his own expense. On his return he wrote a record of his discoveries but unfortunately it was lost, so we have to rely on the account of it given by Polybius, who had seen the original. He says that after passing through the Pillars of Hercules Pytheas sailed north, and that not only did he visit Britain but "traveled all over it on foot."

He certainly walked over some of it, for he compares the daily life of the people of the "Tin Islands" with that of the Greeks and notes that they drank mead instead of wine. He would have found warlike tribes using domestic animals and iron and dwelling in lake villages or in caves. Their shields, horned helmets, and bracelets were of finely worked enamel on bronze; they wore simple, woven clothes, threshed corn, and used wheeled carts. He would have seen Cornish miners tunneling in the earth for tin ore and smelting it into blocks for export.

On the coast of what is now Helgoland, he would have seen people picking up amber, so prized by the Greeks, from the beaches. He observed the strong tidal movement of the sea, so different from the almost-tideless Mediterranean and, sailing farther north, he is said to have discovered an island called Thule, six days' sail from the north of Britain. This might have been Shetland, Norway, or possibly Iceland. In the north he saw the frozen sea—a thing incomprehensible to the Mediterraneans. He described the ice as looking like jellyfish, as indeed it did, for anyone who has seen new ice forming on the sea has noticed that the slightest breeze will break up the flexible film into pieces which, jostling together, form "pancake ice" of small rounded disks.

Example of the "jellyfish" ice which Pytheas saw on his voyage.

Throughout history explorers have been doubted on their return home when they gave accounts of what they saw. Pytheas was no exception. After his records were lost, protagonists and antagonists fought over what he had seen, the pancake ice being a case in point. But there is no doubt whatever that he added greatly to the Mediterranean knowledge of northwestern Europe. But perhaps the most important discovery of Pytheas is that he worked out a way of determining latitude.

When a man leads others to victory, he is a great general. When he must see what lies beyond the conquered lands, he becomes an explorer. Such was Alexander of Macedon, the pupil of Aristotle, who crossed every strange river that bordered the unknown—the Danube, Oxus, Jaxartes, and the Indus. The Egyptian desert, too, excited his inquiring mind and he penetrated it as far as the oasis of Siwa.

On his military adventures—and these have somewhat unfairly overshadowed the geographical significance of his journeys—Alexander took with him land surveyors, scribes to observe and record the natural resources of the countries they passed through and to describe the villages, towns, and their products, and he took men who understood the mining of precious metals. He sent one party up the Nile to find out why the river overflowed every year. He sent others to sail along the shores of the Caspian Sea, the northern end of which was quite unknown. He sent thousands of natural history specimens to Aristotle in Athens.

Darius, the great Persian leader and foe of Alexander the Great.

The twenty-year-old Alexander's wars with the Persians were terrible and long and were based on his father's interest in Greece—the belief that a united Greece could overcome the all-conquering Persians. But he first had to establish his authority in the Greek states, so he marched against Thebes (not to be confused with the Babylonian city of the same name), and destroyed the city completely. In one bold stroke he united the Greek states and became master of their armies.

His pursuit of Darius, which ended with the Persian king's death at the hands of his own men, took Alexander to the foot of the Elburz Mountains. On his march through them he was attacked first by wild, half-nomadic tribes who were to become the ancestors of the Turks, then by the Scythians, true nomads. Still in pursuit of the Persians, now led by Bessus, Alexander continued his eastward thrust. His two campaigns in Afghanistan, under the shadow of the towering Hindu Kush, took him to the gateway of India through the wild mountains near the difficult Khyber Pass. Finally his armies reached the fertile land of the Five Rivers (the Punjab). They had survived the battle of Jhelum, and the rest of vast unknown India lay before him. The general and explorer in him thirsted for conquest and sights of new lands. What wonders might be found in a country where elephants (the first he had ever seen) could be used in battle?

But the patience and endurance of his men had reached the breaking point. A mutiny decided his return. So bitter was his disappointment that he shut himself in his tent and flung himself on the ground and cried, so we are told. But it was now that Alexander showed all the instincts of the true explorer. He was determined not to return by the same way he had come but by the shores of the Arabian Sea, crossing country entirely unknown to the Western world. But before he moved on he built twelve altars to mark the limits of his conquest, and he founded many cities, one of which he named after his celebrated charger, Bucephalus. It took him nine months to reach the Indus delta. He had sent some of his men in fleets of ships, while others had marched along the banks as far as they could. At the delta he divided his forces into three sections, two armies going by separate routes through Baluchistan and southern Persia, while the third, under Nearchus, was to sail round to the head of the Persian Gulf.

Alexander himself took the middle and hardest route across the barren stretch along the Makran coast, five hundred miles of wild and forbidding country. Even today it is rarely traveled, but it is well known to passengers looking down on it while flying between Baghdad and Karachi. Of the legions who marched with him, Alexander lost many. He followed the coast as far as possible then turned inland, and it was along a 150-mile stretch before he again reached the sea that, ill-equipped and with little food and less water, men and beasts dropped dead on the scorching heat

Two hundred years before Alexander, Greek merchant galleys were sailing the Mediterranean.

of the desert sands. Plutarch says that "of an army of 120,000 foot and 15,000 horse, he scarcely brought back above a fourth." From the beginning of the campaign until he returned to Babylon more than seven years had passed.

Never before and rarely since has there been such a mass exploration, an unknown region being scientifically examined by three separate and very large bodies of men not for conquest but for knowledge. Heartened by his expedition, particularly the part Nearchus had played by ship, Alexander ordered an even larger fleet of ships for the circumnavigation of Arabia, but his untimely death at the age of thirty-three ended all such thoughts. Alexander's empire stretched from Macedonia and Egypt in the west to the Hindu Kush and the Punjab in the east. On a modern map the countries either conquered by Alexander or subject to him would read Greece, Bulgaria, Rumania, Turkey, Armenia, Persia, Afghanistan, Pakistan, Arabia, Iraq, Syria, Jordan, and Egypt.

Among his other achievements Alexander founded in 332 B.C. a city which was intended to form a trading link between his native Macedonia and the Nile Valley. The city, Alexandria, was to be a new Athens, a cultural center to reflect the intellectual splendor of Greece. It was governed by a Macedonian general (Ptolemy) who became Pharaoh. Greek was spoken at his court, and even before the final decline of Greece the cultural leadership of the eastern Mediterranean had passed to Alexandria.

It was here that Ptolemy conceived one of the noblest ideas of the human mind, that of gathering and distributing knowledge by means of books. In successive generations the Alexandrian library fostered some notable sons—the mathematician Euclid, Apollonius, who wrote on conic sections, Hero, who invented a steam engine, Hipparchus, who

Coin showing Alexander the Great.

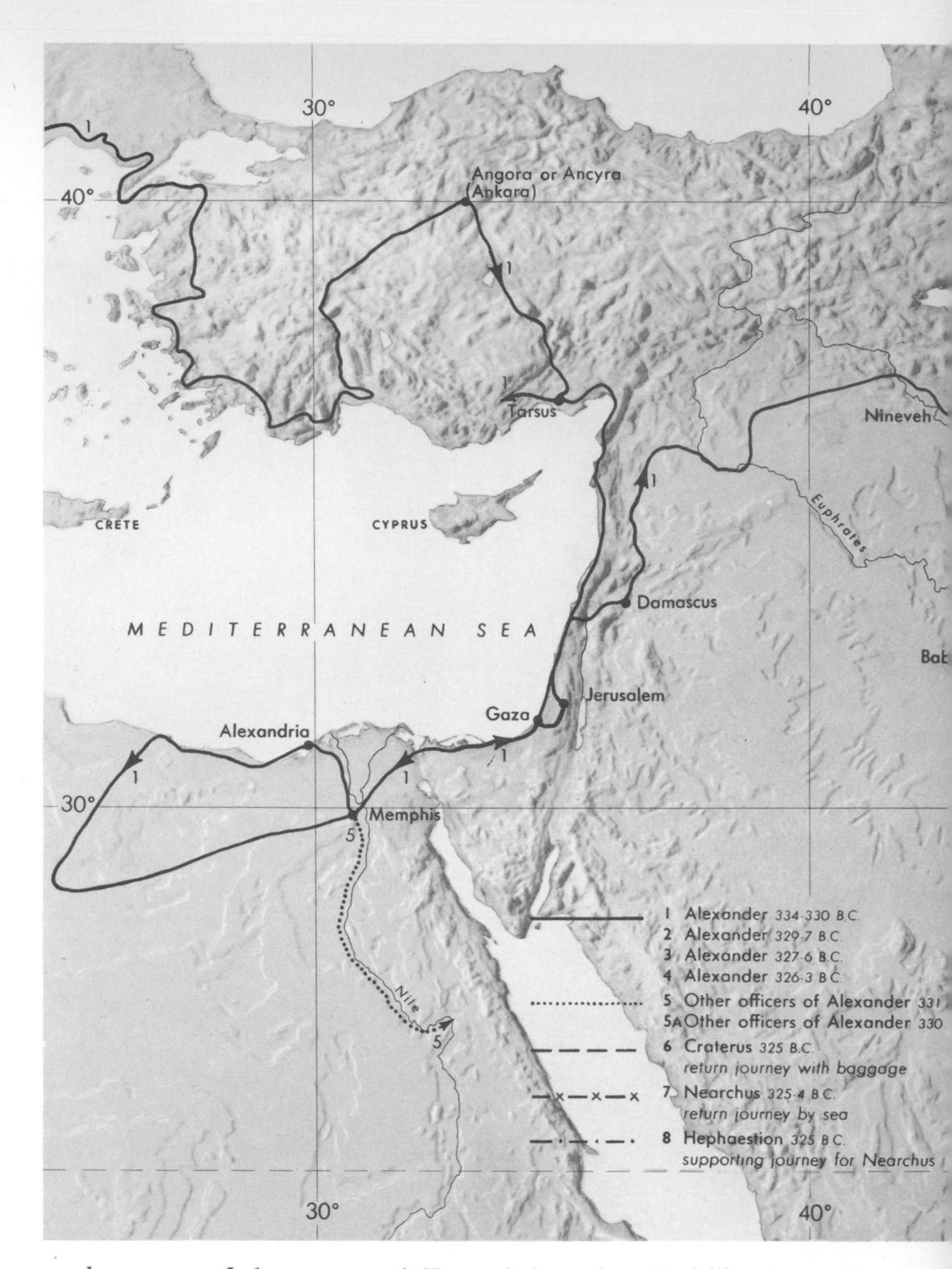

made a map of the stars, and Eratosthenes, the chief librarian, who calculated the size of the earth with amazing accuracy.

Ptolemy's great library ignited a blaze of knowledge such as the world was not to see again until the sixteenth century. Brilliant though the conception was, it was of limited use. Because there was no paper, books could be made only on clumsy papyrus rolls, which were so expensive and difficult to store that only the wealthy could afford them. Eratosthenes' writings on the geography of the world were so explicit that it was possible to construct a map from them, and from this it is clear that the Greeks had no idea that beyond India lay China.

The early story of China will be dealt with later in this book, as will that of India. Here it is necessary to say only that while Alexander was extending his empire the Chinese were consolidating theirs, fighting off invaders from the north. Meanwhile in India the princely Asoka was encouraging his people to dig wells, build hospitals, to cultivate herbs, and even to educate women. In neither of these two great countries is there evidence that their peoples, like Alexander, sought to explore the lands that lay beyond their own.

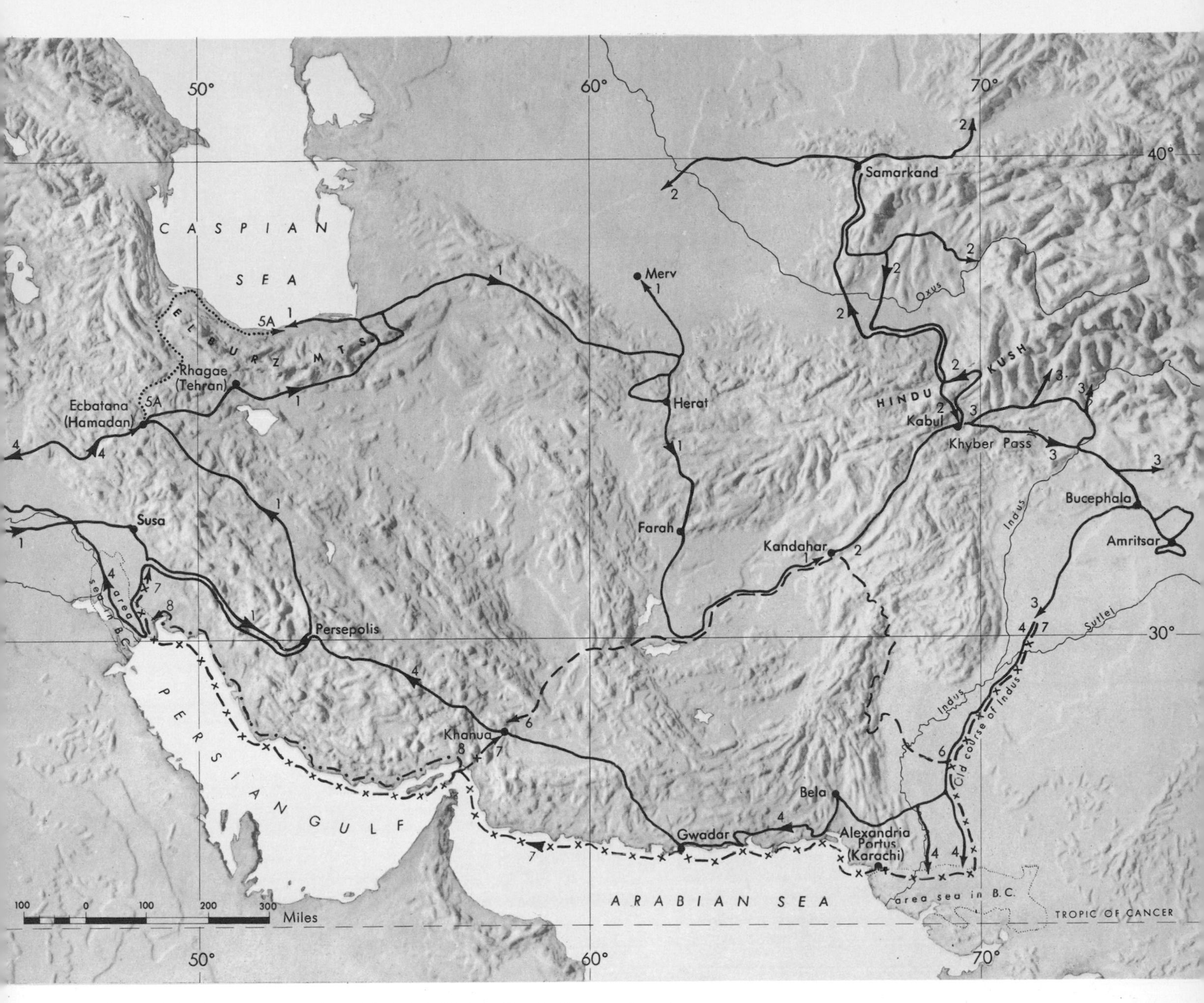

About this time, among the tribes inhabiting the Italian peninsula was a group of Latin-speaking farming communities whose settlements, on the south bank of the Tiber, faced lands long held by the Etruscans whose origins are obscure. The Etruscans were seafarers and may have come from western Asia Minor to settle on the coasts and in the central part of Italy as far back as 900 B.C. By 600 B.C. they had formed an alliance with other communities and become a strong and fearless power. The Greeks called them Tyrrhenians; to the Latins they were Etruscans, or Tuscans, but they were thought of as pirates by both.

The Latins were forced to trade with the Etruscans, their usual meeting place being on marshy ground near a stone bridge built on both sides of an island in the river. Etruscan ships could sail only as far as the bridge. Here they would unload their goods and display them in an open-air market called the Forum; and here the peasant farmers of Latium could exchange corn or cattle for metal tools and weapons—no longer of bronze but of iron. But it was an uneasy situation. Skirmishes between the Etruscans and Latins were constant, and Rome, which grew up on the old trading site, was long a city-state under an Etruscan king.

One of Alexander the Great's horsemen, carved on the sarcophagus at Sidon.

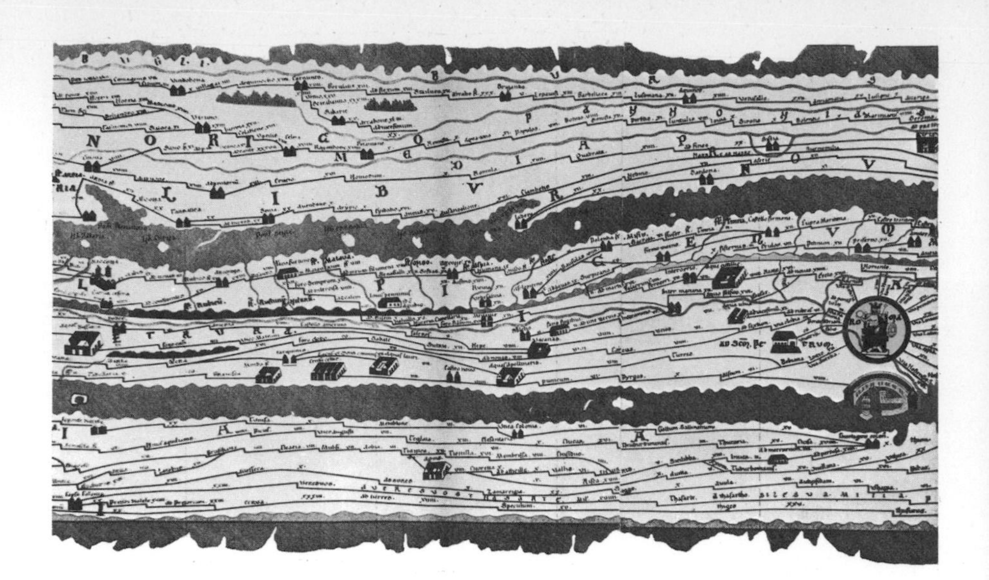

When eventually the Etruscan kings were driven out, the Latins had ceased to be small farmers. By this time they had become a highly civilized people, culturally and politically centered in Rome. But their lives were not destined to be peaceful ones.

The Carthaginians, known also as the Puni or Poeni, had no love for Rome, and when that power began to look dangerous, the long and bitter struggle of the Punic Wars began. To the Romans, the Carthaginians were a treacherous, untrustworthy people. Power and revenge were the two main motives in the three wars which finally exhausted both sides. The first began in 264 B.C. and was for the possession of Sicily. Finally, after twenty three years of fighting, the Carthaginians had to withdraw.

The second, 218-201 B.C., was notable for the bold bid by Hannibal to surprise the Romans from an unexpected quarter. This remarkable and resolute young leader took his troups, their cavalry, and elephants to Carthaginian Spain, from where he marched toward the Rhone. The feat of crossing it with so numerous and heavy an army has become overshadowed by his crossing of the Alps, which was a feat of the greatest endurance. Over unknown and extremely difficult country he marched along tracks so narrow and precipitous that in places his men had to hack away rock so that the elephants could pass.

The third of the Punic Wars—149-146 B.C.—was no less than the wanton destruction of Carthage, leaving Rome as the leading power in the ancient world. The picture of Rome itself in the last century B.C. is that of a very rich city, one that prospered by virtue of money handling rather than by industry. Money could hire mercenaries to fight Roman wars; it could bribe where bribes were acceptable; and it could send large fleets, manned by subject peoples, down the Red Sea and probably across to India for rich cargoes. As the Roman Empire expanded, it constantly had to establish new frontiers in order to defend the last ones, which meant that there was constant exploration, mostly for reconnaissance. An example was the expedition sent by the Emperor Nero to find the sources of the Nile, which certainly reached the marshy land or Sudd region of the White Nile. On the whole, however, their incurious outlook did not encourage exploration for exploration's sake.

As the boundaries of military occupation spread farther and farther afield, so did the boundaries of trade. Roman merchants and their agents

Roman aqueduct, Pont du Gard, at Nîmes; and a Roman road map (top of page) with Rome shown by the yellow dot.

were, in fact, responsible for more discovery than Roman generals. For their own use the merchants compiled guidebooks of a sort, of which the best known was the *Periplous of the Erythraean* [Red] *Sea*, drawn up in the first century A. D. With great exactness it listed the ports and their products, including modern Aden; it also described the Arabian and Indian coasts and gave some account of Ceylon. Trade and traffic along these routes had made considerable progress in the three centuries since the voyage of Alexander's general, Nearchus. Distant travelers had spoken of Malaya, and even the silk trade of China was not unknown.

The Romans left many reminders of their achievements in Europe, including their vast system of roads which circled the Mediterranean and stretched from Mesopotamia to the north of England. This road network encouraged communications with the fringe of the unknown world in a way that sea routes could never do.

Rome itself had enough to do establishing and defending her frontiers without embarking on plans for discovering new lands she would be unable to control. Her great gift to the world was not discovery, but administration; her aim was to consolidate what she held rather than to explore for the sake of exploration. In any case the Romans' scope for world exploration was somewhat circumscribed. To the west it was limited by the Atlantic. To the south the Sahara was a formidable barrier, and difficulties encountered by the few Roman expeditions that got as far as the marshes of the Upper Nile did not encourage further exploration.

This section of the Trajan Column shows some Roman soldiers taking prisoners.

The map on this page shows the world as it was known, part by the East and part by the West, at the time of the decline of Rome. It does not show areas inhabited by static peoples who showed no inclination to discover, to explore, or to move, and were, therefore, taking no part in the exchange of knowledge which implies cultural evolution.

America, for example, is not shown, for although nomads had crossed the Bering Straits there is no evidence that any of them came back. These people left few records of themselves, knew nothing of Egypt, Persia, Greece, Carthage, or Rome, and it is safe to presume that the civilized world knew nothing of them. And, so far as we know, at the time of Rome's decline many of the people inhabiting the dark areas of the world were still culturally in the Stone Age.

But people were inhabiting the earth everywhere. The Mediterranean expansion attendant upon great empires reached out to lands new to the explorers but already occupied. Because few records exist of the nomads' thousands of years of wandering in Africa, America, or Australia, it is only when these lands were *re*discovered that their recorded history begins.

In the last few centuries before the Christian era, pressure of nomadic groups on the settled peoples of Asia and Europe became more and more evident. To find a cause we must move across Asia to China, where there was a civilization coincident in time and brilliance with that of the Mediterranean area.

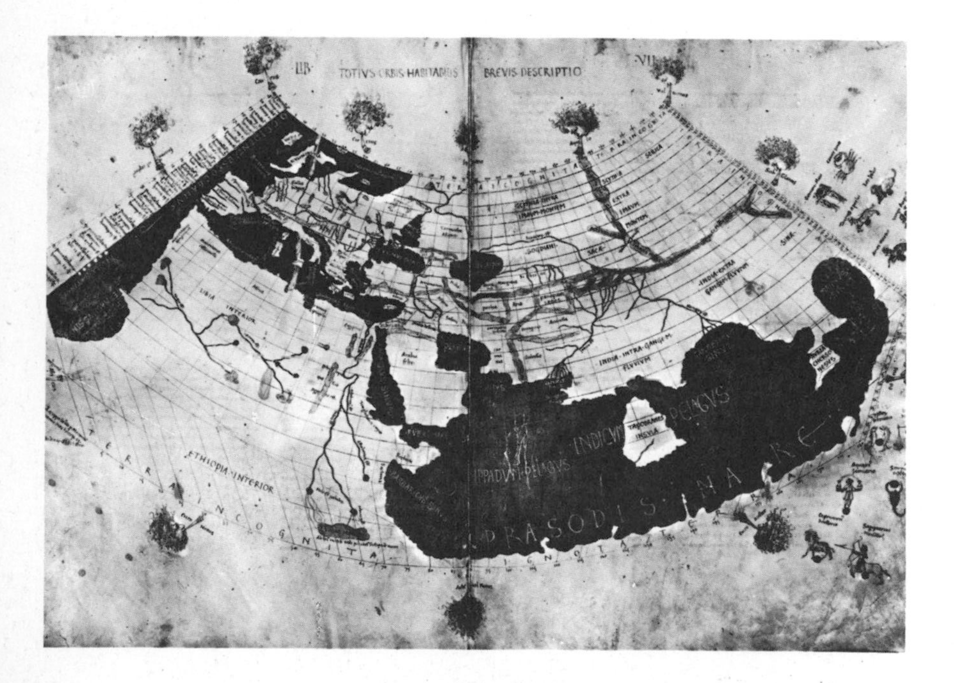

A 1447 world map based on Ptolemy. Notice the sprawling southern continent *terra incognita*.

Areas of the world known up to A.D. 150 by the West and East are shown in relief coloring; the unknown world is shown in indigo.

Danube
ROPE
Rome
Athens
DITERRANEAN SEA
hage
Euphrates
Tyre
Babylon
Alexandria
Kashgar
Peking
90°
Indus
Hormuz
Yangtzu
A
S
I
A
RED SEA
Nile
Aden

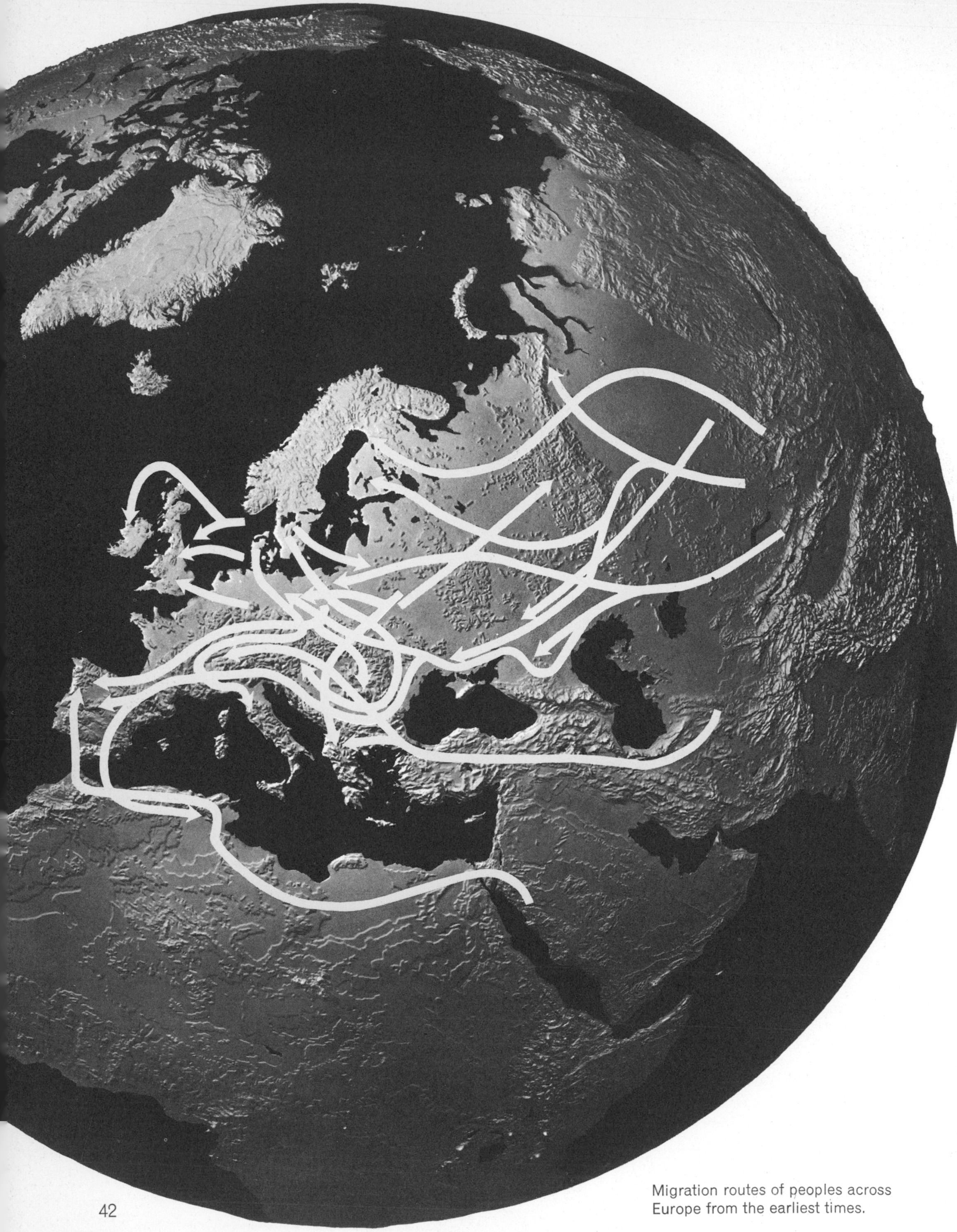

Migration routes of peoples across
Europe from the earliest times.

The world grows larger

Each time the nomads of Central Asia raided the settled farmers the age-old hostilities between Cain and Abel sprang into prominence. The nomads did not want to exchange the freedom and simplicity of life on the plains for the splendors of the city or the security of long-established farms; but they did want the spoils of their despised neighbors.

The origins of these nomads lie far back in Neolithic times. Very few traces of them remain, but they probably wandered over or near the desert zone which extends from Arabia to Mongolia. The slow relentless advance of ice during the last Ice Age resulted in the forest land's receding southward; with its recession grasslands replaced forests north of the Caspian Sea. It may have been through that corridor that the Asiatic nomads trickled into Europe. They moved in mass migration, spreading across Europe as far as Finland and Lapland, where some remained, while others, called Goths, wandered toward the west and then returned, gradually to become assimilated by the peoples they plundered. The nomads' raiding parties on the settled peoples became highly organized.

Greeks and Romans encountered the nomads and spoke of them as barbarians; to the civilized they were wild and uncouth, skilled only in the art of mobile warfare. But the fact that the Mediterranean peoples knew little of them does not mean that the nomads sprang into existence suddenly: the nomadic way of life predates the city way of life that grew out of agrarian societies. Changes in climate and the search for food controlled their wanderings. In Eurasia the camel owners kept to the semideserts, the horse and cattle people to the grassy plains. In the hills, where vegetation is too sparse for soft-mouthed animals, shepherds followed their sheep. For the most part their boundaries were natural ones; but some of the nomad migrations may have been fugitive in nature for the tribes fought each other for the possession of flocks, herds, or desirable territory. Whether by defeat, conquest, or peaceful penetration, the successive waves of nomads, drifting from Asia into Europe, engendered a fusion of peoples, languages and customs.

The Chinese, too, were conscious of the nomads pressing on their northern borders. They called them the Hiung-nu, which may be the same as the generic term Huns; and they had cause to fear these horse-riding, flesh-eating people from the semiarid regions of the Gobi desert. The Huns despised the settled Chinese and described them as "caged-up man-milliners" because of their silk trade. The Huns' boast was that their country was "the back of a horse."

There were frequent wars between Huns and Chinese, some of them on a scale which dwarfed those between the Mesopotamian Empires. But finally about 200 B.C. the Chinese drove the Huns back across the desert and finished building the Great Wall of China, 1500 miles long, 15 to 20 feet thick, and rarely less than 20 feet high. The amount of earth and stone that went into the wall's construction was four times that moved in cutting the Panama Canal. With the help of the Great Wall, China was able by the second century B.C. to deflect the Huns toward the west—a feat which induced a series of raids and migrations which reached all across Asia and Europe. It was then that real unrest began among the nomads, a seething and eddying which was to go on for a thousand years. In a remote sense one might say that the decline and fall of the Roman Empire was due to the rise of the Chinese Empire, which had turned the tide of the aggressive nomads westward. Eventually the nomads' routes became the standard corridors from the East to the West for armies, traders, and men on diplomatic missions.

The Great Wall of China, built to stem the invading Huns, deflected these nomads westward.

China's Great Wall, although breached time and again, gave China the protection she needed against the nomadic Huns. Discouraged, the Huns pushed west in migratory attacks, during one of which they drove a Chinese tribe, the Yuechi, westward from the southern part of the Gobi. In turn the Yuechi displaced a tribe from Kashgar who moved into Bactria, driving its Greek settlers across the Hindu Kush. A later push by the Huns followed a pattern of displacement similar to the earlier one, but the Yuechi finally settled and built an empire based on the city we now call Peshawar. Later this empire was in diplomatic contact with the Romans and sent its envoys to Augustus. Among the things the Yuechi had brought with them from China were the peach and the pear—the latter reaching Europe through Persia, from which its name is derived.

In the second century B.C. lived one of the earliest known Chinese travelers, Chang Ch'ien. He was sent out alone by the Emperor Wu Ti of the Han dynasty to make contact with the Yuechi, but on the way was taken prisoner by the Huns and remained so for ten years. Finally he escaped but, instead of returning home and lamenting his misfortune, he pushed on to Fergana, where he was well received. Eventually he reached the Yuechi, completed his mission, and set out for home; but on his way back to China, via Tibet, he again had the misfortune of being captured by raiding Huns. Twelve more years he spent in exile, after which he managed to reach China safely and was able to supply the emperor with much valuable information. Eleven years later he was sent on another mission to the west, this time to establish Chinese agencies in Fergana. His reports resulted in the opening of a famous silk route. Another route opened up about this time led southward over the mountains into India and followed the course of the Ganges, carrying trading expeditions into the settled areas of India. With the establishment of regular trading routes, Chinese envoys, backed by the growing military forces of a settled China, traveled widely and finally reached Persia. It was at this period, during the second century B.C., that the empire reached its greatest extent, stretching from the Pacific Ocean to the Sea of Aral.

Early Chinese travelers,
a detail from a painting on wood.

China's contacts with the West by sea were mainly due to the enterprise of Arab seamen, and in some of the earliest accounts from Arab sources are references to the frequent appearances of ships from India and China on the Euphrates in the first half of the fifth century A.D. Later Chinese sources of the seventh and eighth centuries describe the route taken by the junks from Canton, where the Arab traders had established a factory, or trading post, to the Euphrates. After making Ceylon, they steered for Malabar and across the Gulf of Cambay. Mention is made of the Indus, and it is clear that they followed the course taken by Nearchus nearly a thousand years earlier, past the Straits of Hormuz and so to the mouth of the Euphrates.

Trade, then, was the primary stimulus encouraging an exchange of knowledge between China and the lands west and south, as it had been for the Mediterranean people earlier. But a new stimulus to travel was making itself felt.

When man embraces a religious belief with passion, he must communicate it to others. With the rise of Buddhism, Christianity, and Mohammedanism came spreaders of the gospels who crossed frontiers to preach their messages of hope. Zeal for evangelization, then, became a new motive for exploration and travel. But it also worked in the reverse. In all three religions, converts, in the course of time, went on pilgrimages—the pilgrimage to Mecca being the best known today.

A small but steady stream of Christian pilgrimages began as early as the third century to become fashionable when Helena, the mother of Constantine the Great, made a prolonged journey to the Holy Land. She was followed by other aristocrats, though the majority of the pilgrims were still simple folk.

As travel in Palestine itself became more difficult, pilgrims visited other scenes from New Testament history—Rome and northwest Spain, for example. This comparative freedom for a pilgrim to travel was something quite new in Europe and it led naturally to a far wider knowledge among the common people.

About 250 B.C., under the great Indian King Asoka, the missionary zeal of Buddhism spread outward to Central Asia, and later to China and Japan by the silk route and to the islands of southeast Asia, probably by trading junks which carried missionaries on their tireless journeys.

A significant, though tangled, series of moves within the Christian Church around A.D. 430 led to communications across national boundaries such as armed forces could not have achieved. The story begins with

In the fourteenth century Jên Jên-fa, a Chinese official in the service of the Mongols, made this painting of a group of Mongols tending their horses.

the tradition that the apostle Thomas went to India and became a missionary and martyr. The next phase of the story involves Nestorius, a bishop of Constantinople who was excommunicated for his unorthodox beliefs but continued vigorously to preach, to such effect that his followers established strong centers in Persia and in southern India. Here they became associated with a group who believed in the apostle Thomas story.

Later on, around the 1100s, the Nestorians were linked with the legends of Prester John, a Christian potentate of great power and wealth in Central Asia. However vague and even fabulous these stories may have been they were current in Europe, and the growing Roman Church was naturally interested in a branch of Christianity—even a splinter group—which was so powerful in far away countries. Investigators were sent to find out what was going on.

Saint Brendan, one of the Irish Monks who reached Iceland ahead of the Vikings. Significance of the large fish is a puzzle.

So it was that religion played an active part in encouraging travel in China, India, and Europe, and that many missionaries of various faiths became explorers whose journeys added to the total sum of knowledge.

For missionary travel which was truly bold exploration we must go to the far west of Europe, where we find a group of Irish monks. Columba's journey to Iona, off Scotland, led to one of the most extraordinary cases of discovery that we know of, for there is good evidence that a group of Irish monks reached Iceland as early as 795—a voyage of 500 miles in the open sea if they sailed from the Hebrides, or more than 300 miles if they touched at the Faeroes on the way. They are believed to have sailed there in wicker-frame boats covered with hides. The Norsemen found the monks in Iceland when they settled there in 874; either there were later reinforcements from Ireland or the monks the Norwegians met were close to a hundred years old.

While men in the northwest of Europe were pushing out boldly to Iceland, Greenland, and beyond, there was very little discovery from the Mediterranean region. As in Central Asia, there was a great deal of traveling for trade, especially from Alexandria, the great emporium for goods from the East. Cosmas was one of the leading merchant-travelers in the sixth century; he later turned monk and wrote of his journeys. He probably got as far as Ceylon, where he may have seen Chinese junks which were regularly coming there at that time and occasionally reaching as far as the Persian Gulf. Cosmas also knew the southern end of the Red

Sea. His ideas about the shape of the world were quite absurd and well illustrate Alexandria's intellectual decline since Ptolemy's time.

By the year 1000 Islam ruled from Spain to India and had became the natural heir to the civilizations of Egypt and Mesopotamia. The constant struggle between Christendom and Islam led eventually to the Crusades. For centuries thousands of nameless pilgrims had been making their way to the Holy Land. Organized by Popes and kings, the early Crusades were the outcome of a surge of religious fervor never before known to Europe. There was even a moral and chivalrous side to the Crusade movement, so that it became known as the Age of Chivalry. The knights with their badge of the cross had a code of honor unknown to the classical world.

Long before the Crusades began a people known as the Vikings had settled in Europe's northlands which were unknown to people of the Mediterranean area. They were men of a Nordic race who battled against stormy seas and coaxed an unproductive soil. The poverty of the soil forced the Vikings to turn to the sea for food, which bred in them both courage and bold seamanship quite outside the Mediterranean experience.

The exploits of these Norsemen still ring in European ears. Their deep-sea voyages were of a dramatic and striking kind, ranging from Norway to America, to Spain and the Mediterranean, even as far as Constantinople. The ships they used were long open boats called "serpents," usually with a carved figurehead at the prow. The sailor-warriors carried their shields in slots along the gunwales, each man's lying alongside his own oar. There was one sail, useful if a favorable wind aided their journey. A small deck at the extreme end of the stern was the only fixed shelter, but the mast could be taken down and propped up horizontally so that with the sail lashed across it a rough and ready tent could be made for inclement weather. In such simple boats these intrepid Norsemen struck out across uncharted seas on missions of conquest.

Their expeditions were carried out during the summer. In winter they repaired or built their boats, fished, and prepared for the next summer's

An early Viking ship, taken from a ninth century tombstone. In ships like this the Vikings sailed to Greenland and America.

forays. Many of their exploits they recorded in sagas, one relating how they navigated by relying on the instincts of birds. They took with them a number of ravens, and when they had sailed well to the west they released one. If the raven flew back along the course they had steered, they sailed farther west for a few days, releasing more birds from time to time. Only when a raven flew forward would they change course and follow its flight path in search of new land. Apart from this, they had certainly discovered how to navigate along a given latitude.

Under the general name of Vikings, these men from the fiords and bays of Norway, Sweden, and Denmark early discovered the Faeroe Islands. About A. D. 780 they began their summer raids on Scotland and Ireland, a few years later reaching the south of England. Their mission was to plunder and return to their homes, but in some cases they settled on the lands that they conquered; for example, the Orkneys, the Shetlands, and Ireland saw settlements which might well be called colonization. The Europeans saw Viking fleets sail up the Rhine and the Seine sacking capital cities as they went. Raiders the Vikings may have been, but they were also traders—across Europe and as far afield as Baghdad.

More than a thousand years ago the Norsemen built this church, the remains of which were discovered at Hvälso, Greenland.

One of the earliest of Norwegian explorers was a man called Ohthere, or Ottar, who sailed around the North Cape and along the coast to the White Sea. In his own words he was "desirous to see how far the country extended north and whether anyone lived there."

Their first and chief colony was Iceland, which the Irish monks had already discovered. Next came Greenland, where hot-tempered Eric the Red spent three years exploring the southwest coast. He had left Iceland for various "domestic reasons"; reportedly, he was outlawed because he quarreled with most of his farmer-neighbors and killed several of them. To escape his enemies he sailed west in search of islands he had heard of. The result was that he discovered a land, the south end of which had deep fiords with grassy valleys at their head. Having found a suitable harbor, Eric returned to fetch his family and friends to settle on Greenland. But the little colony had to depend on the mother country for supplies. On one of their voyages to Iceland a ship was blown off course and sighted the coast of Nova Scotia but, in spite of the entreaties of his crew, the captain refused to land. Later, Eric's son Leif fitted out a ship and with thirty five Greenlanders set out to prove to himself that land lay to the west. He reached Labrador and Newfoundland and, sailing farther south, came to a great river swarming with salmon where he said "day and night were more equally divided than in Greenland." He and his crew stayed in "Vinland," as they called it, until the following spring. From his observations the settlement could have been on the coast of New Jersey or Virginia.

In boats like this the Vikings carried out their raids and explorations. The above "Gokstad ship" is 17 feet wide 75 feet long.

Other expeditions followed, including those carrying men and women as colonists, and stories of their adventures were handed down from father to son, later to be written in the famous sagas. These tell of fights with Indians, whose silent warfare the Norsemen found little to their liking. For this or some other reason they did not persist in their attempts to colonize the new country. For a while they continued to sail to Vinland for timber, but gradually their visits ceased altogether.

Nothing of this major discovery was known to anyone in any other part of Europe. The stories and songs describing the voyages were not put into writing until some two or three hundred years after they had taken place. The Norsemen's failure to exploit their discovery will always remain a puzzle. If they had remained in America how different the history of the world would have been!

Voyages of the Norse

Norse voyages & journeys in the 5th-8th centuries

Norse voyages & journeys in the 9th century

Norse voyages in the 10th century (including those of Eric the Red)

Norse voyages in the 11th century (including those of Leif Ericson)

The growth of monotheistic religious beliefs led gradually to the new idea that groups of the same faith should unite politically. This sort of idea was the origin of the Arab Empire, which plays an important part in our story of exploration.

It began in the fertile Yemen at the southwestern tip of the Arabian peninsula. Overpopulation of the area began to press groups of wandering, pastoral people northward. They drifted until they reached the fertile crescent and the coastal districts of the Mediterranean. These scattered groups of warlike nomads became a powerful unified force of one race, one language, and one religion, under the leadership of a man called Mohammed (A.D. 570–632). By sheer force of arms the Mohammedans spread the new Islamic religion far and wide, marching against the crumbling empires of Egypt, Rome, Byzantium, and Persia. Finally the whole of North Africa from the Atlantic shores to the Red Sea, all of Spain, parts of southern France, the Mediterranean islands, Inner Asia as far as the western borders of China and through the Indus Basin to the shores of the Indian Ocean, came under Moslem rule. In the course of time this great empire was divided into distinctive countries under different Arab dynasties, but the Moslem religion remained and is to this day the greatest unifying force of this area.

The rapid dispersal of the Arab peoples was followed by an equally remarkable development in learning. In the great Moslem centers—Spain, North Africa, and the Middle East—academies and universities were built, and scholars from all over the known world came there to learn and to teach. Enormous advances were made in the study of natural sciences, (zoology, botany, geology) and in mathematics, chemistry, medicine, astronomy, and geography. Arab navigators had polished up their practical astronomy and learned about tides, currents, and the cycle of the monsoons by sailing time and again round the shores of the Indian Ocean on missions of trade. The Arabs also improved the rigging of ships, their lateen fore-and-aft sail superseding the heavy trireme and quinquereme (three-bank and five-bank) system of oars used for so long by the Romans and Carthaginians. The lateen sail proved particularly good in trade wind areas.

Idrisi's map of the world shows Europe, Asia, and a half-moon-shaped Africa. The shiplike figure, lower left of center, shows Mountains of the Moon and three lakes feeding the Nile. All of the dark, heavy lines on the map represent mountains.

The vast conquests of the Moslem Empire after the death of Mohammed gave it control from Gibraltar to India, and the Arabs, being primarily coastal sailors, were not slow to take advantage of the long seaboard of the Indian Ocean. Under the caliphate, usually centered at Baghdad, travelers were required to record what they had seen on their journeys; and about the middle of the ninth century a sort of geographical library began to be collected.

Among early Arabian geographers were Soleyman (about 850) and al-Masudi (about 920), who, among other things, recorded much information about China, including the making of tea. At this time China had not yet adopted the isolationist policy which she later assumed.

Al-Masudi left records of journeys which took him from Spain in the west to Turkistan in the east; he mentions also Zanzibar, Sind, and China, but it was his successor, the Spanish-born Arab called Idrisi, whose work had more influence on Europe than that of any of the earlier geographers. Idrisi traveled widely in Europe. He visited France and England and worked his way eastward through Asia Minor, finally returning to the Mediterranean where he settled in Sicily and around 1150 wrote a geographical treatise and produced a famous map engraved on a silver tablet. This map shows the Nile with its source in three lakes far to the south; it also pictures a great river flowing from these lakes, but westward,

A thirteenth-century manuscript shows this Arab boat, which is probably manned by slaves.

to the Atlantic—a composite river which could have been the Niger and the Senegal.

The greatest Moslem explorer of them all was Ibn Batuta—a westernized Arab from Tangier, who was destined to become an even more traveled person than Marco Polo. Batuta set out when he was quite young, and in 1325 began a remarkable series of journeys lasting the best part of thirty years, at the end of which time he could boast that he had been everywhere in the Islamic Empire, and to many infidel countries as well.

In his writings he does not attempt to hide his faults—his many marriages and as frequent desertions, his greed, his borrowings and forgetting to repay, and his plottings against employers he was supposed to serve. On the other hand he was a courageous and devout man. His first intention had been the usual one of making the pilgrimage to Mecca, so he set off by land across North Africa to Alexandria and Cairo, turning south into Upper Egypt with the object of crossing the Red Sea to Jidda. When he found that no ships were available he traveled north again and then east, intending to make his journey overland from Damascus. He spent a good deal of time on this pilgrimage and was in fact the first real explorer of Arabia. He stayed in Mecca as a student for three years but, always restless and footloose, he set out again, this time for Medina and Baghdad, traveling along the pilgrim route across the peninsula. Making Baghdad his base, he journeyed extensively into Persia and then moved south to explore the Yemen. Taking a ship at Aden, he sailed down the east coast of Africa as far south as Mombasa. By this time he had become a prosperous trader, and on his return he set out eastward for the Persian Gulf where he landed on the Arabian coast, making excursions inland and finally crossing Arabia on his way home.

On other journeys he went to Anatolia and the towns of Asia Minor, across the Black Sea, and east to Bukhara and Samarkand. His route to India took him across the Hindu Kush and, working his way southward, he reached the Indus Valley. In India he was received everywhere as a distinguished Moslem traveler and scholar. His experiences during his extensive travels make fascinating reading. He was a keen observer and was interested in all that he saw, taking the ups and downs of travel calmly. He had a post at the court of the Sultan at Delhi, where he lived for seven years, and later was sent as the Sultan's ambassador to the court of China. Batuta's embassy set out with a large escort of troops but was attacked on the way and lost many of his possessions. Glad to have escaped with his life, he finally reached the coast of India and embarked at Gandhara. The ship called at Goa, at Malabar, and finally docked at Calicut to await favorable weather for the journey to China.

But the ambassador's troubles were not to end here. Shipwreck followed and Batuta was left stranded on the shore while his ship, his personal goods and presents for the Chinese Emperor, and many of his slave girls and boys were scattered over the eastern seas. Eventually he reached Peking, only to find that the Emperor was not there.

An Arab caravan traveling to Mecca, taken from a thirteenth-century manuscript.

He made more than one journey to the Maldive Islands, whose queen welcomed him and gave him a job, and where he settled down and married several wives. But he soon became restless again and set out, this time to Ceylon which he explored extensively; then he crossed over to the Coromandel coast where he again was shipwrecked. Ultimately he arrived back at Calicut a poor man. He returned to the Maldive Islands, sailed on to Bengal, where he landed at Chittagong, and then made a trip across Assam. Back in Bengal, he embarked for Java, a voyage of forty days and, after touching the Malay peninsula, he reached an unidentified port in China before starting his long homeward journey to Fès, where he wrote his great book entitled *Travels in Asia and Africa.*

In his journals Batuta mentioned a voyage by Idrisi into the Atlantic, then known as the Sea of Darkness, where his sailors discovered an island far removed from Europe and inhabited by "red men with smooth hair." This might have been Madeira or perhaps one of the Azores, although there were no inhabitants on those islands when they were rediscovered later. If the story is true it is the only instance of exploration by Arabs to the west of Europe.

Batuta also crossed into Spain, where he had a brush with Christian raiders, and after his return he undertook his last journey, one of the most important. He crossed the Sahara and entered the valley of the Niger which he explored carefully, visiting the towns of Timbuktu and Gao. He then crossed the desert east to explore the western Sudan. On his return he was received with great honors by the Sultan of Morocco and settled down at Fès for the rest of his days.

The accounts of Ibn Batuta's travels are remarkable for their accuracy of description of people and places and for their frankness and lack of exaggeration. Together they contribute a detailed description of the Moslem lands. Batuta lived to the age of seventy-three and is said to have traveled at least 75,000 miles.

Toward the end of the Crusades, which stretched from 1096 to 1291, affairs in Mongolia took a sudden turn which was to affect the world from China across Asia to the Holy Roman Empire.

Near the end of the twelfth century a new tribe of Mongols, the Tartars, kindred of the earlier Huns, suddenly sprang to prominence in the region of Lake Baikal and the Amur River. These people had developed a method of fighting which was entirely original and which carried all before it in much the same way as a division of tanks. The Tartars used no infantry; instead they relied on swift, mounted armies, always on the move and able to attack from the rear. They were too much for the slow-moving Chinese and even for the more mobile forces of the Huns in the western steppes.

Central Asian nomads breaking camp. As the illustration shows, their equipment was designed for mobility.

By 1215 their great leader, Genghis Khan, had subdued (but not conquered) China and married a princess before turning toward the west, overcoming or absorbing peoples as he went. When he died he was Emperor from the Yellow Sea to the Persian Gulf and the Black Sea, by conquest which had been even more rapid and decisive than that of Alexander the Great. Within forty years the Tartars had overrun Poland, and only the wooded country of Germany prevented them from sweeping on to the Atlantic. The three great Khans—Mangu, Hulagu, and Kublai—were all leaders, and in 1260 Kublai became the sole Emperor. Of the lands they attacked, China alone remained fully unconquered, as she has repelled all invaders throughout history.

Eager to learn about the Mongol Empire, in 1245 the Pope sent an elderly Franciscan friar named John de Carpini to the Great Khan as his personal representative. Carpini traveled 3000 miles on horseback across south Russia and Turkistan to the northern silk route, passing Lake Balkhash, in less than four months reaching the Khan's court which was established on a river running into Lake Baikal. The friar tells us that he had a stout body; he must also have had a stout heart to have ridden an average of thirty miles a day. After a stay of some sixteen months he returned by the same route, but this time he had to face the hazards of winter. He was the first real explorer from Europe, and his *Book of the Tartars* was a plain statement of what, to the Western world, was a real discovery.

Six years later Carpini was followed by another Franciscan, William of Rubruquis, younger than Carpini but just as stouthearted. Sent to the Great Khan as envoy of Louis, King of France, he traveled mainly by cart on a route similar to the one taken by Carpini and saw the Great Khan at the same place. His book contains a detailed account of life among the Tartars, but neither he nor Carpini mentioned China since the khanate had not yet moved to that country.

Initial letter E from a manuscript of Rubruquis, showing him top right.

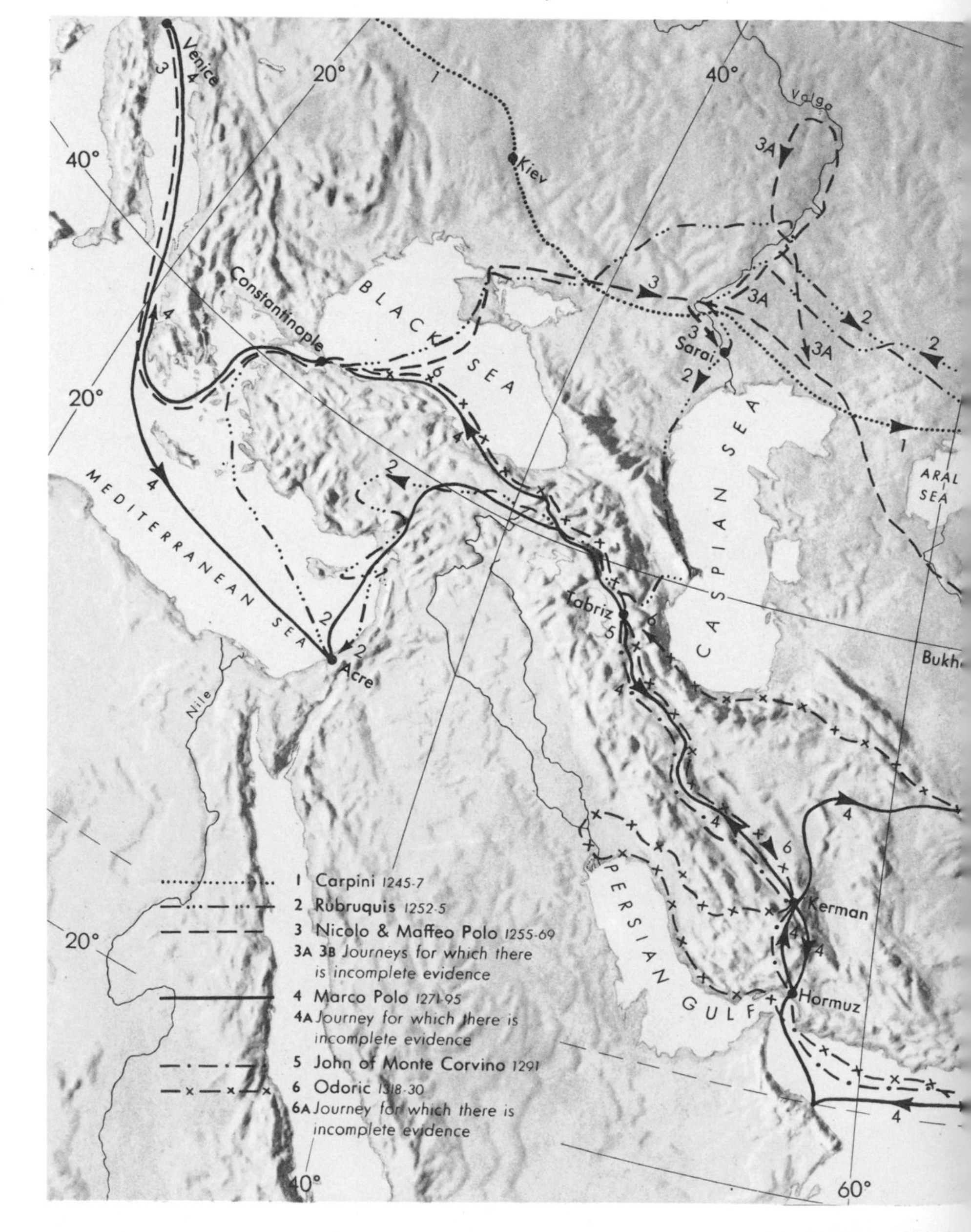

While Rubruquis was still among the Tartars two Venetian merchants were also making their way eastward—the Polo brothers, Maffeo and Niccolò.

They were businessmen who began to travel for the purpose of buying and selling jewels. In 1260, finding themselves in Constantinople, they decided to cross the Black Sea and visit a Tartar dignitary, a Khan, at Sarai where, from all accounts, they profited greatly. Travelers in those days did not make all speed to reach a destination, nor did they leave it in haste. Maffeo and Niccolò remained in Sarai for a year and may well have stayed longer if war had not broken out among the Tartar chiefs. To avoid it the Polos set off once more, but the fighting prevented them from returning the same way they had come so they turned eastward and traveled across the desert to Bukhara, where they remained for three years.

The arrival in "the great and noble city" of a Tartar caravan turned the Polos' thoughts further eastward, and they joined it on its journey to visit the Great Khan. Their way took them through Samarkand, Turkistan, and on to Cambaluc, near present-day Peking, a known and comparatively simple route on the north side of the Tarim Basin. They

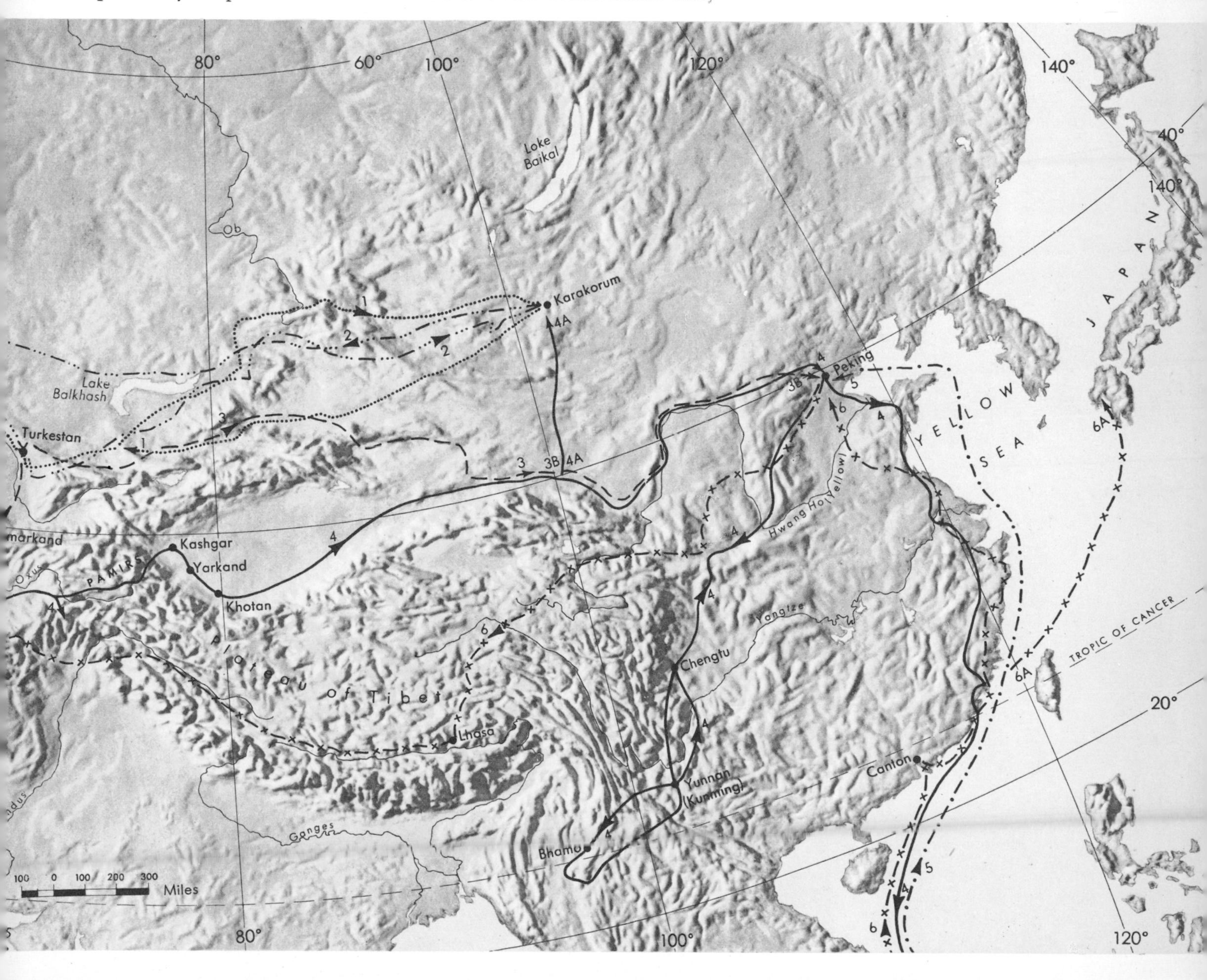

were well received by Kublai, who expressed much interest in their ways and manners and was particularly anxious to know more of the Christian religion. When the Polos finally began their homeward journey, they carried a message from the Khan to the Pope with instructions to bring back a hundred men of "learning and ability" to inform the Mongols on the Western way of life.

It took the Polo brothers three years to get as far as Acre, north of Jerusalem, where they learned that the Pope was dead. This meant that they could not deliver their message so they returned to Venice, some nine years after they had set out. They had crossed Asia from west to east and back again.

Two years later there was still no Pope. Not wishing to delay their return to the Great Khan any longer, the Polos started out again, but on hearing that a new Pope had at last been elected, and had summoned them to return to Acre, they retraced their steps. When they arrived in Acre papal envoys met them and gave them splendid presents for the Great Khan, among which was a flask of sacred oil. The envoys also assigned two preaching friars to accompany the Polos and convert the heathen Mongols. And so the Polos set out again, but during the trip the friars excused themselves when they began to see the perils of such a journey; whatever chances there had been of carrying Christianity into

The Polo brothers on their way to Peking from Bukhara to visit the Great Khan. They are shown traveling with an embassy caravan.

China at that time were lost. Although the two monks turned back, a third traveler in the party continued the journey with eager delight. He was Niccolò's seventeen-year-old son, Marco.

It is curious that among the more illustrious of explorers the name Marco Polo shines with continuing brilliance and yet, in the true sense of the word, he was not an explorer at all. The journeys he made all had been made before, dozens of times. Why, then, has his name habitually been given so much attention? It is because he faithfully described in writing the people and places he saw—people and places his countrymen had never heard of. For this reason he finds an honored place in our story of exploration.

On his first journey, with his father and uncle, the young Marco traveled through Persia and crossed Alexander's route to the port of Hormuz where Nearchus had beached his ships some thousand years earlier. The three wanted to reach China by sea but they could not find a ship, so they turned back north to Kerman and followed the mountain route to Balkh, then journeyed along the valley of the Oxus to enter the desolate Pamir—"the roof of the world." For twelve days they went without seeing another human being, animal, or bird; and ahead of them were an additional forty days' travel across the lofty barren desert to Kashgar.

Throughout this difficult country everything they needed to sustain life had to be carried. Their caravan consisted of camels to carry supplies,

The Polo brothers presenting Kublai Khan gifts on arriving at his court.

camel drivers, and servants. The Polos and their attendants rode horses, but there were many places in the mountains where the animals had to be led. Before starting for Kashgar young Marco fell ill. The journey was delayed for a year so that he could be taken to the highlands of Badakhshan to recover. His notebooks tell of the sweet mountain air, the horses, and the precious stones he found there. He speaks also of the rams with curling horns which roam the high Pamirs.

After Marco's recovery the Polos reached Kashgar, with its cool vineyards and cultivated fields. From here they followed the ancient route through Yarkand, Khotan and Lob Nor to China. An escort was sent by the Great Khan to meet them forty days' journey from Peking. The Khan was delighted to see them and he made much of Marco, who was given a post in the Khan's court. Their journey from Venice had taken them three and a half years.

A new world opened to young Marco. His gift for learning languages, his pleasing manners and his intelligence soon marked him as a man the Khan could trust. Time after time the Khan sent Marco on diplomatic missions. He saw things he had never dreamed of—a civilization equal to, if not beyond, his own. In China he saw people using paper money; he also saw block printing, elaborate buildings, countless ships on great rivers, huge cities with thousands of people. For the first time he saw coal burned and he saw asbestos, which would not burn at all. He went to Shansi, Szechwan and Tibet, Karakorum and Cochin China, and his reports pleased Kublai Khan so well that he kept Marco at his court for twenty years. The only way Marco Polo was released from the Khan's court was through his wish to send a young princess to marry a Persian prince and Marco offered to escort her.

Their return journey was by sea in a fleet of fourteen ships ordered by the Khan. Marco wrote of spices and of cannibals in Sumatra, where they were delayed for five months. His family interest in jewels appears in his careful description of a royal ruby in Ceylon; on the Coromandel Coast he saw pearls. At Gujarat he met Brahmins, but at Hormuz he was back on familiar ground. Of the 600 who had set out with the Polos and their princess, only eighteen survived. When finally, after about two years, the small group arrived in Persia, the princess' suitor was long since dead, but as she had never met him she was perhaps equally happy to marry his son.

Marco Polo as an old man.

From Persia the Polos returned to Venice by way of Tabriz, Trebizond, and Constantinople after an absence of 24 years. Although Marco kept records of his journeys, his book might never have seen the light of day if it had not been for a strange chance. Three years after his return war broke out between the Venetians and the Genoese. With 7000 others Marco was taken prisoner, and while he was detained he dictated his story to a fellow prisoner. It is said that his captors allowed him to send to Venice for his notebooks, and this would account for the close detail he gives of journeys which began more than 25 years earlier. For example, when he briefly describes his crossing of the Pamir he mentions that because the region is so lofty the "fire does not give out so much heat as usual nor does it cook food effectually."

Marco's book was widely read and widely disbelieved. Years later, when he was on his death bed, some of his friends begged him to recant "all the lies he had told." He replied, "I have not told half of what I saw."

Marco Polo's book bridges a gap between East and West. After him the northern trade route to China became popular. Many missionaries, however, followed the southern routes and one of these, John of Monte Corvino, reached Peking by sea. He remained for more than thirty years and established a church there. His letters to the Pope describe his life, his school, his Chinese choirboys and his pleasure that the Great Khan liked to hear them sing. For all that he was unable to convert the Khan.

Another missionary, Friar Odoric, spent fourteen years traveling from Constantinople to Canton by sea and returning overland through Shensi and Tibet. He was the first European to describe Lhasa.

At this time a steady trickle of Christian missionaries were entering China and India in spite of Moslem attempts to prevent them. The West was beginning to know the East, but the driving force which sent Europeans into the Orient did not work in reverse. Neither Chinese nor Indians were sea rovers and they do not seem to have thought the attractions of the West sufficiently great to risk the hostility of the Moslems, whose rapid expansion was proving an effective barrier.

Perhaps it was partly because of this that in later years China became cut off from the West, to remain for centuries in isolation. Another reason was that after the death of the Great Khan and his followers new and less enlightened rulers took their place. As the proud Mongol Empire crumbled, anti-foreign ideas spread; trade routes no longer provided a safe conduct for travelers. Turks and Saracens stood in the way. But the maritime peoples of Europe felt the magnetic force of the Orient. If they could not go by land, they would go by sea. The very closing of the Asiatic door acted as a spur to the adventurous. So began for Europe the great age of exploration.

Looking back on man's achievements since he began his random wanderings thousands of years ago, we see that they took place at different times in different regions. Ten thousand years passed before he entered the Stone Age, in Europe at least; and in the next ten thousand, during which great empires rose and fell, man spread across the land masses of the world, acquiring different racial and cultural tendencies. Major inventions such as the wheel, the development of bronze, iron, and in some places even steel, had already taken place. Greece left the splendor of her intellect as a glorious legacy to man. Rome's gifts to the world were administration and a superior network of roads that circled the Mediterranean. The Hebrews had written the Decalogue and gathered their ancient literature into a composite whole. All this was accomplished long before the beginning of the Christian era, as were the organization of government and trade. Man was interested in man, and movements to and fro across the continents of Europe and Asia heightened that interest. But after the first century A.D. a curious kind of apathy seems to have deterred men from adventure; the pace of discovery slackened and did not accelerate for thirteen hundred years.

A map by Fra Mauro which shows the Chinese imperial city of "Chambalech" and summer palace.

To Europeans the known world by this time included the Orient, but Africa was still the Dark Continent. The early discovery of America was lost; and the continents of Australia and Antarctica had never even been dreamed of by civilized men of Europe and Asia. For two hundred years the Norsemen had carried out raids on Britain, France, Germany, and Russia, and in some of these countries they planted stable governments. In all they left a legacy of strength, vigor, and courage. Their American excursions pale into insignificance when measured against the mark they made on Europe.

In Asia vast unrest in a vast continent prevented the Chinese from spreading outward. Wars were common but there were intervals of relative peace when small groups of traders or missionaries were able to move from Europe into Asia. The assimilation of the conquered or the conquerors led to the fusion of peoples and the diffusion of ideas.

The three main religions inspired people to take long journeys as pilgrims to visit distant shrines, and to propagate the various gospels in foreign lands. In Arabia scattered nomadic people, fired by the teachings of Mohammed, united and sprang into prominence as accomplished warriors. Ibn Batuta traveled to China and India, explored Arabia and the western Sudan, and Arab seamen navigated the coasts of the Indian Ocean. The Polos crossed Asia and sailed from China to the Persian Gulf.

As civilization in European centers became more complex, the needs of the populations increased. Trade expanded, three-masted ships built of oak and decorated with wrought iron sailed the European seas. Man was about to become cosmopolitan.

Areas of the world known up to 1420 by the West, East, and Islamic Empire are shown in relief coloring; the unknown world is shown in indigo. Pale blue sea extending west from Norway shows Norse voyages.

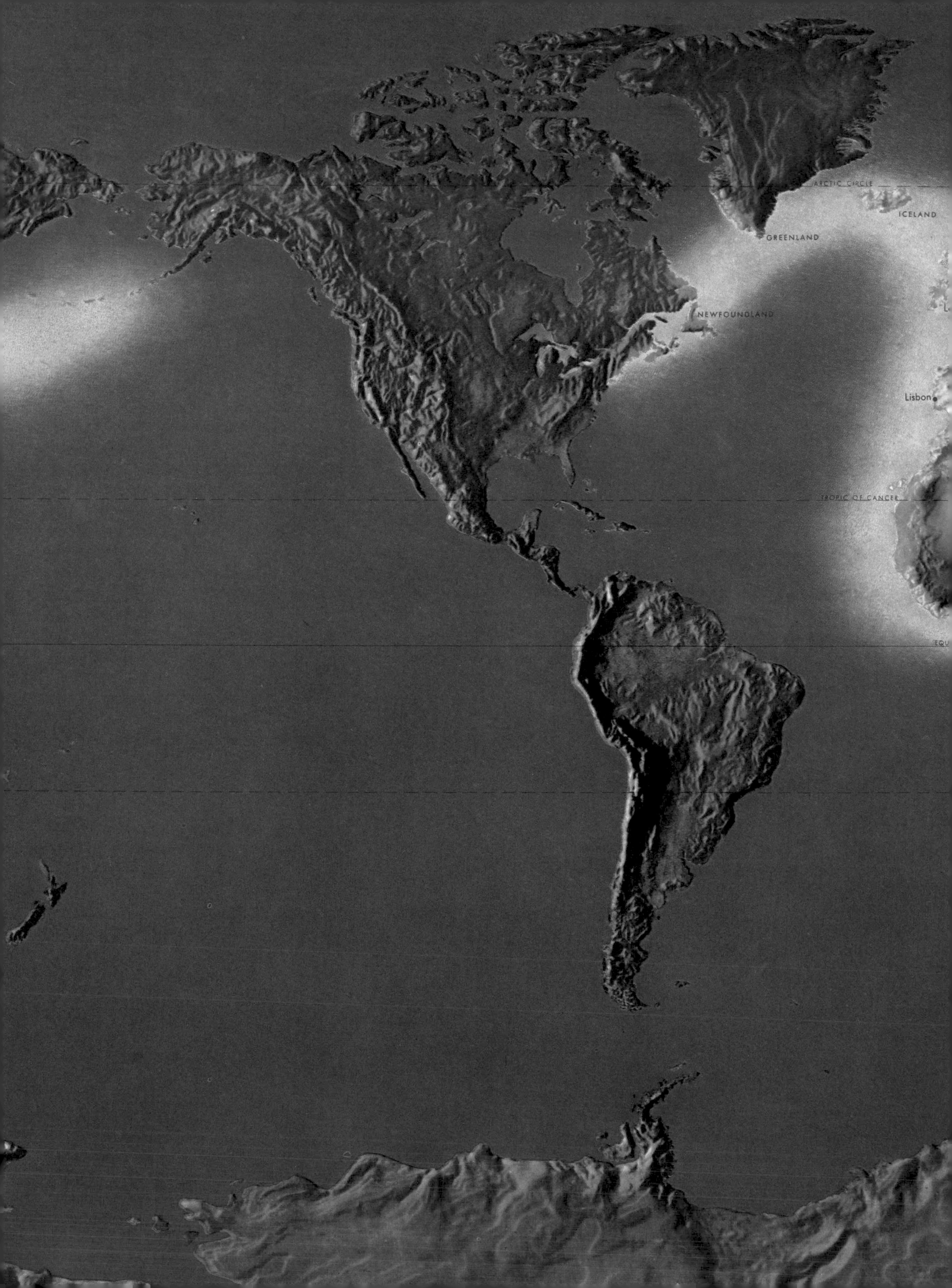
ARCTIC CIRCLE
ICELAND
GREENLAND
NEWFOUNDLAND
Lisbon
TROPIC OF CANCER

U R O P E
Oslo
Moscow
90°
Venice
Genoa
Danube
Constantinople
Karakorum
A S I A
Kashgar
Peking
DITERRANEAN SEA
Euphrates
Jerusalem
Indus
Delhi
Yangtze
R I C A
Nile
Mecca
Canton
Calicut
INDIAN OCEAN
JAVA

The great age of discovery

With the exception of the Viking excursions and the energetic seafaring trade of the Arabs, most discoveries up to the thirteenth century had been overland. But now that the Moslem Empire stood between East and West, European traders were determined to find a sea route to the Orient. There is no evidence that people of the Orient had any strong desire to find a sea route to the West.

Much of the knowledge gained by earlier mariners, such as the Phoenicians, had been lost; even so, European navigators felt that there must be a way around Africa and they were determined to find out. On the eve of what has since been called the "great age of discovery," Prince Henry of Portugal in 1416 established a school of navigation at Sagres, near Cap St. Vincent. A scholar and a scientist, a soldier and crusader, he abandoned the splendid life of a medieval prince to study the art of cartography, to plan voyages, and to equip expeditions which were to be of world-wide importance. But like every other of man's advances, exploration depended on the excellence of tools. With wide experience in fishing-boat construction, the Portuguese had already designed a sailing ship of some 200 tons called a "caravel"—broad of beam and capable of carrying plenty of water and provisions. Lateen rigged, she had high castles fore and aft of the mainmast, carried a mainsail and a topsail, but since these masked the foresail, the foremast was usually very small. Although slow, the caravels were seaworthy ships.

They probably carried some sort of compass, since the properties of the loadstone had been known for centuries in both Europe and Asia, and it is likely that the Portuguese already knew of the Italian device of mounting a needle on a card, although the actual date of the first use of the loadstone as an aid to navigation is not known.

Another instrument was the astrolabe, which had been used for more than a thousand years to find latitude and tell the time, and which now came into use at sea. It consisted of a heavy metal circle which was directed toward the sun or a star in order to find its height above the horizon. With this reading and a simple table of the position of the sun or star at any given date, both latitude and time could be worked out.

By this time seamen were making their own charts. Drawn on stretched sheepskin, they followed a set pattern which was faithfully copied for years. They were known as Portolano charts and the original ones came from the Balearic Isles. Ports were shown primarily, and capes and shoals were often magnified to give prominence to their danger. A geometrical network of lines was ruled across the charts to assist the mariner in setting a course, but the lines had nothing to do with latitude or longitude. Under this system some distortion was inevitable; in the Mediterranean this was of little consequence, but it had serious drawbacks when applied to the much larger Atlantic or Indian oceans.

Prince Henry's captains' most notable feat was the discovery of the Azores, a journey of 800 miles with no coast line to guide them. They had to rely for the first time on their primitive compass. The islands were colonized and, had the Portuguese known anything of the Norsemen's adventures, the Azores might well have become a starting point for the rediscovery of America, but Prince Henry's hopes were centered on finding a way round Africa to the east, and every year he sent caravels with this object in view. Ever since his crusading days his natural enemies had been the Moors, and it was his ambition to outflank them by sea. He was also much influenced by stories of Prester John, whom he identified with the Prince of Ethiopia; the possibility of joining him and crushing Islam in Africa seemed to him most attractive.

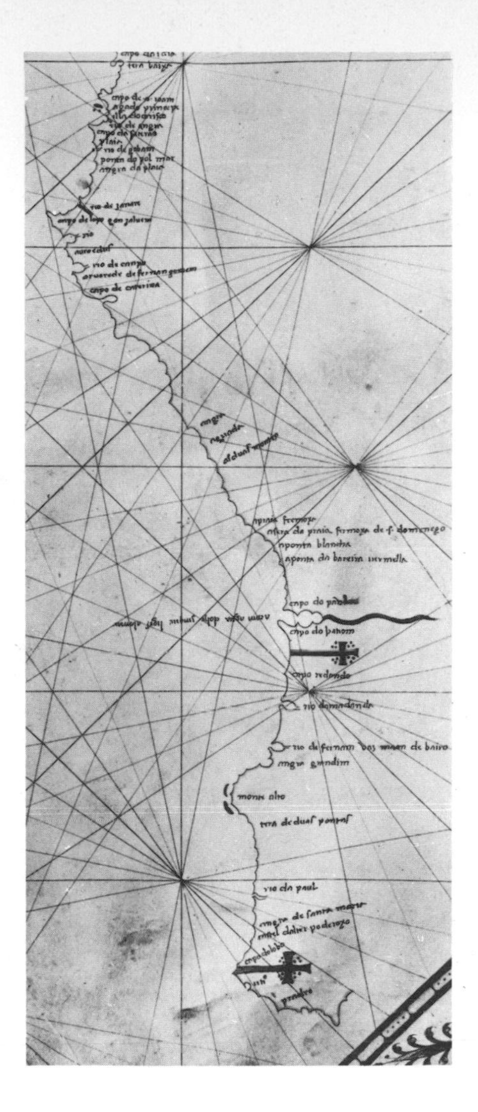

Detail from a Portuguese map of the West African coast, drawn in 1490. Long crosses show where Diego Cam set up two pillars on his voyage of 1482–84.

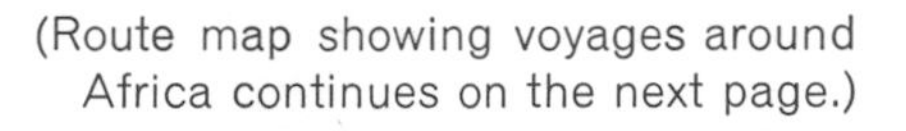

(Route map showing voyages around Africa continues on the next page.)

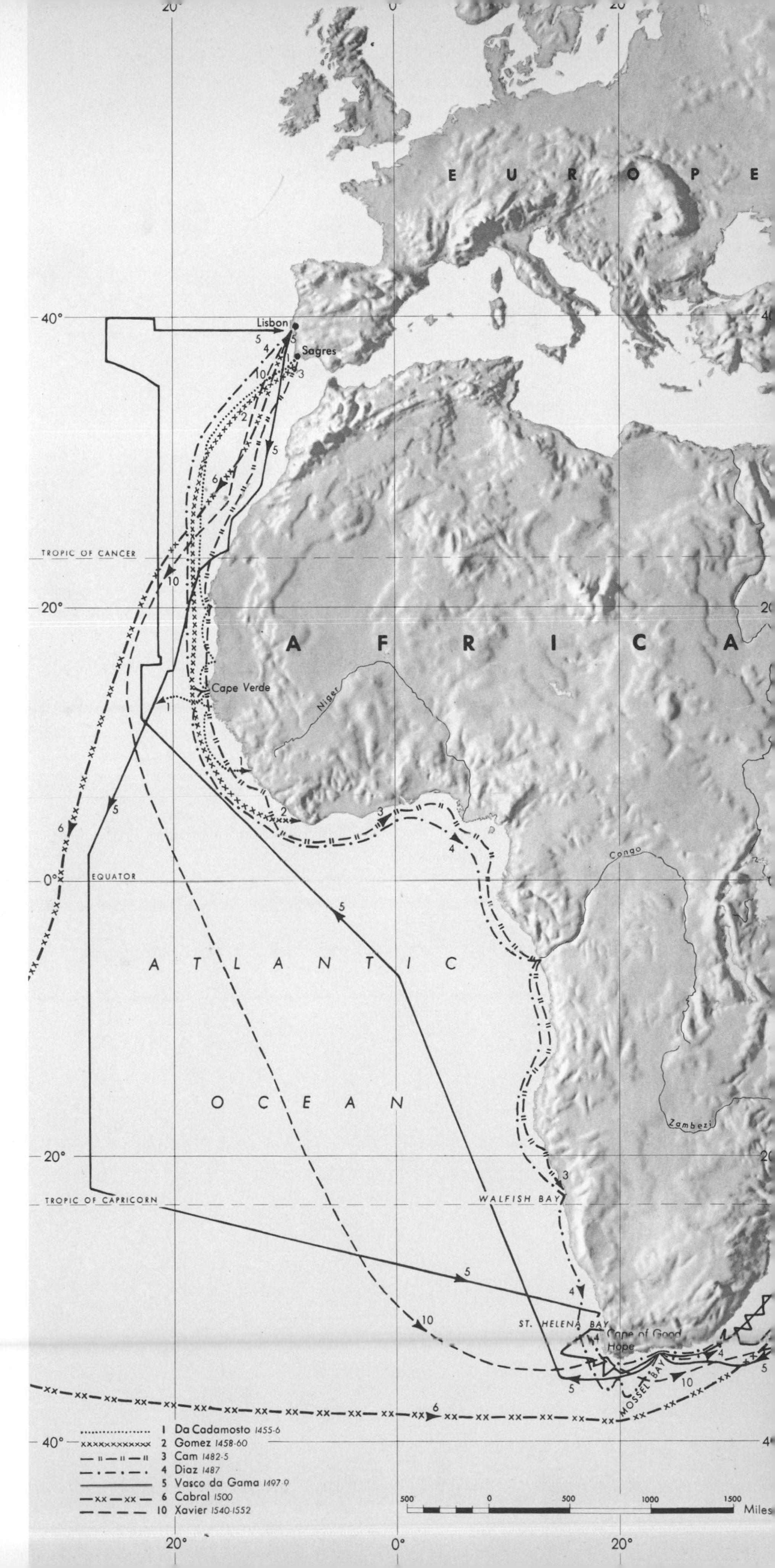

A S I A
INDIAN OCEAN
EAST INDIES
TROPIC OF CANC
EQUATOR
TROPIC OF CAPRICOR
Indus
Ganges
Mekong
SOCOTRA
CEYLON
Bombay
Goa
Calicut
Cochin
Negapatam
Malacca
Canton
Kagoshima
Kyoto
Tok
Ternate
Malindi
Zanzibar
Mozambique
5 Vasco da Gama 1497-9
6 Cabral 1500
7 Sequira 1509
8 Serrano 1511
9 Pinto 1540-52
10 Xavier 1540-1552
500 0 500 1000 1500 Mile
60° 80° 100° 120° 140°
40° 20° 0° 20° 40°

Piracy and piety have often traveled hand in hand, and Prince Henry's expeditions were no exception. Desirous as the prince was to carry Christendom into foreign lands, he found that companies set up along the African coast paid Portugal very handsomely. His captains were not above scuttling or taking as prizes any Moslem ships they sighted. Nor were they above engaging in the African slave trade, a new idea in Europe but one which had flourished for centuries in Arab lands. Portuguese merchants were quick to see the value of this trade, and Prince Henry's captains were commissioned by them to land at convenient places on the coast of northwest Africa to seize Negroes for sale abroad. Because of these delays twenty years were to pass before Henry's men managed to get as far as Hanno had a thousand years earlier.

Even by the time Prince Henry died in 1460, the great bulge of Africa had only just been rounded, Da Cadamosto having reached Gambia in 1455 and Diego Gomez reaching it in 1460, but Portuguese trade had expanded tremendously, and for a time what had been a relatively small and insignificant European country dominated the western seas with a chain of ports from Madeira to Cape Verde and beyond.

Of the Portuguese captains who led these ventures to circumnavigate Africa, two are outstanding. One was Diego Cam, who, during a voyage in 1482–84, pushed farther down the coast than any of his predecessors and found the mouth of the Congo River. He set up a stone pillar at the mouth of the Congo and then, before altering course for home, sailed another 500 miles south and left another pillar. Two years later he returned and pushed his discovery as far as the Tropic of Capricorn [illegible] the present Walfish Bay, but unfortunately he died on the voy[illegible]. All his pillars have recently been found, and one or two of th[illegible] very little the worse for nearly five centuries of exposure. The [illegible] on one of them begins, "In the year 6681 of the world and in [illegible] the birth of Christ ..." In these two voyages Cam sailed [illegible] 1400 miles farther than anyone else of his day, and so in a sense he laid th[illegible] foundations for the final step of rounding the southern end of Africa.

Henry the Navigator

A detail from an atlas of 1556, showing a Portuguese ship sailing around Cape of Good Hope.

The second man to deserve a niche in the list of great explorers is Bartholomew Diaz. In 1487 he left Lisbon in command of three ships with the purpose of continuing the work of Diego Cam. Only one brief account of his voyage exists. Having followed Cam's route down the coast, he passed the last pillar and set up one of his own on a cape just south of the present Lüderitz Bay. A storm carried him south for thirteen days before he was able to turn east, hoping to find land. When he failed, he altered course and sailed north to land at Mossel Bay, then followed the coast as far as the Great Fish River.

By this time his crew was becoming restive, so he turned for home and was surprised to find that in following the coast he came to a cape—the Cape of Good Hope. Without knowing it, Diaz had rounded the tip of Africa. On his return he was put in charge of building and outfitting a fleet of ships that were to sail around Africa under Vasco da Gama.

It was left to Spain to rediscover America, and this had already taken place on Columbus' voyage before Vasco da Gama set out on his expeditions. The rivalry between Spain and Portugal was none the less for the Treaty of Tordesillas in 1494, in which the reigning Pope agreed that Spain and Portugal should share the world between them. He divided the world by designating a meridian as a boundary running from the southern end of Greenland to the mouth of the Amazon, neither of which points was known with any certainty at the time. Point was matched with point: Columbus claimed America and Bartholomew Diaz claimed the Cape of Good Hope. It was now Vasco da Gama's turn to put Portugal further into the lead by finding a route to the East and setting up trading posts along the way.

Vasco da Gama

Instead of sailing into the unknown, as Columbus did, Da Gama was heading for land already discovered, but he had much farther to go than Columbus, whose whole journey was only about 6000 miles and who sailed no more than 80 days on the open sea. Da Gama's fleet, with 180 men in four ships, each about 120 tons, and with Diaz as pilot, covered 24,000 miles and spent more than 300 days on the open sea. On one stretch he was out of sight of land for 96 days. Da Gama's was perhaps the first major expedition to suffer from scurvy.

Scurvy is a disease of vitamin deficiency caused by a lack of fresh food and vegetables. It is of interest because only in relatively recent times have we learned to combat it successfully. The early stages are not easily diagnosed for, as another explorer wrote, "It frequently puts on the form of many other diseases but the common appearances are large discolored spots over the body, swelled legs, putrid gums and, above all, an extraordinary lassitude of the whole body. The disease is likewise attended with a strange dejection of the spirits, shiverings, tremblings and a disposition to be seized with the most dreadful terrors. ..."

Da Gama called his first landfall in Africa St. Helena Bay. It lies about a hundred miles north of the stormy Cape of Good Hope, which he had difficulty rounding in the early spring gales. When he came to the farthest point reached by Diaz he stopped to unload and burn his stores ship which the pounding gales had made unseaworthy. He then sailed 800 miles north along a coast entirely unknown to him, his passage slowed down by the Mozambique current; and at Quelimane he first met Oriental civilization in the person of "two gentlemen; they were very haughty and valued nothing which we gave them." In a land where presents exchanged between the high and mighty included gold, ivory, and precious jewels, the trinkets he had brought from Portugal were insulting.

The captains received more pointed rebuffs at Mozambique and

Mombasa, and learned the hard fact that Moslem merchants and seamen were astonished to find that these "dogs of Christians" had found their way into an ocean which for centuries had belonged solely to them. A more friendly chief at Malindi helped Da Gama find an Indian pilot, who took them eastward across the sea to Calicut in 23 days.

When at last he set sail for home he lost thirty three men from scurvy, leaving a total of sixty. With a light crew he had difficulty managing his ships, so back at Malindi he burned one, leaving only two of the original four to complete the long journey back to Portugal. His hardships had been severe, but he had found a way to the East and Portugal was undisputed mistress of the sea route.

The entry of European nations into the Indian Ocean was an event of world importance. It meant the first continuing contact between East and West. With the arrival of Western ships it was discovered that the East—China in particular—welcomed the idea of trade. But the significance of Vasco da Gama's return was not only to hail Portugal as trade mistress of the seas, but to mark the beginning of the long period of a dominance of the sea by European nations.

The year following Da Gama's return a fleet of thirteen ships under Pedro Cabral set out to follow up the Da Gama expedition. For spiritual guidance the ship's company included a group of Franciscan friars. In addition many merchants were aboard to represent the trading side of the venture, and in case of attack the fleet carried the best cannon to be had. An unexpected event made the voyage successful beyond expectation. Whether by accident or design, Cabral hit upon the coast of Brazil and so won for his country a good portion of South America.

A tragedy during the voyage claimed the life of Bartholomew Diaz. Along with three other ships the one carrying Diaz went down during a storm off the Cape. In grim prophecy he had originally named it Cape Tormentoso.

Seventeenth-century engraving of
Indian boats used on the
Malabar coast and seen by Da Gama.

The daring Portuguese expeditions established permanent fortress-factories in India, some of which still remain today. Their conquest was by acts of cruelty and savagery matched only by the Spanish in the West Indies. At one time the Portuguese set fire to a pilgrim ship returning from Mecca. These western nations soon learned that they had to depend on superior seamanship during their early years of discovery. In the thickly populated civilized countries, and with the Chinese and Arabs dominating much of the land, it was impossible to conquer, occupy, and extend areas. Their hold, like their future exploits, depended entirely on their command of the sea.

The early Portuguese Viceroys—Da Gama, then Almeida and Albuquerque—promptly seized strategic trading points in the Indian Ocean: the entrance to the Red Sea, the island of Hormuz in the Persian Gulf, Goa, Malacca, and even Ternate in the East Indian archipelago. They held the key to all traffic from farther east. One of the Portuguese captains, Ferdinand Magellan, established headquarters in the Spice Islands as early as 1511.

This was at the peak of the Great Age of Discovery, when, in a brief half century, nearly all the unknown parts of the world were unveiled by bold explorers from the Atlantic fringe of Europe. The broad waters of the Atlantic and Pacific so completely isolated North America that neither Asia nor Europe had any notion that a rich, vast land was waiting to be explored.

The inhabitants of this new continent were lean, dark, straight-haired men with aquiline features. When they were first discovered by Europeans, the Indians of the north were still mainly nomad huntsmen living in crude shelters, dressed in animal skins, and dependent on the bow and arrow. Although skilled in canoeing swift rivers in frail birch-bark boats, they had no knowledge of the wheel. In many ways they had advanced little beyond the Stone Age.

Farther south the picture was different. When Europeans discovered Peru and Mexico they were astonished to find that elaborate civilizations —later to be conquered by Pizarro and Cortéz—had existed for centuries.

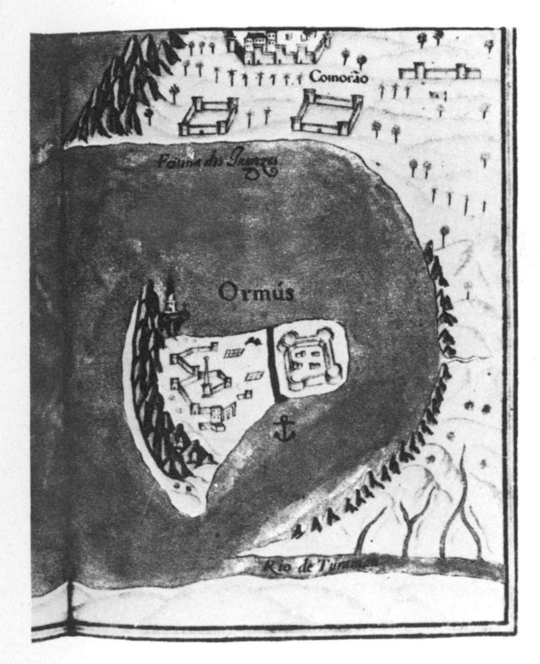

Painting of the Portuguese port, Hormuz, on the Persian Gulf, from a book about the Viceroys of India.

With the landing of Christopher Columbus the American scene changed. This grimly determined man, clever and with a craving for dignity and power that made him vain and boastful, was convinced that if he sailed west he would find Asia—probably India. The map makers of the time deserve at least part of the blame for Columbus' error. They had dotted the Atlantic with islands mythical and real. For example, there were Antilia and Cypango, neither of which has been clearly identified with real places.

His first task was to finance the expedition. Rebuffed by King John of Portugal, it took him six years to persuade Queen Isabella of Spain that a small investment would bring in return spiritual and financial gain beyond their dreams. Columbus promised great rewards, but in return demanded great privileges—for example, that he be appointed governor of any lands that he discovered. He approached and won the support of the three Pinzón brothers, who were ship owners at Palos, the little port from which Columbus finally sailed with his three caravels on August 3, 1492.

Only the flagship the *Santa Maria* was fully decked and of 100 tons burden. Both the *Pinta* (50 tons) and the *Niña* (40 tons) were open amidships. The two smaller ships were commanded by two of the

Japanese screen which shows Portuguese Jesuits landing in Japan.

Pinzóns. Their complements were 52, 18, and 18 respectively. The voyage itself was straightforward in those trade-wind seas. The leader's difficulties were chiefly with the faint hearts of his men, who thought they would never see Spain again, and a certain independence in his two captains. But his crew took courage when they saw birds flying toward the west; Martin Pinzón advised Columbus to follow them, and on October 11, about thirty three days after leaving the Canaries, he sighted land—an island in the Bahamas which he claimed for Spain under the name of San Salvador. He mistook Cuba for the mainland (Cathay) and sent an expedition inland where, for the first time, Europeans saw men smoking tobacco. In an account of a similar inland journey on the island of Hispaniola he wrote:

"In it there are many harbors on the coast of the seas, and many rivers, good and large. Its islands are high and there are very lofty mountains. All are most beautiful, of a thousand shapes, and all are accessible and filled with trees of a thousand kinds and tall, and they

Christopher Columbus

seem to touch the sky. And some were flowering and some bearing fruit. And the nightingale was singing, and other birds of a thousand kinds. There are six or eight kinds of palm, which are a wonder to behold on account of their beautiful variety.

"The people all go naked, men and women. They have no iron or steel or weapons. ... They are so guileless and generous with all they possess that no one would believe it who has not seen it."

Before returning to Spain, Columbus' flagship was wrecked, so he left forty two of his men behind to look for gold. At home he was greeted in the old style of victorious Roman generals and met with Diaz, who had sailed around the Cape of Good Hope six years earlier. A few months later he fitted out a second voyage, which led to his discovery of Jamaica, but it was not until his fourth voyage, in 1503, that Columbus touched on the mainland of America.

In all his journeys Columbus was looking not for new lands, but for a sea passage to the East. Map makers and seamen alike thought that such a route must lie between the "islands" separating Europe from the East. They never dreamed that the enormous land mass of the Americas stretched almost across the globe from north to south.

Having "discovered" the new continent, Columbus made no attempt to explore it. He was determined on all his later journeys to find a passage to India or some other of the eastern lands. His accounts of his last voyage, during which he sailed along the Central American coast, tell of a country which he thought must lie near the river Ganges.

During his second voyage Columbus hired a provision-contractor named Amerigo Vespucci, who later ventured out on his own. His first

A ship of the *Santa Maria* type used by Columbus on 1492 voyage.

discoveries included Honduras and the Gulf of Mexico. His second voyage was along the coast of Brazil. He returned to Spain with a cargo of slaves and on his next expedition found the site of Rio de Janeiro. That his name was given to America may have been because Columbus, overanxious to press his claims with Ferdinand and Isabella, fell into disgrace. Vespucci's claims, on the other hand, have provided geographers, cartographers, and explorers with countless arguments. For instance, he claimed that during one of his voyages down the South American coast he sailed within "thirteen degrees of Antarctic pole"; this would have put him close to where Sir Vivian Fuchs made his recent journey.

By the time Columbus was on his fourth voyage, in 1503, the English had rediscovered the Vinland that the Vikings had visited 500 years earlier. John Cabot, a Venetian living in England, and his son Sebastian share the honor of leading three expeditions from Bristol. They were backed by the cautious Henry VII, who was anxious not to offend Ferdinand of Spain by sending his men anywhere near the Columbian discoveries. That fear may be partly responsible for the fact that very little is known of these voyages. We know that John Cabot discovered land near Nova Scotia in 1497, thinking it was part of Asia. Three years later Sebastian recognized that Nova Scotia was part of a new continent.

Like Columbus, the Bristol merchants were determined to find a passage to the East around the new continent. Again they tried, this time in 1500 backing the brothers Corte-Real in an expedition during which the brothers saw Eskimos—either in Greenland or Labrador—and found evidence of the Cabot's journeys. On later voyages both brothers mysteriously perished.

Cod fishing in Newfoundland was stimulated by John Cabot's voyages. This detail is from a map of 1698.

The voyages of Columbus.

Columbus' 1st. voyage 1492-3
Columbus' 2nd. voyage 1493-6
Columbus' 3rd. voyage 1498
Columbus' 4th. voyage 1502-4

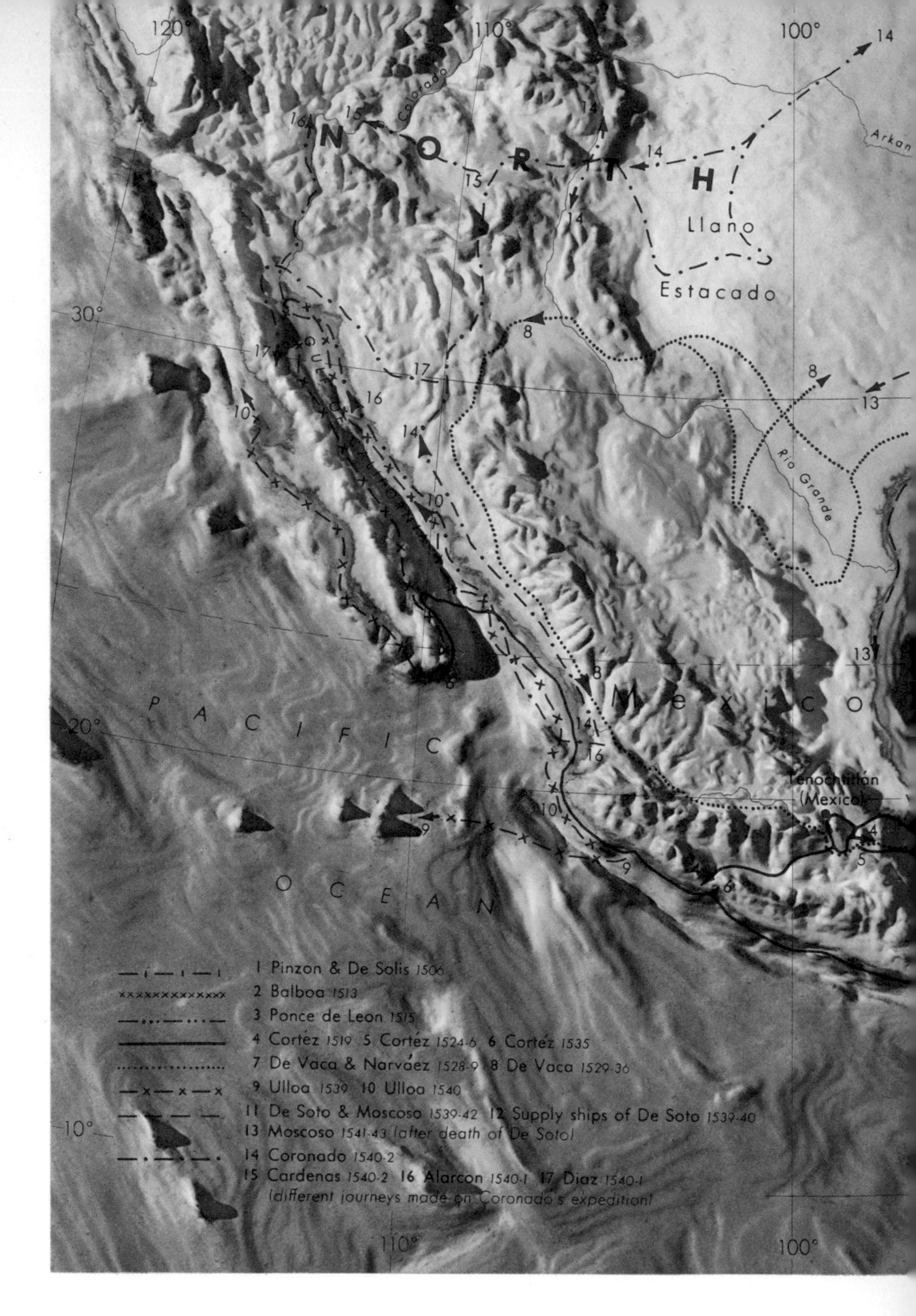

Map shows area of Central America which attracted so many explorers after Columbus. The exploration routes which extend from east to west cross deserts, jungle, and mountains.

Following on the heels of Columbus' exploration of the American coast, the European nations eagerly and swiftly continued the exploration, and with extraordinary results. In less than thirty years the entire eastern shore of both the Americas was known. During that short time voyages akin to that of Columbus became commonplace.

The concern of the Spaniards who followed Columbus was to find a passage through the vast continent that lay between them and the coveted trade of the East. It was Balboa and not "stout Cortéz" who in 1513 crossed the narrow Isthmus of Panama,

> ... when with eagle eyes
> He stared at the Pacific—and all his men
> Look'd at each other with a wild surmise—
> Silent, upon a peak in Darien.

a significant moment in man's discovery of the world, aptly chosen by Keats as a simile to his own discovery of an English translation of Homer.

For Spain the immediate result of Atlantic crossings was more territory

on either side of the Isthmus of Panama. This new source of riches turned her attention from the Far East and led her to concentrate on opening up the new continent. Under appalling physical conditions the Spaniards performed amazing feats of exploration over impossible territory but, unhappily, these exploits were combined with ruthlessness and plundering of the native peoples. Hernando Cortéz was outstanding in employing ruthless, nevertheless brilliant, tactics in his conquest of Mexico.

In 1519 he sailed with a mere 500 men and 16 horses, landing where Vera Cruz now stands. He carried out an incredible two-year campaign during which he conquered the country, partly by skillful use of disaffected tribes, partly by wholesale cruelty, but mainly by consummate leadership. At one time he was desperate with fear that his men would abandon him and sail home, so he burned his ships to prevent retreat. Another time he arrested the amazing Emperor Montezuma, and in rapid succession crushed Narváez, a Spaniard sent by the king to displace him, and he lost and recaptured the great city of Mexico.

For sheer audacity the campaigns of Cortéz challenge all. In a series of marches with a few hundred soldiers he trooped over every geographic obstacle from near desert to tropical jungle. He reached the Gulf of California to the northwest and Honduras to the southeast.

His success, coupled with the riches he was sending back to Spain, led others to explore the great Gulf of Mexico, which then began to take shape on maps. Among these adventurers was Cabeza de Vaca who, as a junior official, landed with an expedition in Florida in 1528. He marched inland until he lost touch with his ships. Then he turned west and crossed the Mississippi, next wintering on an island off the coast of Texas. Here De Vaca left his men, returning to the mainland, where he lived for five years with the Indians. From tribe to tribe he moved through the territories of the settled Pueblos and the wandering bison hunters of the great grassy plains. He eventually reached the Gulf of California. From there he journeyed to Mexico City, then in 1537 he sailed back to Spain after nine years of adventurous wanderings. He had managed to cross the continent from Florida to the Gulf of California—a distance of about 3000 miles.

One of the first drawings of the people of the New World, Indians of Brazil, published 1505.

When De Vaca reported what he had seen, other expeditions were sent to America. One commanded by Hernando de Soto, who had been with Pizarro in Peru, landed with 600 infantry and 150 horsemen on the west coast of Florida in 1539. His quest for gold was unsuccessful, but in his travels he covered the modern states of Georgia, Alabama, Mississippi, and Arkansas. De Soto died somewhere near Memphis on the Mississippi, leaving his men stranded. Finally, after many hardships, the men built boats and drifted down-river to the Gulf of Mexico. At the time the expedition was accounted a failure, but it was the first great penetration by Europeans of the southern United States.

Inspired by De Vaca's stories of fabulous wealth around modern New Mexico, an expedition of several hundred men under Coronado set out from the Gulf of California in 1540. Their wanderings led them to the astonishing Grand Canyon of the Colorado. Southeast of the Canyon they came upon the vast grassy plains teeming with enormous herds of bison and populated by the Indian tribes with whom De Vaca had lived —"people who lived like Arabs" in tents made of tanned skins. Like the nomads of the Old World they followed their herds, killing them for food when necessary. The discovery was of mutual help because the Spaniards found a much needed source of food. In exchange the Indians learned that the horse could be tamed, which meant a more efficient means of hunting bison. Coronado himself got as far as Kansas, not much farther west than De Soto. Between them they had explored all the southern states, but mere exploration meant little to the officials in "New Spain." Coronado found himself in disgrace when in 1542 he reached Mexico City without gold. Both expeditions were splendid failures.

The Spaniards next turned their attention south. Vague stories of the Indians told of a fabulously wealthy kingdom belonging to the Incas. Still hungry for gold, the Spaniards began building ships at the newly founded city of Panama in 1519, but their first voyages south brought them little more than headwinds at sea and swamps wherever they touched land.

The first real clues to the existence of Peru came from Francisco Pizarro, a veteran of Balboa's party. Illiterate and illegitimate, this soldier of fortune had little to help him but matchless courage and ruthless determination. After exploratory expeditions which convinced him that the Incas existed, he set out in 1531 with three ships, 180 men, and

Cortéz arriving in Mexico in 1519, accompanied by Mexican porters.

27 horses. In his pocket he carried a contract commissioning him to conquer Peru. He landed in the Gulf of Guayaquil, and the story of that conquest is as incredible as the conquests by Cortéz.

He announced himself as a friend coming to establish relations between a far-off Christian king and the Emperor of the Children of the Sun—the Incas. He was permitted to cross the high mountain ranges to Caxamarca, an outlying Inca city. From the pass above the city he and his party of a mere hundred Spaniards looked down on the ordered tents of thousands of the Inca's army. His only hope was to capture the emperor, Atahualpa, by surprise. This he did by massacring the court officials and leaders without a single loss of his own. He promised freedom to the emperor in return for a roomful of gold, a ransom which amounted to about three million pounds sterling, or close to nine million dollars. On receiving the gold, he staged a mock trial, after which Atahualpa was basely murdered. By the end of 1533 Pizarro was master of the capital city of Cuzco.

Historians have tended to harp on the cruelty and the lust for gold of the Spanish conquistadors, often forgetting their astonishing courage and the physical hardships they endured. Cuzco, for instance, is over 11,000 feet above sea level, and to be reached only by crossing still higher snowy passes with only pack llamas for transport. Yet it was from that chilly center in the northern Andes that Pizarro sent out two expeditions and formulated plans to discover even more riches.

In 1535 Pizarro sent Almagro, his veteran partner of earlier days, to explore southward over the still higher country in Bolivia and Chile. Almagro was over sixty at the time. He mustered a force of a few hundred Spaniards and several thousand Indians and set out. First he threaded his way over the high Andes, then skirted the deserts of what is now northern Chile. Along the way he lost more than half of his men from cold, privation, and battles with hostile tribes through whose territory he passed. By the time he reached the latitude of the present Concepción

Francisco Pizarro

Jungles along the Amazon are the same today as they were when the Spanish crossed the continent.

he felt only disgust at finding no such treasures as he had left behind at Cuzco. There was nothing to do but return. On returning to Cuzco he had covered more than four thousand miles over country far more rugged than young Alexander had had to cross on his famous journeys a thousand years earlier. There was, however, a tragic ending to Almagro's courageous journey. Back at Cuzco he rebelled against Pizarro, was captured, imprisoned, and garroted.

Pizarro, then nearly seventy years old himself, next sent out an even more extensive expedition, this time to the north, commanded by his much younger half brother, Gonzalo. Pizarro told Gonzalo to try to locate the rich country rumored to exist east of Ecuador. The expedition began with a march of at least 1000 miles from Cuzco to the coast, then north to Quito, where Gonzalo assembled 4000 Indians and about 300 Spaniards. During his trek from Quito across the Andes, Gonzalo lost hundreds of men, who perished from the cold and fatigue. The mountain snows were followed by continuous tropical rains, and the men had to hack their way through thick forest. Those who could struggle no farther were sent back; the fate of many others will never be known.

When the survivors reached the river Napo they were so desperate that they had to kill their horses for food. Here they decided to continue by boat, making nails out of the horseshoes. While some of the party

went by water, the rest struggled through the thick tropical undergrowth along the bank of the river. Terrible heat now succeeded intense cold, and they were within two degrees of the Equator. After wandering for 400 miles without finding food or settlements, Gonzalo decided to send his lieutenant, Francisco de Orellana, ahead with the boat to search for food. Orellana followed the Napo till it joined a large river, but he failed to find food and decided to go on downstream. We will never know whether this was base desertion or simply inability to return against the current. A few of his men protested, refusing to go on, so they were left behind.

Drifting downstream with the current, Orellana and his men achieved what has become an epic voyage through dense, steamy, tropical vegetation infested with insects and snakes and open to attack by hostile tribes, some of whom they reported as having women warriors. Amazons, they called them, and so the name was given to the great eastward-flowing river.

Eventually Orellana's men had to build a new boat, and in it they finally reached the sea—an achievement not to be repeated for centuries, for the Amazon Basin has since defeated many expeditions far better equipped. At the mouth of the Amazon the hardy survivors raised makeshift sails and headed north for Trinidad, adding another 1000 miles to the 2000 of their river journey. But of treasure they had found none.

Amazon Basin seen from the east coast of South America and looking westward over the Andes.

After waiting in vain for Orellana, Gonzalo pursued him down the river until he had gone too far to return against the current. The jungle along both banks was impenetrable. Finally he stumbled onto the stouthearted Spaniards who had chosen to be left behind rather than be disloyal to Gonzalo. On hearing that Orellana had continued down-river Gonzalo ordered a march back through the jungle. Day by day, hacking their way through dense undergrowth, men dropped from famine, fatigue and fever. Eventually they reached the snowy passes of the Andes and, finally, Quito—with only eighty men out of the four thousand who had set out two years before. Rarely has an expedition returned with so few men and with such great results. A way had been found across the broadest part of South America, and it was accomplished nearly three centuries before a crossing of the northern North American continent.

While Pizarro was working his way down the Pacific side of South America, other Spanish expeditions were landing on the Caribbean coast. The post of Santa Marta was established in 1525, and a dozen years later Quesada pushed his way up the Magdalena River to the plateau of what was then called New Grenada, now Colombia, where, after conquering the Chibcha tribe, he founded the city of Santa Fe de Bogotá. There he met other parties all searching for rumored gold, mainly in the region of the Upper Orinoco and the northern most part of the Andes.

Mexican drawing of a Spaniard burning a captured Indian.

Orellana's report of the Amazon did not excite further exploration, and the Pope's dividing line between the claims of Spain and Portugal left the tropical part of eastern South America open to the Portuguese. But Spain well understood that the Tordesillas line, established by treaty in 1494, must cross the coast near the southern tropic, thus giving her rights southward where the merchant-adventurer Vespucci claimed to have been in 1501. In 1516 De Solís discovered the great estuary of the Río de la Plata, where he and most of his crew were killed and eaten by cannibals. Sebastian Cabot, who divided his services between Henry VIII of England and Charles V of Spain, sailed in 1526 to the South Atlantic on a mission to find a way to the Spice Islands of the East. Near La Plata (a few miles from Buenos Aires) he met some survivors of the De Solís expedition and eagerly listened to their reports of riches in the hinterland, which diverted him from his original purpose; he journeyed 500 miles up the estuary and beyond.

Following Cabot, several small Spanish expeditions were sent out to explore the coasts beyond the wide mouth of the Río de la Plata. One of these parties, under Mendoza, founded the town of Buenos Aires; another went north up river and settled at Asunción on the Paraguay River. Cabeza de Vaca, the man who had made the extraordinary journey from Florida to California many years before, was sent out in 1541 to settle Buenos Aires and Asunción, both of which had been attacked repeatedly by hostile Indian tribes and weakened by poor Spanish leadership. From the island of Santa Catarina, De Vaca made an unusual journey by land all the way to Asunción. From there he worked his way up the Paraguay River to the marshy regions well within the tropics, where fever reduced the strength of his party. De Vaca had far more interest in true exploration than the majority of the Spanish adventurers. Unhappily his valuable services were lost when, because of hardships, his officers mutinied in 1545 and sent him back to Spain a prisoner.

In the meantime, on the Pacific side of the continent, Pizarro had succeeded in conquering Peru, and even more permanent results were to come from a renewal of the exploration of Chile, which he had awarded to his lieutenant, Valdívia. That leader founded Santiago in 1541 with hopes of finding great mineral wealth. But those hopes soon died, so he began the nearest attempt at colonization by settling parties of farmers. Farmers, however, also had to be soldiers to resist the many rebellions of the native tribes, so settlement proved to be slow and difficult. In 1545 the Spaniards in Bolivia discovered the great silver mine of Potosí, 13,000 feet above sea level. This brought the Spaniards far greater riches than the gold they had taken from the Incas.

Next, Valdívia's men turned eastward and crossed the Andes as far as the great plains of the Pampas regions, conquering the province of Cuyo, which is now part of Argentina. Another expedition worked southward and founded the town of Valdívia in 1552, near latitude 40° South. At the same time, expeditions traveling by sea reached the Strait of Magellan. Valdívia's plan to explore the whole of the southern coastline came to an end when, before it could be launched, he was killed in a skirmish with Indians.

The achievements of Da Gama, who had opened the sea routes from Europe to the East, and of Columbus, who had shown the way to countless expeditions westward across the Atlantic, were linked by the exploits of a third great explorer—Ferdinand Magellan.

Map of South America, engraved in 1562, shows extent of Spanish exploration along the coasts and river valleys. The Amazon is given common serpentine form; vignette above words *Gigantum Regio* shows belief in Patagonian giants.

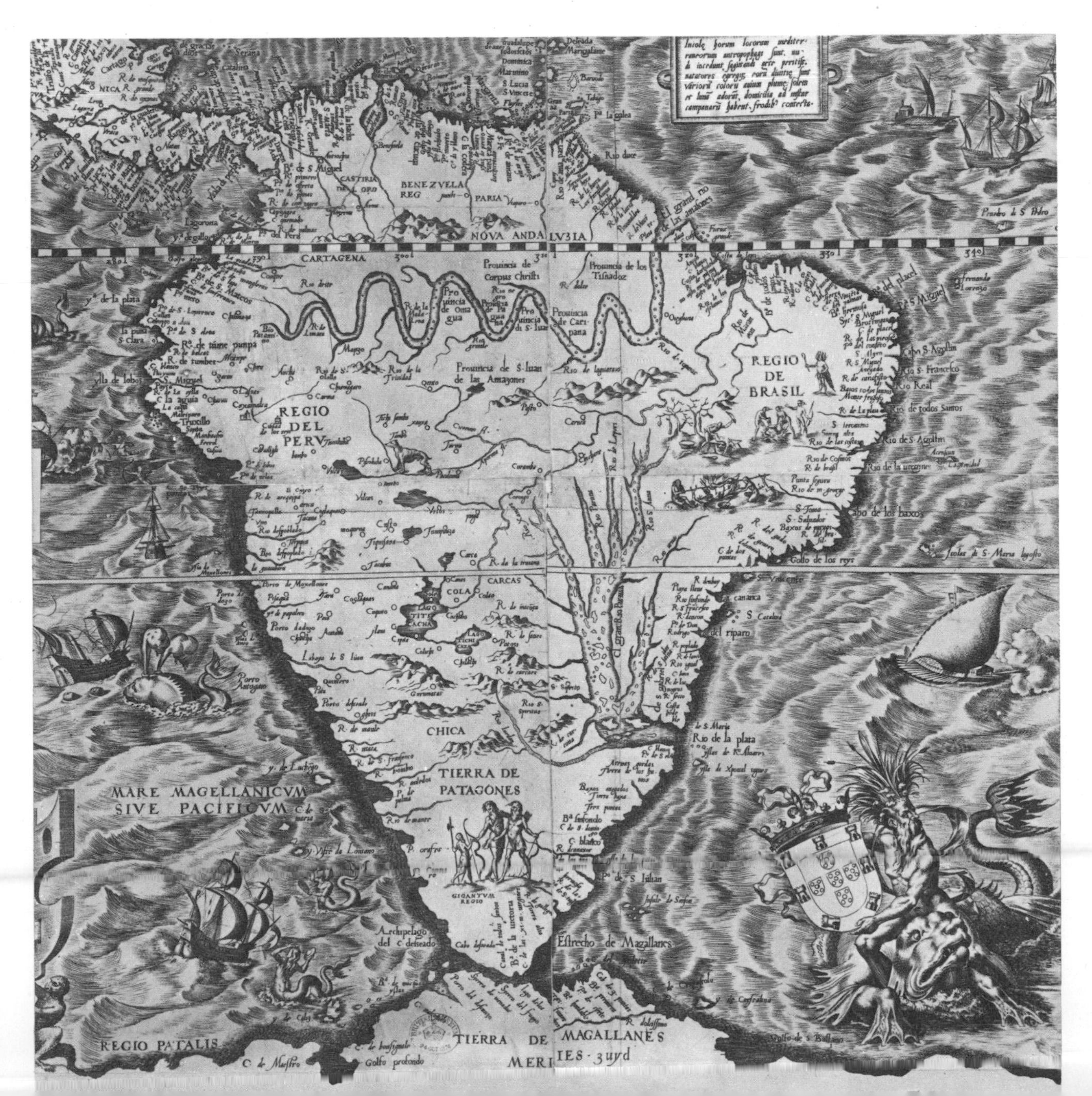

Ferdinand Magellan

Ferdinand Magellan—seamen, geographer, explorer—was the first to circumnavigate the earth.

Magellan came from a noble Portuguese family, had acquired his seamanship and his fighting spirit under Portuguese viceroys in India, and had served in the East for seven years, sailing the waters off the Malay peninsula and of the South China seas. From Cochin China and Malacca he led trading expeditions, and may have gone as far as the Moluccas—the much-sought-after Spice Islands.

For four years he had dreamed and planned of sailing completely around the globe. When his plans were rejected at home he decided to leave Portugal, and offered his services to the King of Spain. Charles V supported his project, and Magellan finally set sail in September, 1519, with five ships, in rather poor condition, manned by about 280 men. Tensions among the senior officers were high, the Spaniards being jealous of the Portuguese, of whom there were 37 all told. Of the ships two were just over 100 tons; another, the *Victoria*, was only 90 tons, and was the only one to complete the voyage. All had high poops and forecastles and were probably fully decked. According to records, the expedition was outfitted with 2½ tons of gunpowder, 21 quadrants, and 7 astrolabes.

One of those who completed the voyage was an Italian named Pigafetta, who fortunately kept a diary from which he later wrote an account. An adventurous man, he wanted to go on the voyage "to experiment and see with my eyes a part of the very great and awful things of the Ocean."

A drawing by Pigafetta showing two of Magellan's crew trying out a native pirogue. The large island may be Guam.

Magellan's ship, the first to circumnavigate the globe.

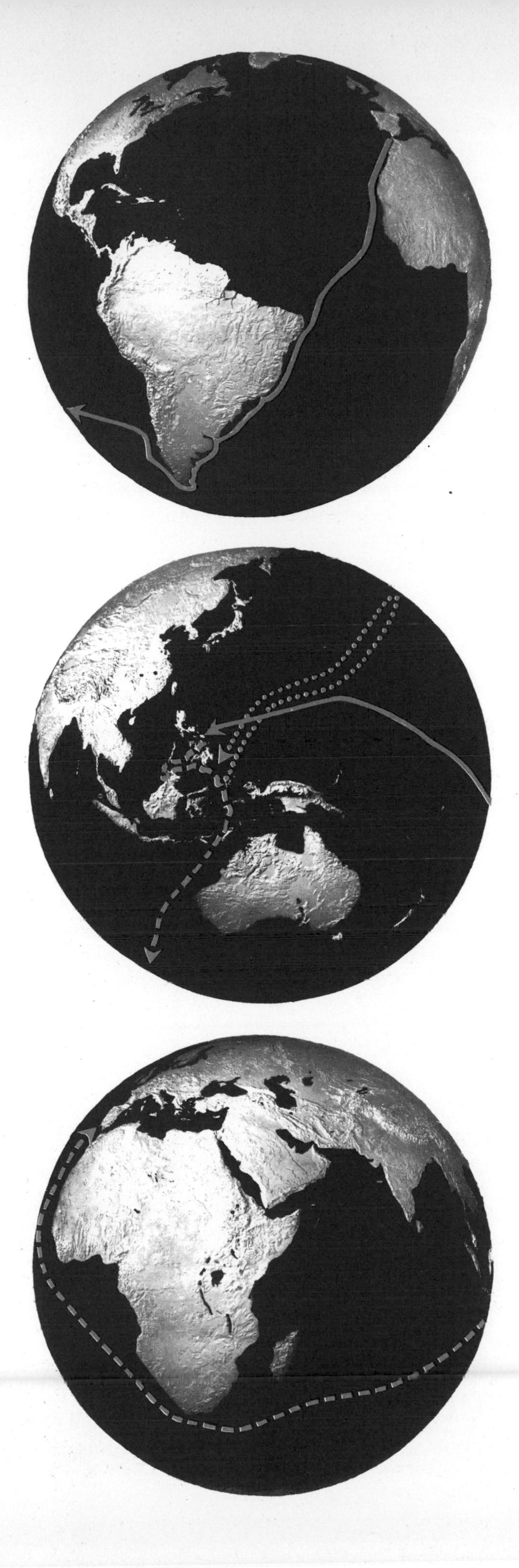

Magellan's voyage around the world.

——— Magellan *1519-21*
— — — Del Cano *(in the "Victoria") 1521-2*
········ Voyage of the "Trinity"

The fleet made very slow passage as far as the estuary of the Río de la Plata, taking five months, during which some of the officers tried to displace Magellan from command. He decided to winter in the bay of Port St. Julian, latitude 49° South. Supplies were running short and the men were disheartened by the wreck of one ship and repeated failures to find a passage through to the Pacific. But Magellan remained firm in his belief. Toward the end of August another attempt was made and on October 21, 1520, he discovered his strait at Cape Virgins: "We found, by a miracle, a strait ... a hundred and ten leagues long, which are four hundred and forty miles ... and it issues in another sea, which is called the peaceful sea."

Halfway through the winding strait one ship deserted, so that when Magellan found an outlet into the Pacific Ocean, after sailing for 38 days, his fleet was reduced to three ships. Even then there were some who wanted to turn back, but Magellan was determined to go on; he set a northwest course and for 96 grim days they sailed with the trade winds behind them and no sight of land except two small atolls of the Tuamotu Archipelago. Pigafetta is brief but dramatic about this period: "We ate old biscuit reduced to powder and full of grubs, and drank water that was yellow and stinking. ... We ate the oxhides from under the yardarms, also the sawdust of wood, and rats, which cost half a crown each. ... The worst misfortune was that the gums of our men grew so much that they could not eat, and nineteen died."

Riddled by scurvy, the expedition at last reached the Ladrone Islands, 15° north of the Equator. Ten days later they reached the Philippines, the other side of which lay the familiar South China Sea. They had filled in the gap between the Old World and the New. One member of Magellan's crew was from the Moluccas, so was the first man to sail around the world. But from that time on misfortune dogged the explorers, who underrated the power and intelligence of the islanders. On a miserable little expedition to a small island called Mactan, Magellan was killed.

Part of world map drawn by Juan de la Cosa in 1496. Spain and Africa are at right; Central and South America are left and center.

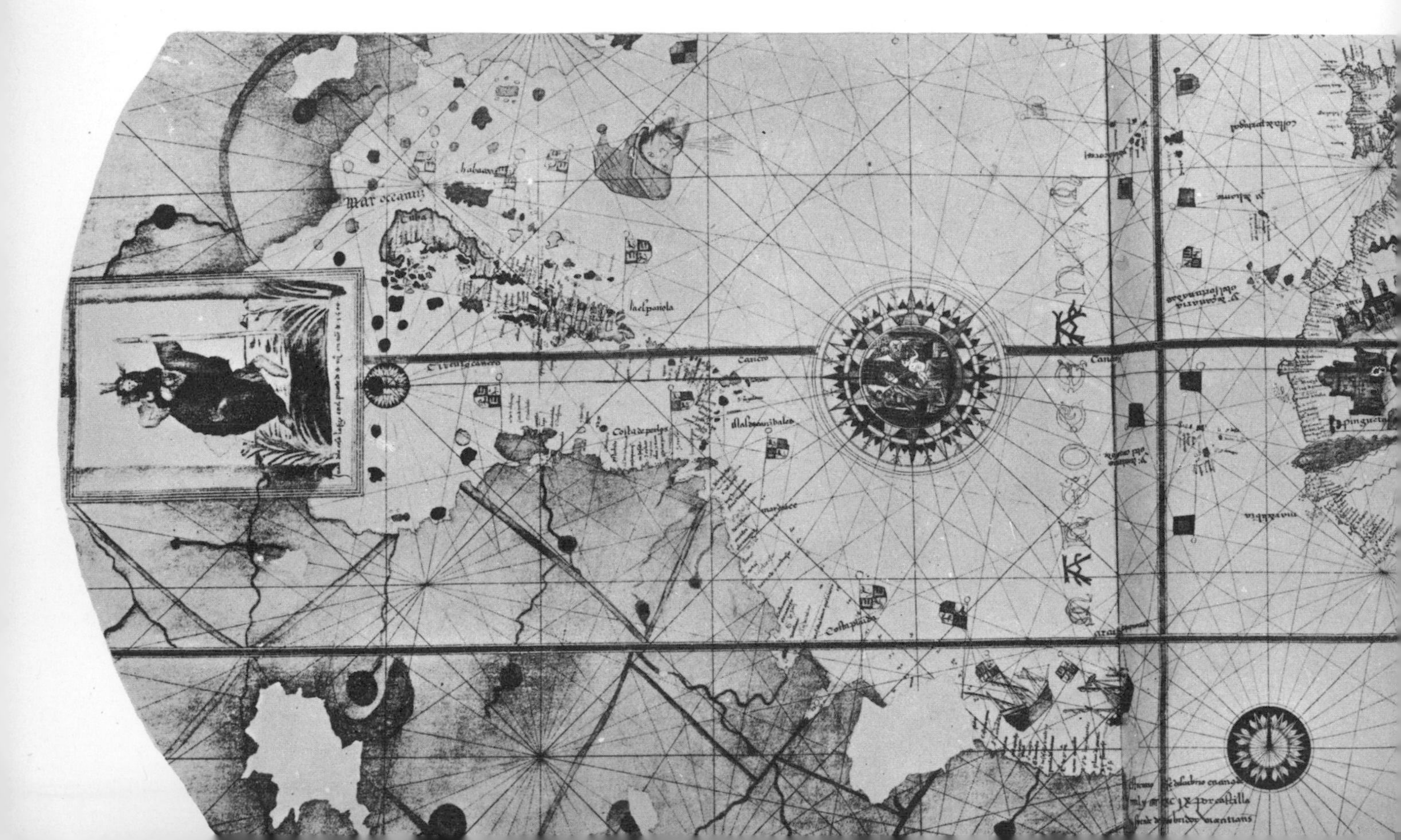

When Magellan died the expedition fell to pieces. The islanders, who had been regarded trustworthy, massacred several senior officers and so reduced the crews to 115 men. Burning the least seaworthy of their remaining three ships, they set out for the Moluccas, visiting North Borneo on the way and capturing several junks, acts of piracy which Magellan would never have permitted. At the Moluccas they filled the ships with spices and prepared to sail homeward, but the flagship *Trinidad* developed a bad leak so only the *Victoria* could leave.

Sebastian del Cano, who mutinied back at St. Julian, was elected captain, and he set sail with a crew of only 47 Europeans and a few natives. For fear of the Portuguese they did not dare to go through the Strait of Malacca, so they came into the Indian Ocean via Ombai Strait and Timor and set a course for the Cape of Good Hope.

It was as dangerous a voyage as that across the Pacific, for scurvy took 25 of the pitifully small ship's company. Pigafetta's interest in all that took place still remained, for he recorded: "A curious thing in throwing the bodies overboard: the Christians remained with face upturned to Heaven, the Indians with face downward." They found it necessary to stop at the Portuguese Cape Verde islands, where they pretended that they had come from the Americas, but they were discovered and 13 of their men were arrested. This left only 18 Europeans to work the ship back to Spain. Finally they anchored at Seville—three years after they had left.

Del Cano was heaped with honors by Charles V. Magellan was all but forgotten, except during the trial of the mutineers, but Del Cano lied and showed disloyalty both to Magellan and to his memory. There is an element of sadness in the whole story of Magellan. Not only was he killed at the peak of his success, but his achievements and his true quality as an explorer and leader were not realized until long afterward. His brother-in-law was killed shortly after him, his small son died at birth, and on receiving the news of Magellan's death his wife died also.

Western half of Mercator's world map of 1585. Notice sprawling North America and lack of northern coast line for Canada.

The year 1550 is a proper point in time for us to review the Great Age of Discovery. Mastery of the Atlantic and Pacific opened the Far East to the ever expanding markets of the Old World. Little land travel could take place in Asia because of the nomadic hordes barring all possible routes. But in little over 60 years the Western World, also hemmed in on land by those same hordes, had broken out toward the west by sea, opening a new world and a new ocean. In that brief period the outlines of all the continents except Australia and Antarctica were drawn on maps and were remarkably different from those of Henry the Navigator. A glance at the map of Juan de la Cosa of 1500 shows the advance of world discovery. Although map makers were still at the mercy of faulty longitudes of shipmasters, there were fewer sea monsters and imaginary islands. Conquest of vast distances by sea meant that a Da Gama could appear in the East as a conqueror as well as a trader.

Shipbuilding reacted to the new stimulus. Where formerly a merchant had to buy distant goods in small lots through a host of middlemen, he could now obtain silks and spices by the shipload direct from the Far East, and, from the distant west, anything from cod from the rich grounds of Newfoundland to gold and silver from the Spanish Main.

By 1550 the two great empires that had ruled for years—Asian and Moslem—were suddenly faced by a third: Western Europe, which was immensely more mobile by its mastery of the world's seas.

Areas of the world known up to 1550 by the West, East, and Islamic Empire are shown in relief coloring; the unknown world is shown in indigo. Pale blue streak of sea circling world represents Magellan's voyage.

ARCTIC CIRCLE
180°
Quebec
Boston
Cape Cod
90°
Mississippi
NORTH
ATLANTIC
OCEAN
Lisbon
Cadiz
CENTRAL
AMERICA
New Orleans
TROPIC OF CANCER
Mexico
WEST INDIES
Timb
EQUATOR
Quito
Amazon
SOUT
ATLAN
OCEA
Cuzco
TROPIC OF CAPRICORN
Buenos Aires
STRAIT OF MAGELLAN

ROPE
ASIA
Moscow
90°
180°
Karakorum
Kashgar
Peking
DITERRANEAN SEA
Indus
Yangtze
RICA
Mecca
Nile
Canton
Calicut
PHILIPPINE ISLANDS
INDIAN OCEAN
Ternate
Zanzibar
EAST INDIES
Good Hope

Migration routes of peoples across South America from earliest times.

Exploration of South America

The first men to arrive in the New World must have come from Asia in Neolithic times, crossing the Bering Strait—either by land bridge or across a narrow, shallow sea—at a time when men lived by hunting and gathering wild plants. Many centuries of wandering or deliberate exploration must have slipped by before these early men gradually worked their way southward through the plains and valleys of North America, across the Isthmus of Panama, and eventually into South America. The dense forests and jungles probably kept them to the highlands or forced them to assemble primitive rafts, which carried them along rivers and down the coastline of the Pacific. We have traces of early Americans in different parts of the continent—in caves and rock shelters in the mountains, and in primitive earth buildings on the coastal plains. In the New World maize formed the basis of Stone Age agricultural economy; in the Old World it was bread wheat.

Several primitive empires evolved in Middle America roughly about the same time. The first to reach its peak was the early Mayan culture, which rose and fell about the time of the Roman Empire. The Mayans showed remarkable parallels with the early civilizations of the Nile and Euphrates basins. They learned controlled agriculture; they were pyramid builders, astronomers, calendar makers; and they developed their own form of written language. The cities built by the Mayans, now buried in dense jungle, were ceremonial centers used only during religious and other festivals. Their "pyramids" and certain other buildings have paved courts and temples with immense flights of stone stairs leading to other small temples on the roof. These were astonishing achievements for a simple farming people living in a tropical environment of fast-growing jungle and swamps. They used stone tools only; their knowledge of metal ended with the little gold working they did for ornamental purposes. They neither discovered the use of the wheel nor, in spite of their skill in calculations, did they apply their mathematics in practical ways. In their buildings they never achieved a true arch. Their elaborately carved pillars of stone with dated hieroglyphs have provided scholars and research workers with fascinating material, yet much of it still remains a mystery.

The "classic" period of the Mayan civilization lasted roughly from A.D. 325–925, and produced the best of their buildings, sculpture, hieroglyphic writing, painted pottery, and their greatest progress in astronomy and advanced arithmetic. Its decline and sudden collapse is a mystery; it may have been the result of tribal attacks from Mexico combined with internal revolt of the peasants against a ruthless priestly hierarchy. Whatever the cause, the empire lingered on in slow decay in the more remote parts of the Yucatán Peninsula until it was finally crushed by Spanish invaders of the sixteenth century.

The great empire of the Incas was based on a culture already far advanced and covering the whole central Andean area. The Incas developed intensive agriculture in and near the river valleys, devising an elaborate system of irrigation, but their tools were nothing more elaborate than the digging stick, hoe, and clodbreaker. The importance of water for irrigation united the people of each valley and led to a strong, centralized type of state. While people in the valleys were engaged in agriculture, those living in the grassy uplands tended valuable herds of llamas and alpacas. To the east of the Andes the ground falls rapidly away to dense tropical forest unsuited to agricultural or pastoral peoples. With rare exceptions, there is little evidence that even the hardiest of the mountain tribesmen tried to penetrate east of the Andes.

Incas had no knowledge of the arch; they built doorways as shown here. Stone blocks were cut to nestle in a firm position.

All the Central Andean peoples were skilled in the use of simple tools. Weaving of an extremely high standard is still a feature of the area today. Pottery, produced without the aid of the potter's wheel, was skillfully made and beautifully decorated. The more we unearth the products of these cultures, the more evidence we find that they made use of all materials around them—wood, stone, rushes, and, among the metals, gold, silver, and copper, but not iron, for it was unknown in America at this time.

The Peruvian civilization is marked by the full flourishing of these arts and crafts; also by the regrouping of certain tribes which produced highly organized and aggressive states to the north and south. This social unrest along the coastal regions was taking place about the time of the collapse and decline of the Mayan Empire in Central America. Eventually it led to the building of large urban centers and concentrations of population along the Pacific coast of South America. This period was one of great political and administrative energy. Even in the highland areas, not particularly suited to large concentrations of people, the grouping and regrouping of tribes were taking place and led to the construction of walled towns.

Among these highland peoples were the Incas. Exactly where the Inca Empire originated is unknown, but it may have been in the highland zone around Cuzco, which later became Pizarro's headquarters. From this region the ruling chieftains planned their campaigns of conquest and struck down neighboring tribes. Their great period of conquest began early in the fifteenth century, soon after which they seized the states on the coast and so weakened the overcentralized state administration that nearly all of the people were left helpless. Over the following century the Empire of the Incas spread beyond the limits of modern Peru into Ecuador to the north and into Chile to the south.

The Inca Empire lasted no longer than some of the empires in Mesopotamia, reaching its peak just about the time the Spaniards arrived. The Incas' material culture—masonry, pottery, textiles—amazed the Spanish, as did their stepped roads, unique in the Americas, with embankments crossing marshlands and rope bridges spanning rivers. For a culture so advanced it is curious that its technicians never invented the wheel, evolved an archway, discovered iron, or developed a written language. For transport of goods they depended on human muscles and the pack llama; for long-range communication they relied on professional runners situated at resthouses linking key centers. For counting, so necessary in an organized state, they used a system of knots tied in cords, the secret of which still eludes scholars.

Sculptured Peruvian head, A. D. 400.

The organization of the state was even more progressive than the Incas' material culture. All property belonged to the state, a system that required close supervision by the ruling class and one we would call a vast civil service. It was a very successful system for a young, expanding empire, but the suppression of the individual in favor of the state made it vulnerable to schism of any kind. This particular weakness the Incas themselves had taken advantage of in their conquest of the coastal states, but they failed to avoid it in their own government, the result being that the Spanish were able to break the system in a very short time.

In addition to the Incas there were other major groups of peoples on the South American continent. One of the more remarkable were the Araucanians of central Chile. They lived in a dense forest region and were extremely primitive in their ways, compared with the Incas, but they were a people renowned for their independence and fighting spirit.

The Incas had been unable to conquer them, and even the Spanish struggled with them for more than a century.

Although the Spaniards were rulers of the Caribbean coasts and islands and the northwest coast of South America (known as the Spanish Main), they were not without rivals. Trading ships from the Netherlands and England, and later France, contrived to slip into the area, expecting and often inviting the hostility of the Spaniards. The stern and brutal measures adopted by the Spaniards to discourage foreign shipping encouraged sailors and soldiers of all European nationalities to unite in perpetual warfare against the common enemy, although none of them was in fact acting with official government backing. Queen Elizabeth put the case very plainly when she wrote to the Spanish ambassador in answer to a complaint of interference that "the Spaniards had drawn these inconveniences upon themselves, by their severe and unjust dealings in their American commerce, for she did not understand why either her subjects, or those of any other European prince, should be debarred from traffic in the Indies."

She went on to state a requirement for right of possession which has become a basis of a kind of international law: "As she did not acknowledge the Spaniards to have any title by the donation of the Bishop of Rome, so she knew no right they had to any places other than those they were in actual possession of, for that their having touched only here and there upon a coast, and given names to a few rivers or capes, were such insignificant things as could no ways entitle them to a property further than in the parts where they actually settled, and continued to inhabit."

View of Truxillo (Trujillo) Bay. "B" marks the remains of a city sacked by the buccaneers.

The bond of unity among the European intruders was strong, and they called themselves "the brethren of the coast"—the coast in question being part of the island of Hispaniola, which we now call Haiti. The island was thickly wooded and had many wild cattle and swine, which were hunted by the brethren whenever they were provisioning their ships. They cut the meat into strips and cured it by laying it on *boucans*, or barbecues, and smoking it over a wood fire fed also with the bones from the carcasses, so improving the flavor of the meat. The French called these hunters *boucaniers* and the English applied the term to themselves as "buccaneers."

In addition to harrying the Spanish ships and towns of the West Indies, the buccaneers explored every hole and corner of the Caribbean Sea. Although few of their exploits ever found their way into print, there were some careful diarists among them who recorded what they did and where they went. One of them, Ringrose, gives an account of their raid-and-run tactics up and down the west coast of South America, refreshing themselves on occasion at the islands of Juan Fernández. Bartholomew Sharp, one of the buccaneer leaders, commanding a hit-and-run voyage lasting from 1680 to 1682, discovered and named some of the islands just north of the Strait of Magellan. Earlier, another buccaneer, Henry Morgan, a ruffian, had sacked the city of Panama.

Portuguese landing in Brazil.

The next buccaneer expedition was a much bigger affair. It started from Virginia in 1683, sailing across to Africa, where the crew pirated a Danish ship near Sierra Leone and renamed her the *Bachelor's Delight*. One member of this expedition was William Dampier, a strange explorer. He became a pirate simply because he wanted to see the world and to satisfy an insatiable curiosity in natural history. His journals are a mine of information about the countries he visited, but he was not popular with his companions, for he found it boring when they captured ships and got drunk on the loot. The *Bachelor's Delight* sailed through the Drake Strait to Juan Fernández to pick up reinforcements, and they then pursued their raiding profession up the west coast of South America as far as the Galapagos Islands on the Equator, where they named several of the islands and made a chart of the area which was used for two centuries. The most farsighted of the buccaneers was Edward Davis. At one stage he planned to occupy part of the Isthmus of Panama, the territory of the Mosquito Indians who were hostile to the Spaniards. At that time, 1685, there were nearly 1000 buccaneers on the west coast of South America and the plan would not have been absurd had there been more unity and discipline among that hardy and unscrupulous band.

The successful exploits of the buccaneers lasted nearly two centuries and are excellent examples of the element of surprise in raiding from the sea. It was guerrilla warfare waged from the trackless ocean on which the raiders had only to disappear over the horizon to be beyond pursuit.

The buccaneers provided Spain with clear proof that she could not hope to retain so vast a part of the New World unless she made permanent settlements there, peopled by farmers rather than by soldiers of fortune.

The first serious attempts at occupation had been made earlier by Valdívia under the direction of Pizarro. After exploring the coast of Chile as far south as the Strait of Magellan, then across the high Andes eastward into the plains of the Pampas region, his plans for a colony in the densely forested area of southern Chile were checked by the Araucanian Indians. This was the tribe which earlier had stopped the Inca invasion of Chile. The Araucanians had no real social or political structure and were little more than nomadic family units living an independent life and uniting under military chieftains to resist attack from the outside. Their first skirmishes with the Spaniards, who meted out their usual brutal treatment of prisoners, welded these tribesmen into a meld of fierce, courageous warriors under a succession of almost legendary hero-leaders. Their bravery in the face of almost impossible odds touched the imagination even of their enemies. One of the Conquistadors, Don Alonso de Ercilla, who celebrated the conquest of Chile in an epic poem, *La Araucana*, wrote in his foreword to it:

A fully armed buccaneer.

"And if there were persons who thought that I show myself somewhat partial to the Araucanians, dwelling on their deeds and exploits, more extensively than would be required in the case of barbarians, we shall see that, considering their upbringing and habits, their ways of waging war and training in it, few have excelled them and few are those who have defended their country with so much constancy and firmness against such fierce enemies as the Spaniards. And to be sure it is a thing to be admired that the Araucanians—with such small territory and means—by sheer valour and steady determination should have redeemed and maintained their liberty, shedding in sacrifice to it so much blood, theirs as well as Spanish."

Valdívia was killed in a skirmish with them, but not before he had settled Spaniards on both sides of the Andes, pioneers who had to handle both the plow and the sword and who produced a sterner stock than did the soldier-miners of Potosí in Bolivia.

Under Mendoza the initial exploration was continued, and by 1600 all the hinterland down to the bleak islands near the Strait of Magellan was known, though not explored in detail. The very fact that settlement was the main object prevented the Spaniards from exploring farther to the east than the foothills of the Andes, leaving that side of the continent to be explored from the Atlantic.

The link between Peru and the settlements along the Río de la Plata and the Paraguay had been made in 1548 by De Irala, who followed routes first attempted by De Vaca, and a little later communications were established with Chile across the plains of the Pampas.

After the first burst of exploration by soldier bands, who found little in the way of mineral wealth east of the Cordilleras, the careful examination of this vast area fell to the Catholic missionaries who moved up the rivers into the basin of the Amazon itself, often followed and hindered by slave-raiding parties from the coast.

Sir Walter Raleigh

The other spur to exploration to the north of the Amazon was the legend of El Dorado, the supposed home of the Gilded One, a potentate said to be anointed daily with oil and sprinkled with gold dust, ruling over a fabulously rich country called Manoa. For many years stories of the Gilded One lured parties from Peru and Ecuador and from towns along the north coast. An early expedition to find El Dorado was led by Pedro de Ursúa and was typical of many others in that it was ruined by mutiny. Ursúa set out from Lima in 1560 on an official mission to reach the Caribbean Sea, crossing the headwaters of the Amazon into those of the Orinoco. Some of the party did in fact complete that long journey, but in the course of it Ursúa was murdered by his officers, and another leader, Aguirre, became a bandit in Venezuela.

The last expeditions to seek the land of the Gilded One were those of Sir Walter Raleigh, in 1595 and again in 1617. The second expedition is of more interest because Raleigh was released from prison and promised freedom by James I on condition that he should find a source of South American riches not already claimed by Spain. Needless to say, he failed because he could not avoid encroaching on Spanish settlements during his search. Exploration on pain of death if unsuccessful was not a new practice, but this was a very late example of it, and Raleigh was duly executed on his return to England.

The continued interest of the British and French in the coastline between the Orinoco and the Amazon spurred both the Spanish and the Portuguese toward further exploration. In 1637, with a party of Portuguese, Teixeira made the first continuous journey up the Amazon to its source, finally arriving in Quito, a journey of ten months. Along the way they made some kind of survey, greatly exaggerated, of the population and the products they found. On reaching Quito the accounts of their achievement roused the jealousy of the Spaniards, who ordered Teixeira to return by the same route and take two Jesuit priests who would make a survey of their own.

By this time in our story—the late seventeenth century—the Amazon Basin was fairly well mapped, and in both the north and south serious exploration was being done by Jesuit missionaries.

Map shows area of northwest Andes and Amazon Basin. Exploration routes lead from the difficult mountainous side of the continent and extend inland.

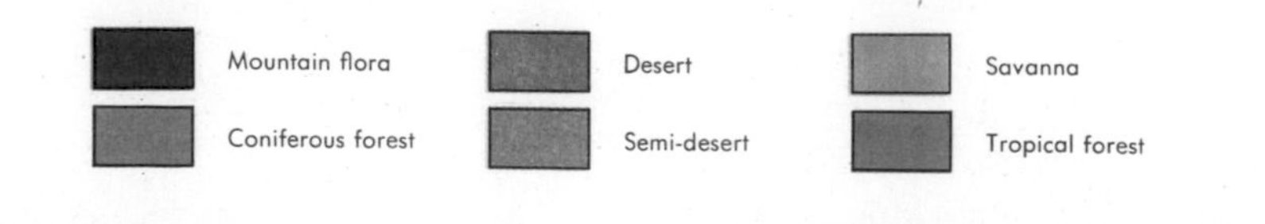

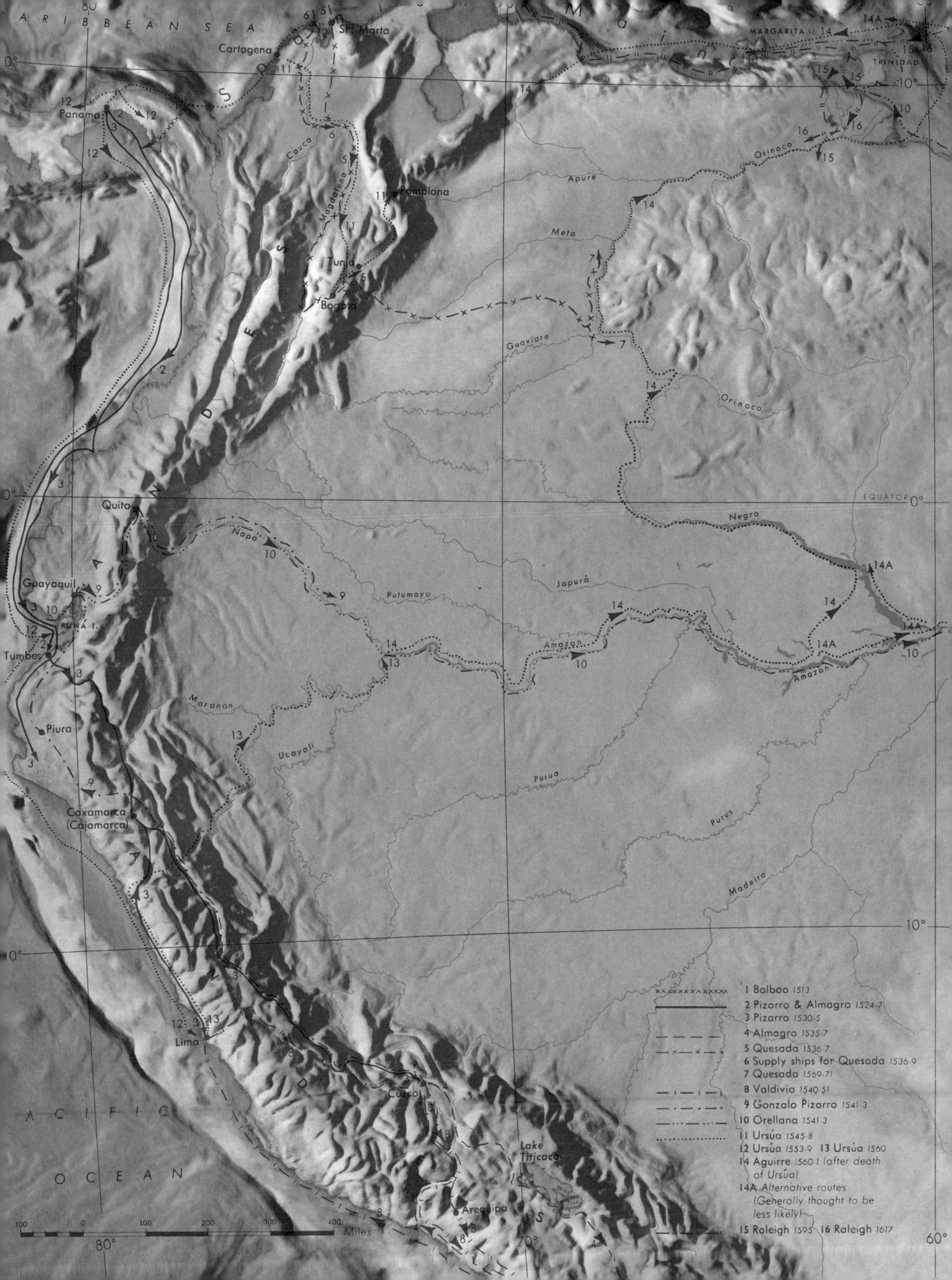
ARIBBEAN SEA
Cartagena
St. Marta
Panama
MARGARITA I.
TRINIDAD
Orinoco
Apure
Meta
Guaviare
Cauca
Magdalena
Pamplona
Tunja
Bogota
Quito
Napo
Putumayo
Japurá
Negro
EQUATOR
Amazon
Guayaquil
PUNÁ I.
Tumbes
Piura
Maranon
Ucayali
Purua
Purus
Madeira
Caxamarca
(Cajamarca)
Lima
Cuzco
Lake Titicaca
Arequipa
PACIFIC
OCEAN
Miles
1 Balboa 1513
2 Pizarro & Almagro 1524-7
3 Pizarro 1530-5
4 Almagro 1535-7
5 Quesada 1536-7
6 Supply ships for Quesada 1536-9
7 Quesada 1569-71
8 Valdivia 1540-51
9 Gonzalo Pizarro 1541-3
10 Orellana 1541-3
11 Ursúa 1545-8
12 Ursúa 1553-9 13 Ursúa 1560
14 Aguirre 1560-1 (after death of Ursúa)
14A Alternative routes (Generally thought to be less likely)
15 Raleigh 1595 16 Raleigh 1617

Among the missionary explorers of South America was a Jesuit named Samuel Fritz. He might well be called the David Livingstone of South America for, like the Scotsman in Africa, Fritz devoted himself to the Indians of the upper Amazon, constantly moving among them and trying to protect them from the Portuguese slave raiders and traders. Father Fritz died in 1728.

The parallel can be carried still further in that the fate of the Indians along the Amazon tributaries was repeated along the rivers of the Congo Basin in Africa in the nineteenth century. The Amazon Indians were either taken as slaves or forced to find rubber for their masters. Father Ramon, another missionary, in 1744 journeyed with slave traders from the upper Orinoco to the Río Negro under precisely the same conditions as Livingstone traveled with Arab slave traders from the Zambezi to the Congo a century later.

In 1740 there was a curious instance of exploration by accident in the famous voyage of Anson. The voyage also represents a transition between the sheer buccaneering of earlier years and the truly exploratory voyages

Humboldt's lithograph of 1810, which shows his party at the foot of Mt. Chimborazo. Humboldt is seen collecting plant specimens.

of Captain Cook which were to follow. Anson's voyage was intended as a punitive expedition against Spain on the west coast of South America, but a series of accidents turned part of it into exploration of the maze of islands known as Chonos and the Chiloé Archipelago north of the Strait of Magellan. Of the squadron of six ships only four managed to round Cape Horn and sail into the Pacific. Of these, one met rough seas and had to run for shelter behind the islands in about 45° South latitude, and remained there for two months, after which time she joined the flagship *Centurion* at Juan Fernández Islands. The *Centurion*, with Anson, had had a difficult enough voyage in the depth of winter, but it was further complicated by attacks of scurvy. In those days a ship's master regarded scurvy as one of the natural hazards of the sea. To lose part of a crew from it was regarded in much the same light as losing a spar or a sail—inconvenient, but unavoidable.

By the time the *Centurion* reached Fernández she had been ten weeks at sea and had lost more than half her crew of 450 men. Eighty of them died in the last days while Anson was searching for the islands. He had lost all account of the ship's longitude during their long voyage. Another ship, the *Wager*, suffered a worse fate: she was driven ashore about sixty miles north of Fernández and demolished. The disasters suffered on this journey were a high price to pay for the exploration of a few coastal islands; however, after Anson regrouped what was left of his men he continued the voyage and finally sailed around the world, taking four long years to do so.

So far in our story of discovery and exploration we have had little need to speak of scientific exploration. The Amazon, curiously enough, was one of the earliest regions in the world to attract scientist-explorers in large numbers. Perhaps it was partly the romance of a new continent that attracted them; stories of the Gilded One and reports of exotic natural wonders—red-faced spider monkeys, crab-eating raccoons, sloths and kinkajous, orchids and mimosa, quicksilver, gold and diamonds. Why shouldn't the scientist be attracted to this exciting new continent? It offered a wealth of variety to geographer and naturalist.

To find out if the earth was flattened at the poles the French Academy of Sciences sent La Condamine to Peru in 1736 to measure the length of an arc of the meridian. He and some of his party returned to Europe by crossing the continent down the Amazon. Scientific interest in South America blossomed fully at the end of the century when the great German scientist, Alexander von Humboldt, traveled through Venezuela, Colombia, and Peru for more than four years. Primarily a botanist, he was knowledgeable in most branches of science, including geography. His first long journey was to the little-known swamp area where the Orinoco and the Río Negro are joined by a curious natural canal nearly 200 miles long and rarely less than 100 feet wide. Later he ascended the Magdalena River in the northwest, climbed several of the higher peaks in Peru, and went from Lima on the coast to Mexico. The results of his expedition were published in eighty volumes. It was Humboldt's enthusiastic report that inspired later scientists such as Darwin and Wallace.

Natives of Tierra del Fuego, visited by Darwin on his voyage.

Charles Darwin's voyage in the celebrated *Beagle* in 1831 was a model of its kind for exploration, especially because Fitzroy, his captain, knew the Patagonian coast along southeast Argentina and was an accomplished hydrographic surveyor. Darwin's own travels inland to within sight of the Andes and his coastal exploration of Tierra del Fuego at the tip of the continent were as productive as those of Humboldt in Venezuela. They were both capable of close examination of detail, whether biological or geographical, yet never lost sight of the larger issues arising from their discoveries in both fields. In Fuegia, Darwin and Fitzroy were in a little-known region. During a previous voyage in 1830 Captain Fitzroy had captured several Fuegians as hostages because some of their compatriots had stolen one of his boats. He had taken them to England where he had them cared for at his own expense, and returned them in 1831 with curious results. Apparently outcast, they were robbed by their own people. Darwin's study and later account of the Fuegians' culture and stage of civilization was of great interest to anthropologists. He regarded them as the purest descendents of people who first crossed the Bering Strait and took up life in the New World.

Darwin's ship *Beagle* in Jemmy Button Sound near Tierra del Fuego.

The systematic and scientific exploration of South America went on throughout the nineteenth century, some of it along specialized lines as carried out by Alfred Wallace and Henry Bates along the Amazon from 1848–52. These two naturalists started out together on the great river but separated, and each wrote his own account of his travels. Although their explorations do not rank highly as actual discovery, since they were over country already known in outline, their books gave a new meaning to travel for geographical purposes.

Wallace went up the Amazon as far as Manaus, then branched off, going up the Negro and returning to the east coast by coming down the Orinoco. Along the way he collected thousands of specimens, but lost many of them in a fire during his homeward voyage. Bates remained in the Amazon Basin for eleven years, his special interest being butterflies and other insects; but his book is a thorough geographical account of the lower half of the basin.

The pioneer exploration of Patagonia was carried out by Chaworth Musters, an Englishman, in 1869–70. He lived among the native peoples and with them traveled great distances, from Magellan's strait up to the Río Negro at 40° South latitude, a distance of nearly a thousand miles. A much more continuous and thorough exploration of the Patagonian region was later carried out by Francisco Moreno over a period of some twenty five years. More recently the American explorer Dr. Hamilton Rice in five expeditions made accurate surveys of the region round that curious channel connecting the Orinoco and the northern Río Negro. Farther south, in the uplands of the Mato Grosso of Brazil, Colonel P. H. Fawcett spent many years exploring, only to be lost without trace sometime after 1925.

South America was discovered for the second time by Europeans within a period of forty years some four centuries ago. It is still being explored today, so massive are its plateaus, so impenetrable its tropical jungles. In spite of the long occupation of the continent by people from the Old World there are probably more unexplored areas in South America than in Africa, mostly in the Amazon Basin, where travel away from the rivers is difficult and where strange and hostile tribes are still being discovered. Nevertheless there is a steady, if slow, penetration of even those recesses, and it can be only a matter of time before the continent is mapped thoroughly, though perhaps mainly from the air.

The penetration and conquest of South America by a comparatively small nation, Spain, was the first large-scale clash between peoples of the Age of Steel and peoples still in the Age of Stone and Copper. It was a struggle waged with tools of an advanced people and tools of a people 6000 years behind in technique. But there was no such wide gap in intelligence; the organization of the Peruvian Empire was in some ways equal to that of most European nations, even though the Peruvians had not developed a system of writing. The outcome of the struggle was

A page from the diary of Henry Bates, naturalist-explorer of South America.

a foregone conclusion, but it was due mainly to the better weapons of war in the hands of the Spaniards and the psychological advantage which a superior technology provides.

There are certain similarities between the early Roman state and the Inca Empire. Both built roads and developed swift communications. Much of the rapid success of the Spaniards in taking over the country lay in their ability to adapt these advanced features of a somewhat backward civilization to their own purposes without inciting large-scale rebellions. Only a few years after his conquest, Pizarro was able to launch vast expeditions for discovery with the willing help of Indians, who far outnumbered the Europeans. It was not the Indians who slowed down exploration of South America, but jealousies and treachery among the Spanish leaders.

In judging the Spanish by modern ethical standards historians have perhaps been too hard on men who endured untold hardships in the cause of exploration; history has emphasized the traitors at the expense of those, like Almagro, who pressed on against all odds. But it is inevitable that the baser motives for discovery should provide the highlights. The greed for gain shines luridly, as do the deeds of treachery and massacre, and it is hard to believe that there was an element of crusade, a twisted notion of fighting for Christendom, which was not merely the selfish human desire to prove that Might is Right. Even the illiterate Pizarro took priests with him, and in his company there were men such as De Soto, who drew a line between the needs of war and the treachery of murdering the Inca Emperor.

In the great explorations following conquest the lure of gold remained strong, but the hope of glory for Spain and the hope of winning souls for Christianity eased the hardships when treasure hunts failed. History must pay tribute to the incredible bravery of the early Spanish leaders, ready to cross deserts or launch themselves down dark rivers without the least knowledge of the dangers before them. Mere greed cannot account for such fanatic courage.

While the Spanish were in the west and northwest of the continent, struggling across the Andean barrier and pushing into the jungle-infested river valleys, the Portuguese along the east coast were meeting with fewer hardships. The British and French were given their introduction to the new continent when they were attracted by the myth of the Gilded One and found themselves in the dense jungle region between the Orinoco and Amazon.

In the end Spain lost all her hard-won territories, but not before she and Portugal had impressed on all South America the spirit of their homelands. Part of that spirit was the readiness to mix both physically and intellectually with colored races, a willingness they may have acquired from their own long occupation by the Moors. Whatever the reason, South America is the classic example of the successful mixing of races on a very large scale. Today from the oil wells of Venezuela to the sheep ranches of Tierra del Fuego, it is the blood of medieval Spain and Portugal that is guiding the destinies of the great continent, much of which is still unexplored.

Tones of coloration show different stages of penetration of South America. Lightest color shows earliest penetration; darker colors, later penetration.

before 1550 | 1550-1700 | 1700-1800 | 1800-1850 | 1850-1900 | 1900 & after

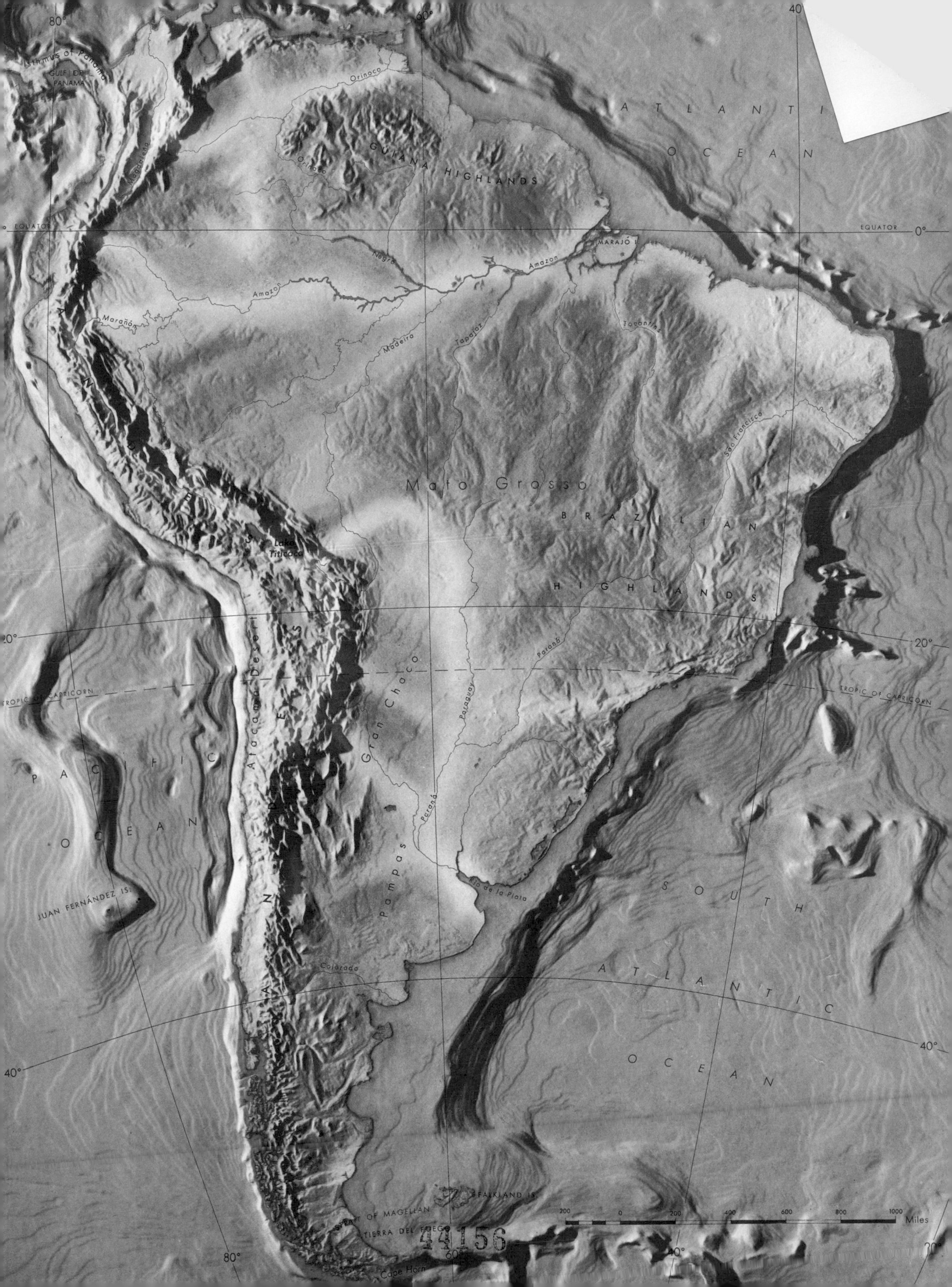
Isthmus of Panama
GULF OF PANAMA
Orinoco
GUIANA HIGHLANDS
ATLANTIC OCEAN
EQUATOR
MARAJÓ I.
Negro
Amazon
Marañón
Madeira
Tapajoz
Tocantins
São Francisco
Mato Grosso
BRAZILIAN HIGHLANDS
Lake Titicaca
ANDES
Atacama Desert
Paraná
Paraguay
Gran Chaco
TROPIC OF CAPRICORN
PACIFIC OCEAN
Pampas
Rio de la Plata
JUAN FERNÁNDEZ IS.
SOUTH ATLANTIC OCEAN
Colorado
FALKLAND IS.
STRAIT OF MAGELLAN
TIERRA DEL FUEGO
Cape Horn
Miles
44156

Migration routes of peoples across North America from earliest times.

Exploration of North America

Earlier we suggested that the original inhabitants of the Americas came from Asia. The fact that Alaska is separated from Siberia by a shallow strait only forty-five miles across, with islands in the middle, is only one of many reasons for believing that long ago people of Asia crossed into the New World by the Bering Strait.

But *why* must we suppose that the first Americans came from Asia? Isn't it possible that they originated on their own continent? The major reason for thinking that man did not develop independently in North America is the absence of any early Paleolithic finds. So far archeologists have found tools dating back only to early Neolithic man. The absence of earlier tools strongly suggests that the first Americans had learned their lessons in tool making on the Asian continent.

The map showing the undersea relief of the world illustrates how, with a small change in sea level, the Americas would become a peninsula of Asia. On the other hand, they are everywhere separated from Europe and Africa by a deep ocean. We can suppose, then, that some time between 10,000 and 20,000 years ago there was a trickle of people of Mongoloid type across to Alaska to begin the Age of Man on an empty continent. They were hunters who probably brought the dog with them, but no other domestic animals or seeds—which places them in early Neolithic time.

The routes these people followed as they spread all the way down the 10,000 miles to Patagonia in Argentina are a matter of guesswork; but, since they were hunters, the mountainous country on the Pacific side, where they could find game on land and fish offshore, would not be so difficult as one might suppose.

The route of the Eskimos, who may have been later comers, and are more Mongoloid than the Indians, is plain enough. Their mode of life kept them to the seashores as they spread across to Greenland carrying their peculiar culture with them. They reached their farthest point from the Bering Strait when they arrived in east Greenland, passing round the northern end of the island. Their last migrations, which might have brought them to the south shores of Davis Strait, took place after the Norsemen had established their temporary colony there about A.D. 1000.

Carving of Eskimo migrants.

Whatever their origin, the men of the New World took thousands of years establishing themselves over the two continents. Their cultural advance followed the pattern of their forerunners in Asia: hunters eventually began to sow seasonal crops, and finally their economy was based on agriculture. But agrarian societies were well established in only a few places when the Europeans arrived in the Americas, though there were various degrees between the pure hunters and established farming peoples. The civilizations of Mexico, based on such settlement, began possibly about 1000 B.C.

There were little more than a million people north of Mexico when the Europeans came, and perhaps three million in Central America, so there was never any pressure of population, as there was in Asia, to force migrations. What caused the early Amerindians to push down the long isthmus into South America remains a mystery; possibly the earlier tribes were constantly displaced southward, pressed on by later arrivals. The Incas may well have been one of these earlier tribes.

Part of the puzzle is understanding how two advanced cultures—the Mayan and the Aztec civilizations—should have arisen in such very different environments. The Aztec state seems to have begun on a lofty plateau as a small village on an island in a lake. The Mayan culture, earlier in date, flourished in the jungle region of Honduras, where recently their city ruins could be studied only by cutting away dense vegetation which had smothered them for centuries.

With the Aztecs, the impact of white men and their ruthless conquest was so sudden that most of their civilization was swept away before it could be properly studied. Their legends, and some concrete evidence from buildings, place the Aztec civilization about the time of the Norman conquest of England. Like the Incas, they may have been pushed southward by tribes in the north and settled on their high, fertile, and well-watered plateau. There they developed irrigation and the unity of purpose implied by irrigation. There they achieved wealth and a kind of luxury, built a form of pyramid temple for sacrifices, constructed aqueducts, viaducts, developed something akin to writing, and acquired a great facility in astronomy and calendar making on stone. It was a priest-ridden community of a bloodthirsty kind, with human sacrifices a prominent feature. The Aztecs never had an empire in the sense that the Incas had, nor did they have an urge to explore; at least they did less exploring than the Incas. Possibly they found no need to move; once they were settled in communities there may have been little pressure from peoples farther in the north.

We can find no evidence of communication between the Central American people and those of the great continent to the south, as though, in moving down from the north, the tribes never looked back. There is, however, a significant link: maize was known as the mainstay cereal all the way from Canada to Chile. Quite likely it was carried south by tribes migrating from North America. If so, then not only hunters wandered southward; there must have been agricultural tribes among them.

Further contrasts among early settlers of the New World are found among Indian cultures of North America. The Pueblo Indians of Arizona and New Mexico lived in communities based on maize agriculture in a semidesert region. To the east of the Pueblo tribes were the Plains Indians, pure hunters and nomadic to some extent, living on and with the bison. Still farther east were Indians, best typified by the Iroquois federation, who were still hunters but lived mainly by agricultural means and were living in something approaching towns.

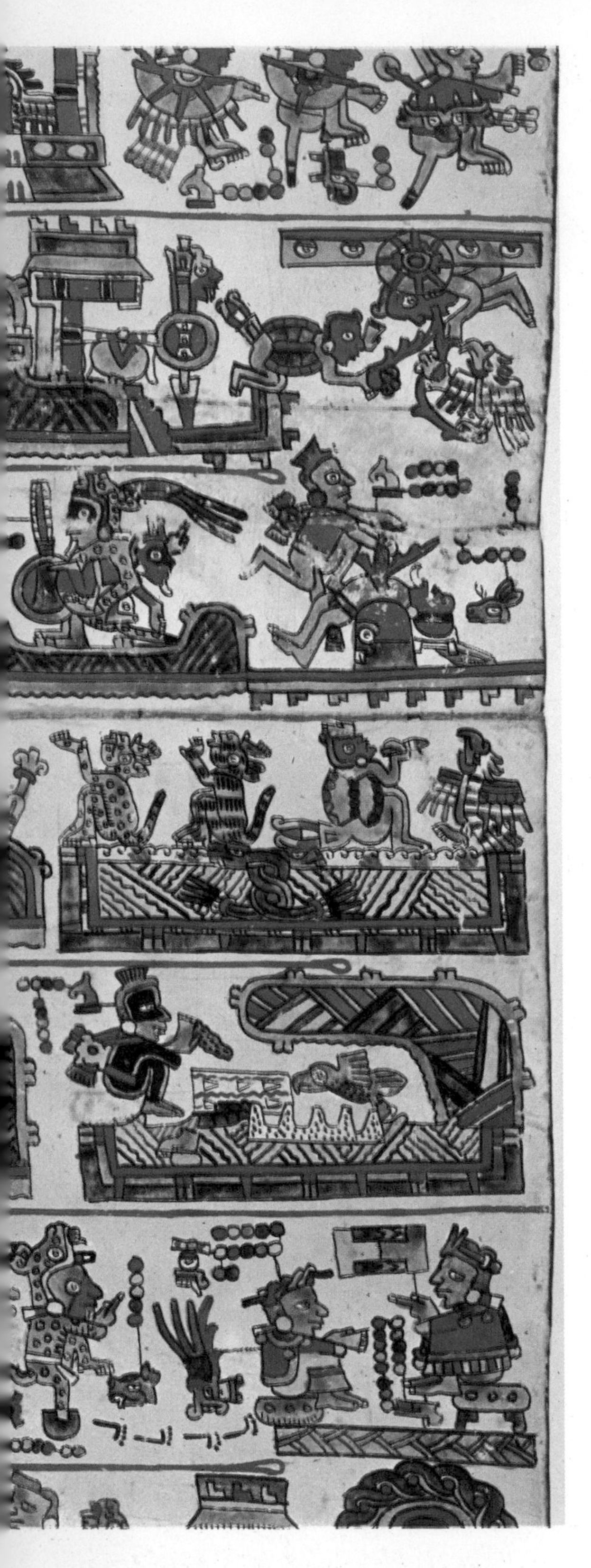

Section of a Mexican manuscript relating the history of the thirteenth-century Mixtecs chief.

Franklin's lithograph of Cree Indians.

The different stages of Indian civilization were very much the result of their surroundings—the cult of the canoe and the trap for the Canadian lakes group, the hillside caves and adobe granaries for the Pueblo peoples, the tents and leatherwork for the bison tribes. But there was room for all in this vast new land, so there were no decimating wars, only border incidents among relatively small groups.

The culture of the Eskimo was more individual and original than any of the Indians. The barren grounds of the tundra formed a zone of more or less neutral ground between them, not often crossed by either. The Eskimos may have brought their mode of life over with them from the shores of Siberia, but in their ingenuity and adaptation to their difficult environment they were far superior to the Indians. Their kayaks alone are proof enough; these boats rank with the catamarans of the central Pacific as the most perfect form of native craft known. Their use of dogs and sleds, their sewing of skins, their igloos, their use of blubber for fuel are all signs of a high degree of intelligence. Eskimo contact with Europeans has been over so long a period; and even today we can see them living in their original manner. So far as we know, these hardy and ingenious people were the last arrivals in the New World.

An early engraving of North American Indians and their canoes.

Neither England nor France dared to defy the Treaty of Tordesillas openly—that famous treaty that divided the world between Spain and Portugal. But both England and France felt that a route to the East might be found well to the north of the sphere of Spanish America. In a sense they were forced to think so. The Portuguese dominated the route to the East via Africa, while the Spanish had their foothold in Central America; England and France, therefore, were left with no alternative but to try either in the extreme north or south.

The reports of the Cabots in the fifteenth century and the Corte-Reals in the early sixteenth century projected little hope of success, but the fishermen of France and Portugal, returning each year from the Grand Banks of Newfoundland with cod, spoke of great bays and inlets in that region. The French were the first to look for a strait through to the Pacific. With two small ships of sixty tons, Jacques Cartier sailed from Saint-Malo in 1534. He navigated to the north of Newfoundland and entered one of the rumored bays by the narrow strait of Belle Isle. After examining the Gulf of St. Lawrence he sailed back home by Belle Isle, not realizing there was a much shorter route to the Atlantic by Cabot Strait, south of Newfoundland.

Frobisher's drawing of Eskimos hunting.

Two years later he was back again, this time with a larger company. He took his ships up the St. Lawrence as far as modern Quebec and continued another 150 miles by boat to Hochelaga, a large Indian settlement which he named Mount Royal (Montreal), from the noble view he had from the top of that hill. But he felt only disappointed when he discovered he was looking down on a river and not a strait. Nevertheless the optimist in him led him to name the rapids beyond Montreal after China (La Chine), trusting that the river would lead to the East.

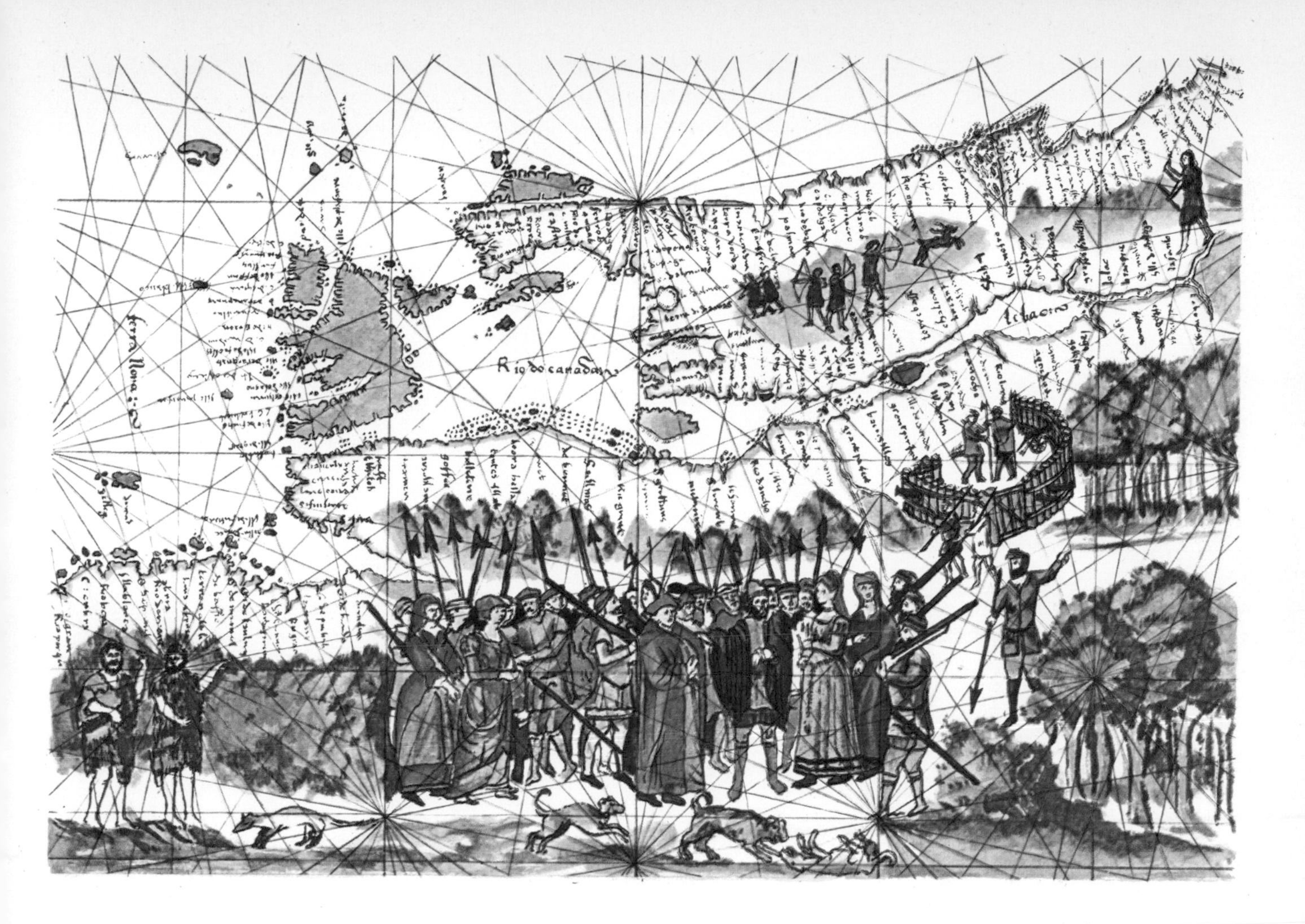

Cartier and his party arriving in Canada—from a map of 1546. To orient the map, hold it upside down.

Beyond all doubt Cartier's voyage ruled out the Gulf of St. Lawrence as a northwest passage to China, but the hope of finding a route would not die. The idea of trying farther to the north was taken up by the English, in particular by the enlightened and chivalrous Sir Humphrey Gilbert, half-brother of Sir Walter Raleigh. He wrote his famous *Discourse of a Discoverie for a New Passage to Cataia*, which, with his influence at Queen Elizabeth's court, was responsible for sending Martin Frobisher to put the theory to a test.

Frobisher's first voyage illustrates what bold and skillful seamen there were in those days. His own ship, the *Gabriel*, was only twenty tons, his

Voyages in search of a northwest passage.

- .... Voyages of Frobisher 1576, 1577 & 1578
- — — — — Voyages of Davis & his fleet 1585, 1586 & 1587
- ———— Voyages of Hudson 1607, 1608, 1609 & 1610-11
- —·—·— Voyages of Baffin & Bylot 1615, 1616

consort, the *Michael*, twenty five tons, and they had a small pinnace of a mere seven tons. In a storm off Scotland the pinnace was sunk and the *Michael* deserted, but the *Gabriel* sailed on across the Atlantic with eighteen men. Heading for what we now know as Baffin Island, Frobisher entered a broad gulf, which he took to be a strait. Fortunately his seamanship was better than his geography. He described his position as follows: "Having upon eyther hande a great mayne or continent; and that land upon hys right hande as he sailed westward, he judged to be the continent of Asia." He was the first Englishman to make contact with the true Arctic. He wrote that he had seen Eskimos and "their boates made all of seales skinnes, with a keel of wood within." Five of his crew were captured by Eskimos and never again seen. Triumphantly he returned to England, thinking he had found a way to Asia, but the whole scheme was diverted from its original purpose by a curious piece of chicanery.

A heavy black stone which he had brought back was examined by an assayer, who said that it contained gold. When Frobisher sailed again the next year he was "more specially directed by commission for the searching more of this golde ore than for the searching any further of the passage." Accordingly, on arrival he loaded up "almost two hundreth tunne of Ore" and returned without any further attempts at discovery. His third and largest expedition of fifteen ships found by accident the opening that is Hudson Strait, but made no other discoveries. The whole enterprise ended with ignominy when they were told that their precious ore was worthless.

Gilbert, despite these false starts, pressed his own conviction of the existence of a northwest passage to the East, and in 1583 he was given personal command of five ships to found a colony in Newfoundland as a base for further search. Gilbert was not as talented at leadership as he was in council, and the expedition turned out to be a failure, the largest ship being wrecked with all hands lost. On the way back to England Gilbert himself went down in a gale. He had insisted on being in the smaller vessel of ten tons, and in a storm off the Azores they were "neere cast away, oppressed by waves, yet at this time recovered; the General sitting abaft with a booke in his hand cried out to us in the *Golden Hind*, 'We are as neere to heaven by sea as by land.'" That night the small tender was swamped by a giant wave and, like the expedition's largest ship, went down.

The next attempt to find a northwest sea route was also fated to find only a blind alley, the large sound (Cumberland Sound) to the north of Frobisher's "strait." The commander was John Davis, and in two voyages he sailed far up the west coast of Greenland, but ice prevented him from going to the west, as it was to block the passage of other explorers after him.

All during this period of flirtations with the Arctic there were fishing vessels off Newfoundland every year, yet none of them was interested in visiting the land only a few miles to the west. It was not until 1609 that Henry Hudson first charted the coast from Cape Cod down to Chesapeake Bay and sailed up the Hudson River more than a hundred and forty miles beyond the site of New York—seventy five years after Cartier had entered the Strait of Belle Isle. The very next year Hudson sailed through his strait far to the north into the huge bay now named after him. He wintered at the southern end, where his crew mutinied. Half his men took the other half prisoners and set them adrift in an open boat, one of the basest actions in all exploration.

Sir Martin Frobisher

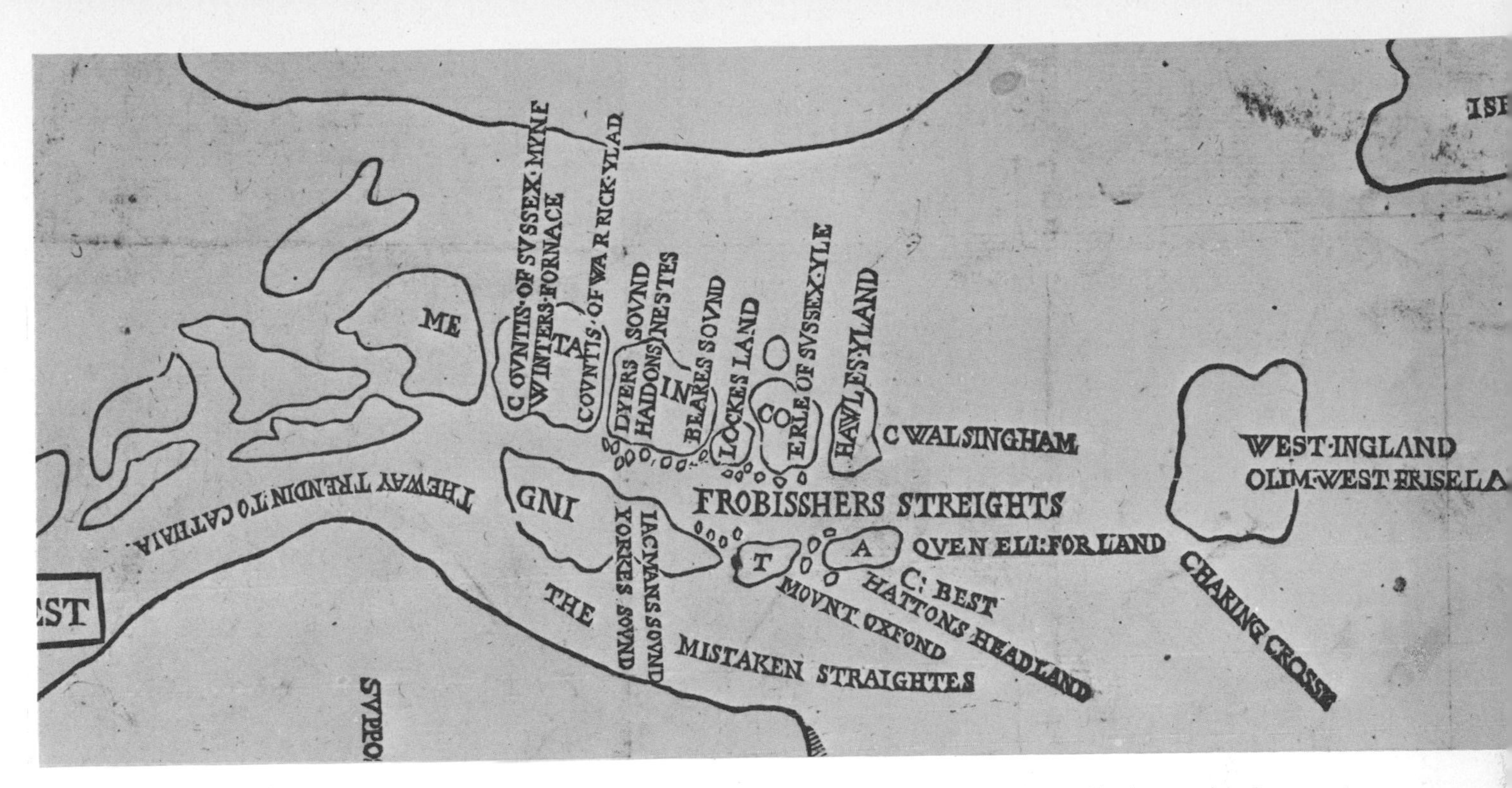

A crude woodcut map showing coasts and channels seen by Frobisher. Compare map with that on page 104.

By this time there was a company of merchant adventurers in London putting up capital to search for the northwest sea passage; William Baffin in two voyages got as close to success as anyone for the next two centuries. In 1615 he sailed across the northern end of Hudson's Bay but was turned back by ice before he could get near Fury Strait. The next year he broke all records by sailing round Baffin Bay, seeing two possible passages on the western side; but both were blocked by ice and he reported the search a failure.

By now it was evident that even if there were a passage, it could not become a practical route to Asia. The nations of northwest Europe began to direct their attention to the new continent for its own sake rather than as a steppingstone to the East.

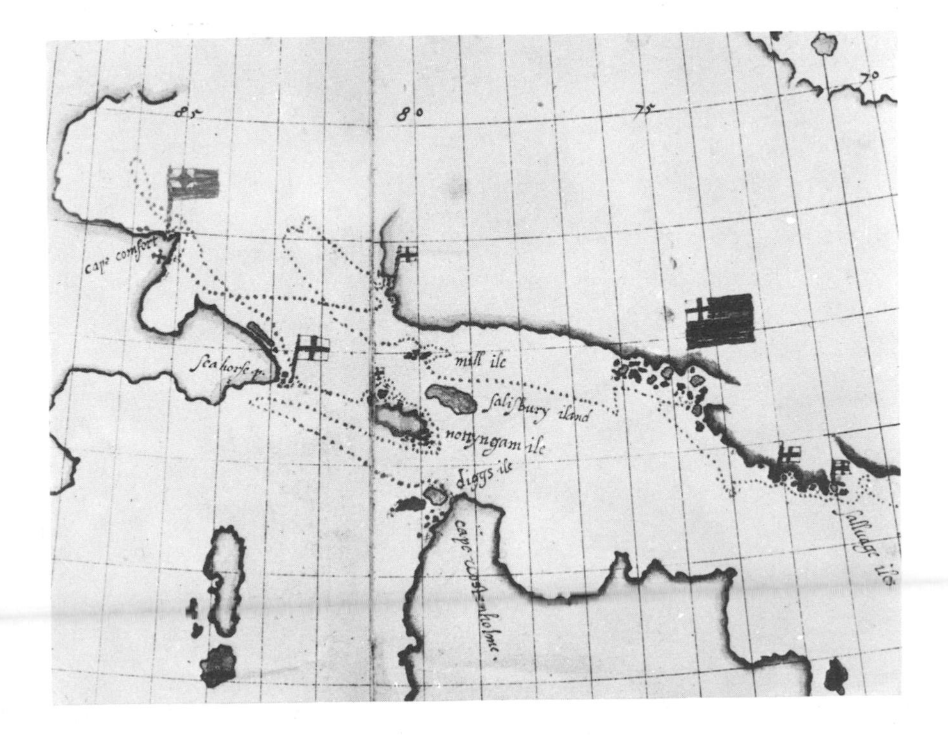

Route map of Baffin's 1616 voyage. Apparent lack of tides in Hudson Strait convinced him that the strait did not offer a passage through to the Orient.

This early view of Niagara Falls appeared in Hennepin's book, 1697.

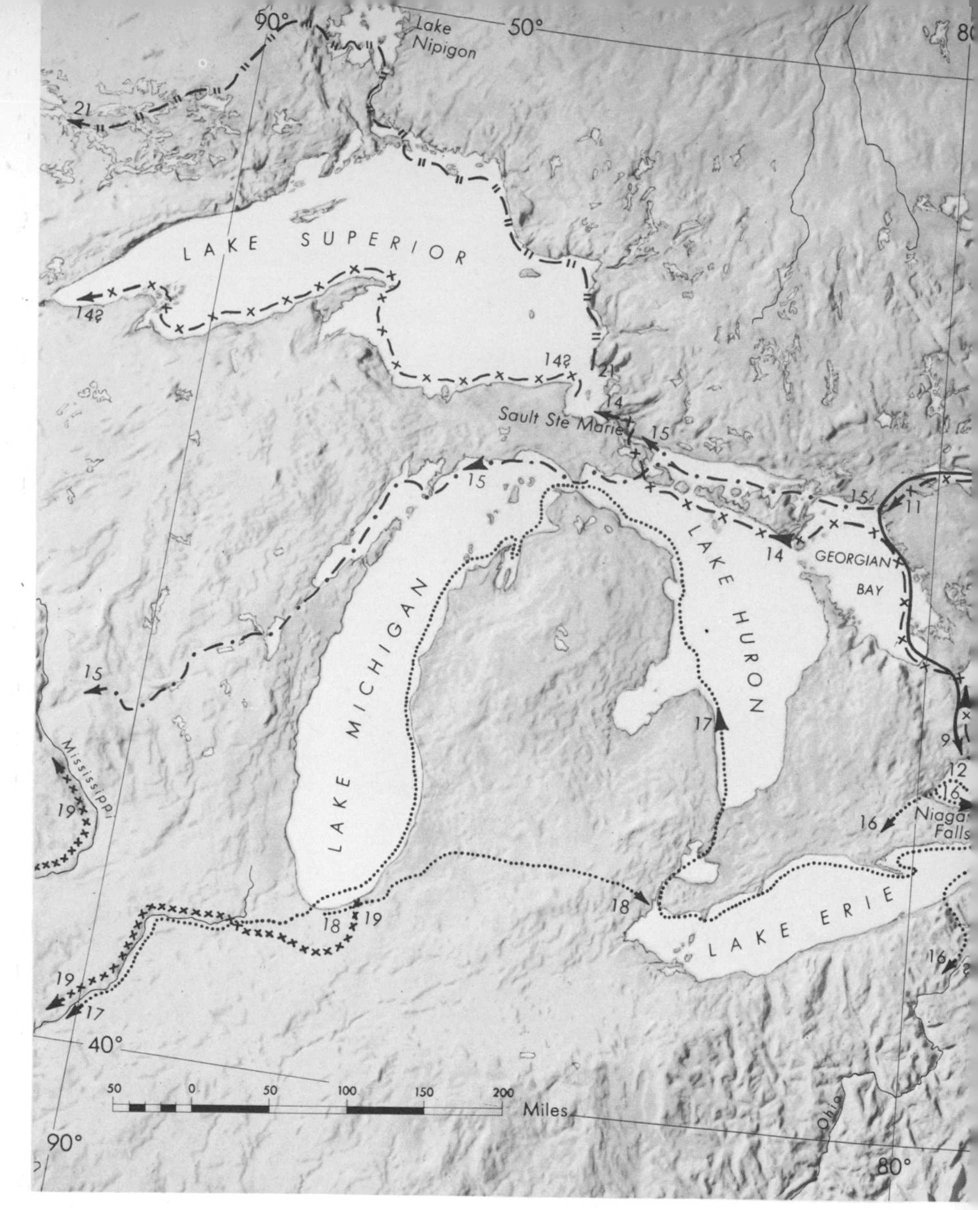

With the lead set by Cartier's discovery of the St. Lawrence, the French began to explore the vast new continent, pushing inland in small groups rather than by militant expeditions. Samuel Champlain was one such man who preferred to travel that way.

In his youth Champlain had been to the West Indies, and was the first one to suggest that a canal might be cut through the isthmus of Panama. After he founded Quebec in 1608 he began a series of small group expeditions west and south, traveling on foot and by canoe, living with and learning from friendly Indians he met. When he met the Huron tribe he helped them to some extent in their continual wars with the Iroquois, but usually he tried to avoid such alliances, which might involve him in a major clash.

On one of his early expeditions he discovered Lake Champlain and explored as far west as Lake Ontario and Lake Huron. Champlain was to devote his life to planning the colonization of New France, as Canada came to be called.

He was not, however, the first white man to gaze upon the Great Lakes. The lakes were visited earlier by an interesting French *voyageur* named Étienne Brulé who loved adventure and was perfectly at home in the rugged Canadian forests. He reached Lake Huron in 1611, Lake Ontario in 1615, and then went down to Chesapeake Bay. In 1621 he was

on Lake Superior and about ten years later, while still a young man, he was killed and eaten by the Huron Indians.

Rumors of still greater lakes to the west gave some promise to the stubborn belief in a route to the Pacific, and in 1634 Jean Nicolet was sent to investigate. Skirting the northern shores of Lake Huron, he came upon the Sault Ste Marie, the channel linking Lake Superior and Lake Huron. He paddled down the west side of Lake Michigan, then came to the divide between the St. Lawrence and Mississippi rivers. Since he was still less than 2000 feet above sea level, he believed that the "Great Water," as the Indians called the Mississippi, must flow into the Pacific; but it was not Nicolet's destiny to be the first white man to follow that mighty river to the sea. That feat was left to La Salle who, in 1682—four years after his visit to Niagara Falls—navigated down the Mississippi to the Gulf of Mexico, where he named the region Louisiana after his king. Following his voyage he returned to France, but came back to America a second time; he was determined to repeat his river journey, but in reverse. For some reason he could not find the entrance to the great river and he was murdered in Texas by his own men.

For the French there was still the mystery of a western sea and they continued to search for it. The La Vérendryes, father and four sons, based at a trading post at Lake Nipigon just north of Lake Superior,

were the chief pioneers. Frustrated fur traders who wanted to be explorers, they went westward and discovered Lake Winnipeg and Lake Manitoba. From there they turned south and went up the Red River, then overland to the Missouri River. It was along the Missouri that, in 1742, two of the sons made a journey which may have taken them to the Rocky Mountains, but at what point we do not know. Their journey of more than a thousand miles proved to the French that there was no easy way to the Pacific across the vast continent. Nevertheless they had pioneered a river route across a large section of North America, but not without misadventure: One of La Vérendrye's sons was killed by Sioux; his head was cut off and wrapped in beaver skins, which the Frenchmen had been so eager to find, a grim instance of Indian humor.

On the east coast of America the English had been trying their hand at colonization since 1585, when Sir Richard Grenville, on behalf of Sir Walter Raleigh, had landed a number of men. After a difficult year on short rations they were picked up and brought back to England by Sir Francis Drake on his way back from the sack of Cartagena on the north coast of Colombia. It was that party that brought news of "an herbe which the Spaniards call Tabacco. The leaves thereof being brought into powder they use to take the fume or smoke thereof by sucking it thorow pipes of clay into their stomach and head from whence it purgeth superfluous fleame [phlegm] and other grosse humours."

Gradually the English established several small settlements between Nova Scotia and Florida, but their way to the west was effectively blocked by the long line of mountains known as the Blue Ridge. Beyond that barrier were the French on the Mississippi and the Spaniards along the Gulf of Mexico and on the West Coast as far north as San Francisco.

Spanish missionaries by land and sea explorers along the coast by the mid-1500s were pushing their way north into the dry country from Middle America. They reached San Diego, near the head of the Gulf of California, in 1542; and in 1602 they were just south of Texas.

Canada was a thin line of French forts stretching from Cape Breton

When Drake returned to England in 1586, he brought news of an herb which the Spanish called tobacco. The Spanish had learned about it from the Indians.

North America seen from the east coast looking west to the Rocky Mountains. Explorers had easy access to the east coast region by sea, but the west region presented a mountain barrier.

Island off Nova Scotia across to the Great Lakes; as a result, the English could not push far northward until wars in Europe weakened the French Navy. French Canada finally fell into English hands after Wolfe's victory at Quebec; from that time onward the St. Lawrence route was open to the English for exploration to the west and the north—even after the American Revolution had crushed the older English colonies.

As a footnote reminder of the ever-present dangers of scurvy, and how survival in wilderness country depends on good leadership, we might mention here an abortive voyage made by a Danish expedition in 1619. Led by Jens Munck, the small expedition of about thirty men sailed in two ships into Hudson Bay where they wintered at Fort Churchill. By June all but three of the expedition had died of scurvy; somehow the three managed to sail back home in the smaller of the two ships.

Undeterred by reports of such misadventures and by the tragedy of Hudson and the failure of Baffin to find an exit to the west in Hudson Bay, the English persisted in searching for a way to the Pacific. Twelve years after the Danish episode an English expedition led by an able but conceited man named Luke Foxe got as far as Foxe Channel to the southwest of Baffin Land; but ice prevented Foxe from getting through and finding a northwest passage and so foiled his plan to return to England with a cargo of pepper, as he had arranged with the East India Company. Still the English persisted. In the charter granted in 1670 by Charles II for the formation of the Hudson's Bay Company, its purpose was defined as "for the Discovery of a new Passage [leading] into the South Sea." Little happened during the first century of the company's founding, but in 1770 Samuel Hearne set out from England and made two journeys to the north and west. When he reached Canada he chose to travel alone with Indians only, dragging a one-man sled overland or in summer following the rivers by canoe. He was the first white man to reach the Canadian Arctic Ocean, at the mouth of the Coppermine River south of Victoria Island. At Coppermine he saw a gruesome example of hatred between the Indians and the Eskimos. His own Indians ambushed

The stone inscribed by Mackenzie when he reached West Coast in 1793.

a party of Eskimos and massacred every one of them, including a young girl who clutched Hearne's legs in the hope of being spared, but Hearne was unable to protect her from his bloodthirsty companions. He was the first explorer to give a clear account of the barren lands of the tundra and of the Eskimos' mode of life in these parts.

A thrust still farther west, during an even more remarkable journey than Hearne's, was made in 1789 by Alexander Mackenzie. At Lake Athabasca, midway between Hudson Bay and the West Coast, he outfitted his party with six canoes. At the southwest tip of the lake he found a river outlet which led him into Great Slave Lake; and from there he followed the river now named after him all the way to the Beaufort Sea (part of the Arctic Ocean), a journey of nearly 3000 miles in 100 days. As Mackenzie was moving down-river he had been uncertain whether he would come out into the Arctic or the Pacific Ocean. On reaching the delta of his river, he wrote that "these waters emptied themselves into the Hyperborean Sea." Discouraged, in spite of a remarkable journey, he was determined to reach the Pacific by going westward from Lake Athabasca, so back he went, retracing his steps.

Party of explorers negotiating rapids of the Mackenzie River. This water color was made by an adventuress who followed the Mackenzie expedition route.

At Lake Athabasca he took his canoes west up the Peace River and wintered on it until spring. In spite of many long portages he continued up river, crossing over to what is now the Fraser River where he thought he would find a clear path to the sea. But again he was disappointed when he was stopped by fierce, foaming rapids and steep canyons. Finally he found a way westward along small streams which eventually led him down to the Pacific at what is now Dean Channel. There in July, 1793 he marked his name with grease pigment on a rock which has since been found. Mackenzie's was the first crossing of the continent since that of the brave De Vaca in 1536.

Mackenzie was an independent explorer, but about the same time there were surveyors of the Hudson's Bay Company who were undertaking great journeys. One of these was Simon Fraser, who in 1807 succeeded in getting most of the way down the difficult river now named after him, though he did not reach the sea. Another was David Thompson, who spent twenty seven years traveling between Lake Superior and the West Coast.

Occupation of the country west of the Appalachian Mountains went on slowly but steadily; gradually settlers in Ohio and Kentucky began sending their products down the Mississippi. This brought them in touch with the rather ill-defined boundaries of the Spanish area in the south. The population of the United States at this time was somewhere around four million, although not more than five per cent of it was west of the eastern mountains. The several small trading posts along the Mississippi and Missouri rivers, mainly of French origin, by 1800 were becoming small centers of settlement. The government, appreciating the dangers of an undeveloped western region, gave full encouragement to pioneers to settle to the west of the great river.

That the people of the newly created United States were not so advanced in their explorations westward as the Canadians was due in part to the shadowy claims of Spain to the Pacific coast and land to the north of the present Mexican boundary. The young nation could not afford to offend a European power at that stage, especially one in alliance with France. But in 1801 Napoleon sold Louisiana to the United States for fifteen million dollars; he needed the money to help in his war with England. For that small sum the Americans doubled their territory and gained the freedom to explore to the mountains far to the west, mountains which they knew only by rumor. The treaty for the Louisiana Purchase was vague and could not include unknown territory, so the United States hurried ahead with exploration in order to extend its indefinite boundary.

The leading spirit in the plans for immediate exploration was the President himself, Thomas Jefferson, but he had to invent reasons other than the true ones to "prevent the obstructions which interested individuals might put in its way"—meaning, presumably, the Spaniards, who had claims to the south and west. At this time the Spanish had a string of missions along the West Coast, but their political and economic significance far outstripped their religious fervor. The United States owes more than half its present territory to the acumen of Jefferson, both for his purchase of Louisiana and for his successful assumption later that the term "Upper Louisiana" included the territory as far as the Rockies and perhaps to the Pacific, north of Spanish claims.

In May 1804 Lewis and Clark set out from St. Louis on an official government expedition numbering forty five men. Their mission was to open a new way to the Pacific. Although Mackenzie had crossed the continent on the Canadian side of the boundary eleven years earlier, the land between the Pacific coastal regions and the frontier country just west of the Mississippi was unknown wilderness; maps of the time showed it as a great white space. The expedition set out in three boats and followed the Missouri up river a thousand miles before wintering. Although not one of particular hardships of the kind experienced by other explorers, the Lewis and Clark expedition is outstanding if for no other reason than the careful description of wildlife recorded by the two officers.

From the early stages of their journey food was the least of their problems. They continually saw "immense heards of Deer" along the

A Currier & Ives lithograph showing the wagon-train migrations that took place around 1848.

banks and daily feasted on "4 deer, an Elk and a deer, or one buffaloe." Farther up river they entered buffalo country, not realizing the fantastic size of some of the herds they were to see. Benteen, hero of the Custer massacre, reports looking down from a high peak and seeing 300 thousand of the animals in a single herd. Lewis and Clark were awed by the beauty of the prairie country that looked "like a bowling green" abounding with animal life—buffalo, deer, elk, antelope, bear, turkeys, ducks, and wild pigeons. At one stage of their journey up river they saw coal burning with a "strong sulphurous smell." Later travelers were to see similar veins burning for years on end; some continued to smolder into the twentieth century.

The winter of 1804–05 was spent in North Dakota with the Mandan Indians. Here Lewis and Clark heard tall tales of grizzly bears, a new animal to these white men. In spring, when they left the Mandans, the tall tales suddenly seemed less tall when they saw one grizzly track measuring eleven inches long and seven and a half inches wide. Lewis was confident that in "the hands of skillful riflemen they are by no means as formidable or dangerous as they have been represented." But he changed his views when he met one and found that it took ten bullets to kill the beast. Lewis concluded that the animals were "hard to die."

These three woodcuts appeared in Patrick Gass' journal of the Lewis and Clark expedition. They show an encounter with Indians (top), being swamped by rapids on the Snake River (middle), and making agreements with the Shoshone Indians.

At the spectacular falls of the Missouri one of the enlisted men left Lewis's side and searched for food. In a surprisingly short time he was back with a large number of trout, sixteen to twenty three inches long. Food had been abundant since their setting out; according to Lewis, "two good hunters could conveniently provide a regiment with provisions," but this good fortune was about to change. During the five months since leaving the Mandans and arriving at the foothills of the Rockies, they had not seen a single human being, not even an Indian sign. The number of beaver dams in the streams leading down out of the foothills staggered the imagination. Some, five feet high, backed up water that covered five acres. Trappers—the fearless "mountain men"—who were to follow Lewis and Clark discovered this area to be the richest beaver country in North America.

In Montana, the group found that two rivers joined the Missouri at "Three Forks," which Lewis and Clark named. Anxious to get over the great Continental Divide ahead of them before the Rockies' severe winter set in—it was already September—they failed to notice the tiny, bright shining pieces of metal covering the stream beds they sloshed through. They were in the heart of Montana's gold country. At this stage the long spell of good luck took a turn. The country so rich in food lay behind them now, and their boats were useless. Their only hope was to get horses from the Shoshone Indians and try to scale the Rockies before the early mountain snows became severe.

By the time they had crossed the Bitterroot Mountains and reached the treacherous Lolo Trail they were buffeted by snowstorms, rain, and sleet. Their pack horses slipped, fell, and tumbled down the mountainside and food was hard to come by. They ate wolf meat, eventually some of their pack horses, and finally were reduced to munching roots. At the height of their hardship Clark, leading an advance party in search of food, climbed a peak and rejoiced at seeing far below him the Clearwater Valley, Idaho. From the Clearwater and the Snake the expedition canoed down the Columbia, which empties into the vast Pacific. For the first time in history men had explored the length of the Missouri, crossed the Rockies at the widest part, and reached the Pacific.

The Lewis and Clark expedition was of enormous importance to the

Opening of the New World attracted millions of emigrants from Europe. Here, a group is about to leave Liverpool in 1856.

young nation, since it constituted a claim to country which ultimately almost doubled the area of the United States. Trappers and traders soon followed the trail of Lewis and Clark, though there was considerable friction between them and the Indians and real overland treks did not begin until 1840.

Prior to that there were many penetrations by picturesque travelers into what might be called the Spanish zone, leading to border incidents with Mexican authorities. From the United States point of view, these were discoveries. Thus, in 1807 Lieutenant Zebulon Pike examined the Rio Grande and New Mexico thoroughly before he was seized by Spanish authorities. In the middle 1820s Jedediah Smith covered most of the territory between Salt Lake City and the California coast. The same region was examined more thoroughly twenty years later by Frémont in semimilitary reconnaissance between the Mexican wars.

Early in the 1800s England showed a renewed interest in finding a northwest passage, and after the Napoleonic Wars the British Admiralty sent expeditions both by land and sea. In 1820 Lieutenant John Franklin and his small party reached the Arctic coast, where Hearne had been before, and explored the coast eastward. But on returning to their winter quarters they met disaster. Game was scarce and they had to eat lichens from the rocks, and leather. On top of their food problem, a Canadian *voyageur* murdered two of Franklin's men, and a Dr. Richardson had the unpleasant duty of shooting him to save the rest of the party. George Back, the strongest man in the small group, hiked overland and saved the party by sending back Indians with food, he himself having lived on a pair of leather trousers and an old shoe.

Five years later the same party, but this time with more men, was back again to explore the coast west of the Mackenzie. In two expeditions they surveyed about 1000 miles of the Arctic coastline. This kind of exploration, well organized and disciplined, is of particular interest to us because it bred a type of Arctic explorer later to figure in the discoveries of the Canadian Arctic—Parry, for instance. This was because Arctic conditions demand a special kind of technique.

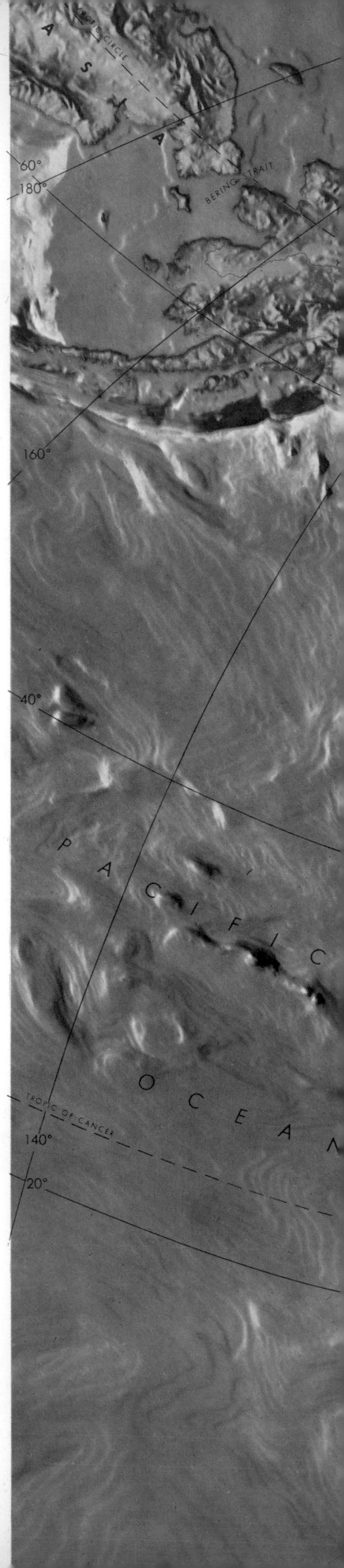

The system of wintering ships in the Canadian Arctic began when, in 1819, the Admiralty commissioned the *Hecla* and *Griper*, strong naval vessels, under the command of Lieutenant William Edward Parry, to attempt a northwest passage by sea. Sailing up Baffin Bay, he made for Lancaster Sound, which two years earlier John Ross had thought to be closed by mountains. Parry found it to be a strait, and before the winter set in he had sailed past the 110th meridian west of Greenwich and won the £5000 bounty offered by the British government. Though he could get no farther west, Parry had proved that there was a passage in that latitude and it might be navigated in an exceptional ice-free season. The Admiralty therefore sent him again in 1821 to try farther south along the northwest corner of Hudson Bay. They did find a strait and named it after their ships, *Fury* and *Hecla*, but it, too, was blocked by ice.

The exploration in North America, in contrast to that in South America, is singularly free of wars of conquest and from exploitation of the native peoples. There was international rivalry, but it was mainly in the cause of occupation and settlement instead of a search for temporary riches. Another notable difference is that penetration was from the Atlantic side of the continent instead of from the Pacific side. The occupation of North America came from a surge of immigration from Europe with spearheads of penetration along the great rivers. The lure to begin with was the fur trade, but that was soon combined with the desire for land to occupy and settle. In North America the Europeans had found a temperate land similar to their own homelands, a land sparsely populated. They adopted it almost at once as an expansion, a sort of Europe overseas. The course of history in Europe at the time ensured that it was for the most part an Anglo-Saxon expansion rather than a Mediterranean one, as in South America.

It may seem difficult to understand how the early explorers of North America could have been so misled in thinking that the great western sea was just overland a few miles from the Great Lakes. Long, long before any of the explorers of North America pushed west, the true dimensions of the earth had been worked out, but the early western explorers were ignorant of the great distance across North America—even though the distance across Asia to Europe was known, as were the distances across Europe and the Atlantic. Although the brave Magellan had circumnavigated the globe and determined the distance across the southern Pacific, there was no knowledge of the distance across the north Pacific. As a result, hopes of the North American explorers of seeing the Pacific at any moment—even before they reached the Rockies—seemed justifiable.

By the time Queen Victoria came to the throne in 1837 the entire continent of North America was known in outline; but there were still mass movements of people to come—immigrants from Europe, a drift to the West by covered wagons in the United States, important gold rushes in California and Alaska—but discovery, in the geographical sense, was ended.

Varying tones of coloration show different stages of penetration of North America. Lightest color shows earliest penetration; darker colors show later penetration.

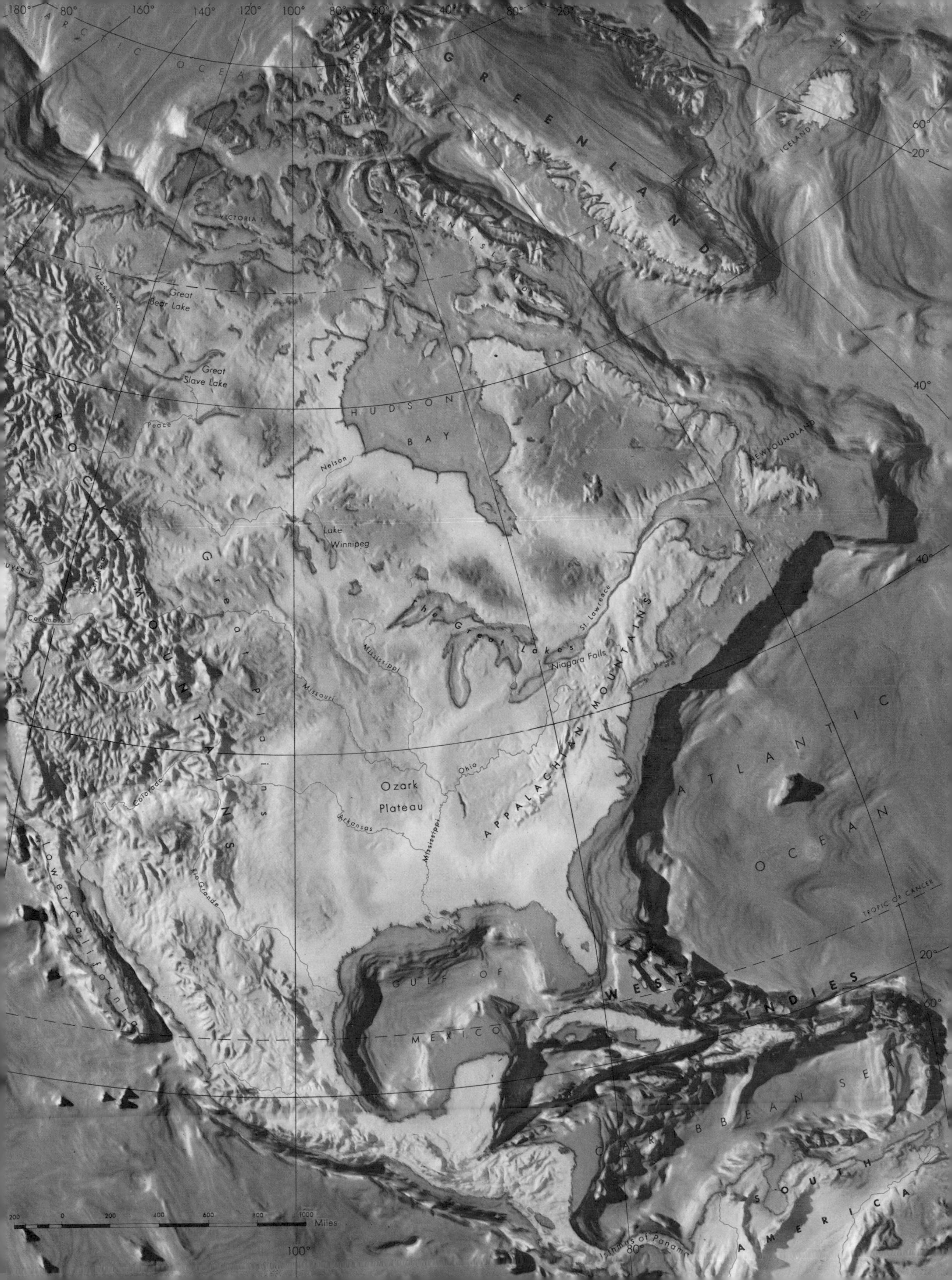
ARCTIC OCEAN
GREENLAND
ICELAND
ARCTIC CIRCLE
ELLESMERE LAND
VICTORIA I.
BAFFIN ISLAND
Mackenzie
Great Bear Lake
Great Slave Lake
Peace
HUDSON BAY
Nelson
NEWFOUNDLAND
Lake Winnipeg
ROCKY MOUNTAINS
Great Plains
Columbia
The Great Lakes
St. Lawrence
Niagara Falls
Mississippi
Missouri
APPALACHIAN MOUNTAINS
Ohio
Ozark Plateau
Colorado
Arkansas
Rio Grande
Lower California
ATLANTIC OCEAN
TROPIC OF CANCER
GULF OF MEXICO
WEST INDIES
CARIBBEAN SEA
SOUTH AMERICA
Isthmus of Panama
Miles
200
0
200
400
600
800
1000
180°
160°
140°
120°
100°
80°
60°
40°
20°

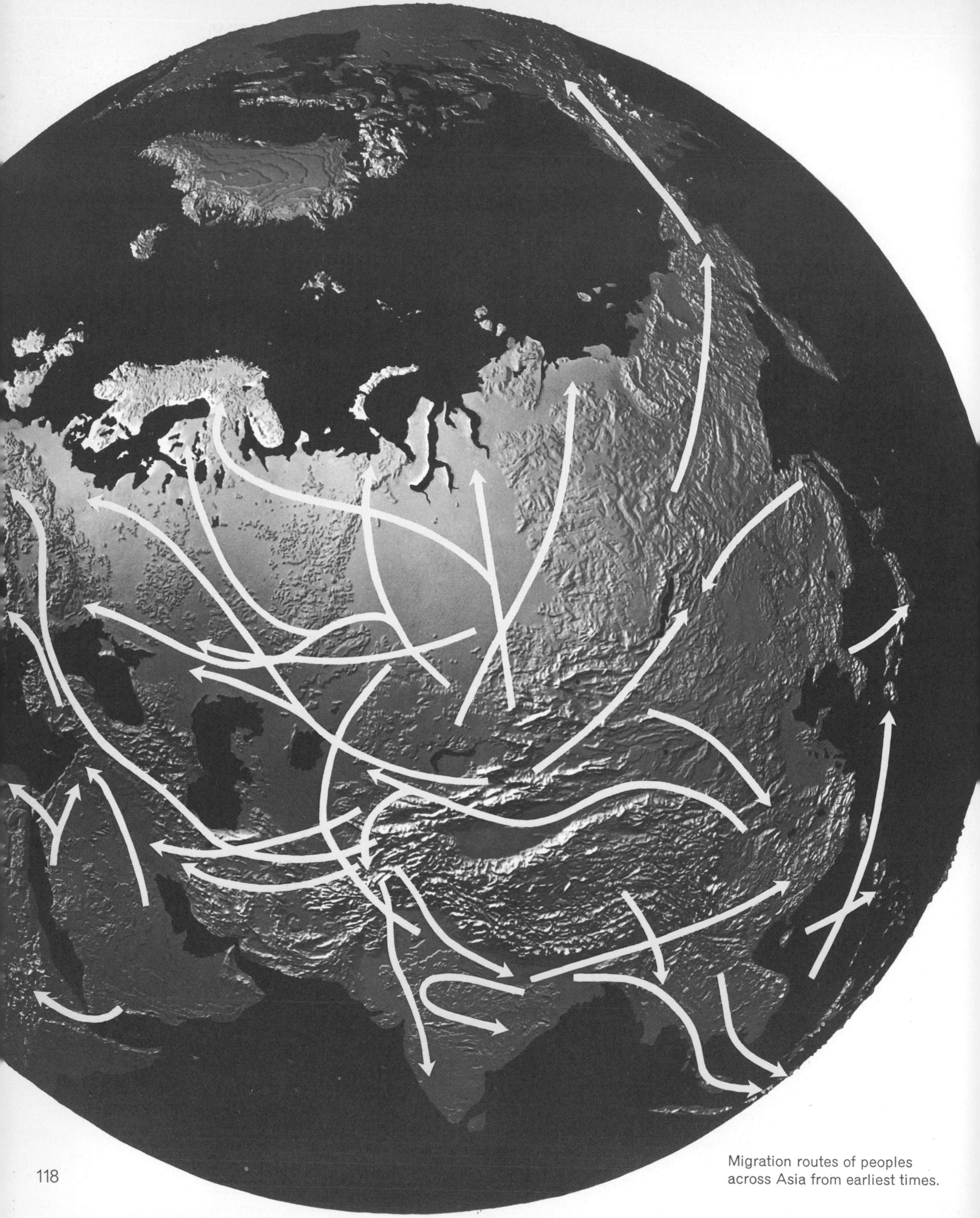

Migration routes of peoples across Asia from earliest times.

Exploration of Asia

Turning from the virgin continents of the New World back to the oldest of the Old World, we again meet the difficulty of deciding what is to be called "discovery." We are returning to that period when the once separate centers of civilization in Asia—China, India, and the Fertile Crescent region—were in close contact, long after the nomadic tribes had begun to intermingle. In a sense the story of discovery in this part of the world becomes inevitably the history of invasion and the record of mass migrations.

In ancient times the basin of the Tarim River in Sinkiang was densely populated along the thousand miles of its course, and the Tarim was one route from China to lands westward. There was also a branch of the river that ran north across the great Takla Makan Desert and from the Kunlun Mountains. These routes led to the ancient city of Kashgar, meeting point for all caravans passing to the west between the high mountains of the Tien Shan in the north and the Pamirs in the south. The caravans traveling along the southern route, known as the silk or jade route, took silk to the western people and jade from the Kunlun Mountains back to China. But over thousands of years climate changes gradually made this route unsuitable for mass movements, since water became scarce. For the same reason the Tarim Basin could no longer support large numbers of nomads, so the main corridor for their migrations was to the north between the Tien Mountains and the Altai Range. Here there were wide grassy valleys leading down to the steppes of southern Siberia or to Lake Balkhash and rivers running into the Sea of Aral. For the nomads, therefore, with their large numbers of animals, their huge wheeled carts, this broad northern corridor was the natural one to follow in their mass migrations. But the Chinese preferred the Tarim Basin, especially in the early summer when the rivers were running strongly, their banks overflowing with floodwater from the high mountain snows.

From the beginnings of time man's movements were governed by his physical needs—food and shelter for himself, pasturage for his animals, barter, conquest, and racial domination, and, as he became a sophisticated trader, sources of merchandise. But during the period from about 600 B.C. to A.D. 600 another motive for exploration and travel emerged and has been a driving force ever since—man's intellectual curiosity and the spread of new ideas, particularly of religious ideas. Establishment of the three great religions (discussed on page 44) took place against a background of violent political change all over the known world. The great dynasties of Egypt and the Middle East declined, making way for the rise of the powerful Arab groups. And Europe, after the fall of the Roman Empire, was overwhelmed by waves of barbarian invaders. China, too, was caught in the upheaval; during the fourth and fifth centuries she was invaded by Turko-Mongol hordes.

In spite of the turmoil of wars and migrations across the breadth of Asia it was possible to travel in small parties. The Chinese often traveled that way, sending what we would now call diplomatic or trade missions as far as the Caspian Sea during the first centuries of the Christian era. For instance, in the first century A.D. a Chinese general named Pan Chao became Viceroy of the province of Kashgar and pushed his command as far west as Syria. Then, or a little later, Chinese missions reached Constantinople and made a brief contact with the Roman Empire. The Nestorians, too, sent their missionaries to the Tartars and Mongols as early as the fourth century. Their monasteries were seen 800 years later by Marco Polo.

Early in the seventh century A.D. we find one of the greatest explorers of the ancient world—Hsüan-tsang. A scholar and a fervent Buddhist, he was disturbed by gaps and discrepancies among the sacred books and manuscripts available to him, so he was determined to "travel in the countries of the west in order to question the wise men on the points that were troubling his mind."

Although he was refused permission to leave China, he was encouraged by a dream and set out in A.D. 629 to cross the Gobi Desert with all its known and unknown dangers. But before he had traveled many miles his guide and companions abandoned him; nevertheless he rode on, picking his way by animal trails and camel bones. He was in constant danger of attack from the watchtowers and forts that guarded the frontier and at one point lost his way in the wild and desolate country. Eventually his horse, scenting water, took him to Hami, in Turfan, where he was welcomed by Chinese monks. At that time Turfan was an important state ruled by the Great Khan of the western Turks. Hsüan, "the Master of the Law," as he was generally known, was received by the local ruler with great honors, and when he was ready to continue his journey he was given an escort and presents to take to the Great Khan.

The scholar-explorer Hsüan-tsang

Passing north of Kashgar and crossing the icebound Tien Shan, he reached the camp of the Great Khan, who treated him with respect and arranged for the next stage of his journey to Tashkent and Samarkand, southeast of the Aral Sea. Here he found a culture and religion which were Iranian, but his next stage across the Oxus took him into a stronghold of Buddhism where he visited monasteries and seats of Buddhist learning. He then crossed the Khyber Pass to Peshawar, in what is now northern Pakistan, explored the Swat Valley, and crossed the gorges of the Indus. Eventually he reached Kashmir, which he described as a country of great beauty and where he found a venerable and learned monk with whom he spent the next two years to complete his philosophical training.

Hsüan traveled far and wide over the plains of India, and in the valley of the sacred Ganges he met doctors of the law and saw great libraries filled with sacred books. Next he visited the cities of Benares and Patna, and Nalanda, which was a great monastic city where he studied for a further year. At one time in Bengal he gave up the idea of a sea voyage to Ceylon on receiving reports of civil wars and famine there. Instead he traveled overland across the Deccan and returned northward along the west coast of the Bay of Bengal, noticing as he passed that the merchants of Gujarat traded with the Persians for brocaded silks and carpets.

Hsüan was now ready to return home, but first he accepted an invitation to visit Assam, with whose king he traveled up the Ganges and visited the king of Northern India. On his way back across the Punjab he had the misfortune to lose fifty manuscripts and his collection of flower seeds. His homeward route took him up the valley of the Oxus to the Pamirs and from there to the oasis of Kashgar. He then followed the caravan route southeast to Khotan, the "Kingdom of Jade," where he found an important Buddhist center, and where he waited several months for his emperor's permission to return to China. Finally in the year 645, sixteen years after he had left his country against the orders of the emperor, he was given a tremendous official reception, and he handed over to his monastery the manuscripts, relics, and treasures he had gathered during his long and arduous journey.

A companion journey to that of Hsüan-tsang was taken by the monk

I-Ching, who left China in the year 671 in a Persian ship bound for India. He reached Sumatra, where he studied Buddhism for a while, then set out across the Bay of Bengal in a Sumatran ship which, along the way, traded iron for fresh fruit with the savage inhabitants of the Nicobar Islands. In 673 I-Ching landed at Tamralipti on the northeast coast of India, where he remained for a year learning Sanskrit before traveling inland to visit shrines and other holy places. On leaving India he took with him thousands of Sanskrit texts; and on returning home he settled down, spending the rest of his days translating the texts into Chinese.

Under the first Ming Emperor, Hung Wu (1368–98), China regained her supremacy at sea. A century earlier Chinese shipping suffered from the disastrous loss of Kublai Khan's fleet, which he had sent out against the Japanese in 1281. From that time on Chinese ships had been at the mercy of Japanese pirates. The need for a rebirth of strength on the seas produced the man—a Chinese Vasco da Gama—who was to journey far to the west with fleets larger than those of the Portuguese, though with poorer armament and less warlike intent. The man was Cheng Ho, a Chinese Moslem from Yunnan who, as a child, was brought to Nanking

Chinese travelers making their way down the Yangtze. (From a thirteenth-century woodcut).

Some believe that the Chinese reached Africa early. This painting on silk of a giraffe was done by Shen Tu in 1414.

and, as a eunuch, became a servant of a prince who later became emperor. Cheng Ho was a striking man, tall and burly, and in Chinese history he is described as having "a stride like a tiger's and a voice clear and vibrant." His father and grandfather had been on pilgrimage to Mecca, and when he had risen to high office at court he was a natural selection to further the development of trade by sea toward the west.

His first voyage was in 1405, a century after Marco Polo had written his description of his voyage from China to India in 1292. Although journeys to the west by Chinese junks were not new, Cheng Ho carried them out on a far larger scale than ever before. Even allowing for some exaggeration on part of Chinese chroniclers, whose accounts were liable to have titles such as *Marvels of the Ocean Horizon*, *Marvels of Star and Mast*, his ships were enormous by western standard. Ibn Batuta mentioned one capable of carrying 1000 passengers. We have to doubt some of the figures of historians who describe vessels 600 feet long and 250 feet broad. (The *Queen Elizabeth*, the world's largest liner, is only 1030 feet long and 118 feet broad.) A wooden vessel of that size would hog badly in a head sea and be battered by a beam sea. Nevertheless the fleets commanded in seven voyages by Cheng Ho must have dwarfed any of that date in Europe.

His ships went as far as Jidda on the coast of the Red Sea, some loaded with pilgrims bound for Mecca; others went to Hormuz in the Persian Gulf and down the Somali coast beyond Mogadishu near the Equator. They were principally trading voyages, carrying porcelain ware, silks, and pepper in exchange for Arabian spices, ivory, and rhinoceros horn, among other things. Chinese pottery is still dug up occasionally as far south as Malindi, just south of the Equator in East Africa. The Chinese duly recorded what they saw on these voyages and they were impressed by many aspects of the cultures they found in India, Persia, and Arabia.

The voyages of Cheng Ho mark the peak of China's maritime trade in the Indian Ocean area. After him trade tended to slacken and the Chinese were satisfied with visits to ports nearer home, Malacca being the chief port. Cheng Ho's name in the East is generally written as San Pao, and is still used as the name of a suburb and a well in Malacca.

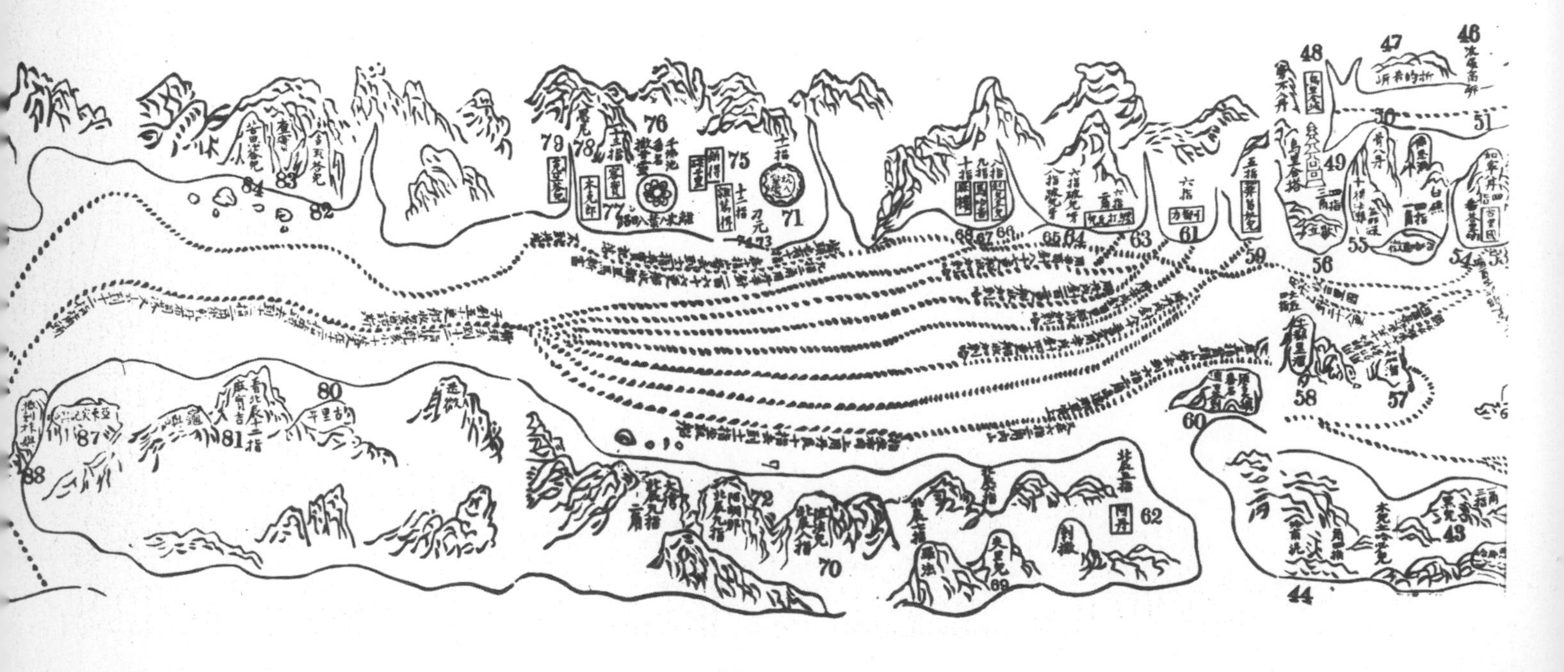

This Chinese navigation chart of 1420 shows sections of the coasts of India (top) and Arabia (bottom). The Indian Ocean is squeezed into a schematic corridor.

The outburst of China's maritime trade occurred when the Turko-Mongol Emperor, Tamerlane, was effectively blocking the land routes to the west. Overland trade, then, was too risky to be attempted on a large scale. But there was another reason for turning to the sea, and it is the essential difference between exploration by sea and by land. Not only was travel by sea much quicker than by land, but you traveled in an organized unit, self-supporting to the extent that you carried your own provisions and you had complete freedom to choose your course and destination.

By land the picture was different. You most often needed help along the way, you had to use gentle persuasion rather than force to get such help, and you could rarely run away once you found yourself in trouble. You also had to have a reason for crossing boundaries, one that would satisfy the people you were among. On land you were a stranger and were usually suspect wherever you went. At sea you were master of your own fate, with no one to interfere or question your motives until you reached your destination. There is no private property at sea and you leave no trail of your passing. The freedom of the open seas is a term which has a wider meaning than that we commonly attach to it.

In the heartland of Asia, therefore, there was always restriction of travel. If you were stout of heart and had a zealous purpose, like Hsüan-tsang in the year 630, you could travel alone from northern China to India, though at great personal risk. If you were bearing a message from one potentate to another, like the friars or the Polos, you could get through. But if you were seeking knowledge only, like Ibn Batuta, you were suspect. Your best hopes for safe travel were by joining caravans or going by sea. On land you had to be so small a unit as to be harmless, or so large that you could fight your way through. There was no such thing as a scientific expedition in the modern sense; the very idea of a party's wandering through a territory to find out about it and its people was suspicious in itself. So it is not surprising that exploration in Asia was the business either of bold individuals or of armies, nothing in between.

The routes in Central Asia, too, were strictly limited by its geography. The Arctic tundras lay to the north and the Himalayas to the south. That left only the route by the upper Irtysh River north of the Tien Shan or that by the lower Tarim River south of them, going either round or across the great Takla Makan Desert.

Earlier in this book we suggested that the Asians seemed to have little need to explore; also, they apparently lacked an urge to do so. During the period of the "Great Age of Discovery" the western nations were almost cutting each other's throats to reach the East by whatever route they could, yet during this same period the seaboard nations of Asia were making no attempt to reach the West. For China the explanation is a simple one. Under the Ming Dynasty she had no need for conquests to the north or west; she was self-sufficient, highly civilized, and hemmed in by mountains to the west and ocean to the east. When her traders went to the southeast in their junks they found nothing half so good as their own land could supply.

In Central Asia the nomads were as restless as ever, but they were never again welded into an empire like that of Genghis Khan. Their mobile armies had been halted when they reached the densely wooded lands of middle Europe, and there was either retreat or assimilation when gunpowder and fortresses were at hand to challenge the horse and the arrow.

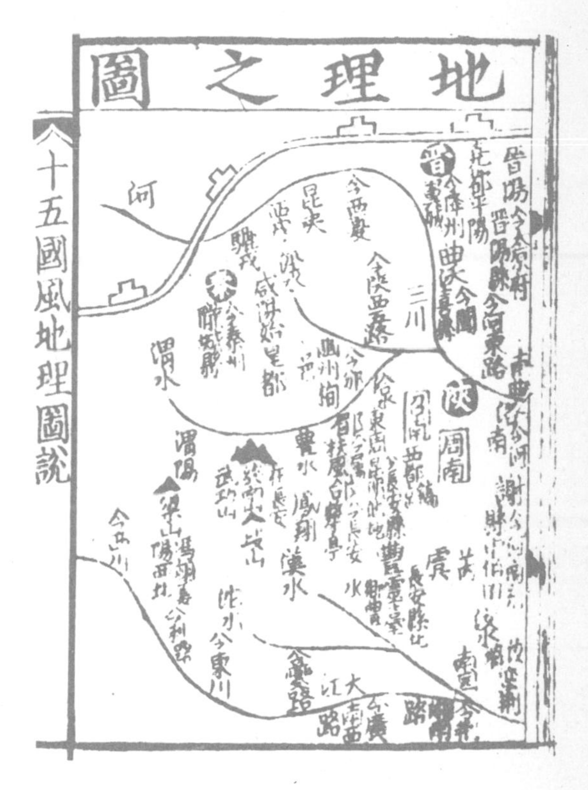

This map, the oldest printed one known in the world, shows west China in 1155. Part of the Great Wall appears at the top; the dark lines are rivers.

A woodcut of St. Francis Xavier (seated) and a pupil named Loyola.

Moscow is represented by St. Basil Cathedral, a detail from a seventeenth-century Russian map.

India was in somewhat the same position as China. She, too, was hemmed in by mountains and sea and had a civilization further advanced than her neighbors. Under the greatest of the Moguls, Akbar, India was achieving a kind of unity not unlike that brought by the Ming period in China. Religious toleration was one of the strongest features, even though India was Moslem and not Buddhist.

In the Indian Ocean and the China seas regions both the Chinese and Indians were passing on elements of their own cultures, particularly around the Malay Archipelago, where both countries carried on trade. For example, the great Borobudur Temple of Buddha was built in Java about the year 800. A little later Islam penetrated and drove Buddhism on to Bali. By the fifteenth century the Moslem religion had spread to the Philippine Islands, carried most likely by Malayan traders, but the Chinese had authentic accounts of the Philippine Islands as early as the tenth century, although they had never made any attempts at conquest or colonization.

Into these strongholds of Buddhism and Islam there stalks the strange figure of the Jesuit priest, Francis Xavier. He was one of the founder-members of the Society of Jesus formed by Ignatius Loyala in 1534. Xavier began his missionary work at Goa, the Indian port, but he went on to Malacca, then to the Moluccas off New Guinea, the center of the spice trade.

For two years he traveled among the islands of the Banda Sea, living with and baptizing the islanders, but he returned to Malacca disappointed with the type of simple folk he had dealt with. At Malacca he met a native Japanese and realized that for a sure foundation of the Christian Church in the Far East he must seek out such intellectual people as the Japanese. He went to Japan in 1549, the first Christian missionary to that country of whom we have any record. For two years he carried on his missionary work, and his letters home gave the first clear accounts of that nation to European readers. He died when just about to journey to China.

Associated with Xavier was a strange Portuguese adventurer, Fernando Pinto, who had gone out to the east with the son of Vasco da Gama and had traveled, fought, and traded in those seas for more than twenty years. Though he was a gay and debonair cavalier, he traveled with and eventually fell under the influence of Xavier, and for a while he even took the vows of that missionary order and revisited Japan. His book, called *Peregrination*, was published after his death and is, on the whole, a truthful account of his wanderings.

Halfway into the sixteenth century the English were still determined to get a share of the trade with the Far East. Having already attempted to find a northwest passage around the North American continent, and meeting with failure, they began to search for a northeast passage. The Portuguese, remember, controlled the African route to the East and the Spanish controlled the South American route, so it was left to other nations to look for a northwest or northeast passage. In 1553 a company of London merchant-adventurers (later to be known as the Muscovy Company) sent ships around the north of Norway to see what chance there might be of a route. One ship got through to the White Sea and its commander, Richard Chancellor, found to his surprise that he was in Russia. Summoned to the Emperor Ivan's court at Moscow, he was very well treated, and trade relations, which had a strange sequel, were arranged.

In 1557 another Englishman, Anthony Jenkinson, was sent as agent to Moscow by way of the White Sea. From Moscow he made an incredible journey—the first by an Englishman—to find an overland route to Cathay (China). He set out armed with letters from Ivan to the various princes he would meet along the way. First he went to the Volga via Kazan, then down the great river, noting as a key point the town that is now Stalingrad. From Astrakhan at the mouth of the Volga they coasted round the northeast shores of the Caspian. He and his assistants, the Johnson brothers, were largely responsible for the navigation and flew the cross of St. George on their ship. With a caravan of a thousand camels they went overland to the Oxus River, but not without skirmishes with robbers. Finally they arrived at Bukhara, where they spent the winter among the "Mahometists."

Jenkinson's report to his principals is a model for its time, and there is something delightful about these three matter-of-fact commercial travelers who were as ready with their "hand gunnes" to repel robbers as with their yardsticks and rolls of Kersey cloth. Wars in the region prevented them from traveling farther east and denied them the pleasure of meeting caravans from China; but they managed to gather a great deal of geographical information which they soberly recorded and later embodied in a map published in 1562.

Jenkinson's was a really great journey, not made any easier by an Iron Curtain of a sort between Russia and the Baltic; a barrier of Finns,

Scene from a cotton wall hanging (1540) showing English in India.

The city of Canton, an engraving from a book about the Dutch East India Co. (1665).

Livonians, and Poles, and another barrier toward the Mediterranean where "the Mahometists stopped up the way." The most interesting point about his journey is that his route had to be by the White Sea to Archangel then via Vologda to Moscow. The worthy agent-explorer had to report that trade any farther than Moscow would be "of little utterance and small profite," for the merchants from Persia, whom he met in Astrakhan, would have none of his Kersey cloths, saying "they had them as good cheape in their countrey."

Blocked along that long and complicated overland route by the Tartars and blocked along a sea route by the Portuguese, the English continued to look for a northeast route. In the process they found the long island of Novaya Zemlya and even the straits between it and the Pechora coast, but unhappily they were turned back by tightly packed ice in the Kara Sea.

The Dutch, too, joined in the search. The three voyages of Willem Barents produced good charts of the northeast region and a dramatic ending. On his last voyage in 1596 Barents discovered the small Bear Island and the larger Spitsbergen and, sailing east, he managed to get round the north end of Novaya Zemlya into the Kara Sea. But there his ship was frozen in the ice and his sixteen men and a cabin boy were forced to winter at latitude 76° N., a record for a northerly wintering up to that time. Unprepared for such a trial, they built a house out of driftwood and timbers from their ship, set up beds and a Dutch clock, and made a steam bath out of a cask. Outside they set traps for foxes and had encounters with polar bears. The seaman's plague—scurvy—gripped them, killing the cabin boy and making Barents very ill. With the coming of summer they set off toward the White Sea in two open boats. Barents died within sight of Novaya Zemlya, but the rest of the party carried on, sailing for an additional 600 miles until they reached the Kola Peninsula and safety.

The account of the expedition was written by the mate, Gerrit de Veer, in quaint detail and with illustrations, but the accuracy of his narrative had to wait more than 270 years for proof. In 1871 a Norwegian sealer, Carlsen, reached the Ice Haven of Barents and there saw a hut still standing. Beds were placed as de Veer had described them; the Dutch clock was still on the wall, and bath cask complete. In a museum in Amsterdam these relics can be seen today, including the flute and a shoe of the little cabin boy who died on what probably was his first voyage nearly four centuries ago.

One of Barents' earlier supporters was van Linschoten, who was determined to find alternative routes to the East on behalf of the Dutch. He was a sort of Marco Polo on a small scale. In 1583 he went out to Goa in a Portuguese bishop's retinue and lived there for five years. The book he wrote of his travels and what he observed was translated into English in 1598 and influenced a race between Dutch and English traders to take advantage of the waning power of Spain and Portugal in the profitable spice trade, a trade which was destined to result in discovery on a grand scale.

The first English voyage around the Cape along the Portuguese-controlled route was under James Lancaster in 1591 and was disastrous. He lost all but an eighth of his men but managed to return to England with a precious cargo of pepper. Holland, however, won the race, ousting the Portuguese from Java and sending fifteen fleets around the Cape between 1595 and 1601. The famous Dutch East India Company was founded in 1602 and established a Dutch maritime empire in the East which extended from Madagascar to Japan.

The English had also formed an East India Company of their own, which was granted a royal charter by Queen Elizabeth in 1600. The early voyages of their ships reached as far as Japan. But friction with the Dutch finally led to an agreement: the Dutch were to have a monopoly in the East and the English in India. The Company survived for two and half centuries, and for knowledge of the East generally we owe a great deal to its traders and agents. Like the Hudson's Bay Company, the two East India companies played an important part in the story of discovery. Many members of their staffs were engaged for the majority of their lives mapping and exploring.

A good instance of such a trader-explorer is John Jourdain, who went out with the fourth East Indian voyage in 1608 and was the first Englishman to give an account of the Seychelles group of islands off the coast of East Africa. From there he visited Aden, at the southern tip of Arabia, and called it "an uncomfortable cittie, where onely your delight must be in cragged rocks and decayed house." He was also the first Englishman to visit Yemen in southwest Arabia. After spending some time in India he was buying pepper in Sumatra and cloves in the Moluccas. There he met "an English sailor which had secreetlie brought a letter from Mr. Adams in which there was a draught by him drawn of the countrye of Japan." The mysterious "Mr. Adams" was one William Adams, who reached Japan as a pilot in a Dutch ship and who became so useful to the Japanese that he was kept there until he died about 1620. Since the Japanese discouraged his communicating with friends, he could send news out only "secreetlie."

In the first years of the 1600s the struggle for the eastern trade between Dutch, Portuguese, and English was keen. The eventual arrival of European merchants and missionaries in Japan was the signal for an outburst of commercial and religious activity which was astonishing in a country which a century later refused all association with nations of the West.

De Veer's woodcuts show Barents' hut (top) and his party hunting polar bears.

By the middle of the sixteenth century Russian adventurers and explorers, under Ivan the Terrible (1503–84), turned the tide of invasion and therefore discovery toward Asia. It was Russians who opened up Siberia.

The conquest was begun by the Cossack leader Yermak in 1580, but many other soldiers and traders followed his lead, advancing across Siberia at an astonishing rate. Their general route was that now followed by the trans-Siberian railway, that is to say, well to the north of the classic routes of the Mongols, who had migrated westward centuries earlier. So any resistance which the Russians met came more from natural barriers than from the backward tribes they encountered. Nevertheless it was an extraordinary feat for these unknown explorers to cross that broad and desolate land mass, gripped by a hostile climate, and reach the Pacific at the Sea of Okhotsk, founding towns along the way.

Detail from a map of Siberia drawn for Bering in 1729. This section shows some costumes and customs of the Tibetan tribes.

They had pushed eastward initially, then went down the great rivers to the Arctic coast, and then traveled south many miles until they reached the Amur River, the border between Siberia and China. Here they were finally stopped by the Manchus who were just about to conquer and rule over China. The Cossack Dezhnev supposedly sailed from the mouth of the Kolyma River around the northeast tip of Asia in 1648, passing through Bering Strait. If he did, he did not realize how close he was to America. In the seventeenth century exploration across Siberia by the Russians was a parallel of sorts with exploration across Canada.

Gradually the expeditions along the Siberian coast became more scientific in nature and were carried out by the western nations. Such were the two expeditions of Vitus Bering, a Dane, sent by Peter the Great in 1724 to find out whether Asia was joined to America. He went overland to Kamchatka, where he built a ship and sailed northward, but not quite far enough. In 1741 he returned again, and both his ships sighted that part of America lying south of the Aleutian Islands. Bering died on the island now carrying his name. By 1742, when Chelyuskin reached the most northern cape, the Arctic coast had been surveyed in outline.

The exploration of Tibet needs a section to itself. It is not only the most forbidding region in the world for travel, but for long periods it has been a forbidden land, closed to nearly all strangers. On any relief map the vast wrinkled plateau of Tibet catches the eye at once. It is truly the "roof of the world," averaging 13,000 to 15,000 feet in height, which is only slightly below the snow line for that latitude. In area this tableland is only slightly less than that of peninsular India. It is a land of high-level east-west valleys, of arid belts leading to salt lakes, and its plants, animals, and human inhabitants are as strange as its structure. It is an almost inaccessible land: to the south and east are the Himalayas and great valleys of the Mekong and Salween. To the east the valleys are separated by high ridges which make travel extraordinarily difficult. To the north are the Tarim Basin and desert; and to the west are the barriers of the Hindu Kush and the Pamirs. Yet in spite of these barriers Tibet had to be explored. In exploration it is often the inaccessible which is the lure—mountains, deserts, jungles, and the warning that "it can't be done."

The people of Tibet are of Mongol rather than Indian origin, since the least difficult approach to the region is from the north, not the south. Chinese literature has many references to the Tibetans. The country was first explored by the Chinese, who have usually held a loose sovereignty over the northern and eastern part of the plateau.

Yet Tibet is a stronghold of Buddhism, which came to the area from India in the seventh century and developed into the special form known as Lamaism, in which the priests became the temporal as well as the spiritual rulers. Its history consists largely of conflicts between two sects—the Red-Hat Lamas and the later Yellow Hats, and between the Dalai Lama and the Tashi Lama, both of whom are believed to be reincarnations of the earliest followers of Buddha.

The politico-religious system was in itself as effective a barrier to travelers from the West, as was the ruggedness of the country. Nor was the mode of life of the Tibetans an easy one for a westerner to fit into. Though they are, like the Eskimos, a cheerful, pleasure-loving people, their obsession with religion (nearly a quarter of the males are lamas) and their diet of meat and barley, with endless drinks of tea mixed with butter and salt, all set social barriers to strangers from other lands. It is, therefore, not to be wondered at that Tibet has been the last and most difficult region for exploration in Asia, and is even yet incompletely known to the West.

In a sense there is a parallel here with the Chinese culture, in that the Tibetans and the Chinese did almost no exploring beyond their own back yards. The material culture of the Chinese was so far in advance of any they were in contact with that there was little for them to covet or emulate. The Tibetans were hemmed in by physical barriers and so were discouraged from exploration. The social structure of both countries was so rigid that neither one had the desire to learn new ways from outside cultures—which would imply travel—nor did they particularly welcome strangers into their midst.

There are, of course, exceptions to such generalities. Jesuit priests had successfully entered China and had been allowed freedom of movement. For example, there was Matteo Ricci. In 1582 he reached Canton and was welcomed by the Chinese, but mainly for his superiority in astronomy and mathematics. From Canton he went on to Nanking and, finally, to Peking, where he settled and made a name for himself. He and his fellow priests were allowed to move about China year after year, and they even taught two lamas (Buddhist priests) to make a rough survey of Tibet.

The Jesuit Matteo Ricci as he appeared in Chinese costume at Emperor Wan-Li's court, 1603.

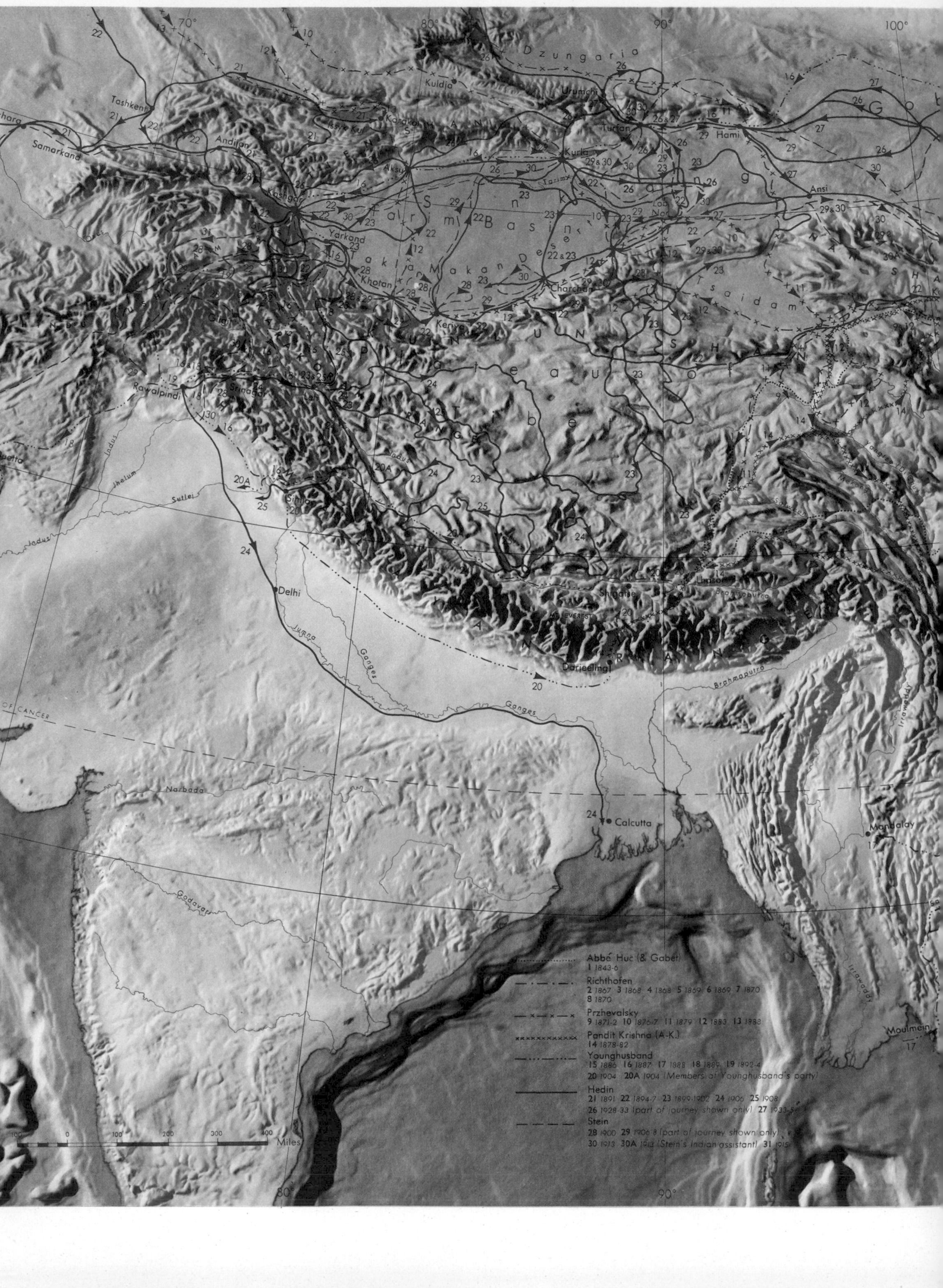
Dzungaria
Kuldja
Urumchi
Turfan
Hami
Gobi
Tashkent
Bukhara
Samarkand
Andijan
Kashgar
Aksu
Kurla
Tarim Basin
Lob Nor
Yarkand
Khotan
Takla Makan Desert
Charchan
Kenya
Tsaidam
Ansi
Gilgit
Srinagar
Leh
Rawalpindi
Plateau of Tibet
Quetta
Simla
Delhi
Karachi
Shigatse
Lhasa
Darjeeling
Mt. Everest
Calcutta
Mandalay
Moulmein
Amu Darya
Indus
Jhelum
Sutlej
Jumna
Ganges
Brahmaputra
Narbada
Godavari
Irrawaddy
Tropic of Cancer
Miles
Abbé Huc (& Gabet)
1 1843-6
Richthofen
2 1867 3 1868 4 1868 5 1869 6 1869 7 1870
8 1870
Przhevalsky
9 1871-2 10 1876-7 11 1879 12 1883 13 1888
Pandit Krishna (A-K.)
14 1878-82
Younghusband
15 1886 16 1887 17 1888 18 1889 19 1892-4
20 1904 20A 1904 (Members of Younghusband's party)
Hedin
21 1891 22 1894-7 23 1899-1902 24 1906 25 1908
26 1928-33 (part of journey shown only) 27 1933-5
Stein
28 1900 29 1906-8 (part of journey shown only)
30 1913 30A 1913 (Stein's Indian assistant) 31 1915

Map shows exploration routes across Tibetan plateau, Tarim Basin, and Gobi Desert—areas which drew many explorers during the last half of the nineteenth-century.

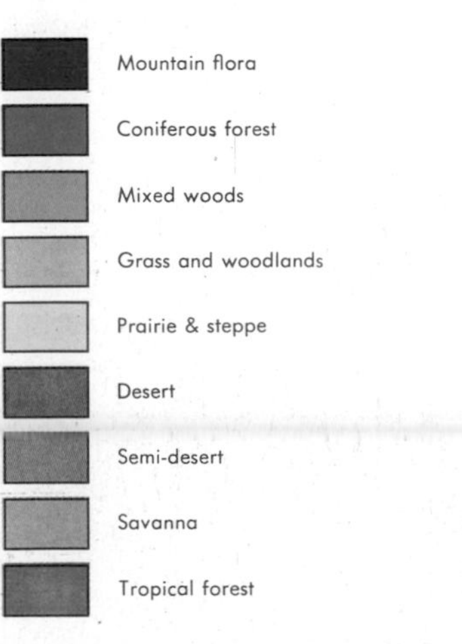

The Jesuit sketch maps were finally published in Paris a century and a half later, the first well-documented maps of China to be circulated in the West.

The first Christian penetration of Tibet itself was made by Friar Odoric two centuries earlier, but it is doubtful whether he reached the heart of the land. The next was not until 1624 when the Jesuit De Andrada crossed the barrier separating Tibet from India. Surprisingly enough he was allowed to set up a mission, which lasted for sixteen years, on the upper waters of the Sutlej River. Two more Jesuit fathers—Grueber, an Austrian, and D'Orville, a Belgian—were the first Europeans to reach Lhasa. In 1661 they left Peking and traveled overland to Nepal. Their writings give a graphic account of the despotism of the fifth Dalai Lama, then ruling, and of the Tibetans' curious form of Buddhism based on priest rule and on reincarnation. At that time the great palace-monastery of the Potala, overlooking Lhasa, was being enlarged to its present size, over 300 yards in length, and Grueber made a careful sketch of it.

The first English to reach Tibet were agents sent by the East India Company around the end of the eighteenth century. Up to that time travelers had followed the few available routes into the country, and knowlege of regions to the side of them was fragmentary and second-hand. The herdsmen of the high grassy valleys, living with their herds of sheep and yaks, were usually friendly. It was the priesthood of the monasteries and townspeople who resented strangers and who, from the beginning of the nineteenth century, practically closed the country to all foreigners from the south.

Several travelers, however, managed to reach Tibet, of whom the outstanding French missionary, the Abbé Huc, was the most successful. In 1844, encouraged by the vicar apostolic of Mongolia, he left Dolon Nor with a young Tibetan priest named Joseph Gabet. To escape attention, Abbé Huc and his small party at considerable risk changed into the secular costume worn by Tibetan lamas: "We put on a long yellow robe, fastened at the right side with five gilt buttons, and round the waist by a long red sash; over this was a red jacket, with a colar of purple velvet; a yellow cap, surmounted by a red tuft, completed our new costume." They crossed the flooded Hwang Ho, then the Ordos Desert, and in January 1845 arrived on the Tibetan border. Here they remained for eight months to study the Tibetan language and digest Buddhist literature. Part of this period they spent in the Kunbum lamasery, which reportedly accommodated 4000 people.

In 1904 Younghusband took this photograph of the Potala, in Lhasa, the central monastery which so many explorers yearned to see.

Late in September a Tibetan embassy, consisting of 2000 men and 3700 animals and returning home from Peking, passed by. Abbé Huc and his group joined the embassy. They crossed the Koko Nor Desert and the lake of the same name and finally reached Lhasa on January 29, 1846, after having crossed the tortuous track over the snow-covered mount-ains. The regent received him well and allowed Huc to set up a small chapel, but not before a test of sorts during an interview. Curious about the wisdom of the foreign visitors, the regent commanded them to write something. "'In what language—in Thibetian?' 'No, write some letters in your own country's language.' One of us took the paper ... and wrote this sentence: 'What avails it to man to conquer the whole world if he lose his own soul?' 'Ah, here are characters of your own country! I never saw any like them; and what is the meaning of that?' We wrote the translation in Thibetian, Tartar, and Chinese, and handed it to him. 'I have not been deceived,' he said; 'you are men of great knowledge. You can write in all languages, and you express thoughts as profound

Travelers through Tibet sometimes had to build bridges of poles lashed together in order to bypass difficult rock faces.

as those we find in the prayer books.' He then repeated, slowly moving his head to and fro, 'What avails it to man to conquer the whole world if he lose his own soul?'"

Promising as Abbé Huc's introduction to Tibet was, his visit came to a swift end. Before he could get to know the Tibetans well, the Chinese ambassador had the two missionaries sent back to Canton.

The topography of Tibet remained largely unknown until the Indian government sent in surveyors from 1863 onward. They carried out one of the most secret mapping missions yet known. The chief was Pandit Krishna, who went by the code name A–K, the first and last letters of his name transposed. Their supposed prayer wheels contained paper for recording their data and their Tibetan rosaries of beads were used for counting paces. A–K traveled for several years in the forbidden land and lived in Lhasa for an entire year. When the Tibetans discovered that the neighboring Indian power was making a secret survey, they became very annoyed and took great precautions.

The great Russian traveler, Nikolai Przhevalsky, suffered from the Tibetans' growing anxiety over foreign explorers. All four of his journeys aimed at reaching Lhasa ended in failures. An officer of the general staff of the Russian Army, he began his explorations while he was stationed at Irkutsk on Lake Baikal. On his first journey in 1870, accompanied by only three men, he traveled southeast across the Gobi Desert, reached Peking, then went farther west and explored the Ordos, the Ala Shan, and the upper regions of the river Yangtze. Although he managed to enter the closed country of Tibet as far as the Di Chu River, he did not go beyond. On his second attempted journey to Lhasa in 1877, he rediscovered the great Lob Nor; and on his third, in 1879, he visited the difficult area of the great Tsaidam swamps and the valleys to the south. When only 170 miles from Lhasa he was stopped and forced to return by

The *takhtrawan*, or grandee's litter; a colored lithograph from Sir Richard Burton's *Pilgrimage to El-Medinah and Mecca.*

A S I A
MEDITERRANEAN SEA
Tigris
Euphrates
Damascus
Baghdad
Amman
Dead Sea
Suez Canal 1869
Petra
Aqaba
Basra
PERSIAN GULF
Taima
Haïl
Medain Salih
Buraida
Hofuf
Riyadh
Buraimi
Medina
RED SEA
Jidda
Mecca
Sulaiyil
Suakin
Salala
San'a
Mukalla
Aden
GULF OF ADEN
Addis Ababa
Nile
40°
50°
60°
30°
20°
10°
100 0 100 200 300 Miles
Niebuhr
1 1761-3
Burckhardt
2 1812 3 1813-5
Burton
4 1853 5 1854 6 1877
Doughty
7 1875 8 1876-8
Bell
9 1913-4
Philby
10 1917 11 1918 12 1920-2
13 1931-2 14 1936
Thomas
15 1928-9 16 1930-1
Thesiger
17 1934 18 1945-6 19 1946-7
20 1947-8 21 1948-50

order of the Dalai Lama. His fourth journey, begun in 1883, took him through the rugged mountain regions between Mongolia and Tibet. On all four expeditions he proved himself a distinguished naturalist by collecting many forms of animal and plant life new to science. After he set out on his fifth journey he died, on November 1, 1888.

About this time tension between Russia and British India was responsible for a number of expeditions in the Afghan and Pamir region by both nations. The political mission of Sir Francis Younghusband to Lhasa in 1904 led to further knowledge of the terribly difficult route from India. In 1887 he had made the long journey from Mukden in Manchuria across the Gobi and north of the Tarim River to Kashgar, then on to India by a pass discovered by his party.

He was a great authority on Central Asia, on both its mountains and its deserts, and the present writer remembers vividly having a great argument with him in 1925 on the origin of "singing sands," a phenomenon of active dunes due to slides of loose sand. He insisted that those he had seen justified that name, whereas I held that a more exact adjective would be "groaning" or "squeaking."

For the most thorough exploration of Chinese Turkestan and northern Tibet we have to thank two archeologists, the Swede, Dr. Sven Hedin, and the Englishman, Sir Aurel Stein. Their routes crisscrossed the difficult country between the Tarim Basin and the Kunlun mountains and their narratives exposed the past and present history of the region to the European world.

Arabs of the Yemen on a military exercise; from Niebuhr's book on his journeys in Arabia.

Another forbidden land—Arabia—until recently was nearly as unknown in the interior to Europeans as was the high roof of the world—the Pamirs and Tibet. Both its desert and its fanatic religion denied the land to the ordinary non-Arab traveler. It was practically impossible for any non-Moslem to reach Mecca; consequently only those in disguise and completely word-perfect in Arabic dared think of attempting the journey.

The first comprehensive account of southern Arabia came from a Dane, Niebuhr, who spent three years in the regions of the Yemen and of Oman from 1761–63. But it was a Swiss student at Cambridge, John Burckhardt, who was the pioneer of exploration in the Hejaz, the high plateau which includes the sacred cities of Mecca and Medina. His discovery in 1812 of the cave dwellings of Petra, that "rose-red city half as old as Time," led to a detailed knowledge of Arabian life. Successfully disguised as a pilgrim, he passed three months in Mecca in 1814 and went on to Medina.

His successor, Richard Burton, a brilliant but intolerant Irishman sent down from Oxford for dueling in 1840, was also highly successful in his Arabian travels. He was an astonishing linguist, a ready writer, and one of the most brilliant and picturesque characters in exploration, but he was very difficult to work with. As an assistant in the survey of Sind province on the Indus, he mixed with the people in the bazaar so thoroughly that he frequently deceived his own colonel when posing as a native of the lower classes. This was his apprenticeship to joining in the pilgrimage to Mecca, which he carried out in 1853 disguised as an Indian Pathan, a feat which demanded a very detailed knowledge of language and customs, a quick wit, and a good deal of courage.

Burton's narrative of the journey, besides giving an insight into the modes of thought of the Arab, struck out a new line in the literature of exploration, introducing an intensely personal note, couched in uncouth but vigorous phrase, which has made it a curiosity in literature. The title of his book: *Pilgrimage to Al-Medinah and Meccah (1855).*

Equally remarkable a personality was Charles Doughty, who by many has been named the greatest of the explorers of Arabia. A scientist, he left Cambridge in 1865 and set out for the Middle East, partly because an impediment in his speech made him shy in English society. Doughty found himself in Syria in 1876, where he asked permission of the British consul to join the caravan of the hadj, the yearly pilgrimage to Mecca. The reply was, as narrated by Doughty in his quaint Elizabethan style, that the consul "had as much regard of me, would I take such dangerous ways, as of his old hat."

At Medain Salih Doughty was forced to leave the hadj, and he wandered to Teima and Haïl and other scarcely known places in northern Arabia. He took copious notes of everything he saw. His journal is

A photograph by Thesiger, showing the lifeless desert, a region called The Empty Quarter.

now in the possession of his old college—Caius—at Cambridge. When the present writer, also of that college, met him when he presented his journal in 1924, Doughty at the age of 81 had just the same gentle, hesitant manner that had kept him from harm among the wild Bedouins fifty years earlier.

In writing his book, *Travels in Arabia Deserta*, he was less concerned with his travels than with his ideal of writing great English prose. In spite of his biblical phraseology he gives a far better picture of the Arabian Desert and its inhabitants than anyone else, and in my opinion the book will remain a classic of travel narrative for all time. Its style, so reminiscent of the Scriptures, seems to suit the subject to perfection, and has influenced subsequent travelers in Arabia. The writer has challenged three of them, T. E. Lawrence, Bertram Thomas, and Wilfred Thesiger, with some degree of imitation of Doughty. All have confessed that any similarity was unconscious. I am now convinced that any long sojourn with the Bedouins, their thoughts, and their speech induces in the Englishman the power and the need to use phrases of earlier centuries.

The discovery of the largest and culturally oldest of the continents is a composite of the records of warriors, traders, missionaries and inquisitive travelers. Asia was perhaps the earliest continent to be thoroughly known by its own inhabitants, but was one of the latest to be fully recorded in story and on maps. Much of its exploration was by Asians themselves, and we should pay tribute to the travel of countless Chinese and Indians whose work has never appeared in western print.

The greatest empires and, possibly, the greatest generals have held sway in Asia and left records—some still being interpreted. The traders, on the other hand, have less to say; the sands have long since obscured the tracks of their caravans. The salt and the silk they carried could not endure. The real record is in the writings of the travelers.

But there is another record coming gradually to light year by year — ancient history is being dug up and interpreted by archeologists in western Asia. The same thing is taking place in India, and will continue until it reaches Tibet and, in time, Mongolia. Eventually, then, the interpenetration of West and East shown on the maps in this book will have to be redrawn, and the story of the discovery of the most ancient continent will require retelling.

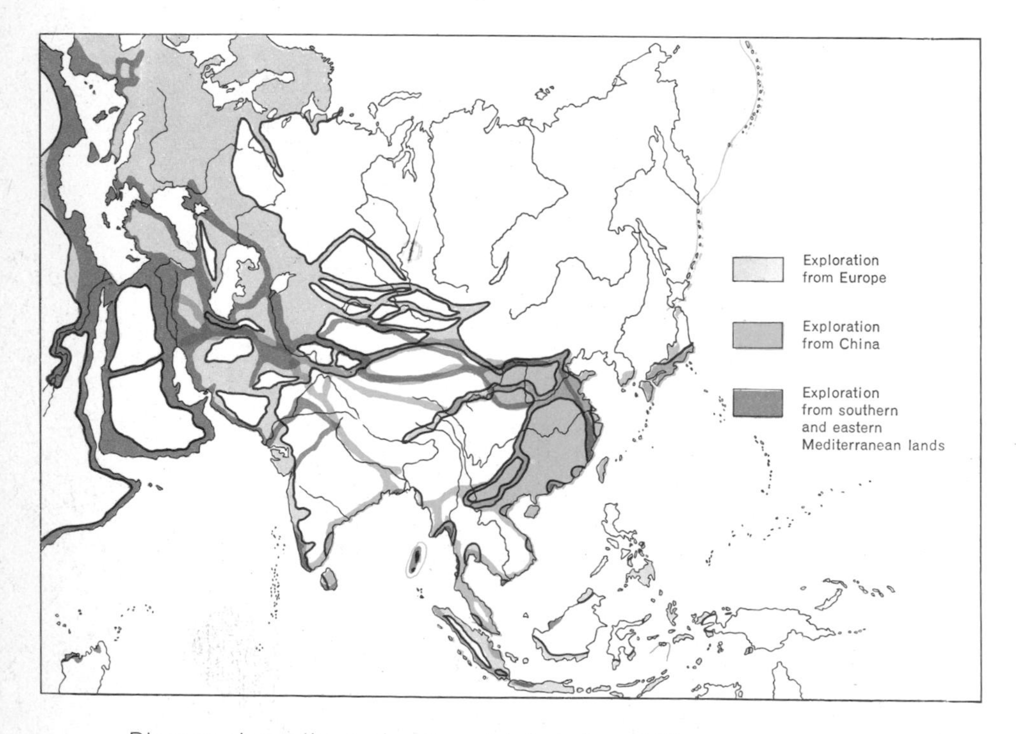

Diagram shows the exploration of Asia before 1550 by people from the three major areas of civilization.

Varying tones of coloration show different stages of penetration of Asia. Lightest color shows earliest penetration; darker colors, later penetration.

before 1550 | 1550-1700 | 1700-1800 | 1800-1850 | 1850-1900 | 1900 & after

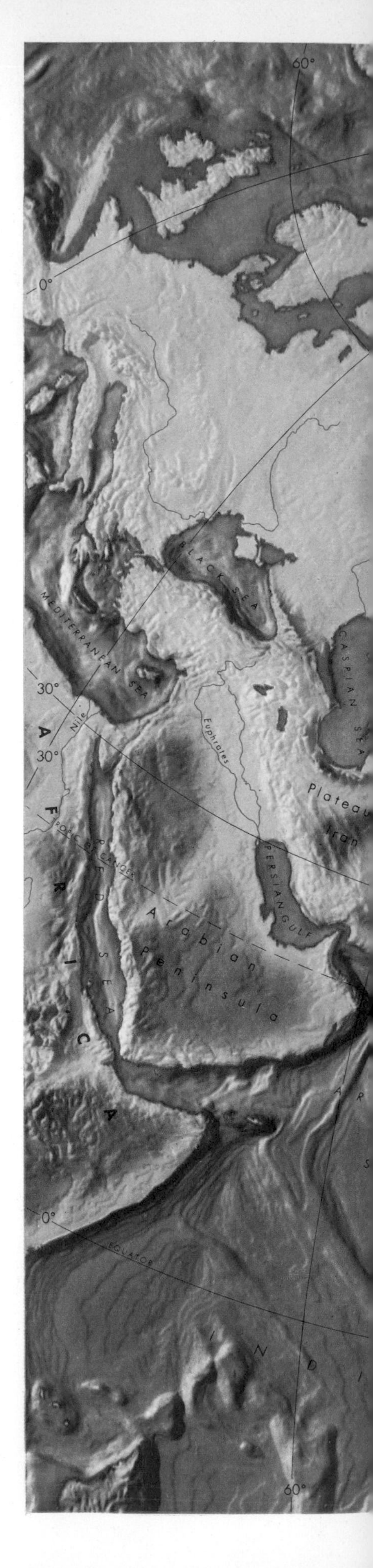

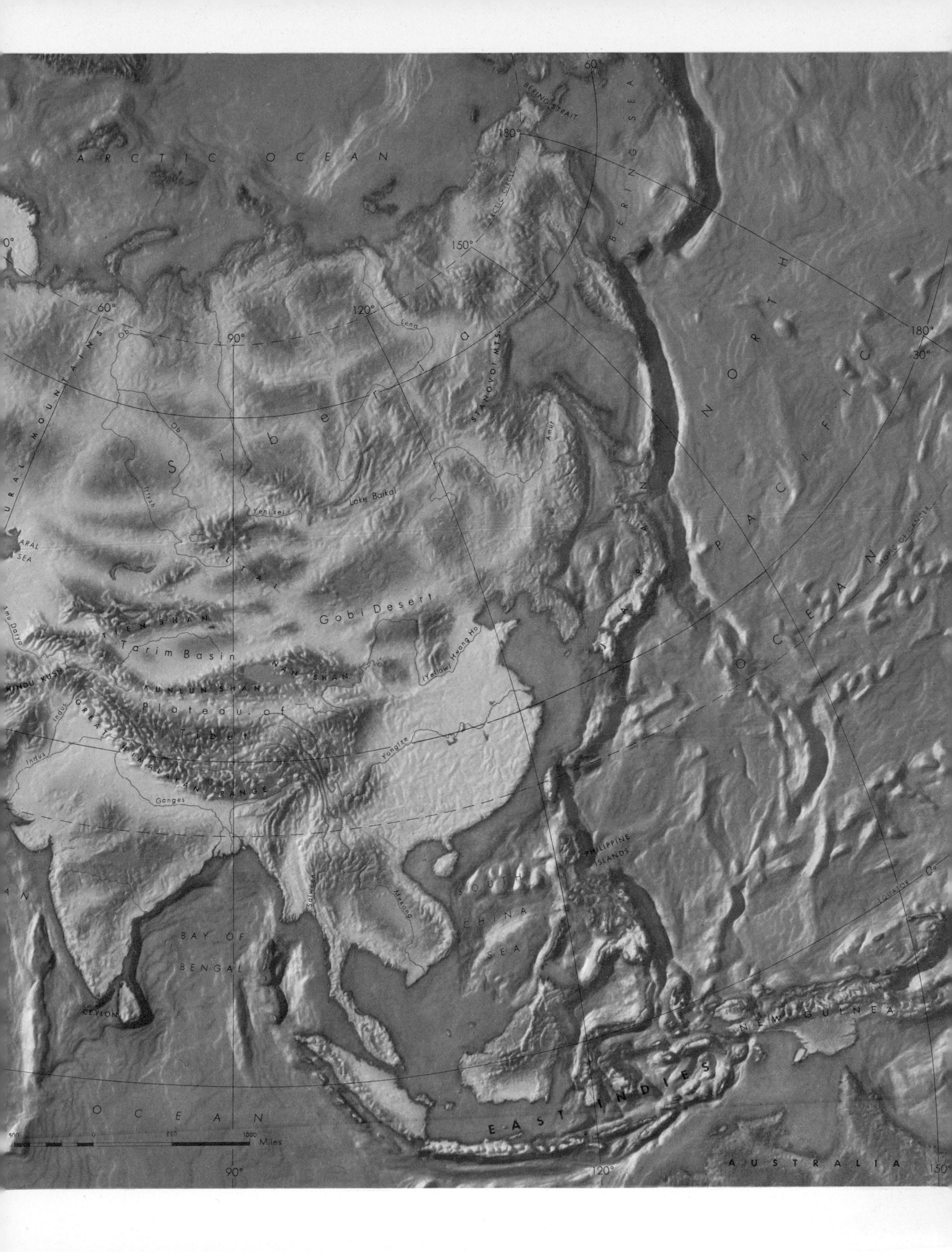
ARCTIC OCEAN
BERING STRAIT
BERING SEA
ARCTIC CIRCLE
STANOVOI MTS.
Siberia
Lena
Ob
Amur
Irtysh
Yenisei
Lake Baikal
URAL MOUNTAINS
ARAL SEA
ALTAI
Gobi Desert
TIEN SHAN
Tarim Basin
NAN SHAN
(Yellow) Hwang Ho
Amu Darya
HINDU KUSH
KUNLUN SHAN
Plateau of Tibet
Indus
GREAT HIMALAYAN RANGE
Yangtze
Ganges
JAPAN
NORTH PACIFIC OCEAN
TROPIC OF CANCER
PHILIPPINE ISLANDS
SOUTH CHINA SEA
Salween
Mekong
BAY OF BENGAL
CEYLON
EQUATOR
NEW GUINEA
EAST INDIES
AUSTRALIA
OCEAN
Miles
1000
90°
120°
150°
180°
60°
30°
0°

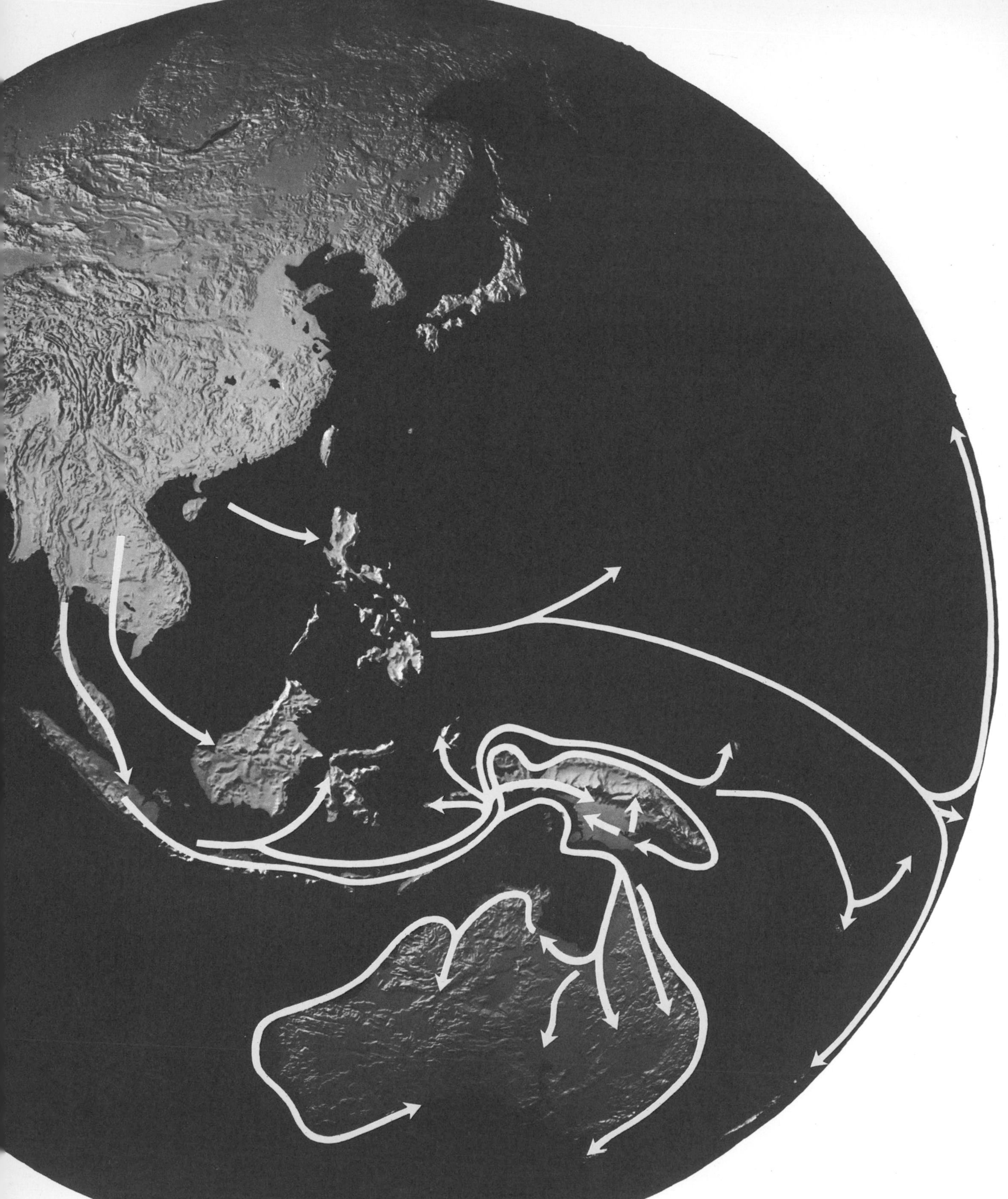

Migration routes of peoples across to Australasia from earliest times.

Exploration of Australasia

Australia and New Zealand must be taken together as the farthest lands that man could reach from southeast Asia proper. Yet we cannot be certain when he reached these outposts or where he came from. Ethnologists think that the Tasmanians—extinct since the middle of the last century—may have been the earliest inhabitants of Australia, but were driven down to Tasmania by later comers while there was still a land bridge linking Tasmania to Australia. The Tasmanians were more Negroid than the straight-haired Australian aborigine and had a more backward culture.

Anthropologists have found certain similarities between the Australians and some of the primitive hill tribes in India. If such an ancestral link exists, then, these groups could have migrated to Australia some time during the Late Stone Age when the seas were shallower and the straits narrower than they are today, and very likely they brought dogs (the native dingo) with them. To this day the aborigines are still hunters and food gatherers.

Lack of competition may have kept them in the Late Stone Age, but they are by no means lacking in intelligence. They have a most complicated system of rituals, marriage rules, and tribal customs, yet they have been consistently underrated by the white man, who has rarely taken the pains to see their point of view. The impact of civilization and our lack of understanding can be seen even today on a journey by train from Perth to Adelaide across the arid Nullarbor Plain.

Stations are sixty miles apart, and some of them have a changing population of aborigines, known locally as the "abos." Their real country is 500 miles to the north, but their passion for wandering, for a "walkabout," leads them down to the white man's railway at times. Travelers in the air-conditioned train look out and see an apparently dirty, cringing figure holding up a hand and saying, "Gibit bacca," (Give tobacco). The tourist turns away in disgust at what he calls a degraded, degenerate beggar, or else gives him an empty cigarette packet. How complete is the lack of understanding! If the places were changed, if the tourist were to walk up to a tribal camp in Central Australia he would be given food by the abo and treated with dignity and good fellowship. Gloriously free in their own territory and splendidly naked, they are told that they must wear a shirt and trousers in the presence of the white man—an act of conformity which they observe but which they do not understand.

Unlike Australia, New Zealand is separated by a thousand miles of deep sea from the nearest steppingstone to Asia. New Zealand, then, could be reached only by a bold and vigorous people. When the Maoris got there they found inhabitants of whom we know practically nothing. Stories handed down among the Maoris relate that around 1350 a fleet of their large double canoes carried the first colonists from Tahiti, bringing with them food plants, dogs, and a great knowledge of the sea. For as far back as we can trace, therefore, the early New Zealanders were cultivators as well as hunters and fishermen, and they had a distinctive social structure. There was ritual cannibalism for enemies and a warlike attitude toward strangers. On the other hand, they are laughter-loving, like all the Polynesians, and are fond of games. The present writer well remembers the defeats at Rugby which his school sustained at the hands of a team of burly Maori schoolboys coming from North Island of New Zealand. Unlike the aborigines, such a virile race was bound to adjust to the arrival of a more advanced civilization, although the Maori wars carried on until 1870. Today the full-blooded Maoris constitute about five per cent of the population.

Map shows the Polynesian triangle which was the sphere of their activity around A. D. 1000.
In boats like the one below, the Polynesians navigated great distances over the Pacific.

Where the Polynesians originally came from is still a problem to ethnologists. Most likely they came from Asia, crossing the seas via the islands of Indonesia. The idea that they may have come from South America, drifting across on balsa-wood rafts as demonstrated by the Kon-Tiki expedition, has not very wide support. Whichever way they came, their canoe migrations constituted long voyages on the open sea and were made by men still in the age of stone implements. This was long before men of the Iron Age were ready to venture into the open ocean, so we must regard the Polynesian migrations as a distinct era in the evolution of man as explorer.

Their large double canoes were wonderful craft, yet they were built entirely with stone tools. But the real mystery is how the Polynesians navigated that spacious ocean and managed to find small and usually low islands. Traditions and languages show that the Hawaiians were able to travel to Samoa, 2500 miles away, and the Tahitians to the Marquesas, 1000 miles distant. Although the secret of their navigation has been lost, they must have had some way of finding their latitude, which implies some form of instrument for measuring the altitude of stars.

The farthest outpost of Polynesian migration was Easter Island, which is 1000 miles east of Pitcairn Island, famed for sheltering the mutineers of the *Bounty*, and 2000 miles west of South America. Local tradition dates this migration as early as the fourteenth century. The Polynesians were not a pure race, but there was something approaching a common language, and migration songs and legends have been handed down by memory all the way from Hawaii to the Maoris of New Zealand. If that is not enough to show a common origin of these seafaring people, there are the stone carvings found all the way to Easter Island, true megaliths, emblems of a cult which died out only a short time before the island was discovered by Roggeveen in 1722.

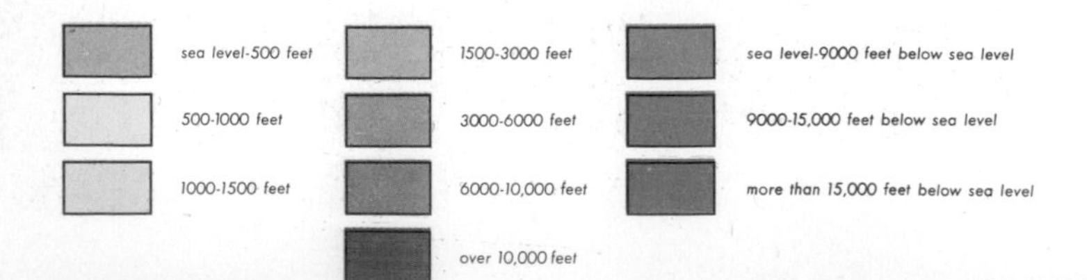

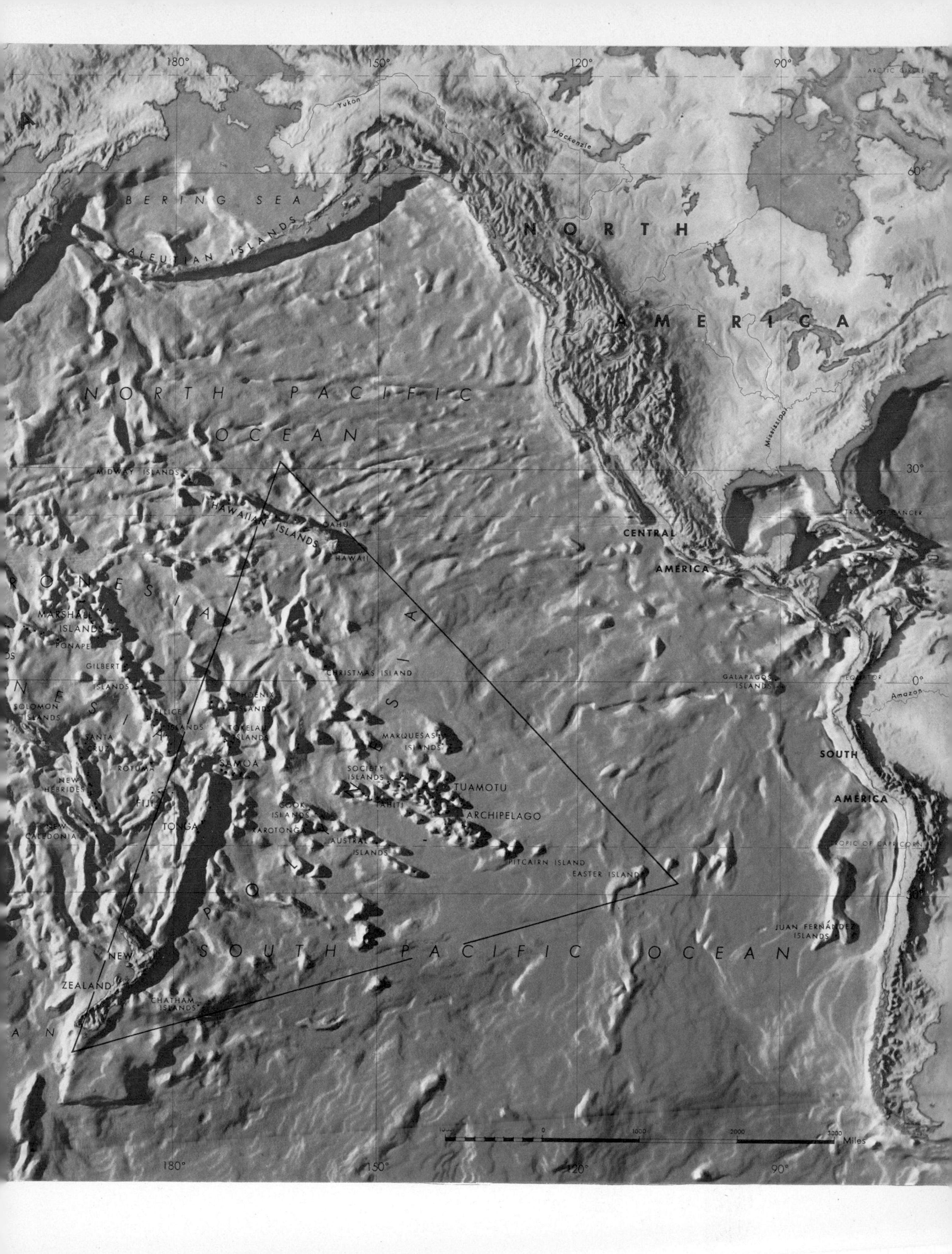

180°
150°
120°
90°
ARCTIC CIRCLE
Yukon
Mackenzie
60°
BERING SEA
ALEUTIAN ISLANDS
NORTH
AMERICA
NORTH PACIFIC
OCEAN
Mississippi
30°
MIDWAY ISLANDS
HAWAIIAN ISLANDS
OAHU
HAWAII
TROPIC OF CANCER
CENTRAL
AMERICA
MARSHALL
ISLANDS
PONAPE
GILBERT
ISLANDS
CHRISTMAS ISLAND
GALAPAGOS
ISLANDS
EQUATOR
0°
Amazon
SOLOMON
ISLANDS
ELLICE
ISLANDS
PHOENIX
ISLANDS
TOKELAU
ISLANDS
MARQUESAS
ISLANDS
SANTA
CRUZ
ROTUMA
SAMOA
SOCIETY
ISLANDS
TUAMOTU
ARCHIPELAGO
SOUTH
AMERICA
NEW
HEBRIDES
FIJI
TONGA
COOK
ISLANDS
TAHITI
NEW
CALEDONIA
KAROTONGA
AUSTRAL
ISLANDS
TROPIC OF CAPRICORN
PITCAIRN ISLAND
EASTER ISLAND
30°
JUAN FERNÁNDEZ
ISLANDS
NEW
ZEALAND
SOUTH PACIFIC OCEAN
CHATHAM
ISLANDS
0
1000
2000
3000
Miles
180°
150°
120°
90°

Broadly speaking, Australia was populated probably more than 10,000 years ago by people from southeast Asia, after which time seas separated the two continents. From this time onward a process of island-hopping went on for centuries; the darker Melanesians from New Guinea going down to the New Hebrides and Fiji, and the lighter Polynesians following more northerly routes through the Carolines, Marshalls, and Gilberts. But there were also the later migrations in A. D. times, some—the Maoris—only four centuries ahead of European discovery.

It may seem strange that Australia was not discovered by the Arabs, who for at least three centuries had made the Indian Ocean their own. They knew Africa down to Sofala and they knew the opposite coast of Madagascar; they also knew the way to Java and Borneo. Why did they not go farther south? For that matter, if Malayan stock managed to get across to Madagascar and mix with those peoples, why did they, too, decline to go due east for a far less distance? The answer probably is that both the Arabs and the Malays did go south but found so little to interest them in northern Australia that they did not repeat their voyages. There is also a belief that the Chinese and Japanese reached Australia before the Europeans.

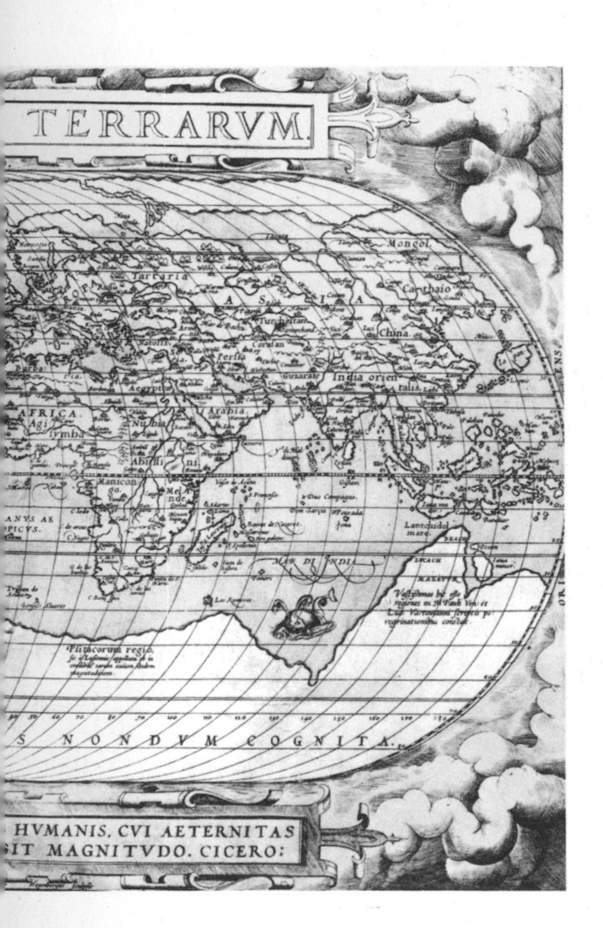

World map by Anthony Jenkinson (1562) shows huge imaginary continent, Terra Australis, which Cook and others proved nonexistent.

It is curious that Australia was on maps long before any of the European explorers had been near it. Encouraged by Magellan's reports of land south of his strait (Tierra del Fuego) and reports of other explorers, European geographers, deducing symmetry north and south of the Equator, drew a huge imaginary continent called Terra Australis. The continent was pictured with a great bulge northward into the Indian Ocean and was labeled Brasilie Regio. Farther east, where Australia actually is, the map makers showed another bulge named Regio Patalis. Both bulges reflected a combination of earlier reports from both Eastern and Western travelers and strengthened the Terra Australis myth which, like the El Dorado and Prester John stories, stimulated explorers.

Once down in black and white on the cartographers' maps, the sprawling continent had to stay there until disproved. Consequently the story of discovery of the southern lands becomes the story of successive loppings-off of great pieces of the continent as explorers became increasingly familiar with the true outline of Australia.

But the first parts of the story began with an increase rather than a reduction of the huge land mass because of a voyage from Mexico across the Pacific to the Spice Islands in 1527. Cortéz had sent ships under Saavedra, who tried to return to Mexico against the trade winds. During the trip he coasted along the northern shores of a great land inhabited by "black people with frizzled hair, who are cannibals, and the devil walks with them." The Portuguese called the land New Guinea because the frizzled hair of its people reminded them of West Africa. For the time being, therefore, the map makers could place New Guinea as the northern tip of the Regio Patalis bulge.

The Spaniards were still anxious to discover lands in the region of the Spice Islands, which were now firmly in the hands of the Portuguese. In 1567 two ships sailed from Peru under the command of Mendaña and remained in the Solomons six months looking for gold and pearls, but found only treacherous cannibals. Mendaña never lost faith that there must be rich lands somewhere near the Solomons. Twenty eight years after his first expedition he sailed again with four ships. The idea was to form a permanent colony, and for that purpose there were women aboard.

The group discovered the Marquesas Islands. As they sailed on, mutinies broke out and one ship deserted. They found an island, Santa

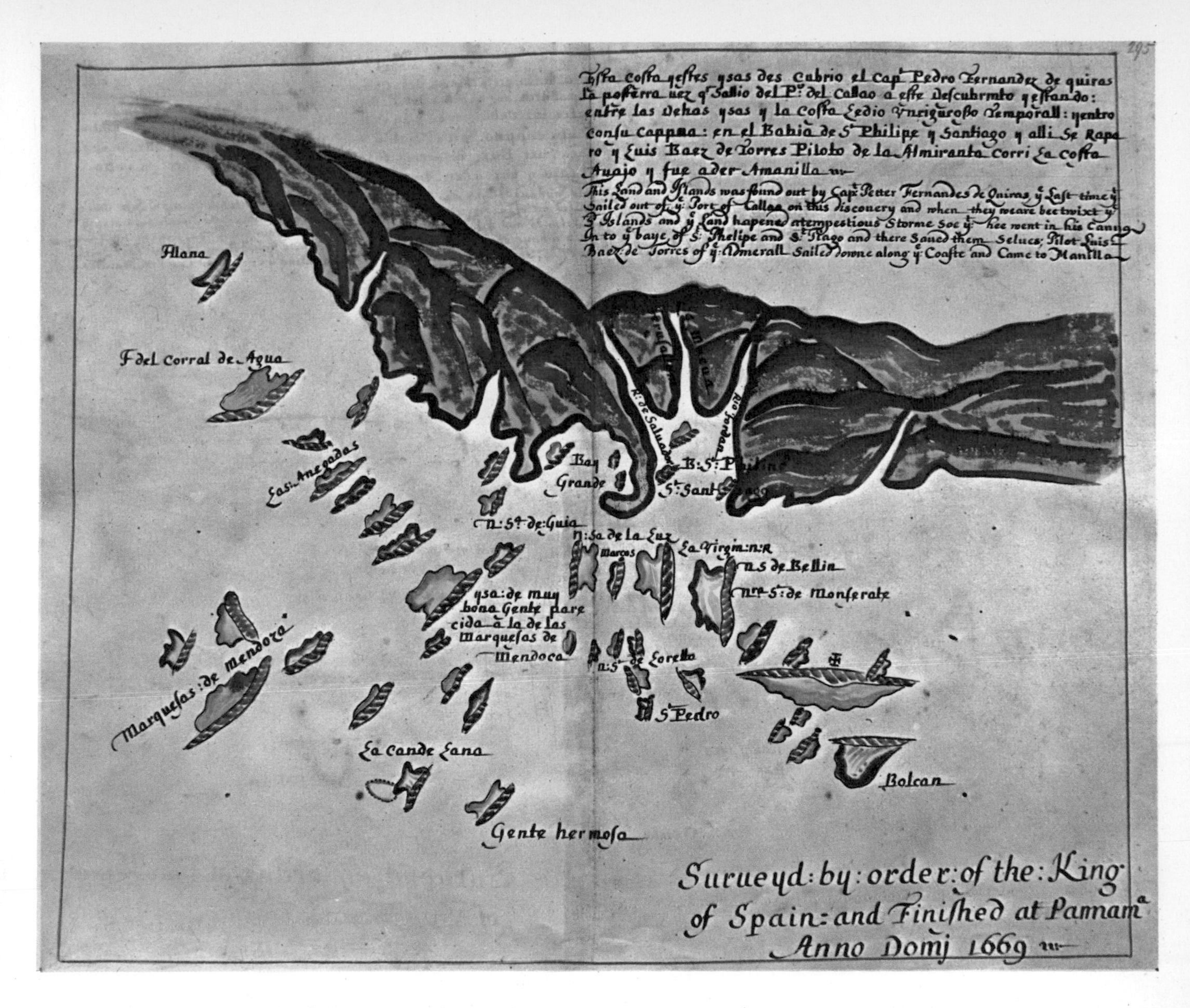

This map, drawn in 1669, shows the discoveries of Mendaña and Quirós on their voyage to the New Hebrides.

Cruz, at the northern end of the New Hebrides, but about this time the expedition went to pieces. Mendaña died and was succeeded in command by his widow, who was called the Governess. In desperation they sailed for Manila. The shortage of food and water made their life hard enough, but their sufferings increased under the Governess, who refused to share her private store of wine and oil and washed her clothes in the precious drinking water. In vain the second-in-command, De Quirós, had told the Governess, "You wash your clothes with their life." A mere remnant of the original 378 reached Manila.

Ten years later, in 1605, Quirós departed from Peru with three ships and 300 men in hopes of finding the new continent. In the eyes of the leader it was to be a chivalrous missionary enterprise, but his men were of another mind. After many arguments over the course they were to follow, they reached the New Hebrides and stayed for five weeks at the major island, which they named Espíritu Santo. Nowhere in the history of exploration is there an expedition so farcical or a leader so quixotic as Quirós. His men began by firing at the natives on the beach, then they beheaded a captive while Quirós was erecting a church to save the souls of the inhabitants. Then his "Knights of the Holy Ghost," marched inland, captured "three young boys and twenty pigs."

A detail from a 1622 chart shows a Dutch fleet sailing the Pacific.

Quirós himself returned to Mexico, probably compelled to by mutiny, but in another boat his second-in-command, Torres, after looking in vain for his leader, set off to the west to carry out his original instructions. He appears to have reached the Great Barrier Reef off Queensland in latitude 21° South, and then sailed north till he sighted New Guinea near its eastern end. From there he worried his way through the reefs and shallows of the present Torres Strait, but apparently without realizing that one of "the very large islands to the southward" was Cape York, the northern point of the great continent they had been looking for.

The Dutch were traders first, fighters next, and explorers only by accident. They did, however, prospect southward from their bases in the Dutch East Indies for gold or trade. In 1606 a pinnace called the *Duyfken* entered the Gulf of Carpentaria, on the north coast, and sailed in as far as Cape Keerweer (Cape Turn-again); this voyage marked the rediscovery of Australia.

Their next discovery came about as a result of finding a better route than the old Portuguese one up the east coast of Africa and across with the southwest monsoon to India and Malacca. In 1611 one shipmaster was bold enough to sail eastward—instead of northward—from the Cape of Good Hope for 4000 miles before turning north for Java, and found he took only six months for the voyage from Holland instead of the sixteen it took by the old route. In doing so he lopped off the maps another great part of Terra Australis—the bulge of Brasilie Regio. After that it was merely a question of time before some ship would sight Australia on that route. In 1616 a ship commanded by Dirk Hartog sighted the island now bearing his name off Shark Bay, halfway down the west coast, though no account of that particular discovery was published at the time.

The Dutch were loath to say much about their discoveries, and of the most important one, in 1627, there is but a single sentence printed fourteen years later and a map on which to base it. A ship from Holland carrying one of the high councilors of the Dutch East India Company, Peter Nuyts, had sailed too far south and east before turning north for Java. On sighting the coast east of Cape Leeuwin they had the sense

to continue sailing eastward for 1000 miles to the Nuyts Archipelago.

Shipwrecks occurred at a regular rate along the west Australian coast, a fact which perhaps discouraged shipmasters from lingering in this region. In 1629 a great ship, the *Batavia*, was wrecked on the coastal islands; the tale is full of horrors. Pelsart, the commander, sailed north for Batavia in a pinnace with a few men to get help, leaving nearly 200 people on the barren, almost waterless islands. When he returned three months later he heard a tale of wholesale murder of one group of the castaways by another group, who planned to capture Pelsart's ship and use her for piracy. This was thwarted and the forty mutineers were executed.

In Pelsart's narrative there is one sentence in lighter vein where he describes having seen there "a species of cat, whose forepaws are very short and hindlegs long and it walks on those alone." In such guise does, that winsome creature, the Australian kangaroo, make its bow to the European world.

In 1642 the Governor General of the Dutch East Indies, Van Diemen, sent out Abel Tasman, a captain of doubtful reputation, in two ships to find out more about this great land which was beginning to be known as New Holland. From Mauritius, a small island due east of Madagascar, they sailed so far south that they missed all Australia but came to the west coast of Tasmania, naming it Van Diemen's Land. They rounded it to the south but made only one landing. They were not very ardent explorers. Instead of following up the coast they turned eastward until they sighted the west coast of South Island of New Zealand. This was the last piece of habitable land in the world to be discovered by Europeans, had they known it. They coasted north till they reached Cook Strait, which they took to be a gulf. There they met the warlike Maoris in their long double canoes and had an affray in which four of the Dutch sailors were killed.

A sketch made by Tasman in 1642 shows his ships and Maori canoes in Murderers Bay, New Zealand.

Tasman continued northward along North Island until he came to three small islands which he named the Three Kings, so familiar now to passengers going from Australia to Auckland. There they saw an impressive number of men "of tall stature armed with clubs" and were afraid to venture in close enough for a landing. New Zealand was to be spared contact with Europeans for another 130 years.

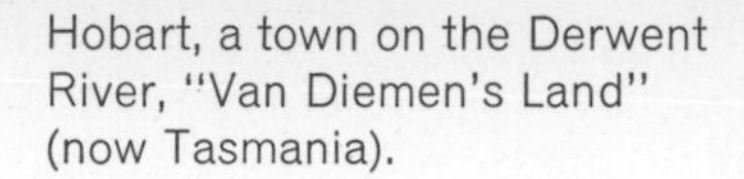

Hobart, a town on the Derwent River, "Van Diemen's Land" (now Tasmania).

William Dampier was a naturalist turned pirate, and one of the strangest of explorers. In 1688 with his fellow pirates he spent five weeks off the northwest Australian coast and wrote a very good account of its barren aspect. About nine years later, back in England, he wrote his book, *New Voyage Round the World*, which introduced him to people of such consequence that he was sent in command of the *Roebuck* to investigate the new continent.

Sailing with a crew of ruffians equal to his earlier companions, the ex-pirate reached the ill-famed west coast and sailed along it to the north, frequently landing for water, which he rarely found. Then, after a rest on the island Timor, he sailed along the north coast of New Guinea, producing a good chart along the way and discovering the long island of New Britain at its eastern end. From there he returned to Timor, then set out for England. But with a rotten ship and a rebellious crew he got only as far as Ascension Island in the middle of the Atlantic, where the *Roebuck* foundered and the crew was picked up by some English man-of-war in 1701.

Dampier was a poor pirate and not a very good captain, but he was a first-class pilot, and as a writer he introduced the Far East to Englishmen. Yet his account of Australia was unpromising, and no more Englishmen were attracted in that direction for another fifty years.

By Dampier's time the great Terra Australis had been severely sliced —Brasilie Regio had gone and Tasman had lopped off Australia proper as a separate land. But there remained the southern Pacific, quite large enough to contain a "large bulge."

In 1721 a Dutchman named Roggeveen set out to discover the southern bulge, but after passing Cape Horn far enough southward to meet icebergs he turned northward to Juan Fernández, discovered Easter Island and, later, Samoa. He had pushed back Terra Australis by many degrees of latitude.

About this time France and England were overtaking Holland in trade in the East, and in both countries a new scientific approach to

Voyages in search of Australia.

Torres' voyage *(first half with Quiros)* 1606-7
Parts of the Australian coast seen by:
A Hartog 1616 B Houtman 1619
C Nuyts 1627 D Pelsart 1629
Tasman's voyages 1642-3, 1643-4
Dampier's voyages 1679-91, 1699-1700
Cook's voyages *in Australasian waters* 1769-70, 1772-5, 1776-8

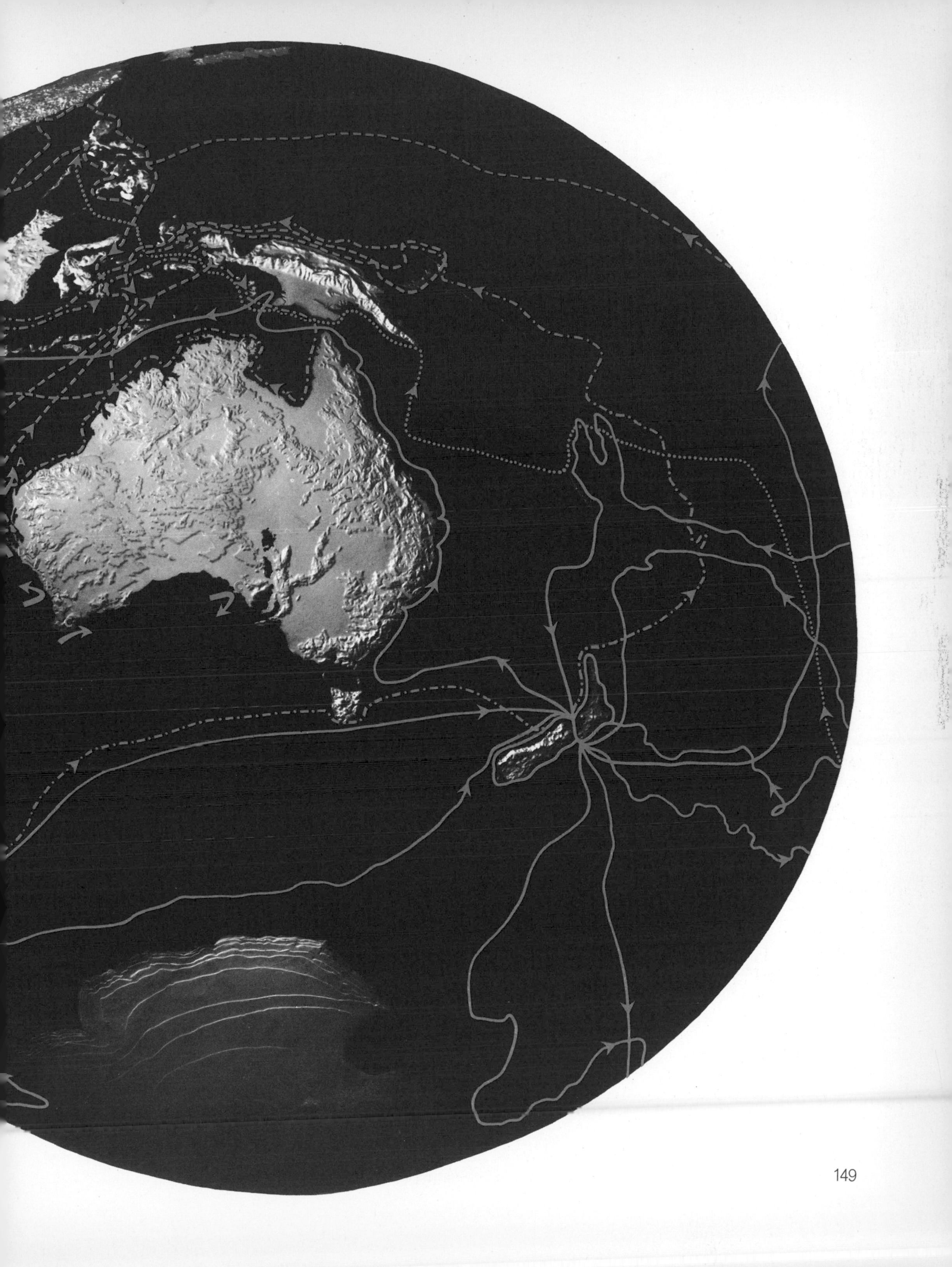

Mr. Banks receives a visitor—the King of Duke of York Island.

world geography was growing. Scientific papers discussed what lay between Cape Horn and New Zealand. The matter was to be settled by one man in two voyages, Captain James Cook. The son of a farmer, Cook entered the Navy at a time when pride of birth was still the best aid to advancement; but he earned his promotions by merit and by his command of navigation and seamanship.

In 1768 British astronomers were becoming anxious to make observations of a transit of the planet Venus which was due in June 1769, when it would be seen best at Tahiti in mid-Pacific. Cook was given command of the operation and was made a first lieutenant at five shillings, or about seventy cents, a day. His ship, the *Endeavour*, was stoutly built for the coal-carrying trade, weighed 370 tons, carried a complement of eighty four, and cost £5000 to buy and refit. Accompanying Cook was a young Eton and Oxford man named Joseph Banks, then twenty five years old. He was an ardent botanist with ample means and was to become "a friend of the King, the adviser of statesmen, the President of the Royal Society for thirty two years, and the father of New South Wales."

After the group duly observed the transit of Venus at Tahiti, Cook sailed south and west on the next part of his mission—to examine Tasman's New Zealand, which was still only a wavy west-coast line on the map and which could be part of the vast southern continent suspected by several writers. They sighted the east coast of North Island and had a brush with the Maoris, who Cook found were not to be frightened off by powder and shot. They passed round the island and refitted in Charlotte Sound, where they were delighted to find that the Tahitian they had with them could talk to the Maoris and establish friendly relations. They continued sailing southward and rounded South Island, disproving any continental connection. Cook was fast removing from the map any great "southern bulge."

The *Endeavour* next headed westward for Van Diemen's Land (Tasmania), but strong southerly gales drove them north so that their landfall was on the southeast corner of Australia itself. Sailing north along the coast and looking for a harbor and fresh water they entered Botany Bay, where their reception by "Indians" was peculiar. Two fishermen in crude canoes hardly looked at them as they passed, but when they tried to beach their small boats two defenders of Australia challenged them with spears and throwing sticks (woomerahs). There was no way of speaking to them and "they disputed our landing to their utmost, though they were but two and we thirty." Musket shot over their heads was too much for them and they ran away. Cook made short excursions inland to where the southern suburbs of Sydney now are. He must have forgotten his training as a farm boy because he reported the soil rich; the present author, 130 years later and at precisely the same place, had great difficulty producing a garden on the sandy soil.

Captain James Cook

The expedition stayed for a week, making a survey of the shallow harbor, then sailed on, but they missed the excellent harbor only twelve miles north which became Sydney Harbor. Provisions were running short as Cook sailed steadily north, surveying as well as he could along the way. Soon he found himself hemmed inside the Great Barrier Reef of coral off Queensland and had a near-serious setback. A coral pinnacle pierced the hull, but fortunately broke off and so plugged the hole. They repaired the ship as well as they could at the mouth of Endeavour River, at which time Banks saw his first kangaroo—"to our surprise it went only on two legs, making vast bounds."

Crippled, the ship sailed on, and Cook carefully worked her through the reef-strewn Torres Strait and reached Batavia. On the way back to England, Cook and Banks decided to name Australia's east coast New South Wales. The voyage had thrust back any southern continent but it had not proved that one did not exist, so the Admiralty sent Cook out again, this time in 1772, to settle the matter.

With two ships—the 462-ton *Resolution* and the 336-ton *Adventure*—Cook made an even more remarkable voyage. In three summer seasons, relieved by winter visits to New Zealand and Tahiti, Cook proved that there was no continent north of 65° South latitude. He was the first man to cross the Antarctic Circle, sailing within it for 23° of longitude. His farthest push south was 71° in the Pacific sector, where he was turned back by dense pack ice and wrote, "yet I think that there must be some land behind this ice, but if there is it can afford no better retreat for birds or any other animals than the ice itself, with which it must be wholly covered," a sage remark. Cook, then, swept away most of the great "Southern Continent" myth and, with Banks, laid the foundation for colonization of New South Wales.

Matthew Flinders, who had sailed under Bligh of the *Bounty* (who had sailed under Cook), began his coast exploration of Australia when the convict settlement at Sydney was only six years old. Bass, a naval surgeon friend of Flinders, in 1798 took six men with him in a whaleboat and proved that Tasmania was separate from Australia; the two men together later confirmed it by sailing completely around the island, discovering King Island, which blocks a good part of the western entrance to Bass Strait. For that reason it has been the scene of some forty wrecks of ships coming from England. The present writer shared in such a hazard when he, too, was wrecked on King Island' swest coast, but later returned to make the first geological examination of it.

Sketch of kangaroos, by Flinders.

Back in England, Flinders got permission to command a sloop named the *Investigator* for a thorough survey of all the coasts of Australia. He set sail in 1801, having as one of his midshipmen John Franklin, who was then fifteen years old. He followed the route of the Dutchman, Nuyts, across the Great Australian Bight and surveyed both the gulfs of Spencer and St. Vincent. When he passed between Kangaroo Island and the mainland, he met a French ship under Baudin, who was surveying in the opposite direction.

Flinders continued with his detailed survey all the way up the east coast until he found himself inside the Great Barrier Reef, where Cook had run into trouble, but he managed to find a passage out to the open sea. Next he threaded his way through Torres Strait and continued his survey by looping inside the Gulf of Carpentaria. By the time he reached Timor his ship was leaking a foot an hour, so there was no chance of his completing his survey down the west coast of Australia. It was all he could do to sail the ship back to Sydney, where he found that he could thrust a stick completely through many of the ship's bottom timbers. He sailed for England in another ship but ran onto a reef 800 miles out from Sydney. Leaving eighty men and young John Franklin on the reef, he and fourteen others sailed in a thirty-foot open boat to Sydney. All he could get there was the *Cumberland*, a ship of only twenty nine tons, but he took her, picked up his shipwrecked crew, and went on to Timor, then to the French island of Mauritius. There he was arrested and for more than six years was held prisoner, becoming so broken in health that when he finally reached England he barely managed to write an account of his voyages before he died, at age forty.

Meanwhile the infant settlement at Sydney was facing problems—first, because the settlers had chosen the one infertile land site on the

Aborigines of Australia quietly watch Captain Stirling's party of 1824 putting up hammocks.

east of the island continent, they had difficulty growing enough food. Second, there was the constant threat that some foreign power (for example, France, represented by La Perouse, who was exploring the Pacific) would discover the slender hold of the British on the infant colony. Exploration inland was imperative.

The search for better land was the leading motive for exploration inland at first, but it was curiously thwarted by the Blue Mountains, which are less than fifty miles west of Sydney. They are low, rarely over 3000 feet high, but are intersected by deep valleys filled with dense forest and ending in cliff faces. What today is a health and tourist resort area could not be reached until someone found a ridge which did not end in a cliff overlooking yet another valley.

It was not until 1813, twenty four years after the first landing, that Blaxland, Lawson, and Wentworth managed to find a way across the barrier and discover good pastoral country and rivers flowing westward. At first exploration of the hinterland was rapid and comparatively easy. There were no really hostile tribes; in fact many escaped convicts were adopted by the aborigines and lived up to twenty years with them. There were no more impassable mountains inland, which made travel with horse and wagon possible, and there was no danger from wild animals. Not until men reached the central region did they meet the real hazards—lack of drinking water and a food scarcity that white men could not tolerate.

The most important journey in the early days of the push inland took place in 1824 when Hume, an Australian-born settler, with Hovell, an English sailor, set out from Sydney to cross the southeast corner of the continent. They discovered the knot of mountains called the Australian Alps and skirted them on the inland side. Next they crossed several rivers flowing northwest and passing through good country. They just missed the large embayment of Port Phillip (north of King Island) and reached the sea at the present Geelong. Hovell's faulty navigation

Charles Sturt's engraving of the river Murray, which he followed to the coast in 1829.

Early settlers of Australia ascending a pass through the Blue Mountains in 1851.

placed them at the poor scrubby country of Western Port, and for some years there was confusion and quarreling over what was a very useful journey.

It was Charles Sturt who solved the problem of where the westward-flowing rivers led. In 1829, with materials for a boat loaded onto his wagons, he headed inland with six men. After building the boat he launched it on the Murrumbidgee, about 300 miles from the eastern coast, and rowed down the river to the point where it joins the Murray. Here he recognized the Darling River, which he had explored earlier. Going down the Murray he found himself deposited at the shallow lagoon of Lake Alexandrina, which the earlier coastal surveyors had not recognized as the mouth of a great river.

The occupation of southeastern Australia by sheepherders and cattlemen began to breed a hardy type of explorer, who learned bushman craft for further inland thrusts. "Overlanding" the cattle across great distances to the ports was good training. Some of the exploration was heroic and not without drama. For instance, when Eyre made a journey from South Australia to West Australia in 1841, his only white companion was murdered by a disloyal black fellow in the party, and Eyre himself survived only by a lucky meeting with a French whaling ship.

The true nature of Central Australia was beginning to unfold as a series of endless plains, stony in some places, sandy in others, rarely quite desert, and entirely dependent on rainfall. What baffled the explorers and the later settlers of such country was that in a good season there was knee-high grass growing between the hardy and graceful trees of mulga and myall, whereas in a drought there was little but bare soil and the stubs of the invaluable saltbush which is normally the stand-by for animals in such a climate. The mobile emu and kangaroo could move to fresh grounds at the onset of a drought, but an explorer could easily press on, erroneously hoping to reach water and horse feed, until it was too late to turn back. Sturt, experienced traveler that he was, very nearly perished in 1844 when he tried to press inland from the Darling River; he barely survived when he temporarily lost his sight from the deadly glare reflected from the "Stony Desert," near Lake Eyre.

One of the unsolved mysteries of Australian exploration is the fate of Ludwig Leichhardt. In 1844 he had made a remarkable journey of 3000 miles from Brisbane halfway up the east coast, to the Gulf of

Col. P. E. Warburton setting out in 1872 to cross central Australia from east to west.

Carpentaria, and on to Arnhem Land west of the Gulf. In 1848 he started on an even more ambitious crossing of the continent, but was lost without trace.

After two unsuccessful attempts to claim the £10,000 prize offered by the government of South Australia for a crossing of the continent from south to north, John Stuart finally succeeded in 1862. But Stuart's success was preceded by a tragedy known as the Burke and Wills expedition, which attempted a south-to-north crossing from Melbourne to the Gulf of Carpentaria. With a full complement of camels and horses they reached Cooper's Creek, halfway to their goal, without incident. Then the impatient Burke decided to go ahead with three others instead of waiting for his supporting party. He got to within sound of the sea at the Gulf but was on short rations when he decided that they should turn back. This was a fatal decision. One man died on the way and the other three staggered into the depot at Cooper's Creek only a few hours after their supporting party had turned back for the south. Of the three men left, Burke and Wills died but the aborigines looked after the last man, King, who told the tale when he was found six months later.

By 1875 the main features of Australia were known, but in Western Australia there were to be many journeys—by prospectors for minerals, by men looking for stock routes, and others by surveyors.

In an odd way the story of inland exploration in Australia is lacking in some of the picturesque details of that in other continents. It is difficult to believe that the Arabs—masters of the Indian Ocean for three centuries —and that the Malayan peoples did not know about Australia long, long before Europeans discovered the continent. Yet until relatively recent times the complete outline of one of the world's major land masses, populated for about 10,000 years, remained unknown.

But gradually the myth of a vast southern continent called Terra Australis attracted men. Beginning with Dutch flirtations with the west and south coasts of the continent and New Zealand and ending with the expeditions of Cook, Flinders, and others, the mystery of the Southern Continent was solved, and the true outlines of Australia and New Zealand found their way onto maps.

Exploration of inland Australia was slow to come. Perhaps it was because there were no wars of conquest, no treasure to be looted, no great scope for missionary ventures, no rivalry from other nations. There was no Wild West period of cowboys and gunmen as in the United States, no safari period as in Africa with the white man marching at the head of a hundred carriers. Yet the "call of the bush" gradually attracted men and still exists for Australians today, even in elderly men such as the present writer, whose earliest memories are of trying to find some muddy creek or some haunt of kangaroos that his forerunners had missed.

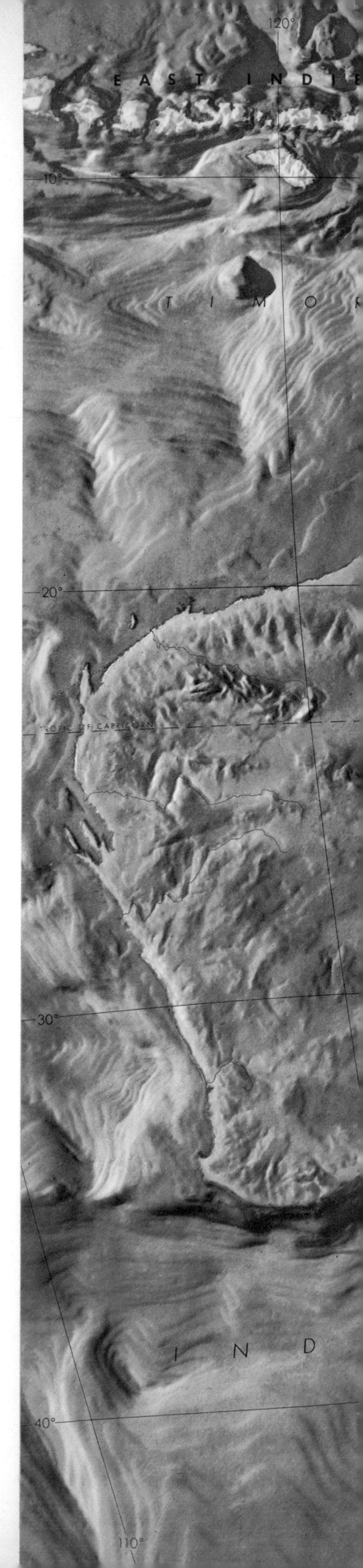

Varying tones of coloration show different stages of penetration of Australia. Lightest color shows earliest penetration; darker colors, later penetration.

before 1550 | 1550-1700 | 1700-1800 | 1800-1850 | 1850-1900 | 1900 & after

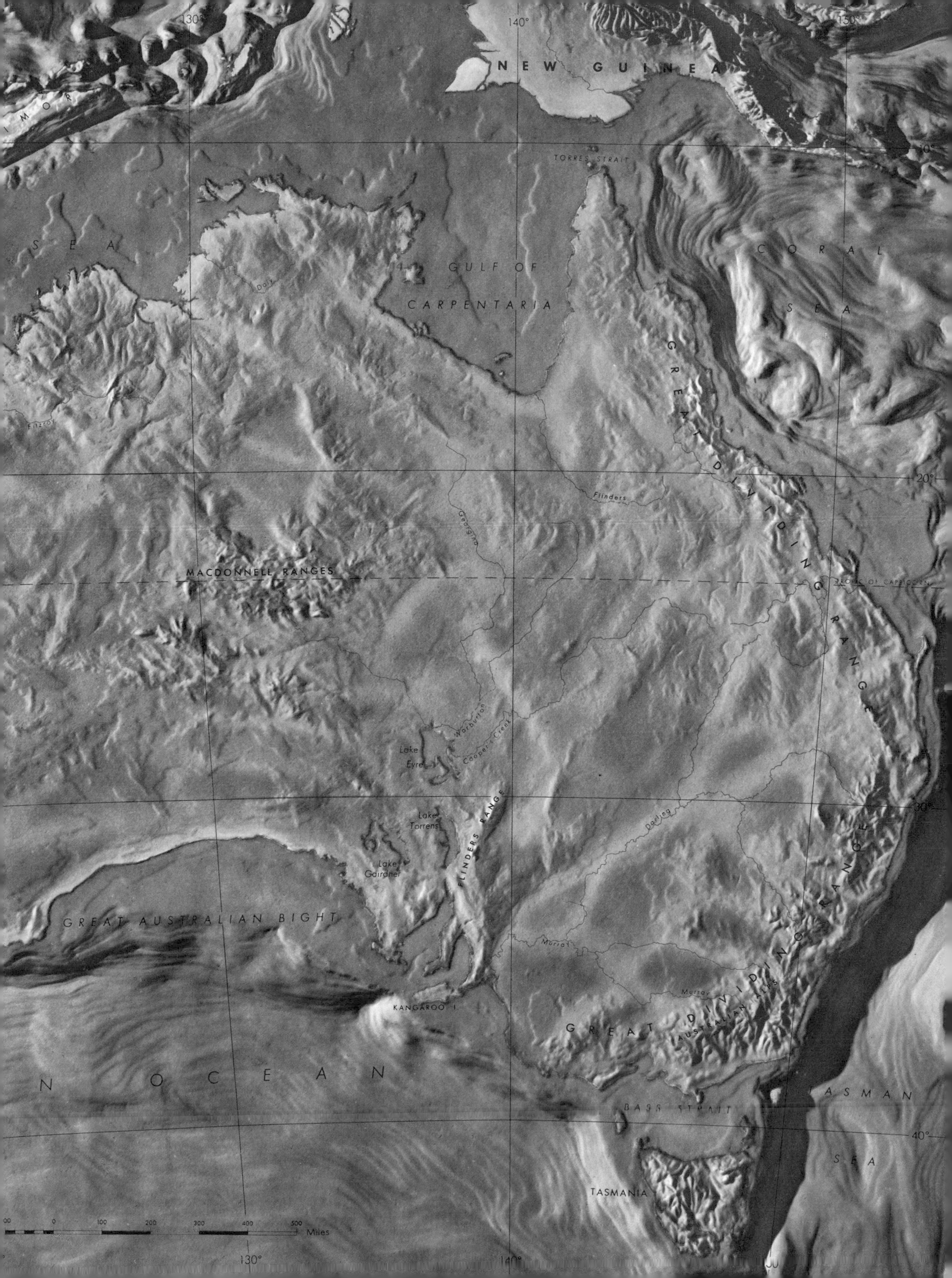

NEW GUINEA
TORRES STRAIT
SEA
GULF OF CARPENTARIA
CORAL SEA
GREAT DIVIDING RANGE
Daly
Fitzroy
Flinders
Georgina
MACDONNELL RANGES
Warburton
Cooper's Creek
Lake Eyre
FLINDERS RANGE
Lake Torrens
Lake Gairdner
Darling
GREAT AUSTRALIAN BIGHT
Murray
Murray
AUSTRALIAN ALPS
KANGAROO I.
N OCEAN
BASS STRAIT
TASMAN SEA
TASMANIA
Miles
100 0 100 200 300 400 500
130°
140°
150°
20°
30°
40°

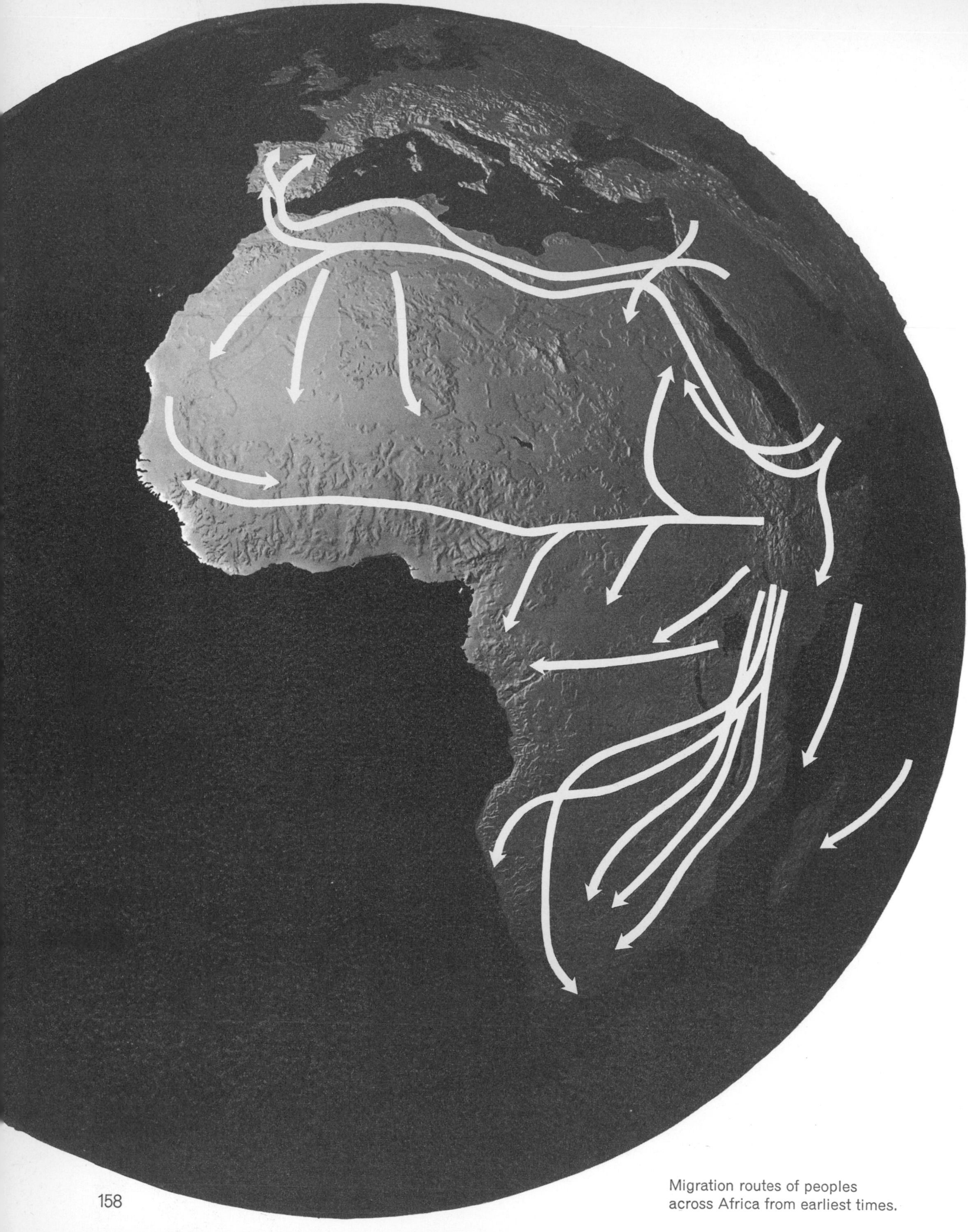

Migration routes of peoples across Africa from earliest times.

Exploration of Africa

Wherever we try to trace the origins of man we meet the same problem, and prehistoric Africa is no exception. We know very little about where its people originated and not much more about what movements or migrations led to their present distribution, especially in that vast region to the south of the Sahara. Quite possibly there may have been more than one center of origin and dispersal of man, and one or more of them may have been in Africa. We simply don't know.

On the theory that the people now in the most remote parts of the earth were the earliest, driven ever forward by later comers, it would be the Bushmen of southwest Africa who were the originals. Yet the Bushmen themselves may have been preceded by still earlier people. The Bushmen probably came from the tropical hunting grounds of East Africa, but one cannot meet them—the last remnant of them in the Kalahari—without thinking of Asia. Their Mongoloid faces with slant eyes, their yellow skin, and their small size remind one of the faraway Javanese, yet their peppercorn hair and their body form seem African rather than Asian. To this day they are still hunters and food gatherers of early New Stone Age type, with no wish or will to change their culture or group themselves in anything larger than family bands.

These shy and skillful hunters are absolute masters of their environment and remain content to do without any of the tools of the white man, though they have been in contact with white men for three centuries. They are highly intelligent but are afraid to go outside their immediate cultural sphere. I once tried to demonstrate the principle of the wheel and axle to three Bushmen in the Kalahari with the wheels of one of our vehicles. I seemed to be making some headway until one of the wheels, jacked up, was spun round by hand. The Bushmen jumped up in alarm. They explained that a wheel which turned along the ground was well enough, but a wheel that turned and "did not run away" was white man's magic, something to be shunned and feared.

Wherever the Bushmen came from, they were followed by a people resembling them in general appearance—the Hottentots. These people may have mixed with Hamitic groups coming down from the Red Sea region. From the Hamites the Hottentots learned to keep animals, grow crops, and live in large communities.

The true Negro, so different in his characteristics, seems to have had his origin in West Africa, far away from the Hamites of the Red Sea. But later the two cultures merged along the upper Nile, and the mixture produced the tall, picturesque tribes on that river, cattle peoples, from the Nuers of the White Nile down to the Masai of Kenya.

In the first millennium of the Christian era, most likely, these racially mixed people we now call the Bantu came into prominence in the region of the great lakes of eastern Africa. The march of the Bantu southward began sometime around the twelfth century; its success stemmed mainly from their ability to combine under warlike chiefs and to learn new tactics of battle while fighting beside professional warriors. Of these chiefs the last and greatest was Chaka. He was king of the Zulus and lived when the two great movements in southern Africa met in a head-on clash: the white men were moving eastward from Cape Colony and the Bantu westward from Natal. The Bantu recoiled and moved northward again in two groups—as the Angoni tribe to Nyasaland and the Matabele to Southern Rhodesia.

Such mass migrations of the Bantu could take place only over the plateaus of the east half of Africa. The dense jungle of the Congo Basin remained undisturbed, and sheltered a more strongly Negroid people living along the rivers and encircled a few small groups of pygmies.

But even on the Congo side of Africa small groups may have trickled south from North Africa. Some anthropologists have tried to find a link between certain southern African groups and the Vandals, a Teutonic tribe which reached North Africa from Europe in the fifth century. The three-pronged hat of the Ovambo and Herero women of southwest Africa and their custom of pretending they have long hair by wearing cow-tails are strongly reminiscent of the Vandals, who took Carthage in the year 439 and Rome in 455.

If this outline of what happened in Africa south of the Sahara is anywhere near the truth, then we can trace a similarity between the events which caused dispersal of man in Asia with those in Africa, though dispersal of man in Africa came many thousands of years later and on miniature scale.

Area near the Nile source, where the Romans explored during Ptolemy's time.

Before the Dark Continent was opened to later surges of exploration there were highly developed civilizations along the northern strip from the Great Atlas Mountains in the west to the Nile Valley in the east. In the Congo jungle area south of the Sahara, in the Kalahari, and in the eastern highlands were the African primitives, living as hunters and food gatherers. But on the eastern plateau region around the great lakes and in the west along the coast of the Gulf of Guinea were cultivators who had been in contact with the northern fringe. And a still more highly developed culture thrived in the Ethiopian massif. The barriers of sea and desert, however, kept the Africans south of the Sahara from sharing the progress of Asia. The camel was late in reaching them, the horse later still, and the wheel never at all.

From the year 700 to the time of Henry the Navigator in the fifteenth century the whole of North Africa was a preserve of Islam guarded against the infidels of Europe. On the east coast there was sea traffic of the Arabs, whose main interest was ivory and another "product" far more valuable—slaves.

In the New World the prime motive for exploration was the search for gold. In Asia it was the age-old struggle between nomads and settled peoples interlarded with the spread of religion. For Australia it was the search for the mythical continent of Terra Australis. If we look for a simple and recurring motive for the exploration of Africa it must be slavery. For more than 2000 years Africa had been furnishing slaves for Europe and Asia, then later for the Americas. Slavery is as old as the pyramids of Egypt or the city of Babylon. It was, in fact, a system devised by early civilized man as soon as he began to form large settled communities. The step from the taming of animals to the taming of other men—usually backward tribes—is a logical one, if not a morally sound one. Slavery was a natural and inevitable development in civilization.

But the slaves had to come from somewhere. Prisoners of war were one source, but these slaves were apt to be too intelligent; they required too much guarding. It was better to find a less tutored group, easy to raid and less likely to combine and rebel. Just as animal husbandry began with the catching of young wild animals to be trained, so man husbandry, or slavery, was best practiced by catching women and young children, the first to breed and the second to be disciplined for labor.

To the advanced peoples of the Mediterranean and the Middle East there was a simple and perennial source for slaves—Africa. All the slave raiders had to do was send their raiding parties across the Sahara, up the

Slaves were packed like cattle for shipment to Europe and America. For each one landed and delivered at least one died on the way.

Nile, or down the east coast and surprise a village or two, capture and shackle those that could stand the journey, and march them back to the slave markets of their own country. As time went on it became easier still, for the coastal African himself became the raider and the "civilized" visitor became a trader and buyer only, just as in any other cattle market. The African has always been the greatest enemy of the African. The emblem of Africa, therefore, should be the manacles of slavery, which were regarded by civilization as "natural" rather than shameful up to a bare century or so ago, an attitude which is still not entirely stamped out. Much of the early discovery of inner Africa, then, is not written in words; it is inscribed as trails of countless caravans across the Sahara, sometimes east and west but more often north and south, the routes of slave gangs to the Mediterranean or the Red Sea.

It would be wrong to suppose that these were always trails of misery and blood. Even when Ibn Batuta visited Timbuktu in 1352 he found that the slave farmers were becoming as careful of their stock as animal farmers taking cattle to market. Slaves had to be delivered in prime condition if they were to command a good price in the market place. There were even chances for a slave to achieve a high position. In Arabia and India there were slave-kings and there were grand viziers by the score who were slaves by origin. There can be no ethical grounds for slavery as an institution, yet it has swayed history to an enormous extent in its various forms. The highly trained Janizaries of the Ottoman Empire and the Mamelukes of Egypt, who carried all before them in their day, were really slaves in all but name.

Africa, then, between the Equator and the Sahara was well known to slave traders at an early date, but this part of its history is for the most part unrecorded. The trade first appears on a large scale in Africa at the time of Henry the Navigator. He was the innocent origin of its spread to Europeans. In 1442 Henry returned some captured Moors to their own country and received a return present from Morocco of some gold dust and ten blacks. This began what may be called the colonial slave trade, the awakening of the Portuguese that slaves were as much an article of trade as ivory and gold dust. We shall find that from the first centuries A.D. the thread of the slave trade runs through the story of exploration almost to the present day. It follows a strange course, at first for the expansion of slavery and later for its suppression.

Figure of a slave, made by the Romans and found along upper Nile.

Domination of all North Africa by the Moors and Arabs was the state of affairs when the Portuguese began to push down the west coast of Africa in search of a trade route to the East. Although the Arabs would allow single travelers to pass through their territory, they would not permit bands of traders or merchant fleets to pass through the Red Sea route to the East for fear of seeing their Moslem domination threatened. There was, however, an important exception to the universal rule of Islam—namely, Ethiopia, a somewhat vague name applied to what we once called Abyssinia.

Christianity had been introduced in Ethiopia as early as the fourth century A.D. Although the conquests of the Arabs in the seventh century cut the Ethiopian Christians off from the rest of their coreligionists for many centuries, Christianity never quite died out. In fact, from the fourteenth century on, the fabled Prester John was thought to be in Ethiopia. The map of Fra Mauro (1459) showed him as residing in a great palace in the Sudan.

Ethiopia, therefore, became a region of great interest to the dawning phase of discovery in Western Europe, and when John II of Portugal sent out a mission in 1487 to discover a route to India he gave Pedro de Covilham letters to Prester John. Covilham gave the letters to the negus, or emperor, after which he was taken prisoner and held there the rest of his life. These emperors traced their descent to King Solomon and the Queen of Sheba, thus reinforcing the link between the Israelites and Africans. Eventually Portugal and Ethiopia exchanged embassies, and the Portuguese even helped the negus resist conquest by the Mohammedans. In that way the penetration of the country by missionaries was begun, and for a long time to come all knowledge of the region came through a succession of Jesuit priests.

African ivory carving of Portuguese soldiers. On top is a ship with a lookout in the crow's-nest.

Because of the missionaries, Ethiopia by the 1600s was better known than any other large area of Africa. The Jesuits' usual route was from ports on the Red Sea up to Gondar. Some of them spent many years in the country. In 1613 one of them, Páez, visited the sources of the Blue Nile and showed that the usual flooding of the great river was due to a rainy season and not to melting snows in the mountains. Discovery of other sources of the Nile soon became a definite object of travelers. A French expedition in 1699 under Poncet was one of the first to reach Ethiopia by traveling up the Nile from Cairo, though the group returned by the more usual route through Massawa on the Red Sea.

Although difficult to reach, Ethiopia became a sort of oasis surrounded by the barren and hostile religion of Mohammed. Also it was a sort of halfway house, either from the Red Sea or up the Nile, for all who were interested in a search for the coy sources of the great river which sustained millions of people who still had no idea of where its endless waters came from. Yet exploration of the region was terribly difficult because neither the Arabs nor the Ethiopians could understand why a European should want to travel through their territory for such an unprofitable reason as curiosity. He was at once suspected of spying or of subversion.

Any explorer who hoped to make any progress whatever in Ethiopia and the surrounding regions first had to become fluent in the languages and customs of those areas; yet even then he had to combine the diplomacy of an ambassador with the resolution of a soldier on a campaign of conquest.

Such a man was James Bruce, a Scot with a leaning to adventure and an accomplished linguist. To some extent he repeated the discoveries of the Jesuits, but he was inclined to disparage what they had done. His journey and his narrative stand out as the first fully recorded exploration in the search for a Nile source, the ultimate aim of his travels. With a good knowledge of Arabic, some acquaintance with medicine and astronomy, and backed by his own reasonable wealth, he set out on a major journey in 1768. On reaching the African continent he went up the Nile about 200 miles to Syene (Aswan). Next he crossed overland to Kosseir, the ancient port on the Red Sea, and from there took a ship down the Arabian coast to Jidda. Here his diplomacy won him friendship and letters of recommendation from the leading people of Arabia to those of Ethiopia. In 1769 he landed at Massawa on the Ethiopian coast. His letters and reputation as a "physician" to royal personages gave him safe, although at times difficult, passage to Gondar, the capital. His graphic accounts of these difficulties, including long conversations with both friendly and hostile people, interlarded with discussions of the past history of the land, were a novel departure in travel narrative and make interesting reading to this day.

James Bruce.

Like many other travelers from Marco Polo on, Bruce found it almost more difficult to get himself released from royal patronage than to attain acceptance. Only by being made a governor of the province did he succeed in traveling to the source of the Blue Nile both above and below Lake Tana. It was not until 1771 that he escaped from Gondar and journeyed to Sennar on his way to Egypt. In spite of the dangers from robbers, thirst, and sandstorms he reached Syene with all his notes and most of his instruments.

Bruce's journey and narrative set a high standard for exploration and influenced to some extent the establishment of the African Association in 1788, the first aim of which was to settle the problem of the other great river of northern Africa, the Niger.

Sixteenth-century portrait of the legendary Prester John, who drew explorers to India, later to Africa.

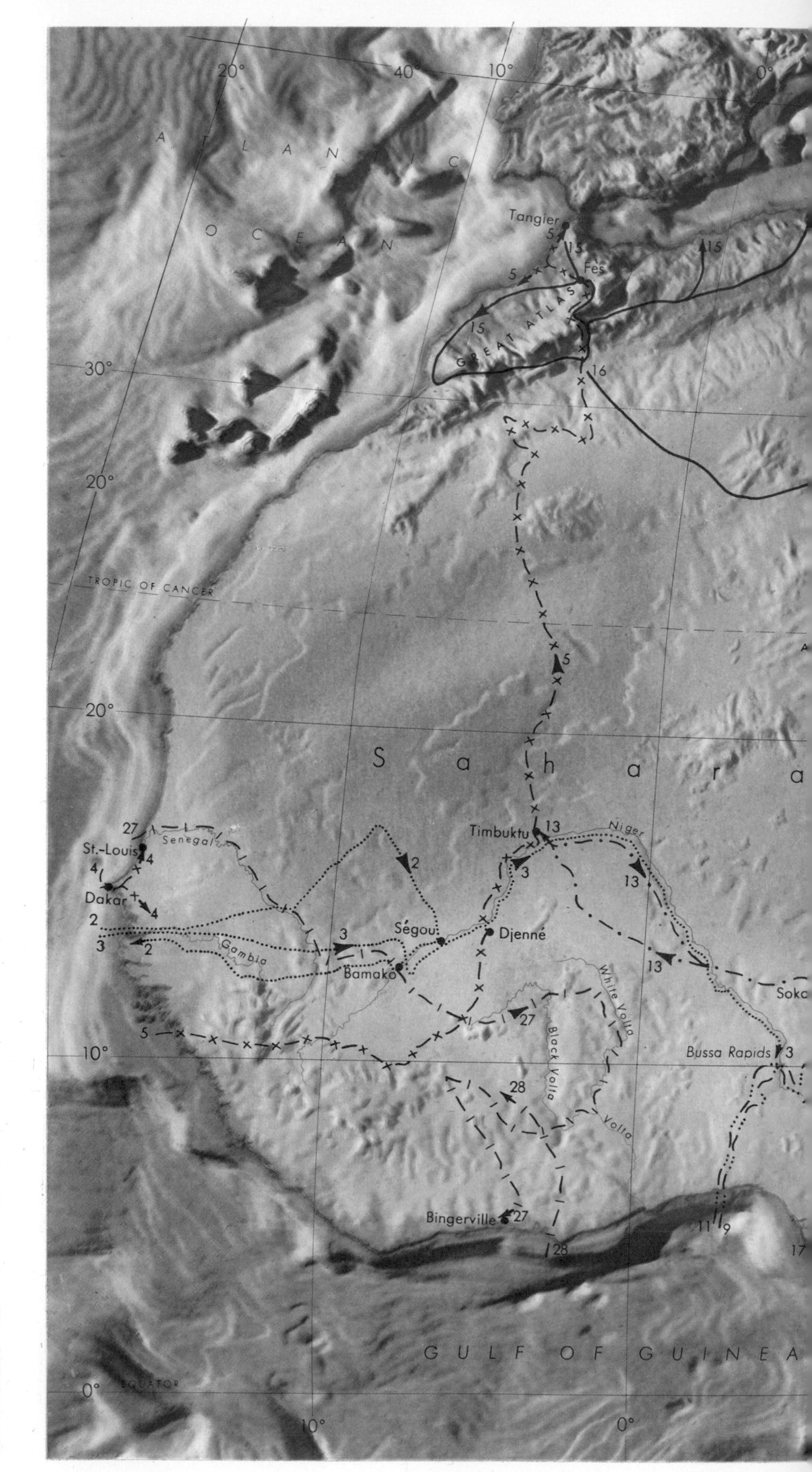

Map shows those regions of northern Africa which have attracted so many explorers—mainly the river areas, the desert, and the towns bordering south of the Sahara.

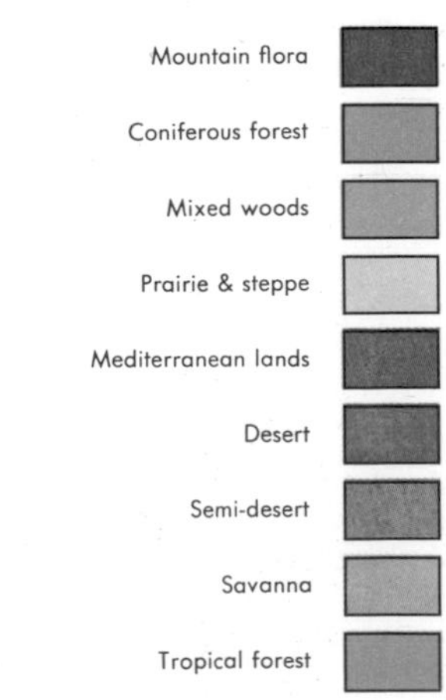

1 Bruce 1768-73
2 Park 1795-7 3 Park 1805-6
4 Caillié 1816 5 Caillié 1827-8
6 Clapperton & Denham 1823-5
7 Clapperton 1825
8 Denham 1825 9 Clapperton & Lander 1825-7 10 Lander 1827-8
11 Lander 1830-2
12 Barth 1844-5 13 Barth 1850-5
14 Baker 1861-4
Rohlfs
15 1862 16 1864 17 1865
18 1867-8 19 1869 20 1874
21 1878 22 1880-1
23 Schweinfurth 1863-6
24 Schweinfurth 1868-71
25 Nachtigal 1869-74
26 Junker 1879-86
27 Binger 1887-9
28 Binger 1892 (probable route)
MEDITERRANEAN SEA
Tunis
Tripoli
Ghadames
Alexandria
Siwa
Libyan Desert
Kufra Oasis
Murzuk
Ghat
Bardaï
TIBESTI
Desert
Faya (Largeau)
Lake Chad
Abéché
Kano
Yola
Benue
Shari
Ubangi
Congo
Uele
Syene (Aswan)
Kosseir
Nile
Khartoum
Blue Nile
White Nile
Gondar
Lake Tana
Jidda
Massawa
RED SEA
Lake Rudolf
Lake Albert
Lake Victoria
TROPIC OF CANCER
Miles

At a Meeting of The Committee of the Association for promoting the Discovery of the Interior parts of Africa held at the Thatched House Tavern the 23d of July 1794.

Present
Sir Joseph Banks
Mr. Beaufoy.

Resolved, That Mr. Mungo Park having offered his Services to the Association as a Geographical Missionary to the interior Countries of Africa; and appearing to the Committee to be well qualified for the Undertaking, his offer be accepted; on the following conditions.

That Mr. Park shall accompany the Consul for Senegambia in his intended Voyage to Fatetenda; for which place the Consul expects to take his departure in the month of September or October 1794.

That as soon as may be expedient,

Before we trace the exploration of the Niger we should mention first that stories of the Nile, Niger, Congo, and Zambezi rivers exerted a strong attraction on explorers, drawing them far inland; and secondly, the slave trade along the coasts of West Africa in its own way acted as a stimulant for exploration. From the time when the Portuguese caravels began sailing down the west coast of the continent the slave trade had become highly developed, and soon other western nations were to join in.

When Sir John Hawkins became the first Englishman to enter the trade there were no English colonies in the New World. He took slaves to the West Indies, at about £25 a head, long before the Virginia colony began to buy slaves for its cotton plantations. The trade assumed vast proportions. In the century from 1680 onward no less than two million slaves were transported by British ships alone, but for every slave landed and delivered at least one died on the way.

Yet this wholesale trade in human livestock produced singularly little direct knowledge of inland Africa. The trade was organized so that coastal tribes acted as the raiders and traders inland, and their produce was handed over to the European "factories" scattered along the coast. The European had no more need to penetrate inland than the butcher of today has to visit the farm where his slaughter cattle come from.

Some Europeans, however, had gone up the Senegal and Gambia rivers and from inland stations had heard reports of a vast river, the Niger, lying to the east. But there were doubts over which way it flowed and at what point it reached the ocean.

The problem of the Niger was put before the African Association, forerunner of the Royal Geographical Society of London, and was even more baffling than the problem of determining the sources of the Nile.

The main object of the African Association was to promote exploration of Africa, but the Association had as a second objective the advancement of British trade and political authority in the unknown continent.

After several attempts which failed to find out which way the Niger flowed, the Association found an able volunteer willing to try his hand. He was a young Scottish doctor named Mungo Park, who had seen service in the East Indies.

On June 21, 1795, Park reached the Gambia and began his journey inland along that river. About 200 miles up river he reached a British trading post and stayed there a few months to prepare for the next stage of his journey and to learn the Manding language. On December 2 he set out again; he crossed the upper Senegal basin, the semidesert area of Kaarta, despite trouble from the Arabs along the way. At Ludamar he was captured by a Moorish chief and imprisoned for four months, but managed to escape on July 1, 1796. Of his original equipment he now had only his horse and a compass. About three weeks later he reached Ségou, a town on the Niger. He reported Ségou as having a population of 30,000 and described the Niger at this point as broad as the Thames at Westminster and flowing eastward.

The jealousy and suspicion of the Moorish element in Ségou were too much for Park, so he left the town by following the river down-stream. By the time he had traveled about eighty miles farther, he had lost his horse and was utterly exhausted. At this point he decided to turn back by taking a route more to the south. The adventures on his return journey were incredible, including fever and being stripped by robbers of everything except his shirt. On June 10, 1797, he reached the British trading post and finally the coast. Park had collected a vast amount of information about the country of the upper Niger, and in 1799 he wrote an account of his journey, *Travels in the Interior of Africa*. Rich with details of his adventures and written in an unaffected style, the book became extremely popular and to this day remains a classic in exploration literature.

In 1803 the British government asked Park to lead another expedition along the Niger. With a captain's commission, and after long preparation coupled with delay, he sailed from Portsmouth in January 1805 with his destination Gambia. The journey up the Gambia River and along the Niger to Ségou proved fatal to most members of the expedition, who died

Mungo Park crossing the Black River.

of fever or dysentery. At Ségou, Park was given permission by the local ruler to continue his journey, and went down-river a short distance to Sansanding. Here he stopped and prepared for the difficult unknown part of the river by converting two canoes into a single 40-foot boat. He called the schooner H. M. S. *Joliba*, the Niger's native name, and launched her down-river November 19.

But the *Joliba* never reached the mouth of the Niger. When news reporting that the expedition had met with disaster reached settlements along the Gambia, the British government commissioned a man named Isaaco to find out what happened to Park's group. Soon after he arrived at Sansanding, Isaaco managed to find the guide who had led the group down-river November 19. According to the guide, the *Joliba* followed the river down to the region of Yauri, where the guide went ashore. Park and three other remaining Europeans plus several slaves continued on until they reached the Bussa rapids not far below Yauri. Here the churning waters pitched the boat against rocks where it remained fast. Hostile natives along the bank began attacking the defenseless men with spears and arrows. Realizing that their situation was hopeless, all sprang into the rapids and, except for one slave, were drowned.

The desolate Sahara appears the same today as it did in 2000 B.C. when Egyptian caravans crossed it.

In his reports Park had referred to a city called "Timbuctoo" north of the Niger, but little was known about it. The "mystery" of this city was solved in 1828 by the brilliant French explorer René Caillié. He spent some time inland in Senegal living with the natives, learning Arabic, and training as a convert to Islam. Then, proclaiming himself an Egyptian Arab journeying home, he joined a caravan in what is now the republic of Guinea and in 1828 reached Timbuktu, where he stayed for a fortnight. Next he picked up a caravan on its way across the Sahara to Morocco, and from Morocco he went home to France, the first European to return alive from Timbuktu.

Another great advance into inland Africa was from the direction of Tripoli in Libya. In 1823 two Englishmen, Clapperton and Denham, crossed the Sahara and discovered Lake Chad, which is near northeast Nigeria. The problem of the mouth of the Niger was finally settled in 1830 by the two Lander brothers, who crossed overland from the Guinea coast to the rapids at Bussa, where Park had been killed, and from there down the great river to its mouth, which empties into the Gulf of Guinea.

Meanwhile the sources of the upper Nile and the upper Congo were still objects of curiosity, attracting the attention of the Royal Geographical Society, which was founded in 1830 and took over the work of the

African Association. The semimythical Mountains of the Moon of Ptolemy and vast lakes associated with them were at last to be investigated. The Society chose the brilliant but difficult Richard Burton and his friend Speke, who had accompanied Burton on a dangerous journey to Harrar, the inland slave-trade depot of eastern Abyssinia. They started from Zanzibar on the east coast, traveled overland, and reached Lake Tanganyika, but Burton was gripped by fever so they cut short their examination of the region and returned to Tabora, halfway to the coast. Here Burton was left to regain his health while Speke went northward and discovered Lake Victoria, which he took to be the source of the Nile.

A year later he returned to Lake Victoria to confirm his discovery by walking round the western side of the great lake. Here he found entering into Lake Victoria the river Kagera, which we now know to be the real source of the Nile. On his way down the Nile, Speke and his party met Samuel Baker and his wife, who a little later discovered Lake Albert and the Murchison Falls.

A few years earlier the problem of the exact course of the Niger was finally settled by a series of journeys of Heinrich Barth, a German explorer. He ranks with Livingstone as a great scientific explorer of Africa, and his narrative is a model for accuracy and interest.

After studying Arabic in London, Barth traveled from Tunis to Egypt in 1844–45 and visited most of the countries of the Middle East, returning to Berlin in 1847. Back in Africa once again, in 1850 he set out from Tripoli and crossed the Sahara. For five years he explored the country between Lake Chad and Timbuktu and south to Cameroon, making prolonged stays with the various sultans and emirs he met. He returned home to become professor of geography at Berlin, and his book describing his travels ranks as the standard authority on the countries he visited. Confusion over the central region south of the Sahara was cleared up by another German explorer, Georg Schweinfurth, a botanist and geologist. Between 1868 and 1871 he crossed the watersheds of the White Nile, Congo, and what he thought was the Chari, which drains into Lake Chad but which turned out to be the Uele, a right-bank tributary of the Congo.

A lancer of the Sultan of Begharmi, drawn by Denham.

The work of these explorers left the upper half of Africa fairly well known. The parts remaining unknown were the Congo Basin, parts of the Zambezi Basin, the Nyasaland area in particular, and parts of southern Africa; although the lower regions of the Zambezi inland from the east coast must have been known to the Arab slave traders of old.

The mystery of Africa's rivers continued to attract explorers. To understand the nature of the mystery requires a few words about the topography of the continent. Most of Africa, particularly the southern half, is a tilted plateau, which means that the rivers are not navigable near their mouths. As they flow across the plateau they are easily navigable, but as they drop over the edge of the plateau near the coasts there are falls and swift rapids. The falls and rapids have been the barrier to penetration inland up the rivers, so to a large extent exploration, except for the coastal regions, has begun at or near the rivers' sources.

The Congo is one such river that drew men inland, and the search for its source was curiously linked with those of the Nile and Zambezi. From 1482, when Diego Cam placed a stone pillar at the mouth of the Congo, until the eighteenth century, very little progress was made up that river. Catholic missionaries soon pushed up the navigable stretch for 200 miles, but there they were stopped by tribal wars. The same was true of the country inland from Luanda farther south along the river Cuanza. The Portuguese, in fact, were not ardent land explorers, and on the east

Speke meeting with tribal chiefs on entering Unyoro.

A sketch by Barth shows the method of crossing the Niger with camels and donkeys; the donkeys were towed astern.

coast at the mouth of the Zambezi they showed little interest in following the river up to the highlands. They did, however, reach the town of Tete, just below the great rapids of Quebrabasa, and even built a fort at Zumbo at the junction of the Luangwa and Zambezi rivers, but they had constant difficulty trying to hold onto it.

To the south of these settlements there was the fabled kingdom of Monomotapa, ruled by an emperor and rich in gold. There was some fact behind the fable, since there was a once-powerful tribe of Bantu there who had worked mines and possibly had erected what are now ruins found at Zimbabwe a long time before the Portuguese arrived.

The most successful of the Portuguese travelers was De Lacerda who, as governor on the lower Zambezi, saw the advantage of establishing contact all across Africa with his compatriots in Angola on the west coast. In 1798 he traveled northwest from Tete, but he missed both Lake Nyasa and Lake Bangweulu, although he heard reports of them. Lacerda died on reaching a tribal chief named Cazembe, whose territory was near Lake Mweru, and his men returned to Tete. This Portuguese journey was the most extensive penetration of southern Africa up to that date, and it drew attention to that remote part of the continent.

But a force which proved to be stronger than the mystery aspect of the rivers in drawing explorers into the unknown hinterland was the awakening of the British public to the evils of slavery. Although the awakening came in the last years of the eighteenth century, it did not immediately promote inland exploration. But the ceaseless watch of the British Navy on the west and east coasts of Africa, which lasted from 1807 until 1837, created an interest in and familiarity with the ports and the practices of the slave trade.

It was the abolition of slavery in Cape Colony in 1833 that stimulated the series of treks of the Boers northward, to some extent exploration by migration. It was also the slavery problem that inspired exploration for religious reasons. There have been many missionary-explorers on the different continents, as we have seen, but the greatest of them all was David Livingstone, who landed at Algoa Bay in 1841 and from that time until his death in 1873 traveled thousands of miles every year.

Livingstone's passion was to push northward into what he called the "Dark Interior," first as a missionary and later as a propagandist against

White Nile
RUWENZORI
Jinja
MT. KENYA
EQUATOR
Congo
Stanley Falls
Lake Victoria
Lake Leopold II
MT. KILIMANJARO
Mombasa
Kasai
Nyangwe
Ujiji
Tabora
I N D I A N
Cabinda
Zanzibar
Lake Tanganyika
Lake Rukwa
Loanda
Cassai
Lake Mweru
O C E A N
Lualaba
Lake Bangweulu
Lake Nyasa
Rovuma
Lobito
Zambezi
Luangwa
Zumbo
Quebrabasa Rapids
Tete
Shire
Livingstone
Quelimane
Okovanggo
Victoria Falls
Lake Ngami
Limpopo
TROPIC OF CAPRICORN
A T L A N T I C
Vaal
O C E A N
Orange
Cape Town
De Lacerda
1 1787 2 1798
Livingstone
3 1841 4 1842 5 1849-51 6 1852-4 7 1854-6 8 1858-60
9 1860-4 10 1866-9 11 1869-73
Speke (12 with Burton, 14 with Grant)
12 1857-8 13 1858 14 1860-3
Stanley
15 1871-2 16 1874-5 17 1875-6 18 1876-7 19 1879-84
20 1888-9
Cameron
21 1874
Thomson
22 1878 23 1881 24 1883
0 100 200 300 400 500 Miles

slavery, and he was always a keen observer and a first-class surveyor.

His first discovery was of Lake Ngami, midway across the continent just north of the Tropic of Capricorn in Bechuanaland. Next with his whole family (threatened by the Boers if he left them behind), he and his friend William Oswell took their wagons northward through to the Zambezi in 1851. Previously there had been no knowledge of that great river beyond Zumbo, the Portuguese station 500 miles up river from the coast. A year later Livingstone sent his family back to England, and for the next four years he was entirely alone in his wanderings. During that time he explored a route up the Zambezi and across to the west coast at Luanda. When asked to return to England, he refused and went back to his friendly tribe, the Makololo, on the upper Zambezi, where he planned to march down to the east coast. These extraordinary solo journeys were typical of the man.

On his first visit to the Zambezi he had come up against the slave trade, organized through the Portuguese of Angola and carried out mainly by Arabs or half-caste Europeans. He at once recognized it as a trade and thought it could be abolished only by undercutting it with more legitimate trade. His exploration, therefore, was to find routes for such trade from the coast. He decided that the route to Luanda was impossible for either wagon or canoe transport, so he turned eastward, placing his hope in the Zambezi.

On this journey in 1855 his first discovery was Victoria Falls, which he had already heard about from his native friends as *Mosi-oa-tunya* (the Smoke that Thunders). The millions of tourists who have since gazed at the majesty of this natural wonder could not realize the disappointment the falls caused Livingstone. They were the first of several blows to his great scheme of finding a navigable route to the interior. Here was an instance of an African river navigable on the plateau but defying navigation as it plunged over a step of the plateau.

Livingstone and his porters crossing the Makata River.

Following the Zambezi's banks as closely as possible, he reached Tete and received a moderate welcome from the Portuguese, having bypassed the Quebrabasa Rapids, which became the second great barrier to his route to the interior. In the spring of 1856 Livingstone left Tete to return to England for a year. He was full of plans for the opening up of the "Dark Interior," but back in England he was persuaded against his will to make his next expedition an official one with white companions.

Livingstone returned to the mouth of the Zambezi in 1858 with his white companions, plus a steam launch for sailing inland. But things went wrong from the start. The launch was too frail and there were quarrels among the members of his party. Livingstone was not a good leader of white men, and the lack of harmony was partly his fault. Once up river he found the Quebrabasa Rapids impossible to navigate, so he turned back and sailed up the Shire River as far as Murchison Rapids, then he went overland and discovered the great Lake Nyasa, which was to become his alternative route to the interior.

With his brother and John Kirk, Livingstone returned up the northern side of the Zambezi all the way to his tribal friends, the Makololo, to

Victoria Falls, described by Africans as "The Smoke that Thunders."

Stanley (beneath flag) arrives at Lake Albert in 1887.

return the natives whom he had taken with him down-river four years earlier. Later he helped the first party of missionaries to settle near Lake Nyasa, explored most of its western shore line, and made a journey on foot toward Lake Bangweulu, which he had heard of from the slavers. When he was recalled by his government, this unconquerable man sailed his tiny launch, the *Lady Nyassa*, from Zanzibar to Bombay before returning to England for his last visit home. The saddest thing about his thorough exploration inland was that he, the archfoe of slavery, opened the way for the Portuguese slavers to Nyasaland.

By the time he returned to Nyasaland in 1866 the slavers had decimated the population of the pleasant Shire Highlands, from which the missionaries had by then retired. He ventured inland as a dedicated man, his chief object being to see the effects of slavery on the unknown interior. But he had a strong secondary purpose—to see whether the true source of the Nile was not farther south than Speke and Baker had thought.

For seven years Livingstone wandered through his "Dark Interior," a solitary white man with a nucleus of faithful attendants, enduring sickness and dangers of every kind. He discovered the southern end of Lake Tanganyika, Lake Mweru, and Lake Bangweulu, and visited the native chief Cazembe, the cruel ruler whose territory was between the two latter lakes, and whose executioner walked round with the despot armed with giant scissors for cropping off the ears of anyone who displeased the chief.

Livingstone found that his small party got on much easier when it traveled with slave caravans, and with one such group he reached Lake

Tanganyika a very sick man and was taken by the slavers to Ujiji, where Burton had been twelve years before. From there he journeyed westward to the banks of the upper Congo, thinking that it might be the Nile. By this time, reduced to near poverty, he could not purchase canoes to go down the river and, horrified by a massacre of the local natives by the Arabs, he returned to Ujiji exhausted and in ill health.

It was in Ujiji that the dramatic meeting with Stanley, the American journalist-explorer, took place, and four months of Stanley's company revived Livingstone's strength. Again he refused to return to England, and after Stanley sent back men and stores from the coast Livingstone started on his last journey, obsessed with the idea that he would find the sources of the Nile to the southwest of Lake Bangweulu. True to his passion for map making, he took the difficult route along the east side of Lake Tanganyika, surveying all the time and ignoring the hardship of traveling during the rainy season. In bad weather, with a faulty sextant, and desperately sick with dysentery, he was lost for a time to the north of the Bangweulu Swamp.

He reached a sandy island in the swamp where he might have recovered his health. This writer has recovered from dysentery at the very same island village and can vouch for it as a healthful site. It was Livingstone's impatience, always a weakness with him, that hastened his death. It was and still is a pleasant village, where he could get plenty of goats' milk and fresh fish. But he rested for only three weeks, then started off by canoe to go round the swamps to the east with his large party and his faithful donkey. The seasonal flood waters were at the worst stage for travel, so he was forced to split his party into a land section and a canoe section. The haste, the coarse food, and constant wading were the worst possible treatment for his illness, and eventually he had to be carried on a litter. But still he continued his mapping, and so well that his route can be followed today.

Livingstone died at a small village in the district of Ilala on the south side of the great swamp of Bangweulu, and his embalmed body was carried all the way to Zanzibar, finally to be buried in Westminster Abbey. The bravery and loyalty of his black servants in making that long march were as great a tribute to the man as his place of burial. He had covered some 30,000 miles in his journeys, most of them on foot and alone with his African servants, every mile mapped or described in his field books.

Mr. Campbell, an early explorer of Madagascar.

The unsolved problem of the Congo was settled between 1874 and 1877 by Henry Morton Stanley in an Anglo-American expedition. By a few weeks Stanley missed the body of his friend Livingstone, being brought back to Zanzibar. By this time Stanley had set out with three English companions and a boat which was carried in eight sections by a large and well-armed retinue. The first half of his journey included sailing round Lake Victoria and Lake Tanganyika; and he confirmed Cameron's discovery of the outlet of Lake Tanganyika. Then with an armed force of 150 men he began to cross Africa, farther north than Cameron's route in 1874. (Cameron had crossed the continent from Zanzibar, Ujiji, Kabambare, Lake Kisale, Bihé, to Luanda.)

The methods of the journalist-explorer were in great contrast to those of the missionary-explorer. Stanley fought his way across Africa, and claimed to have had thirty one fights against great odds during his journey down the Congo. He lost all three of his white companions and 170 of his black followers. Unquestionably his journey was a great one and had important results. Leopold II, King of Belgium, sent a committee to intercept him at Marseilles as he was returning, and commissioned Stanley to lead an expedition two years later. The purpose of the expedition was to help create the Congo Free State under the sovereignty of Leopold himself. Stanley just about completed the exploration of the middle tributaries of the Congo, while von Wissmann did the same for the tributaries coming from the south.

The great journeys of Livingstone and Stanley had led the way, blazing a trail shaped like a great Cross of Lorraine across southern Africa.

As early as 600 B.C. King Necho of Egypt had commissioned a voyage which resulted in the circumnavigation of Africa; and, much earlier, trader-explorers of Egypt had made probes inland with their caravan expeditions across the Sahara and by boat part way up the Nile.

In the fifteenth century the whole of North Africa was under Islam rule. Along the west coast were the Portuguese and along the east coast the Arabs—both well established in the slave trade. Although slavery was the prime motive for exploration of Africa, the "mystery" of the continent's rivers attracted explorers. The four great rivers—Nile, Niger, Zambezi, and Congo—continued to excite men up to the present century.

By the eighties of the last century the hinterland of Africa was being explored in all directions, Joseph Thomson being one of the last and most successful of the pioneer travelers of the continent. A naturalist and geologist from Edinburgh University, Thomson's first expedition was to Lakes Nyasa and Tanganyika, but it is impossible to detail his routes. Wherever you go in East Africa you are bound to cross one of Thomson's tracks. His major journey was from Mombasa in south Kenya up to the Great Rift Valley and its salt lakes and on to Uganda. Twice he crossed the land of the Masai warriors, who until that time had barred the way.

After travels in Nigeria and Morocco, Thomson journeyed to South Africa, from where he was sent on political missions from the east coast to the upper Congo by the British South Africa Chartered Company. Although not so great as the Hudson's Bay Company and the East India Company, the B.S.A. Chartered Company promoted a great deal of exploration, particularly inland in South Africa.

The political matrix of Africa was settled by its partition among the nations of Europe. Although there was much exploration yet to come after Thomson, especially by the French and the Germans, the object of exploration was political rather than geographical. Exploration continued well into the twentieth century, but with such a host of names, particularly French and English, that space will not allow even a list of them.

Although the internal combustion engine has made travel easier, there are still parts of Abyssinia and of the Belgian Congo which are relatively unknown, even though they may have been photographed from the air. Like South America, then, Africa still is a lure to the explorer.

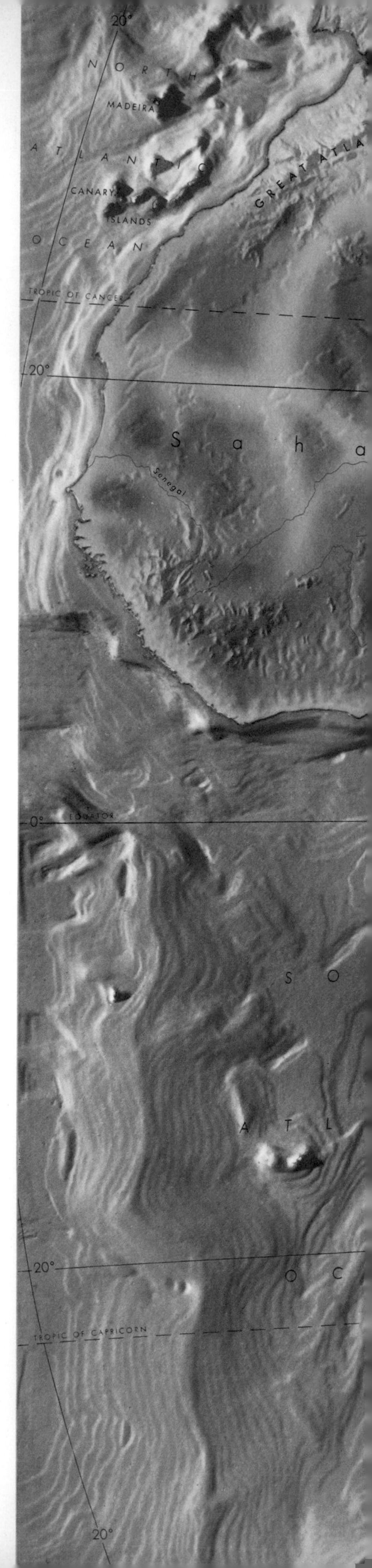

Varying tones of coloration show different stages of penetration of Africa. Lightest color shows earliest penetration; darker colors, later penetration.

before 1550 | 1550-1700 | 1700-1800 | 1800-1850 | 1850-1900 | 1900 & after

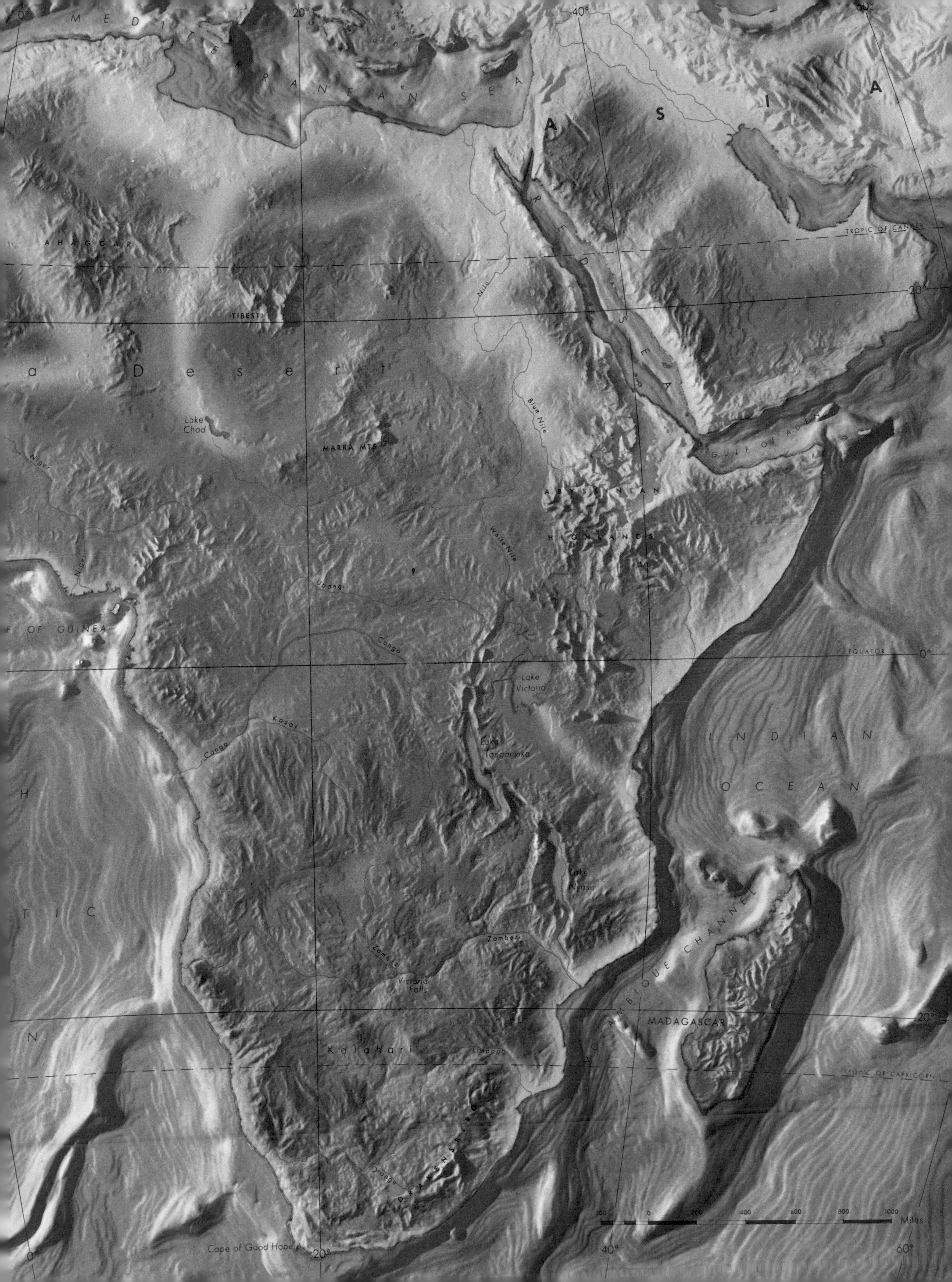
MEDITERRANEAN SEA
ASIA
RED SEA
AHAGGAR
TIBESTI
Desert
Lake Chad
MARRA MTS
Nile
Blue Nile
White Nile
GULF OF ADEN
ABYSSINIAN HIGHLANDS
TROPIC OF CANCER
Niger
OF GUINEA
Ubangi
Congo
EQUATOR
Lake Victoria
Kasai
Lake Tanganyika
INDIAN OCEAN
Lake Nyasa
Zambezi
Victoria Falls
MOZAMBIQUE CHANNEL
MADAGASCAR
Kalahari
Limpopo
TROPIC OF CAPRICORN
DRAKENSBERG
Orange
Cape of Good Hope
Miles
0°
20°
40°
60°

Voyages and journeys in the Arctic.
(See globe key on facing page.)

Challenge of the poles

In the story of discovery we have seen a variety of motives impelling man to explore his world, some of them not greatly to his credit. In polar exploration, however, we can discern purer motives. The profit motive is less in evidence, there are no wars, no slavery, and rather less envy among nations. The abiding love of adventure in man has a nobler outlet, and his deep-seated spirit of curiosity finds a scope less restricted by base incentives.

The urge to explore the Arctic regions could hold no intrinsic attraction at first; there could be little value in it except as a route to some other part of the world. The outburst of maritime activity which followed the discovery of the New World focused the attention of the northern nations of Europe on the Arctic as a possible trade route to the East. With the Portuguese in command of the sea route around Africa to Asia and the Spanish in command of the route around South America, other European nations were pressed to search for a northwest or northeast passage.

Blocked time and time again by ice or disaster, the merchant-adventurers who sailed into northern waters found that there was small prospect of finding a clear passage to the East, but they did begin to find some value in the Arctic region itself. The cod fishery of Newfoundland, the seals and walrus off the west coast of Greenland in Davis Strait, the furs of land animals, and finally the whales of Spitsbergen were all byproducts of the long and difficult search.

By 1620, when William Baffin had discouraged hopes of finding an ice-free northwest passage and, as a result, attention was turned for a while to the northeast-passage region, whaling in Spitsbergen waters came into prominence, at first in the hands of the English but later of the Dutch.

There was a picturesque period in the seventeenth century when rival fleets were in the north discovering new islands, trying to keep them secret, and committing acts of near piracy on each other. In this way the whole of the east coast of Spitsbergen became known, though it was often described as Greenland. Claims and counterclaims to islands and harbors were made. Thus in the narrative of Robert Fotherby in 1614 there is a quaint description of how these claims were made. "I went up to the Harbour, and there caused a Crosse to be set up and the King's Arms on a Sixe-pence to bee nayled thereon, under which also I nayled a peece of sheet-lead whereon I set the Moscovie Companies Marke."

During the seventeenth century all the lands between Greenland and Novaya Zemlya were visited at different times, though they did not all appear on the charts of the period. Thus the island off the east coast of Greenland now called Jan Mayen, first discovered by Henry Hudson in 1607 and called Hudson's Touches, was rediscovered several times and its longitude changed as often as its name. But keeping track of the various northern islands was not an easy task. Many of them, when snow covered, must have appeared very similar to the early explorers, particularly when the coastal waters were frozen and heaped with ice.

Meanwhile interest in the fate of the long-forgotten colony of Norsemen in Greenland was growing. A parish priest of Norway named Hans Egede organized and led a search for traces of them in 1721. He found ruins of their homesteads and churches but only Eskimos were living there. He stayed on the glaciated island as a missionary for fifteen years and founded the modern Danish Greenland.

About the same time that Egede was in Greenland, Dutch and English whalers were sailing the Davis Strait along the west coast of the island

Expeditions within limited areas:
A Nordenskjöld to Spitsbergen *1858, 1861, 1864, 1868, 1872, 1890*
B Nordenskjöld *1870, 1883* C Nansen *1882* D Peary *1886*
E Watkins *1928* F Fuchs *1929* G Watkins *1930-1*
Nordenskjöld *1875, 1876, 1878*
De Long *1879*
Nansen *1888, 1893-6* (. . . . . . . *Nansen's sledge journey*)
Peary *1893-4, 1894-5, 1898-1902, 1906, 1908-9*
Amundsen *1903-6, 1918-20*
Stefansson *1908-12, 1913-8*

Old print shows whalers in the Arctic harpooning sperm whale.

and they revived the stubborn idea of a northwest passage to the East. In 1745 and again in 1776 the British Government offered a reward of £5000 for the first ship reaching 89° North and £20,000 for making a northwest passage.

The Royal Society, inspired by Captain Cook's success in the South Pacific, used its influence on the British Admiralty to fit out an expedition with hopes of reaching the North Pole. Two ships under C. J. Phipps sailed in 1773 but, as the whalers had warned, the explorers failed to find any openings in the ice to the north of Spitsbergen and they narrowly escaped having to abandon their ships. A fourteen-year-old midshipman on one of the ships had an exciting adventure with a polar bear; the midshipman's name was Horatio Nelson. In the same year, 1773, an interesting discovery was made by a Russian fur trader in Siberia. On the coast to the east of the great Lena River he saw reindeer coming over the sea ice. He backtracked them and discovered the low New Siberian Islands and, to his amazement, found deposits of thousands of tusks of the woolly mammoth and horns of the woolly rhinoceros.

During the Napoleonic Wars interest in the Arctic waned, but it was again renewed after the wars, largely through the work of two famous English whalers—the Scoresbys, father and son. The aged president of the Royal Society, Sir Joseph Banks, and the polar-minded Secretary of the Admiralty, Sir John Barrow, talked with the Scoresbys and persuaded the Admiralty to support an expedition. The Scoresbys knew the Spitsbergen seas better than anyone else did—in 1806 having taken their ship to 81° 30′ North, fifty miles farther than Phipps had gone. So in 1818 two ships were sent to Spitsbergen, but they did no better than their forerunners. We need only mention here that Lieutenant John Franklin was in command of one ship and had George Back as his mate, whose voyage we described in the North America section of this book.

Sir John Ross greeted by Eskimos in Greenland, 1818.

Parry's ships frozen in Arctic ice.

In 1818 two other ships, under the command of the breezy but rather obstinate John Ross, were sent to Davis Strait. Ross had Lieutenant Edward Parry as his second-in-command and his nephew, James Clark Ross, as midshipman. It was just two centuries since Baffin had discovered his bay north of Davis Strait, and his work had been somewhat discredited. Ross restored Baffin's good name by following his same course, but Ross made one great error of judgment. When opposite Lancaster Sound at the north end of Baffin Island, he thought he saw high land blocking the way, whereas Parry thought there was a passage. They also discovered Eskimos living far up the west coast of Greenland. Greatly impressed by the cocked hats and epaulets of the naval officers, the Eskimos took them to be visitors from the moon.

The doubt about Lancaster Sound caused the Admiralty to send another expedition the next year to settle the matter. There were two ships with Parry in command, and this expedition won for Parry reputation as the greatest of the British Arctic explorers of the nineteenth century. He was for the Arctic what Cook had been for the Pacific, a bold yet careful navigator, worshiped by his men, and a scientist in all his training.

Lancaster Sound proved to be a strait and Parry sailed through it to 112° West (nearly the same longitude as Salt Lake City, Utah), winning the reward for the ships of £5000 for passing the 110th meridian. The ships wintered very successfully at Melville Island, and although there were symptoms of scurvy there were not any deaths from the disease. From his farthest point west Parry saw that there was a passage through but that the heavy pack ice would prevent any sailing ship's ever passing it, in which he was right.

Sir John Franklin watches his crew bring supplies ashore as they struggle in a heavy surf.

In his next two expeditions he tried to find a passage closer to the mainland of Canada. On both attempts he was foiled by impenetrable ice, but he had trained a group of officers well qualified for polar travel. He had to abandon one of his ships, the *Fury*, which was driven ashore by the ice in Prince Regent Inlet. By this time Parry had such wide experience with ice that he thought it might be possible to get far north by sledging over the drifting ice with boats, and so take advantage of any open water. In 1827 he made an attempt to do just that and managed to reach 82° 45′ North, the farthest north for the next half century.

For the time being the Admiralty lost interest in the northwest passage, but old John Ross, anxious to make up for his original error, found supporters for a small private expedition. He had a poor ship, the *Victory*, of only 85 tons, and he himself was getting old at fifty three for polar work. Among his crew of sixteen was his brilliant nephew James Clark Ross, who had already gained a great deal of polar experience.

They sailed in 1829, taking the route of Parry down Prince Regent Inlet and wintering their ship 200 miles farther south than the wreck of the *Fury*. As the cold set in, Ross's ship was held fast by the ice, frozen in solid so that she could not budge for three summer seasons. During that time the younger Ross made some excellent sledge journeys, including in 1831 a visit to the north magnetic pole, located about 71° North, 96° West.

The *Victory's* crew abandoned their ice-bound ship and sledged north to the wreck of the *Fury*. When they reached her they patched up her old boats, but too late for open water; the ice had already begun to form. After spending a miserable winter on the desolate beach, with the coming of the summer of 1833 they took to their boats and reached Lancaster Sound, where they were picked up by a whaler. During the long ordeal

Ross had lost only two of his men. When he and his nephew climbed aboard the whaler, they were told that the expedition had been given up for lost in England. James Ross had now spent eight winters and fourteen summers in the Arctic.

Ten years later the Admiralty was persuaded to make yet another attempt at finding the elusive northwest passage. By this time James Ross had returned from his famous Antarctic voyage and was offered the command. He declined it on the basis of his age, which was only forty six, but extended exploration of the polar regions takes a lot out of a man. At the time Ross declined, Sir John Franklin had just returned from his assignment as Governor of Tasmania and quickly pressed his claim for command of one ship, the *Erebus*, though he was fifty nine. And F. R. M. Crozier claimed command of the second ship, the *Terror*, a veteran of both polar region. The ships, with a total of 129 men on board, sailed in 1845 and became the mystery of the century when they dropped from sight after entering Lancaster Sound.

Circumstantial evidence showed that the ships had wintered at Beechey Island on the north side of the sound, and presumably Franklin or Crozier left messages there, but if so, they were never found. The Admiralty did not express any anxiety for two years, a normal waiting period for such an expedition; but in 1848 Sir James Ross was sent to look for them. By sledging strenuously he got to within 200 miles of where the *Erebus* and *Terror* were beset, as we now know. Having himself wintered four times in that area, Ross felt that the Franklin group must be safe somewhere, and he expected to meet them when he returned to England.

There then began a long search, extending over ten years and involving forty ships and more than 2000 men. Finally the expedition's fate was pieced together from reports by Eskimos, who had relics from the expedition, but it was not until 1858 that a message was found. Francis Leopold McClintock, in a perilous expedition with twenty four men in a small steam yacht named the *Fox*, found the message written on the edge of an official form in a cairn not far from where Ross had been when he found the magnetic pole. The message stated that the ships had been stranded for two years, that Franklin had died in 1847, and that the survivors were then on their way south to the Arctic coast of Canada. As it turned out, one by one every man weakened from starvation and cold, and died along the way.

The expeditions in search of Franklin taught explorers a great deal about the Canadian Arctic, but perhaps their chief value was that so many men had learned how to travel over the ice by sledging instead of trusting ships to find a clear path through. From that period on, sledging by man or dog power became standard practice.

The continued search for a northwest route had also attracted attention to the north end of Baffin Bay, where Smith Sound turned out to be the lower end of a long strait between Ellesmere Land and Greenland, an avenue leading toward the Pole. Americans pioneered this approach, but it was left to a British expedition in 1875 to make the first sally aimed at the North Pole itself. Under the command of Sir George Nares, the two ships *Discovery* and *Alert* managed to reach the northern end of the strait, one of them wintering at 82° 30′ North. A wholesale outbreak of scurvy, which affected nearly half of the combined crews, dampened the men's spirit, yet they made useful exploratory journeys along the coasts of Greenland and Ellesmere Land. Their hopes of reaching the Pole came to nothing—their progress toward the Pole was only fifty miles.

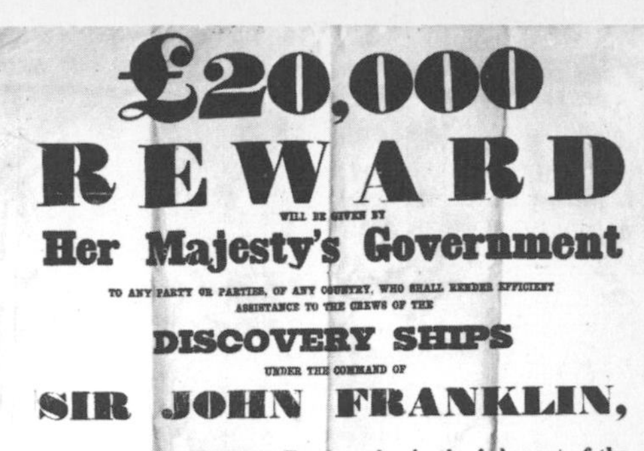

£20,000
REWARD
WILL BE GIVEN BY
Her Majesty's Government
TO ANY PARTY OR PARTIES, OF ANY COUNTRY, WHO SHALL RENDER EFFICIENT ASSISTANCE TO THE CREWS OF THE
DISCOVERY SHIPS
UNDER THE COMMAND OF
SIR JOHN FRANKLIN,

1.—To any Party or Parties who, in the judgment of the Board of Admiralty, shall discover and effectually relieve the Crews of Her Majesty's Ships "Erebus" and "Terror," the Sum of

£20,000.

OR

2.—To any Party or Parties who, in the judgment of the Board of Admiralty, shall discover and effectually relieve *any* of the Crews of Her Majesty's Ships "Erebus" and "Terror," or shall convey such intelligence as shall lead to the relief of such Crews or *any* of them, the Sum of

£10,000.

OR

3.—To any Party or Parties who, in the judgment of the Board of Admiralty, shall by virtue of his or their efforts first succeed in ascertaining their fate,

£10,000.

W. A. B. HAMILTON,
Secretary of the Admiralty

Nares holding morning inspection on the deck of the *Alert* during north polar expedition of 1875.

By 1879 a Swedish scientist and historian, Baron Nordenskjöld, had found the long-sought northeast passage to Asia. He left Norway in his ship, the *Vega*, sailed through the Kara Sea, and rounded Cape Chelyuskin in mid-August. Sailing on, he visited the New Siberian Islands, but was just too late to reach Bering Strait before being frozen in. Even so, he had found a passage into the vast Pacific. For its scientific results the *Vega* expedition ranks high in the history of Arctic exploration.

The very next year an attempt to make the passage in the reverse direction ended in tragedy. An American naval officer, George Washington De Long, sailed through Bering Strait, but north of Wrangel Island his ship, the *Jeannette*, was frozen in and for two winters drifted with the ice across 400 miles before she was finally crushed. In their attempt to reach the mouth of the Lena River more than half the ship's company was lost from a combination of storms and starvation.

The northwesterly drift of De Long's *Jeannette* clamped in ice plus the discovery of relics on drift ice off Greenland encouraged a young Norwegian doctor, Fridtjof Nansen, to devise a bold plan for reaching the North Pole. He reasoned that if he built a ship which would rise to ice pressure and deliberately allowed it to be frozen in near the New Siberian Islands, the ship should drift with the ice across the Arctic Ocean not far from the Pole itself.

Nansen had the famous ship *Fram* specially built, and in 1893 with a party of thirteen men he sailed her beyond Cape Chelyuskin and allowed her to be frozen in. In the first year the ship drifted to 84° North, but Nansen realized the direction of drift would not carry him to the Pole. At this point he followed part two of his plan: He took one man, Lieutenant H. Johansen, with him and set off toward the Pole with dog-sledges carrying kayaks so he could later cross open water. It was the boldest journey ever made in the North. Nansen and Johansen got to within four degrees of the Pole, but at this point were forced to turn back. With great difficulty they reached a northern island in the Franz Josef group and wintered there in a stone hut. The severe cold, loneliness, and strict diet—they lived on a few walrus they had killed—made their lives miserable. In the spring they sledged farther south and met a British expedition which gave them passage back to Norway, where they landed in 1896.

Meanwhile the *Fram* had drifted for more than 1000 days out of sight of land. Finally she broke free from the ice and arrived back in Norway only a few days after Nansen got there. The fifteen-month journey of the two men was a record feat of endurance and skill, and Nansen's name is rightly the greatest in the annals of the Arctic.

Seven years after Nansen's return home another Norwegian explorer, Roald Amundsen, led an expedition which succeeded in making the long-sought northwest passage. With six men and a sloop of forty seven tons, the *Gjöa*, Amundsen left Norway, went south of Greenland, and threaded his way among the islands of the Canadian Arctic. He spent two winters on King William Island, just off the Canadian mainland, and found skeletons of the Franklin expedition. When the ice began to melt, and with only an inch of water under their keel, the group coaxed the ship through the strait which McClintock had found during his search for Franklin and which had been frozen over at the time. After being delayed another winter near the mouth of the Mackenzie River, they managed to round Alaska, sail through Bering Strait, and reach San Francisco in 1906.

About the time of Nansen's great journey the first man to reach the

22 Septemb 1893
7 April 95
86°14.
6 august 95
Vardö
13 august 1896
Fridtjof Nansen

Nansen drew this sketch of his polar route for friends who greeted him on his return.

On his trip to the North Pole, Peary crossed 400 miles of Arctic waste such as this found off Ellesmere Land.

Pole was just beginning his career. Robert Peary, then a young American naval officer, was pursuing a new idea. He had seen a good deal of the Eskimos of Smith Sound and he decided that, led by a white man, they could succeed in the difficult travel over the polar pack ice. After a series of preliminary expeditions, during which he improved his methods of surviving and traveling in the Arctic, in 1909 he set out from Cape Columbia, the northern tip of Ellesmere Land, for the North Pole 400 miles away. Traveling ahead of him, parties broke the trail until the group was within 130 miles of the Pole. From this point he left the group and went ahead with only his Negro servant and four Eskimos.

"I had not dared to hope for such progress as we were making," he wrote in his diary. "Still the biting cold would have been impossible to face by anyone not fortified by an inflexible purpose. The bitter wind burned our faces so that they cracked, and long after we got into camp each day they pained us so that we could hardly go to sleep. The Eskimos complained much, and at every camp [readjusted] their fur clothing. . . . They also complained of their noses, which I had never known them to do before. The air was as keen and bitter as frozen steel."

A day before he reached the Pole he described the countryside in these words: "The sky was a colourless pall gradually deepening to almost black at the horizon, and the ice was a ghastly and chalky white. . . . How different it seemed from the glittering fields, canopied with blue and lit by sun and full moon, over which we had been traveling for the last four days." When on April 6, 1909 he reached his goal he found, as Nansen had suggested, that the Pole was on drifting ice covering a deep sea. In his diary he wrote, "The Pole at last. The prize of three centuries. My dream and goal for twenty years. Mine at last! I cannot bring myself to realize it. It seems all so simple and commonplace."

His technique in polar travel soundly proved, Peary returned home satisfied, willing to let younger men set their sights on the South Pole.

New York Times.

DAY, SEPTEMBER 7, 1909.—EIGHTEEN PAGES. ONE CENT

In order not to miss The New York Times of to-morrow, in which will be printed exclusively Lieut. Peary's own story of his discovery of the North Pole, order a copy from your newsdealer early to-day.

PEARY DISCOVERS THE NORTH POLE AFTER EIGHT TRIALS IN 23 YEARS

COOK GLAD PEARY REACHED THE POLE

Unmoved When, Wreathed with Flowers at Banquet, He Hears the News.

HOPE NOW FOR OTHERS

Believes More Expeditions Will Reach the Pole Within the Next Ten Years.

Notifies The New York Times That He Reached It on April 6, 1909.

HE WIRES FROM LABRADOR

Returning on the Roosevelt, Which He Reports to Bridgman is Safe.

IS NEARING NEWFOUNDLAND

Expects to Reach Chateau Bay To-day, When He Will Send Full Particulars.

McMILLAN SENDS WORD

Explorer's Companion Telegraphs Sister: "We Have the Pole on Board."

SEVEN VAIN EXPEDITIONS

Many Years Consumed in Learning the Feasible Route—Picked Men Were His Assistants.

PEARY REPORTS TO THE TIMES

ANNOUNCES HIS DISCOVERY OF THE POLE AND WILL SEND A FULL AND EXCLUSIVE ACCOUNT TO-DAY.

Indian Harbor, Labrador, via Cape Ray, N. F., Sept. 6.

The New York Times, New York:

I have the pole, April sixth. Expect arrive Chateau Bay September seventh. Secure control wire for me there and arrange expedite transmission big story.

PEARY.

PEARY'S MESSAGE TO HIS WIFE.

SOUTH HARPSWELL, Me., Sept. 6.—Commander Robert E. Peary announced his success in discovering the North Pole to his wife, who is summering at Eagle Island here, as follows:

INDIAN HARBOR, via Cape Ray, Sept. 6, 1909.

Mrs. R. E. Peary, South Harpswell, Me.:

Have made good at last. I have the old Pole. Am well. Love. Will wire again from Chateau.

(Signed) BERT.

In [illegible] Mrs. Peary sent the following dispatch:

SOUTH HARPSWELL, Me., Sept. 6, 1909.

To Commander R. E. Peary, Steamer Roosevelt, Chateau Bay:

All well. Best love. God bless you. Hurry home.

(Signed) JO.

CONFIRMED BY FELLOW-VOYAGER.

INDIAN HARBOR, Labrador, Sept. 6, 1909.

Dr. S. W. Abercrombie, Worcester Academy, Worcester, Mass.:

Top of the earth reached at last. Greetings to Faculty and boys.

(Signed) D. B. McMILLAN.

DR. COOK CABLES THE TIMES.

Voyages and journeys in the Antarctic. (See globe key on facing page.)

When Magellan gave practical proof that the earth was a sphere by sailing completely round it, geographers began to fill in their maps with a vast imaginary continent, "Terra Australis," based on the island Tierra del Fuego, which Magellan described. The idea of symmetry was in the geographers' minds; a land mass in the Southern Hemisphere certainly must exist in order to balance the "excess" of land known to be in the Northern Hemisphere.

They sketched in their *Ant*-arctic shores opposite the south of Africa, so that the imaginary continent included the Australia they knew nothing of and filled the southern third of the great Pacific that yawned wide between Asia and America. As we saw in the section describing exploration of Australia and New Zealand, discovery in the south became that of successive loppings off from this imagined continent as men, more by accident than by design, happened to sail across it in higher and higher latitudes.

Francis Drake in 1578 showed that there was open sea to the south of Tierra del Fuego, and later the Dutch skippers who were looking for a quicker route to Java reduced the amount of land that could be in the Indian Ocean, but they found West Australia. Tasman then proved in 1642 that Australia was a large island apart from the imagined continent, but he left New Zealand as a possible promontory of a continent which might fill the southern Pacific. Then New Zealand was stripped off by Captain Cook in 1770, when he showed that it consisted of two large islands.

In his second voyage Cook was given the specific task of delimiting what was left of a southern continent. He began by sailing due south from Africa and became the first man to cross the Antarctic Circle. We know now that he was turned back by dense pack ice when he was only 100 miles from the true continent. He proceeded to wipe off the map all land to the north of 65° South before he set sail to winter in New Zealand and his beloved Tahiti. In the summers of 1773 and 1774 he again disposed of any land in the South Pacific down to the same high latitude. It was on that voyage that he reached his farthest south, 71°, and still found nothing but ice in front of him. To this day no ship has ever got farther south on that meridian.

Though he failed to find a continent, he shrewdly suspected that one existed, and he prophesied that it would be covered with ice. After his weary crew were refreshed again at Tahiti, Cook sailed directly for Cape Horn, missing Graham Land (Palmer Peninsula), the only part of the continent which is outside the Antarctic Circle. His report of no land of any consequence within the reach of a sailing ship was a revelation to the geographers of the day, but he himself thought his greatest achievement was to have returned home without losing a single man from scurvy, and for this accomplishment he was awarded a medal by the Royal Society in London.

Columbus had discovered a continent which had never been on a map; Cook removed from the map most of a continent which had been largely a product of imagination.

For nearly fifty years Cook had no successors. Then in 1819 a Russian naval captain, Fabian von Bellingshausen, was sent by Emperor Alexander to confirm whether a continent did lie beyond Cook's field of ice. In a brilliant voyage two Russian ships circumnavigated the unknown land and discovered the large island of Alexander I at 69° South. Farther to the north they met American and British sealers who had discovered the extreme end of the Graham Land Peninsula the year before.

Cook's party explores ice islands of the Antarctic during 1773 voyage.

A Larsen 1893 B Larsen & Nordenskjöld (Otto) 1902-3
C Scott, Wilson & Shackleton 1901-4
D Scott & Wilson *to the South Pole* 1910-13
E Amundsen *to the South Pole* 1911-13
F Filchner 1912 G Hillary *to the South Pole* 1957-8
Drygalski 1901-3
Shackleton (& Mawson) 1907-9, Shackleton 1915-6
Mawson 1911-4, 1929-31
Fuchs 1956, Fuchs *to the South Pole* 1957-8

In complete contrast to the Arctic, the Antarctic is a huge continent larger than Australia and covered with an icecap several thousand feet thick. The Antarctic is a perfect example of an ice age in full swing. There is no life at all on this barren land except for a few mosses and some minute insects which manage to survive in spite of being frozen for most of the year. The chief features of the region are wind and cold. It has been truly called the "home of the blizzard."

On the other hand, the sea around the continent is teeming with small marine life which supports the many whales, seals, and penguins that inhabit the belt of drifting pack ice surrounding that vast and inhospitable continent.

In a very few years the antarctic sealers had exhausted the profits of their grisly trade, but in 1831 one of them, John Biscoe, had discovered Enderby Land, that part of Antarctica nearest Africa. For the most part, however, neither the sealers nor whalers took any real interest in discovery or exploration of the lands they passed. All their energies were focused on their trade.

As Cook's exploration in the South Pacific was begun with a scientific mission (to observe a transit of the planet Venus), so was the next assault on the still-shadowy southern continent, and France led the way, although by only a few days. Early in 1840 Dumont d'Urville, on a voyage to study terrestrial magnetism, sighted the continental ice and a few rocky islands some 2000 miles south of Australia and named it Adélie Land after his wife. A few days later, American ships under the command of Charles Wilkes saw ice-covered land on both sides of Adélie Land. Neither the French nor the American expedition was properly equipped for pushing through the pack ice surrounding the continent, and it was left to James Clark Ross with his stout ships the *Erebus* and *Terror* to make the first deep penetration.

Adélie penguins of the Antarctic named by d'Urville in 1840.

Sailing from Tasmania in 1840, he made for that part of Antarctica due south of New Zealand and pushed his way through the heavy belt of pack ice in four days. Once through, he found himself in a sea almost free of ice, the sea now named after him. From here he turned southwest, hoping to sail to the south magnetic pole, but he found his way blocked by high mountains and truly continental land, so he sailed along it for nearly 500 miles, naming it Victoria Land after his sovereign. To the great surprise of the party they discovered twin active volcanos—one 13,000 feet, the other 10,148 feet—which they named Erebus and Terror. Extending eastward from the volcanos was a high cliff of floating ice which they called the Barrier. They surveyed its face along 200 miles and then sailed to the opening of a wide bay which they called McMurdo Bay (after the mate of the *Terror*), and the ship's surgeon drew an excellent sketch of what they saw.

Owing to the clearness of the antarctic atmosphere they took it to be a shallow bay; actually it is a deep sound. Seventy years later the present writer was able to recognize every detail of the surgeon's sketch and to see exactly where it was sketched from. Discouraged by what they took to be only a bay, they decided to turn back to find suitable winter quarters. This decision was their only bit of ill fortune during the voyage. If his ships had gone a few miles farther, Ross would have found good winter quarters under the shadow of Mount Erebus, where Scott was to winter in 1901. For the first time men had discovered that there was open water once the belt of pack ice was passed, and that there was high, ice-capped land beyond.

The next year Ross returned to his sea and completed its survey,

The *Erebus* and *Terror* in a gale amid Antarctic pack ice, 1842.

though the ships narrowly escaped destruction when they collided in a gale and snowstorm while trying to steer clear of several giant icebergs. During his third season of the expedition in the Antarctic, Ross sailed down the east coast of Graham Land, then returned to England after a cruise which had lasted four and a half years. The discoveries of this expedition were momentous from a scientific point of view, but they gave no promise of any "value" in the Antarctic, so it was nearly sixty years more until there was any further serious renewal of exploration in that region.

When the second wave of exploration did come, it was again international in character, and had terrestrial magnetism as its major object. Swedish, German, and British expeditions all set out at the turn of the century. The Swedes, under Otto Nordenskjöld, a nephew of the Baron who had commanded the *Vega*, went to Graham Land, but they ran into trouble. Their ship, which was under the experienced captaincy of C. A. Larsen, was crushed in the ice of the Weddell Sea, and in two separate parties they had to spend the severe winter in stone huts, but they were fortunate in not losing more than one man. Three years earlier a Belgian expedition had been frozen in on the other side of Graham Land and they, too, lost one man. A German expedition under Dr. Erich von Drygalski first went to the Kerguelen Islands and then due south to find winter quarters on the continent. When their ship was frozen in, some forty miles away from the land, they sledged over the ice and found an extinct volcano. As explorers before them had done, they named it after their ship, Mount Gauss.

The British expedition under Captain Robert Scott was more fortunate. In the *Discovery*, specially built for polar exploration and now resting at anchor in the Thames, he arrived in the Antarctic in 1901 and wintered in McMurdo Sound near where Ross had been sixty years earlier. From there during the next two years he organized several sledge journeys inland. On his first one, with Dr. E. A. Wilson and Lieutenant Ernest

Shackleton's ship, *Endurance*, frozen in solid during the winter of 1915. Shackleton's farthest point south was 88° 23′ S. 162° W.

Henry Shackleton, he traveled across the great Ross Barrier and got within 500 miles of the Pole. The following summer he made a journey for 200 miles westward, traveling over the featureless plateau at a height of 8000 feet.

Scott pioneered the way for the many long sledge journeys which were to follow. The immediate effect was a race to get to the Pole. In 1908 Shackleton got to within 120 miles of it on a magnificent journey, discovering that the Pole was on a plateau 10,000 feet high. Most of the journey was done by the four men hauling their own sledges. He turned back just in time to avoid disaster from a food shortage and the severe autumn cold.

In 1910 both Scott and Amundsen led expeditions to the Ross Sea. The British group, of which the present writer was a member, relied mainly on man-hauled sledges, as opposed to the Norwegians, who relied on dogs. Starting from his base at the eastern end of the Ross ice shelf, Amundsen reached the Pole December 14, 1911, and Scott a month later. Amundsen's journey was a triumph for his technique of dog sledging. He started out with fifty two dogs and returned with twelve, having fed the weaker to the stronger as they traveled. The men returned to their ship, the famous *Fram*, fresh and strong, having averaged seventeen miles a day for their journey of 1600 miles.

Scott's ship *Terra Nova* photographed from a grotto in an iceberg during his voyage of 1910–13.

The fate of Scott and his party was grimly different. With the help of supporting parties he reached the Pole only slightly exhausted from the long pull up the Beardmore Glacier and over the plateau, but then fortune deserted him. The long strain had weakened his team and there was probably some incipient scurvy. Coming down the glacier, their strongest man failed and died, and when they reached the level surface of the Barrier, hoping for better weather, they found conditions even worse than on the plateau. Then Captain L. E. G. Oates got frostbitten feet, which delayed the party until he decided to help them the only way he could—by walking off to his death in a blizzard. Finally the last three, Scott, Wilson and H. R. Bowers, with one day's food supply, but when only eleven miles from a large food depot, were held up by a blizzard that howled continuously for nine days. One by one they weakened and died from cold and starvation, leaving brave letters of farewell when the last shreds of hope had gone.

The expedition had, in fact, attempted too wide a program. Another complication was that a second party of six men had been marooned 300 miles up the coast at the same time. With two parties missing and winter darkness coming on there was very little that those of us at the main base could do, though we made searches in each direction. The second party, after wintering for months in the cold and darkness of a cave cut in the ice, made their way back next spring. At the same time a search party looking for the Pole group came upon Scott's tent 140 miles away and brought back the diaries and the specimens the three men had clung to up to the last.

On the opposite side of the continent a German expedition was having misfortunes of its own. Wilhelm Filchner, already a celebrated traveler in Central Asia, had taken his ship farther into the treacherous Weddell Sea than anyone before him and he discovered a vast ice barrier similar to that edging the Ross Sea. He landed a party and built a hut on the floating ice shelf, which then broke up and floated off to the north. His ship was frozen in and drifted north for a whole winter, but fortunately escaped being crushed.

An Australian expedition under Douglas Mawson in 1912 and 1913 made an immense contribution to the knowledge of the continent's coast lines. They set up two stations on the mainland and between them surveyed nearly 100 miles of the coast, the position of which Wilkes, seventy years earlier, had suspected. During the main journey, led by Mawson himself, there was a double tragedy. First, one of his two companions fell into a crevasse and was lost; and then, after Mawson and his surviving companion were reduced to living on their last six dogs, the second man died from food poisoning. Mawson himself staggered on across the bleak ice alone for another 100 miles by sheer will power, an amazing feat of endurance.

Meanwhile the whaling industry in the Antarctic was leaping ahead mainly through the originality of the same Captain Larsen who had been with Nordenskjöld. Then in 1923 he broke all records by taking a steel ship of 13,000 tons into the Ross Sea, towing five small whale catchers through the pack ice. There the catchers found many whales, which were rendered into oil on the mother ship. The whalers made no discoveries

This water color by Wilson shows the Scott party setting off for the South Pole. Men, not dogs, pulled the sledges.

but they pioneered a method by which scores of even larger mother ships assisted in discoveries along the shores of the continent in the southern ocean.

Remote, isolated, and forbidding, the Antarctic Continent has been the greatest challenge to man's urge to discover his world, perhaps because it is far from the great centers of civilization, and because its environment is the most hostile known. It has provided earth-bound man with his greatest challenge of exploration. But modern technology, in the hands of men who know how to apply it, has tamed even the Antarctic. In the past few years about a dozen nations have been engaged in work on the continent. Supplied by air and sea and living in ice vaults, they are maintaining scientific stations along the coast and inland. Their purpose is to wrest from this lonely waste its last secrets.

Challenge of the unknown

No longer is it enough for an explorer to produce a narrative of his travels and a map of his route. Modern discovery and exploration have spread far beyond the earlier geographical aims of discovering new features of the earth's surface to include on maps.

The purpose of exploration today is no longer limited to finding out what is where but also *why* it is there, and for that the sister sciences are being called upon to take a prominent part in the story of discovery. The professional geologist, meteorologist, chemist, and physical anthropologist have become explorers of the twentieth century. The most revolutionary change in exploration is not its purpose, but its modern techniques—for example, the new forms of transport, the submarine, and the airplane, for getting a party to its destination quickly, the helicopter and snow tractor for swift and comfortable travel once at the site to be explored. The general risks in exploration today, however, are not necessarily less; they may be more wholesale, as in the loss of an aircraft or a spacecraft in the future.

Once all the larger areas of the world were known, at least in outline, the intensification of study of smaller areas was a natural development in the history of discovery. It is, after all, a process that is going on in all science, working steadily from the general to the particular, from matter that we can see to matter to be viewed only through a microscope and, further still, to matter that has to be deduced because it cannot be seen at all, like the atom.

We can draw an interesting parallel here with the explorers themselves. About the early migrations of men we know only the general directions and trends—the nomads' wanderings in the Middle East and the Huns' sweep across Asia into eastern and central Europe. At this stage in exploration we have no details or personalities. The second stage in the process is knowing who the individual explorers were, what they did, and exactly where they went. The third stage is represented by scientific exploration today; we know the name of the party but not always the

Skin divers are adding to our knowledge of flora and fauna of the vast undersea world.

names of individuals, and our interest is in the details of scientific value.

To the ordinary reader it may seem enough to explore only those regions where man himself can comfortably exist, the habitable surface of his planet. That does not satisfy the modern geographer. He must go on to explore regions which he cannot see and where he cannot live, the floors of the oceans, the atmosphere, and space beyond.

Man has been interested in the floor of the sea ever since he first "ploughed the vast ocean in his fragile bark"; in fact, because his bark was fragile, he had to plumb the sea's depths for shoals or rocks. The depths he was interested in grew with the size of his ships, but it was not until he thought of using the ocean floor to support telephone cables that he focused his attention on those depths. He then began to explore the new and strange world so graphically described by Kipling in his song of *The Deep Sea Cables:*

> The wrecks dissolve above us; their dust drops down from afar—
> Down to the dark, to the utter dark,
> where the blind white sea-snakes are.
> There is no sound, no echo of sound, in the deserts of the deep,
> Or the great grey level plains of ooze
> where the shell-burred cables creep.

Progress in mapping the floors of the oceans has been slow, and it has surprised us in many ways with the ocean floor's steep canyons, long, winding valleys, and mountains matching in height any of those visible to us. The invention of echo-sounding equipment speeded up hydrographic surveys, and now we have enough data to make maps which show the shape of the land below the sea. When these shapes are shown on relief maps, like the ones in this book, we have the most modern development of the map maker's art. Relief maps tell the story of the continents far better than normal maps, which show the continents ending abruptly at their shore lines and apparently floating in a featureless sea. These new maps reveal the great variety in the offshore features of the sea bottom—mighty cliffs and escarpments such as those off Peru, and abyssal deeps such as those off the Philippines.

The spectacular underwater discoveries being made today were pioneered by Matthew Maury, an American enthusiast, and the long voyage of H. M. S. *Challenger* in the early 1870s. Every year we are reaching greater depths in bathyspheres, steel spheres strong enough to resist the high pressures found thousands of feet below the surface. The recent descent of the United States Navy's bathyscaphe to the greatest ocean depth known was made in the spirit of twentieth-century undersea exploration. Such bathyscaphe descents are of value not only to mappers of the ocean deeps but to marine biologists as well.

A medieval portrayal of Alexander the Great lowered in a glass diving cage to study sea life.

The great difference between land above the sea and land below is that almost everywhere above sea level the winds and rain are eroding the surface, wearing down the land and washing the debris into the oceans, the giant rubbish heaps of nature. Under the sea, on the other hand, the process is mainly one of filling up, of deposition, and the nearer the continent the greater the rate of filling, when the seas are shallow.

With echo-sounding devices we can now measure the thickness of these deposits. In the most remote parts of the great oceans the rate is slower than near the shores. In the great depths of the open sea the ooze coating the ocean floor is made up of the remains of dead sea creatures mixed with cosmic dust from outer space. Over the past few years we have been driving hollow steel cylinders deep into the abyssal ooze and clays and bringing the cores to the surface for examination. There, in a few feet of sea bottom, we have a geological calendar dating back over thousands of years and recording past life in thin layers of reddish clay. Dating such deposits by radioactive methods is now standard.

For the most sterile, changeless, and monotonous region of the undersea world we must go to those parts of the Pacific, where we find the deepest wrinkles in the earth's crust, deeper than Everest is high. Here, at depths more than 30,000 feet, there is no light, little life, and hardly anything moves, since the water itself is nearly motionless, taking hundreds of years to change—a strange place indeed, where in the utter dark and silence change is slow. The occasional arrival of a speck of dust which has survived during its slow sinking adds one more speck to the ooze.

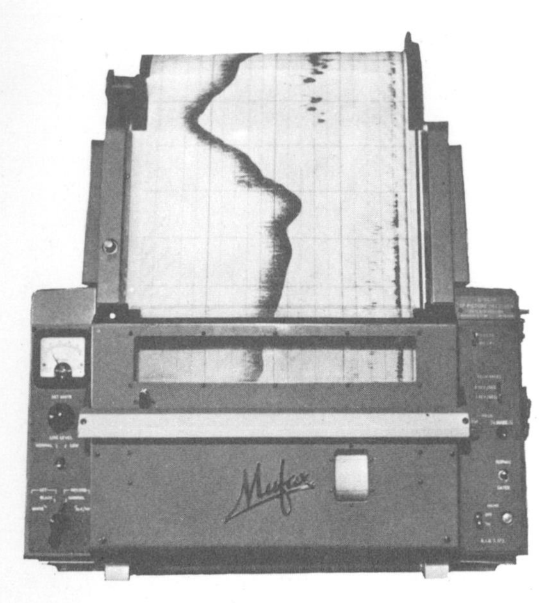

Profile records, made possible with echo-sounding equipment, enable scientists to map the sea floor.

Two features of the earth's surface—mountains and deserts—have long had a peculiar attraction to man, yet by themselves they do not properly belong in our story of discovery and exploration. Mountaineering is a comparatively modern development, only a century old, and began in the Alps of Switzerland, where it is still a thrilling and thriving sport.

When men first began to go far afield in search of mountains to climb, the sport became a form of exploration as well as a competition to collect as many peaks as possible to one's name. Such exploratory climbs include the conquest of South America's Aconcagua (23,000 feet) by Vines in 1897; of North America's Mt. McKinley (20,300 feet) by Hudson Stuck in 1913; and of Africa's Kilimanjaro (19,300 feet) by Hans Meyer in 1889, to mention the highest mountains of these three continents.

In recent years climbers have looked more to the Himalayas, and their climbs usually involved detailed exploration of the best approach. In this activity American, English, French, German, and Swiss climbers pioneered the approaches to Everest, all of which culminated in the successful ascent in 1953 by Edmund Hillary and Tenzing Norkay.

Unlike mountain climbing, the crossing of deserts must usually involve some exploration, and in contrast to mountaineering it relies more on careful organization than nerve and physical ability. For years the Gobi, Arabian, and Sahara deserts have attracted explorers, such as Wilfred Thesiger and Gertrude Bell in our day. Like the sea, deserts enable man to feel the immensity of his world; and like the polar regions, deserts challenge man by offering him a hostile environment. Desert exploration today is nearly all scientific. In areas where settlers followed early desert explorers, the settlers completed the knowledge of a particular region. On the other hand, those desert regions not suitable to settlement remain only partly explored, but the modern aids of powered transport with balloon tires and two-way radio communication have taken something out of desert travel; today it is the machine against the desert, rather than man against the desert.

The deep-diving bathyscaphe, *Trieste*, which has reached a seven-mile depth in the Marianas trench.

Even though polar exploration, too, has become mechanized, it nevertheless is scientific exploration of the highest order. After the First World War the use of aircraft for arctic travel soon showed that the ice-covered ocean had no more islands to reveal. The American Admiral Richard Byrd was the first to fly over the North Pole, in 1926. Later the Russians landed a party on polar ice and drifted with it down the east coast of Greenland. Stationing scientific parties on the drifting ice progressed after the Second World War. Some groups chose a particular kind of ice, known as an "ice island." Sledging along the north coast of

Ellesmere Land, British parties of 1875 and, later, Peary noticed a curious, corrugated type of ice, much thicker than sea ice, the ridges and hollows being very regularly spaced. Quite possibly these ice islands are made of land ice broken off from shore regions. They appear to withstand pressures better than sea ice, and for this reason survive for many years, joining in the general circulation of the Arctic Ocean.

In 1946, during routine flights over the North Pole for weather observations, American planes saw huge islands of this corrugated ice drifting round the polar sea. Parties have lived on these drifting islands for years as a new means of exploring the Arctic. The latest method of all, however, was first accomplished by the American atomic-powered submarine, the *Nautilus*, which cruised under the polar ice for nearly 2000 miles from the Pacific to the Atlantic.

The diverse specialities required of a small group of men taking part in modern scientific polar exploration can be seen in the following example: In 1930 a young Cambridge man named Gino Watkins, a student of the present writer and then twenty three years old, led an expedition to East Greenland to study the prospects for an arctic air route from Europe to Canada via Iceland and Greenland. He took thirteen companions, of an average age of twenty five, most of them from Cambridge and all of them with some special skill—surveying, meteorology, flying, radio, and so on.

Watkins depended strongly on such aptitudes in his men, and after eighteen months the expedition returned with better results than others of twice its size and three times its cost. Nearly all the party learned to use the Eskimo skin kayak, Watkins himself becoming as expert as any of the natives. High on the icecap the group set up a weather station, which had to be occupied by one man alone for five months. Two separate parties crossed Greenland along different routes and there was a 600-mile journey down the coast by kayak and motorboat. Such a record for a small expedition is admittedly unusual, but it shows how wide a scope modern exploration must be prepared to cover.

Today we have reached an age when aircraft and snow tractors have quickened the pace of polar discovery so much that we can mention only a few of the major achievements. The flight of the American, Lincoln Ellsworth, from Dundee Island off Trinity Peninsula to the Bay of Whales in 1935, was one such achievement. He flew 2000 miles across the continent with three landings along the way. Both before and after him Richard Byrd, who had flown over the South Pole in 1929, led large expeditions to the Ross Sea. Byrd's men made many flights over the continent and several surface journeys over the sector south of the Pacific. Americans have made themselves responsible for most of the exploration of that region.

In contrast with the earlier small and inexpensive expeditions, today's operations in the Antarctic are on a huge scale. Americans led the way with many times the usual number of men, tons of equipment, and organization made possible only by wireless and aircraft transport.

In 1946 the United States Navy carried out "Operation High Jump," which involved nearly 5000 men and ninety ships, organized in three divisions. One division set up a temporary base on the Ross Sea from which large airplanes flew from a runway of compressed snow. The other two divisions took carrier ships as close to the continent as possible and sent planes on photographic surveys, for which they took some 70,000 photographs. It was a highly useful preliminary to the International Geophysical Year, during which scientists from at least a dozen nations manned large stations in the Antarctic.

Mountaineering is a special kind of exploration which challenges the adventurous spirit of men. (Peru's Pumasillo—20,490 feet.)

This remarkable photograph shows the United States submarine *Skate* thrust partly through a ceiling of ice forty miles from the North Pole, July 30, 1958.

Of these the most spectacular is a base at the South Pole itself, established entirely through an airlift by the Americans under Rear Admiral George J. Dufek. Even more remote stations were built on the high plateau, both by Russians and Americans, and were supplied by air or snow tractor. The record low temperature so far on the plateau was recorded by the Russians: 144° F. below the freezing point of fresh water, which is not far from the freezing point of alcohol! Scott and the other brave explorers who first set foot on the great southern continent would be amazed if they could see it today.

At the same time as the I.G.Y. there was an important, smaller expedition. Privately organized and planned, it was led by Vivian Fuchs on the Weddell Sea side of the continent and Edmund Hillary on the Ross Sea side. The object of the expedition was a surface crossing of the Antarctic Continent. The Fuchs party of twelve men made the crossing with snow tractors, some 2000 miles in 99 days. They were met at the Pole by the Hillary party, which had laid depots for the second half of the journey.

This crossing of the continent by the Fuchs party represents something between the small private expedition of the past and large government-sponsored ventures. Of the twelve members eight were professional scientists, two were engineers, and there were a photographer and a radio operator. Each man was chosen so that he could dovetail into another's field if required. All had to be expert at tractor driving and maintenance, at navigation, at radio transmission; and each scientist had a shadow man who could assist him or even take his place if necessary. Thus the photographer, who was an eminent mountain climber, found himself navigating aircraft, driving dog teams, taking over meteorological observations, and helping in the seismic sounding.

When the going was bad, everyone had to lend a hand in finding a route through crevasses or in rigging gear to rescue men or machines which had fallen into them. When the going was good, the most strenuous part of the day was when they had camped. On top of all the ordinary chores of pitching camp, tending the dogs, and the mending the gear, equipment had to be set up for sounding the depth of the icecap and weather observations had to be made and sent out by radio. In the middle of all the hustle a large dinner bell would ring out over the snow, a signal for everyone to shut off all engines and to stand still while the delicate instruments responded to an explosion of ten pounds of gelignite, which sent smoke rings high into the air and pressure rings down into the icecap to the rock below. As a result of all this camp activity the party rarely had more than six hours' sleep out of the twenty four, and they came to regard lack of sleep as the greatest hardship of their journey.

The use of modern inventions has forced the explorer to become a specialist as well as a general handy man. Most people could mend a broken trace or patch a tent, but it takes an expert to repair a faulty radio transmitter or weld a cracked engine shaft. Nevertheless, it is the proper blending of the modern techniques with the older ones that obtain the best results. Perhaps an example will make the point clear.

Fifty years ago an area in McMurdo Sound was mapped by a party of four, man-hauling their sledges. The writer was in charge of the survey work and managed to produce a map with a theodolite and plane table. Recently another party of four men, using dog teams reinforced by airplanes dropping supplies, went into the same region and surveyed five times the area in the same time and much more accurately, using a theodolite and air photographs. The principles followed in each case were the same, but the combination of air transport and dog teams increased the rate and the value of the work enormously.

All this is discovery of an exciting kind, though the layman can take little part in it. Still less can he join in or even understand the exploration of the upper atmosphere, which is now in full swing by means of rockets, artificial satellites, and by indirect methods of mathematical physicists. The present chapter in the story of discovery and exploration—now being written by scientists the world over—is becoming so complicated and obscure that only the highly trained scientist can write or read it.

Surveyors of the Fuchs expedition, which crossed the Antarctic Continent during the I.G.Y.

Tractor trains like this United States unit, on its way to Little America, have revolutionized travel in the polar regions.

Conclusion

We know next to nothing about man's first discoveries, of his very earliest wanderings to the four corners of his world. There was, it seems, never a time when man was not, as the prophet Job said of Satan, "going to and fro in the earth and walking up and down in it." Later, when man's journeyings became more organized and more purposeful, there was still little record, so it is but a half-told tale. There is no script of those first bold voyagers by land and sea; their stories are written only in votive mounds or broken shards, or in silent monoliths of stone. What we have of the story is utterly dwarfed by what is missing, just as in history one Caesar lives while a thousand are forgotten. Yet the story is still growing and in ever-increasing volume, for expeditions of one kind or another are constantly in the news, and some of them, even those of schoolboys, add to our knowledge and our maps.

One change that has come about gradually in organized exploration is the younger age of the individual explorers. Today there are many more geographical societies and explorers' clubs than there were a century ago, and the people who belong to these organizations are usually ready to advise and assist university students and other young men who are eager to put their love of adventure to good use. What journalists call the "lure of the unknown" is as active in man today as ever in the past.

There is another change in the aura of exploration, and it has a double-edged effect on the men who explore. Publicity is now a very important factor in most of the activities of man, and whether it is courted or shunned it has to be considered in any expedition. The power of the press is enormous and so are its resources. An early instance was Stanley's search for Livingstone, promoted by a newspaper and written in journalistic style. Stanley told the truth as he saw it, but his example of reporting has not always been followed. Responsible editors always demand the truth from their reporters, but unfortunately "plain truth will influence half a score of men while mystery will lead a million by the nose," and the temptation to garnish the truth or scent a scandal is sometimes too great. The result is that instead of having little or no record of exploration, as in medieval times, we now have an embarrassment of tales of travels. Today we can visit any part of the world by going to a lending library, and we can view most of their landscapes on our television screens.

Today man is master of his globe. He can travel over vast distances and is now planning journeys undreamed of by the Polos, Da Gama, and Magellan. He is reaching out to the moon, and he dreams of ultimate exploration of the sister planets and of solar systems other than his own.

The limited horizon of earliest man has now stretched to infinite space.

Space exploration

In October 1957, when Sputnik I was fired into orbit about the earth, people realized that a new "Great Age of Discovery" had begun. For the first time in human history, man is planning to leave the planet on which he has lived for some half-million years and achieve his age-old ambition to reach for the stars.

Early exploration was usually the work of a few men or even a lone traveler. The Polo brothers traveled from Italy to Turkestan, Mongolia, China, and India—sometimes as members of caravans, other times alone with their porters. Mungo Park, with only a few men, explored the Niger in West Africa; and Livingstone, traveling alone with a few porters, discovered much unknown territory in central Africa. But in the late nineteenth century exploration became much more of a team effort. It was team effort that made the conquest of Everest possible. Systematically camps were established at different heights, and at each one the number of men continuing toward the summit decreased. Finally two men alone, according to a carefully worked plan, were chosen to make the final ascent.

The field specialists required to make the Everest expedition successful included porters, medical men, dietitians, geologists, and meteorologists as well as the actual climbers. Furthermore, without specially devised equipment—oxygen masks, cold-weather clothing, concentrated foods, and climbing apparatus—Hillary and Tenzing could not have reached the summit. If specialized equipment is essential for exploration of the less hospitable regions of our own planet, how impossible it is for man to enter space without very much more elaborate and expensive equipment. The day of the lone explorer discovering new lands is past, for no one man could build a space craft and travel beyond the confines of the earth without hundreds of scientists and technicians to help him.

In 1785 Blanchard and Jeffries became the first men to cross the English Channel by air. Their craft was a hydrogen-filled balloon.

Space travel has interested men for centuries, the earliest fictional story of a journey to the moon having been written by Lucian of Samos in A.D. 160. But it was not until the early seventeenth century, after the invention of the telescope by Galileo, that the subject again fired man's imagination. Toward the end of the nineteenth century the efforts to invent a machine that would fly in the air led to man's first cautious steps into space, although at that time little was known about the differences between aeronautics and astronautics. However eventually it became clear that few of man's inventions for travel through the air would be of use for travel through outer space. For one thing, in space there is no air to hold up the conventional winged aircraft, nor is there oxygen to feed air-breathing jet and reciprocating engines. Lighter-than-air balloons too, would be just as useless in the near vacuum of space. There was only one existing machine that would serve—the rocket.

Until experiments made at the end of the nineteenth century, the rocket had been used mainly for fireworks displays, to a lesser extent in medieval warfare, and more recently for lifesaving at sea. The rocket works independently of its surroundings and can move as well in a vacuum as in an atmosphere; in fact it works best in a vacuum, for there is no air friction to hinder its motion. The explosion of fuel in the combustion chamber exerts pressure on the front and inside walls of the chamber. Since the rear of the chamber is open, the exploding gases escape and in the process produce thrust, pushing the rocket forward whether it is in the air or in outer space. The rocket is not dependent on air because it carries its own oxygen supply with which to burn its fuel.

Early rockets were powered by solid fuels, but these had the disadvantage that the propellant was housed in the combustion chamber, which had to be made extra strong to withstand pressures developed during combustion; also the additional weight limited the range of the rocket. Neither was it possible to control combustion once it had been started. Liquid propellants, although requiring much more complex and expensive machinery, can be controlled and used to cool the combustion chamber. But even with liquid propellants the fuel makes up six sevenths of the weight of the rocket and burns out in a few minutes. Increasing the fuel load in order to increase burning time to achieve a longer period of thrust means a larger and heavier rocket to house the fuel, which in turn means more fuel to move the heavier rocket, a vicious circle. (Recently many of the early disadvantages of solid fuels have been overcome, so these solid propellants have again become popular.)

On December 17, 1903, the Wright brothers made aviation history by achieving sustained powered flight.

To overcome this problem, the step rocket was invented. Two or more rockets are mounted one on top of the other. The first and largest stage takes the assembly into the air. When its fuel is exhausted, it breaks away from the assembly and the second stage, with the momentum of the first, ignites, and so on until a much greater speed is obtained for the final stage.

It was with these multistage rockets that Sputnik I was launched, followed by Sputnik II a month later, and the American Explorer I in January 1958. In December 1958 the "talking satellite" Atlas was sent up, and broadcast Christmas greetings to the world from President Eisenhower. In the first few days of 1959 the Russians launched Lunik I at the moon, but it did not pass near enough and went into orbit around the sun—the first man-made "planet" in the solar system. During 1959 the Russians succeeded in landing a rocket on the moon and in sending another around the moon to photograph the side which never faces the earth, hitherto unseen by man. Animals have been sent into space; the Russians have sent a dog up in one of their Sputniks and Americans have sent monkeys high above the earth and have recovered them alive.

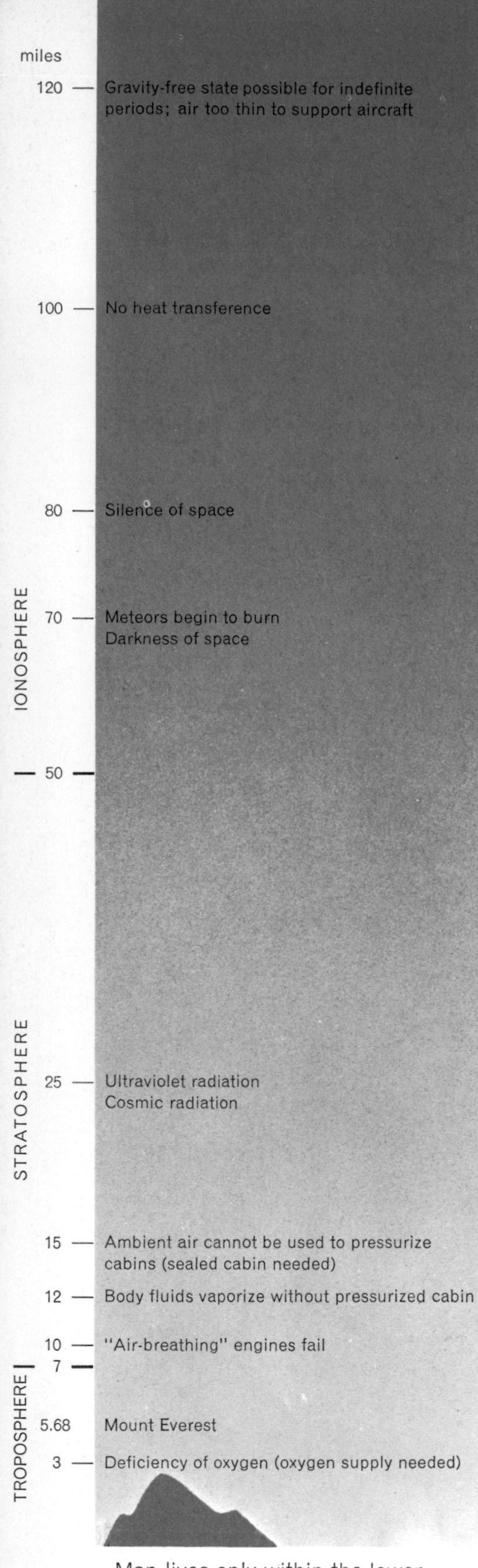

Man lives only within the lower three and a half miles of the earth's atmosphere, where pressure and temperature meet his needs. Above this height, conditions of outer space are found. To enter this hostile region, man must simulate his sea-level environment by artificial means.

Research with high-altitude rockets and artificial satellites is being carried on for many reasons: to learn more about the density and other properties of the upper atmosphere, to learn about the earth's gravitational field and radiation areas surrounding our planet, and to examine the environment of space—temperature, density, number of small meteors, and so on. Eventually all of this information will be used by rocket engineers, who will build the first space vehicle designed to carry man across space.

It is the adventurous spirit of man, combined with his scientific curiosity, that is causing us to reach for the stars. The motives which inspired Stone Age man to explore are fundamentally the same motives that make twentieth-century man want to explore the deserts and dark regions of Mars and gaze on the cloud-veiled surface of Venus. Although most exploration so far in our history has been limited by local or national interest, space exploration on a large scale is likely to be of interest to the whole world, and could have a unifying effect.

The problems that confront man in space exploration are very different from those he has encountered in exploring his native planet. When a space craft leaves the earth, those inside will have no weight and will float about freely unless some means is devised to counteract weightlessness. The absence of gravity will make the directional terms "up" and "down" meaningless, both psychologically and physiologically. To date we do not know whether a man could perform well—or at all—in a long-term state of weightlessness. So far our jet planes have been able to simulate weightlessness for only short periods, from forty seconds up to a minute or so. Some test subjects have enjoyed the sensation and have learned to perform well in the gravity-free state; others have reacted violently to it, developing vertigo and severe nausea. How well a man will be able to tolerate long-term weightlessness is still unknown and will remain unknown until the first men are placed in space.

The deadly silence of space could also pose a problem. All of the familiar background sounds of our planet will be left behind—the wind rustling the leaves, street sounds, the chirping of birds, the bark of a dog, the chatter of children—all the reassuring sounds. To keep man at ease in space it may be necessary to supply him with tape recordings of his familiar sound environment. He will also leave behind his twenty-four-hour day-night cycle. In space there is only eternal night, so periods of sleep, work, and relaxation will have to be carefully worked out in advance. There will also be the problem of confinement—a few men locked into a small cabin for weeks or months on end with no possibility of being alone. The crew for such a flight will have to be chosen with utmost care to reduce the possibility of one man's getting on another man's nerves. Space psychologists have learned much about the problems of confinement from submariners and polar explorers, who have faced the problem for many years but not on the scale space explorers will one day have to face it.

Explorers of the past have always operated within the familiar environment of their native planet. Their problems have been those of water and food provisions in areas where food and water were scarce, of keeping cool in tropical regions and warm in the polar regions, and of avoiding disease. The hostile environment of space demands that the space explorer live in a completely artificial environment of his own making, one that he will have to carry with him everywhere he travels. He will live in a sealed cabin which will have to be provided with the proper air mixture kept at a comfortable pressure and temperature. Maintaining such a closed ecological system is very difficult. The major problem is oxygen. Each inward breath of oxygen means an outward breath of carbon dioxide, which must be kept at a controllable minimum. It will not be possible simply to pump oxygen into the cabin endlessly as it is used up, since this would steadily increase the atmospheric pressure within the cabin. The problem is devising a way to convert the exhaled carbon dioxide back into useful oxygen. Algae may be used to perform this task. In the presence of sunlight these tiny organisms convert carbon dioxide into oxygen; at the same time they are a valuable food source of protein. The biological problems of survival in space are only beginning to be solved; much more research must be done before the first space crew can leave on a prolonged journey.

Astronavigation bears little resemblance to terrestrial navigation. The four-hundred-year accumulation of terrestrial maps and charts will be of no use to the astronavigator. In space the familiar earth co-ordinates are meaningless, for outside a magnetic field the points of the mariner's compass are meaningless. A whole new system of navigation will grow out of space travel.

The type of man selected for space exploration will not be very different from the early scientific explorers. He will have to be in prime physical condition, have a calm disposition, and be of superior intelligence and in command of the necessary scientific knowledge. His closest counterpart in terrestrial exploration perhaps is the polar explorer, who has his primary duties but must be able to take over another man's job in an emergency—he must be a combination of scientist, mechanic, radio operator, and handy man. In space exploration the crew will be largely subordinated to the intricate machines that will carry and guide them to

Putting a man into space is less of a problem than getting him back alive. These photographs show a re-entry capsule of the Project Mercury type being fitted to the booster rocket (left) and being fired to a height of 55 miles (right). Diagram below shows principle of a rocket.

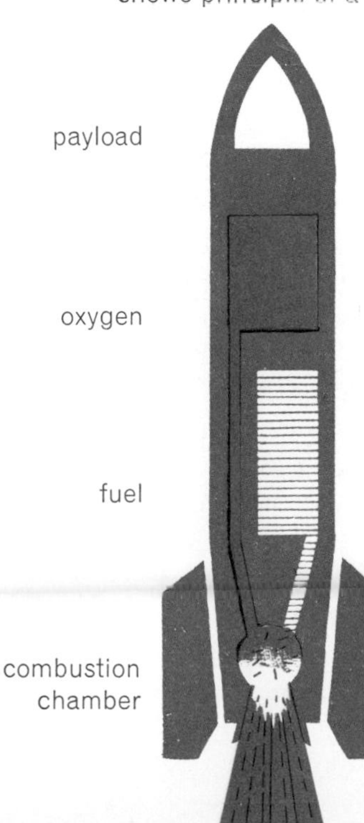

other planets, and these machines will be very costly. The expense of space travel on a grand scale may well mean that every nation will have to contribute toward the cost.

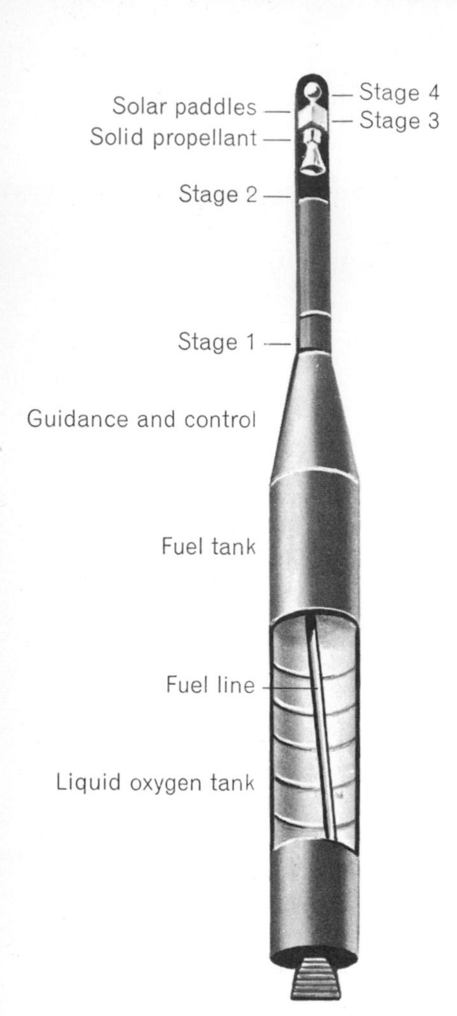

Because the moon is our nearest neighbor in space, at a mean distance of 238,000 miles, it undoubtedly will be our first objective for manned space flight; already we have reached the moon with unmanned rockets. This, our own satellite, is thought to be a dead, hostile world with practically no atmosphere. During its two weeks of continuous daylight the temperature exceeds 200° F., then during the following two weeks of night the temperature plunges to more than –200° F. A small world, the moon is only 2160 miles in diameter. Some astronomers have suggested that the moon's primary use might be that of a steppingstone to the planets. Local rockets would carry space crews to the lunar base, where they would prepare for their interplanetary journeys.

After the moon, manned probes eventually will be sent to the closest planetary targets—Venus and Mars. Venus, regarded as a sister planet to the earth, has always been an object of curiosity and mystery, first because she is so near to us and secondly because she is eternally covered with a thick layer of cloud which hides her surface. We know irritatingly little about Venus. The planet's diameter is thought to be very nearly the same as that of the earth, but we do not even know the rate of rotation or the equatorial plane. Neither do we know if it supports life of any sort, but the possibility cannot be ruled out. At its closest approach Venus is about 26 million miles from our planet.

We know much more about Mars, which is smaller (with a diameter of about 4140 miles) and colder than Earth. On its closest approach Mars is about 35 million miles away from us. What the telescope reveals about Mars makes it an interesting planet. The famous "canals," once popularly believed to be the remains of man-made features, are now thought to be either natural markings or optical illusions. Dark patches on the planet appear to change color, shape, and size with the seasons as the polar cap melts. Many astronomers think that these are areas of vegetation of some sort. Martian temperatures vary widely with day and night and with the seasons. In summer at night the planet is gripped in intense cold, but at

"Paddlewheel" satellites are fitted with solar batteries which are recharged by energy from sunlight. This gives the satellite's radio transmitters a long life. Above is a Thor-Able III rocket with a paddlewheel satellite in place.

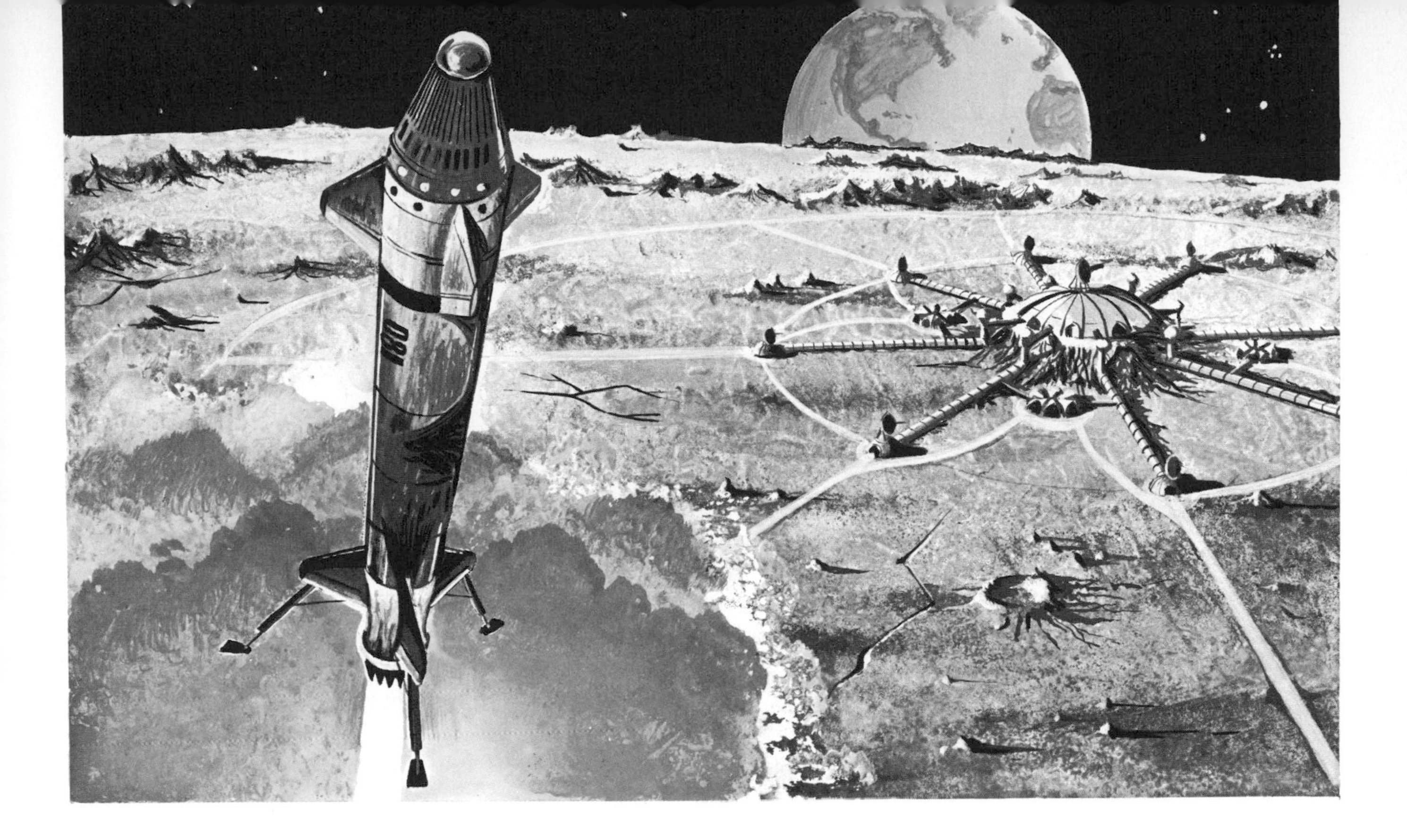

Artist's version of a lunar base. Pot lid structure with radiating arms is pressurized to simulate atmospheric conditions on earth. Roads extending from the central station would be traveled by tractor-type vehicles which would make scientific surveys of the moon's surface. Shuttle rockets, like the one in foreground, would bring supplies from earth and rotate the lunar crew.

high noon it may be in the mid-seventies on the deserts, possibly warmer in the dark areas. The planet's atmosphere, at ground level thought to be no denser than our own atmosphere at an altitude of about 50,000 feet, seems to be composed mostly of nitrogen with only small traces of oxygen and water vapor. Scientist-explorers on Mars would probably concentrate their early attention on the areas of "vegetation," and the very active orange-red deserts.

Of the rest of the solar system, Mercury, the innermost planet, has great extremes of heat and cold (from near absolute zero on its "night" side to 700° F. on its "day" side) and is without an atmosphere. The outer planets—Jupiter, Saturn, Uranus, Neptune, and Pluto—are all extremely cold, and man would not be able to exist in their poisonous atmospheres, which are made up largely of methane. It is thought, too, that the outer planets may consist mainly of liquid or even gaseous matter. Some of the larger satellites of the outer planets, however, may make suitable landing sites for space explorers. There is a wide belt of very small planets, called the asteroids, lying between Mars and Jupiter. The largest of these, too, could be landed upon.

Distances outside the solar system are so vast that measurement is not made in miles but in light-years, the distance light travels in a year. The nearest star, Proxima Centauri, is four light-years away. Other stars are thousands and millions of light-years away. As we see them in our great telescopes we do not see them as they are now, but as they were long before man appeared on this planet. It has taken their light that long to reach us. At present no human invention exists that could transport us over such vast distances, and it seems very unlikely that within the lifetime of those of us living today man's thirst for direct knowledge of the stars will be quenched. But what of the future? In past ages many things have been regarded as impossible, only later to be achieved by man's indomitable spirit.

Ships and Navigation

The ease of traveling by water as opposed to land must have appealed to man early in his career as an explorer. His experiments with boats grew from his observations of objects floating on water—a log floating down a river or ducks on a pond. Early steps in the evolution of boats are easy to imagine, from a bundle of hollow reeds or a rough log to the dugout canoe, and on to the framed coracle.

Boats well illustrate the idea that "necessity is the mother of invention." Otherwise how can we explain the extraordinary efficiency of the Eskimo kayak and the swift catamarans of the Marianas Islanders? Magellan found that catamarans could literally sail rings round his ship's boats, and Frobisher commented on kayaks by saying, "so swift are they in rowing, it had been lost time to have chased them." Both craft are so perfectly shaped for their purpose that the white man has adopted them for his sport, the kayak for running rapids, boats of catamaran type for yacht racing. These early boats are all the more wonderful when we consider that they are both products of the Stone Age and were proportioned by eye alone, without any means of measurement.

Chinese junks

Our earliest record of ships are images painted on vases and cut in stone. From them we know that the Egyptians of at least 5000 B.C. had boats with mast and sail, rising prow and steering oar. These may have been the prototype of the later Minoan and Phoenician ships, by which time there were marked differences in shape and construction between the ships of war and those for carrying merchandise.

Quite possibly the Chinese and Arabs were acquiring skill in shipbuilding at the same time as the Egyptians, but we do not know. By the time we meet people of the Far East and Persian Gulf in history the Chinese junk and the Arabian dhow were as efficient for their own purposes as the vessels of the Mediterranean, the junk for carrying cargoes along coastal routes and the dhow for ocean travel.

From at least the beginning of the Christian era the Arabs and the Chinese had been evolving ships suited to their own purposes, particularly to the monsoon winds. The Arabian dhow has changed little over the past 1000 years, its characteristics being a very sloping stem at the bows and a short, stout mast supporting an enormous yard. Their size was rarely above 200 tons. The Chinese junk has changed even less, so far as we know. With bluff and upright stems and high sterns they were a complete contrast to the dhows, slower but much more capacious. Even in the time of Marco Polo they seem to have been up to 800 tons' burden and carried enormous crews to handle the heavy yards and mats of sails. One peculiarity of the junks was that the stern was set below the hull but could be raised in shallow water.

Whether the East or the West was earlier in shipbuilding, our best records come from Egyptian inscriptions and carvings. The clearest ones show ships of Queen Hatshepsut, about 1500 B.C., on a trading voyage to the land of Punt, somewhere beyond the southern end of the Red Sea. They portray an advanced type of ship with a large central mast, a yard and boom for a square sail, and fifteen rowers on each side. They have a good deal of overhang at bow and stern but the tendency to hog, or bend, was counteracted by a stout cable attached to each end of the ship and passing over forked posts along the center line (see page 25). These ships were probably about sixty feet long.

The Minoans and Phoenicians improved the early Egyptian models, mostly by increasing the ships' carrying capacity and seaworthiness. The Phoenicians, the leading maritime people of the Mediterranean for a thousand years, were not only great traders but they had that *sine qua non* for suc-

A Roman merchant ship with a lighthouse in the background.

cess, a real love for the sea. One great change in design came about during that period. They provided all of their ships with a ram at the bow for use in battle, necessary even in merchant ships to protect their cargo against the many pirates of the Aegean Sea. The Greeks and Romans brought the biremes and triremes into fashion with their two or three banks of oars. These many-oared galleys of the Mediterranean died hard; not until sailing ships grew too large did they cease to carry oars for use when they were becalmed or when they entered a narrow harbor.

The size of Mediterranean ships in late B.C. times was very impressive. The ship in which St. Paul was wrecked on Malta carried nearly 300 people. By that time the large single mast was beginning to be reinforced by a smaller one leaning forward in the bows, which later developed into the bowsprit and spritsail of medieval ships. The seamen of the time were beginning to make more of a beam wind and needed a small sail which could be trimmed hard round to help in tacking.

On the Atlantic coasts of northwest Europe the design of vessels had to be somewhat different to cope with the great range of tides and the long lee shores. When Caesar invaded Britain he complained that his carpenters could not build ships as suitable as those of the native tribes of Brittany. Not long after that invasion, vessels on the German and Scandinavian coasts developed into the famous long ships of the Vikings.

Used mainly for raiding voyages, these boats were double-ended, were of shallow draft, and were stoutly built for frequent beaching rather than for anchoring offshore. Powered by a square sail and by oars manned by the warriors, they were ideal for surprise raids in the shallow estuaries of England and France. By the tenth century these ships were built with a greater beam and were voyaging as far as Iceland and Greenland with families and cattle. Archeologists have uncovered several Viking craft from the long mounds where they were buried with their commanders as part of the ritual of mourning. Even the smaller of these ships were remarkably seaworthy, as was proved at the end of last century. An exact model of the one dug out at Gokstad in Norway was built and sailed across to America by the descendants of the Norsemen.

Seal of Ipswich

From the time of the Norman conquest the nations facing on the Atlantic gradually overtook the Mediterranean peoples in the art of shipbuilding. The stern rudder replaced the clumsy steering oar; a mizzen-mast for fore and aft sail; and a higher freeboard with multiple decks.

The famous caravels and carracks of the fifteenth and sixteenth centuries are represented by the most famous of them all—the hundred-ton *Santa Maria* of Columbus, though she was a slow sailer and not the best of her type. She had three masts (the mizzen, carrying a lateen sail), was ninety feet long, had a twenty-foot beam, and a crew of fifty two.

Though the ships of the Great Age of Discovery had to carry far more stores and water than any before them, they did not increase in size very rapidly. Drake's *Golden Hind* was only a hundred tons and had a crew of about sixty men. His longest voyage was sixty eight days from California to the Philippines. Large ships were a disadvantage in unknown waters; Dampier's *Roebuck* in 1700 was under 300 tons, while Cook's *Endeavour* was only 360 tons. Until the end of the days of sail, so far as exploring ships were concerned, the ships were built and selected for stoutness and handiness above all. Even though the sizes and shapes of ships changed slowly, there were steady improvements in the rigging, in anchors, the sheaves for running gear, and the hundred and one extras that make seamanship the skilled profession it has always been.

The introduction of iron ships powered by steam changed the character of ships enormously, but there is no need to trace their evolution any further. Today we have ten thousand-ton icebreakers which can ram ice ten feet thick at a speed of sixteen knots, and we have atomic-powered submarines which can find their way under ice for a thousand miles.

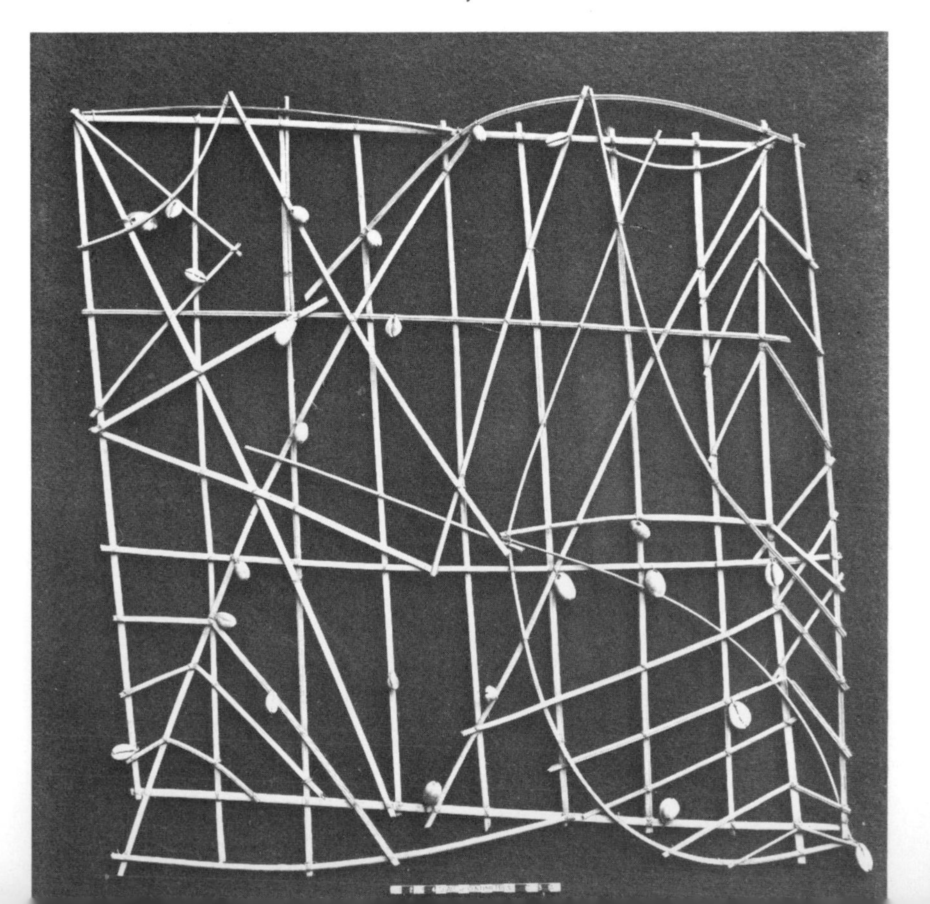

Bamboo and shell navigation chart of the Marshall islanders. The shells represent islands, while the bamboo strips represent ocean swells and complex currents.

When men built craft strong enough to take them far from land they had to develop a system of navigation. The Polynesians and other early seamen must have used all the natural signs that were available—stars and sun, steady winds, currents, flight of birds, and so on. Picturesque stories of such methods have come down to us from earliest times in verse or legend, from Homer's Ulysses' steering by the stars to Noah's sending out the raven and the dove from the ark.

Long before there was any thought of a compass men knew east and west by sunrise and sunset; and they knew north and south by seeing certain stars that circle the North Pole. Steering by the sun or stars meant that the navigator had to allow for the steady motion of these bodies across the sky. His knowledge of celestial navigation had to be gained purely by trial and error.

The early navigators of the Mediterranean had little difficulty finding land, since they were never farther from shore than about 150 miles. So their skill as navigators required experience in recognizing the land they were approaching and in taking soundings. The square sails of that day demanded that a ship be kept well off a lee shore and well out to sea during a voyage. The famous Tower of the Winds at Athens shows how strongly the Greeks relied on the regular winds, of which they named four as being intermediate between the four cardinal points of the compass.

The Greek philosophers and, later, Ptolemy in A.D. 150 had devised a system similar to our latitude and longitude, but it was not used by seamen until more than a thousand years later. Nor during that time were there charts as we know them today, although there were sailing directions. We know of more than one periplous, or description of a "voyage round a coast," simply a list of ports and capes, giving the distances between and an occasional note about which winds would serve best and what trade was to be had at the various places. The only appliance used by the pilots was a sounding rod, or line; everything else was based on judgment or experience.

Although the properties of the loadstone or magnetic iron had been known from the earliest days by the Greeks and the Chinese, the directive property of a magnetized needle was not thought of until about the twelfth century, when it was developed by Mediterranean seamen. The first written record of a needle stuck through a straw and floated in a bowl of water is dated 1218, but the method was spoken of as a regular practice. It was some time before someone thought of balancing a needle on a point and allowing it to swing over a card; and it was still longer before the needle was glued underneath a card so the card itself could swing. The use of the compass meant a way to set and follow a course toward a port, and with the compass came the practice of keeping track of the passage of time along a given course with an hourglass of running sand.

Finding latitude at sea by observing the northern stars may have been first used in the Indian Ocean, for Marco Polo describes some such practice in 1290. The Arabs also appear to have invented the first form of what later became the cross-staff of the western nations. It consisted of a short piece of wood sliding along a longer piece with graduations marked on it. By holding one end to the eye the crosspiece was slid along until it subtended the angle between the star and the horizon, which was then read from the scale.

The European seaman did not take to the astronomers' methods of finding latitude until the time of Henry the Navigator, when the standard instruments became the quadrant and the seaman's astrolabe. In using the quadrant to measure the altitude of a star, the navigator sighted the

Directive properties of magnetized needles were not known until the 1100s. This Chinese ship's compass was made in the 1800s.

This crown compass of 1790 has a free-swinging card. It was hung overhead and read from the bottom.

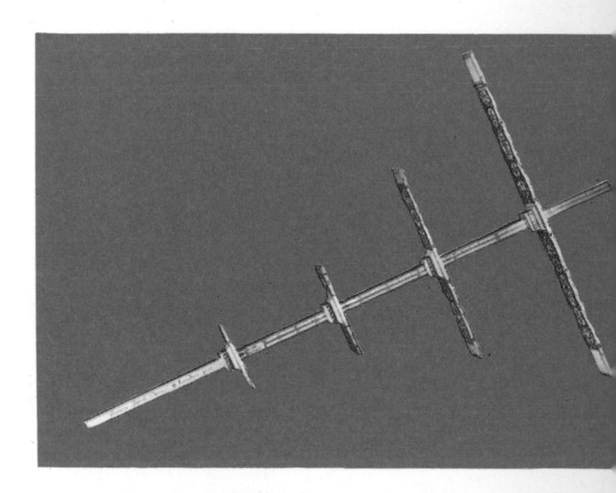

The cross-staff, used to find the altitude of a star, may first have been developed by the Arabs.

The mariner's astrolabe, used for finding latitude. It was accurate to within half a degree.

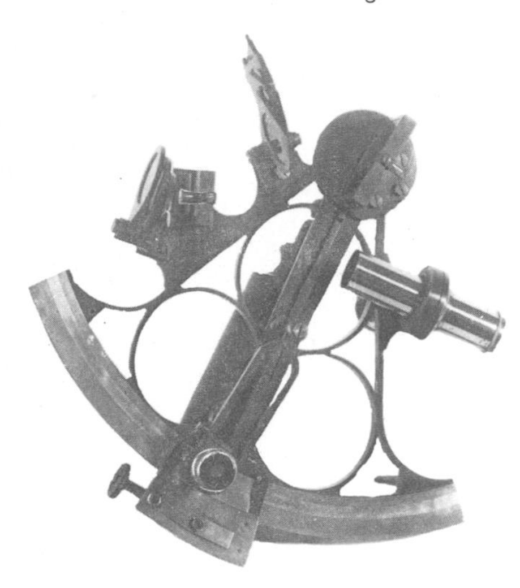

Sextants, developed in the 1700s to measure a star's altitude, were accurate to a sixtieth of a degree.

Harrison's chronometer, which won the famous British prize offered for discovering longitude at sea.

star along one of the sides. A plumb line hanging from the corner of the quadrant showed the angle of tilt on a scale along the curved arc. The seaman's astrolabe was an adaptation of the astronomers' astrolabe for land use. It was made of heavy metal and consisted of a circle inscribed in degrees, across which an arm with sighting holes could be directed to the sun or star. It hung by rings from the thumb or finger and acted as a plumb line.

Both instruments were difficult to use at sea because of the motion of the ship, but a series of observations would give an angle correct to within half a degree. Columbus used both of these instruments on his voyages; but using them meant that he needed two sets of tables, one of the sun's daily movement north or south of the Equator and another of the major stars in the sky. Both sun and stars had to be observed as they crossed the local meridian, so there was only one chance a day with the sun but one for each star in the tables at night.

Because latitude was more easily determined than longitude, navigators developed the habit of making for the latitude of the port well to the east or west and then running along the latitude until the landfall was made. This was a foolproof method which continued until better methods of finding longitude were devised. First they had to invent better instruments for measuring altitude. This came early in the eighteenth century when John Hadley and, independently, Thomas Godfrey, followed by Newton, made the first sextant, an instrument much easier to use on a rolling ship than a quadrant and one capable of an accuracy of a sixtieth of a degree. Latitude was then a simple matter, but longitude was still very uncertain and on a long voyage out of sight of land the ship's captain might easily be a hundred miles off in his calculation of the ship's longitude.

Inability to determine longitude accurately was responsible for many disasters, so in 1714 the British Government offered a reward of £20,000 for "such Person as shall discover the longitude at sea." The annals of the Board of Longitude, created for governing the award, are full of fanciful suggestions for "finding the longitude." When Newton was asked to join the board he replied in an impish mood, saying he was not aware that the longitude had ever been lost.

Difference of longitude is really the difference between local time and Greenwich time, so the real solution to the longitude problem lay in making a clock which would keep Greenwich time to great accuracy. This was done by John Harrison, the son of a Yorkshire carpenter. Since Harrison's time clockmakers have developed the chronometer, a more precise timepiece which has become a standard instrument for both sea and air navigation.

The evolution of the sea chart, which must also be considered an instrument for navigation, tended to lag behind that of other navigational aids. The first true seaman's charts were made near the beginning of the fourteenth century by the pilots of the western end of the Mediterranean. The first one set the pattern for those that followed. These "Portolano charts," as they were called, were used at sea and handed down from one pilot to another for two centuries. They were drawn on sheepskin parchment and in a style all of their own. Only coastal detail appeared on them, with the names of headlands, ports, and so on. Inscribed over the map was a network of lines and circles used for setting a course from one port to another. These portolanos gradually gave way to the maps of land-map makers, of whom Gerardus Mercator was the most helpful to the seaman.

Portolano charts like this one (about 1500) were a crisscross of lines used for setting a course from one port to another.

About 1560 Mercator invented the projection now called by his name. This revolutionized charts for navigation, since from a Mercator projection a pilot could determine his compass course simply by drawing a straight line to his destination, even though the resulting course was not always the shortest route. To this day practically all charts are drawn on a Mercator projection in spite of their distortions of scale as one moves away from the Equator. The projection is also ideal for plotting a ship's position found by the only other advance in navigation we need deal with.

The method was devised in the middle of last century and is known as "position-line plotting." By knowing the altitude of a single heavenly body the navigator can draw a line on a map and know that his ship is somewhere along that line. The altitude of a second star will give another position line, and where the two intersect is the ship's position. It is a method in almost universal use today.

In the present century so many advances in navigation aids have been made that we can mention only a few. The first important result of wireless was that ships at sea could receive time signals to a degree of precision rarely attained by chronometers. Echo sounding was another precision aid giving immediate and continuous information of the depth of water. Radar and other electronic devices gave warning in fog of the presence of other ships, of land, or of icebergs.

When discovery by air was made possible, the same devices were useful for air navigation, while aerial photography developed rapidly as a means of surveying rough or impassable territory. The fact that atomic-powered submarines have navigated with perfect safety under a thousand miles of ice in the Arctic shows the high degree of precision of current methods of navigation.

Famous explorers and their routes

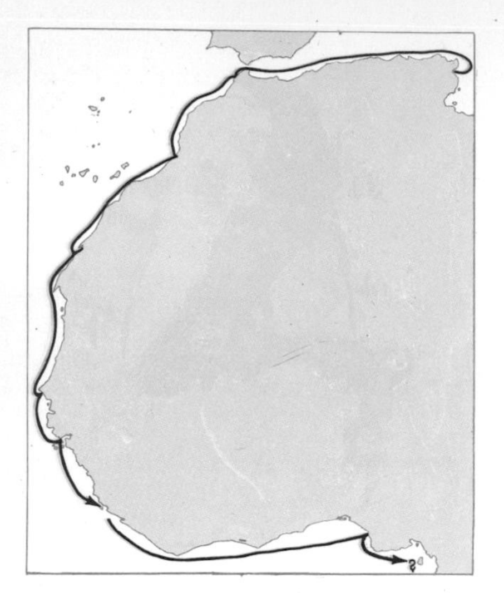

HANNO
(?)–450 B.C. (?) Carthage
about 470 B.C.: Led a voyage of Phoenicians along north and west coast of Africa as far as Sierra Leone; may have gone farther.

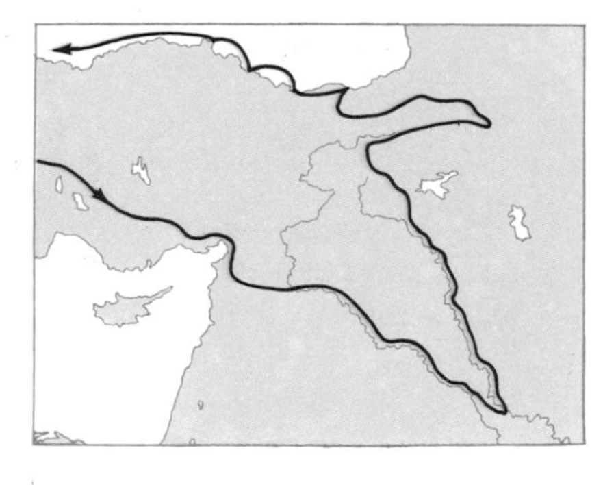

XENOPHON
(?) 430–355 B.C. Greece
401 B.C.: Traveled with Greek army to vicinity of Baghdad; from there he led the army across 3000 miles back to Greece via Kurdistan, Armenia, Georgia, Trebizond, Scutari, and the Black Sea.

ALEXANDER
356–323 B.C. Macedonia
See text on page 33 to 36; map on page 37.

NEARCHUS
(?)–about 312 B.C. Crete
See text on page 35; map on page 37.

PYTHEAS
(?)–310 B.C. Greece
(Born in the Greek colony of Marseilles.)
about 325 B.C.: Left Marseilles, sailed around the Iberian Peninsula, to the Shetlands and possibly farther north. From farthest point north he sailed south, and then visited

Friesian Islands. (At outset of voyage he may have traveled overland from Marseilles to Brittany, because the Carthagenians were blocking the Strait of Gibraltar.) He made several voyages into the Atlantic Ocean and to the west coast of Spain.

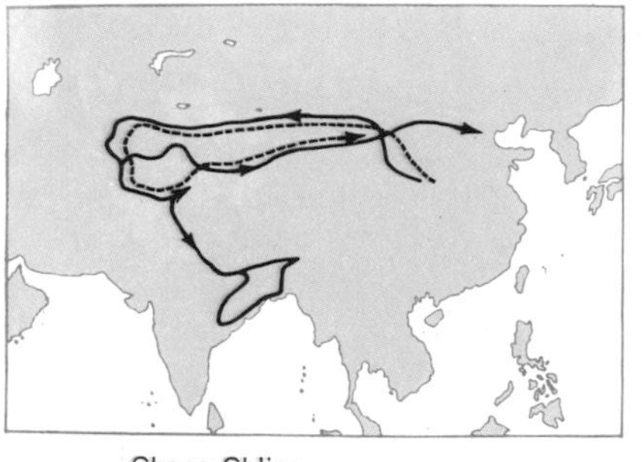

------------ Chang Ch'ien
———— Hsüan-tsang

CHANG CH'IEN
dates unknown China
138 B.C.: Left China but was imprisoned for ten years by Huns. Reached Ferghana, went to Heyuchi near Peshawar. Attempted to return to China via Tibet, but was imprisoned by Huns again. Finally he reached China in 116 B.C.
105 B.C.: Opened up the Silk Route from the Gobi to Khotan, to Yarkand, and Ferghana.

HSÜAN-TSANG
(?)A.D. 605–664 China
A.D. 628–45: Left Li-Chuan, crossed the Gobi to Hami, Lob Nor, north of Kashgar across the Tien Shan to Tashkent and Samarkand. From there he went south across the Oxus into India via the Khyber Pass to the Indus Valley. He also went to Kashmir. Next he went over the Ganges plain and visited Allahabad, Benares, and Patna, then crossed the northeast corner of the Deccan. He returned to China via the coast to Assam and the Punjab to Kashgar and along the south of the Tarim Basin.

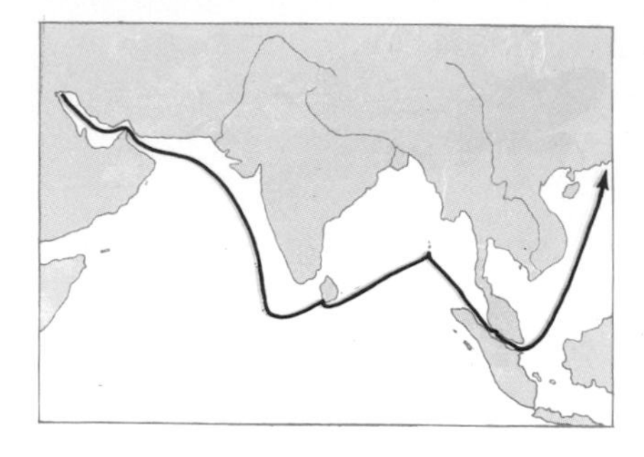

SOLEYMAN
dates unknown Arabia
about A.D. 850: Set out from the Persian Gulf, visited Laccadive and Maldive Islands, Ceylon, Andaman Islands, Malacca, and then on to Canton.

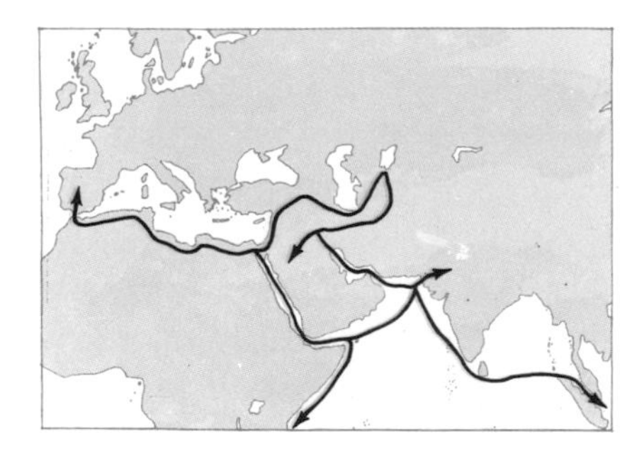

AL-MASUDI
(?)–956 Arabia
914: Born in Baghdad, traveled north as far as the Sea of Aral, west as far as Spain, east as far as China. He spent twenty years wandering about the Islamic world, and is said to have visited every Mohammedan country and lands as far afield as Madagascar, Turkestan, Zanzibar, and Sind.

ERIC THE RED, AND SONS
dates unknown Norway
about 979–82: Went with the settlers to Iceland, then went on to southwest Greenland in 985; he went as far north as 73°. His sons, Leif and Thorvald, voyaged to "Vinland" in 1002 and 1008.
See map on page 49.

IDRISI
1099–1154(?) Arabia
A Spanish Arab who traveled widely in Europe and collated earlier Arab writings of a geographical nature.

CARPINI, JOHN DE
1182–1252 Italy
1245–47: Sent by the Pope to the Great Khan. He went by the rivers Dnieper, Don, Volga, and to the north of the Caspian and to the south of Lake Baikal, to Karakorum.
See map on page 55.

RUBRUQUIS, WILLIAM
1215–70 France
1252–55: Traveled with Friar William of Cremona to Acre, Constantinople; waited a year, then went to the Crimea and across Central Asia to Karakorum. Arrived back at Corycus on the Mediterranean in 1255, having left Friar William with the Great Khan. Returned to his monastry at Acre.
See map on page 55.

POLO BROTHERS (NICCOLÒ and MAFFEO) Venice
See text on page 55; map on page 55.

POLO, MARCO
1254–1324 Venice
See text on page 56 to 58; map on page 55.

FRIAR JOHN OF MONTE CORVINO
1247–1328(?) Italy
1291: Stationed at Tabriz in Persia; went to south India and reached China in 1293. Established Roman Church in Peking.
See map on page 55.

FRIAR ODORIC
1274(?)–1331 Friuli
1318–30: Went to Constantinople and Hormuz in Persia; sailed to China via Malabar, Ceylon, Madras, Nicobar Islands, Sumatra, Java, Borneo, Cochin China, to Canton and Hangchow. From there he went via the Grand Canal to Peking and overland to Ordos, Shensi, Tibet and Lhasa.
See map on page 55.

IBN BATUTA
1304–77(?) Morocco
1324(?): Niger and Timbuktu.
1325–49: Tangier, Egypt, Damascus, Asia Minor, Iraq, Baghdad to East Africa. Also visited Hindu Kush and northwest India, Delhi, Bengal and the Ganges delta, Ceylon, Sumatra, and Peking. During this

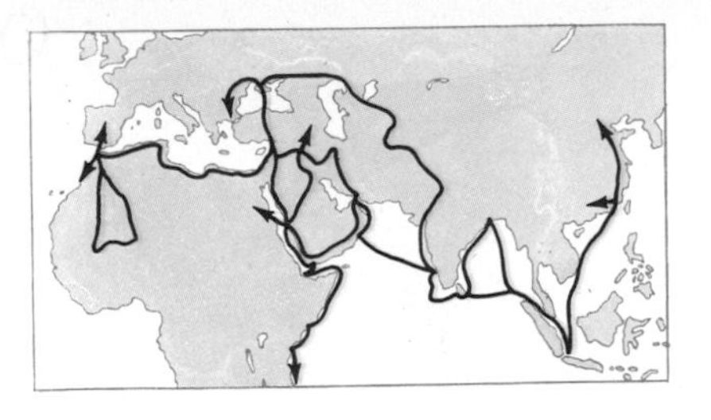

period he also crossed the Sahara to Timbuktu and sailed on the Niger; also visited Moorish Spain.
1350: He made his first trip to Europe by crossing from Africa into Spain, where he visited Moslem outposts, including Andalusia.
1352: Traveled in the western Sahara, setting out from Tangier, Fès, Marrakesh, Timbuktu, Gao, Agadez, the Aïr Massif, Ahaggar, and back to Tangier.
By the time he reached home, he had visited every Islamic country and many infidel countries as well. By the time he died, Batuta had traveled about 75,000 miles.

DA CADAMOSTO, ALVISE
(?)1432–80 Venice
1455–56: Joined the service of Portugal; sailed for Madeira, the Canary Islands, and reached the mainland of Africa near Cape Blanc. He traveled along the coast to Cape Verde and visited the Cape Verde Islands. The Gambia and coast of Sierra Leone.
See map on pages 63.

GOMEZ, DIEGO
1440–82 Portugal
1458–60: Discovered Liberia, sailing under sponsorship of Henry the Navigator.
See map on page 63.
1462: He sailed again for West Africa, but reached only as far as Cape Verde.

DIAZ, BARTHOLOMEW
(?)–1506(?) Portugal
1481: Traded along the Gold Coast.
1487: Sailed to the Congo, then south as far as Walfish Bay to survey the coast. He next sailed around the Cape of Good Hope without realizing it. Landed at Mossel Bay and sailed back around the Cape.
1497: Sailed with da Gama on his voyage to India, but Diaz left the fleet at Cape Verde. On orders from the king of Portugal he sailed his ship to the Gold Coast.
1500: With Cabral he sailed from Lisbon and touched Brazil, but his ship went down on its way to the Cape.
For major voyages, see map on page 63.

CAM, DIEGO
(?)–1486 Portugal
1482: Sailed down the coast of Africa, passed the mouth of the Congo to Cape St. Mary, 13°26′ S.
1485: Sailed down the coast again to Monte Negro, 15°41′ S., and to Cape Cross at about 9°41′ S.
See map on page 63.

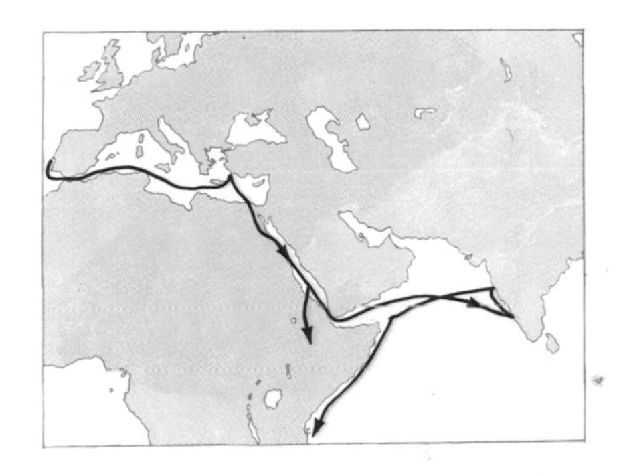

COVILHAM, PEDRO DE
1487–1525 Portugal
1486: Sent to find the abode of Prester John. He first went to India, and from there by ship to Sofala on the east coast of Africa, then possibly by land to Cairo. Went on to Ethiopia where he remained for the rest of his life.

COLUMBUS, CHRISTOPHER
1451–1506 Genoa
1492–93: Sailed on behalf of Spain to Canary Islands, Watling Island in the Bahama group, to Cuba, Haiti, and then back to Spain via the Azores.
1493–96: Sailed along a more southerly course to Dominica, Leeward Islands, Puerto Rico, and Haiti, where he established a colony to explore inland to the Cibao Mountains. He sailed along the south coast of Cuba and went across to the north of Jamaica. Returned to explore the south coast of Cuba more fully. Returned to Spain via Guadeloupe.
1498: Sailed to Cape Verde Islands and then went westward, but had difficulty with calms. Reached Trinidad and saw the coast of South America near Paria and then went on to Haiti, and returned to Spain.
1502–04: Again sailed for the West Indies; reached Honduras and then followed the coast southward to the Gulf of Darien.
See map on page 71.

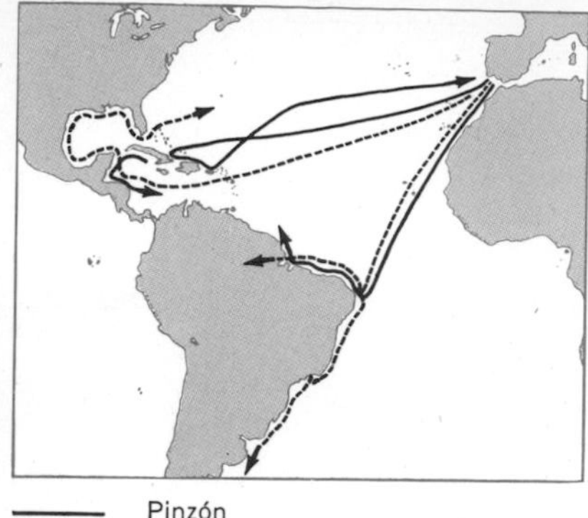

—— Pinzón
------- Vespucci

PINZÓN, MARTIN
1460–1542 Spain
1492: Accompanied Columbus on his journey to the New World.
1500: Touched South America just below Cape St. Augustine and sailed up to the mouth of the Amazon.
1506: With De Solis, sailed along the coast of Yucatán to Trujillo.
Also see map on page 73.

VESPUCCI, AMERIGO
1451(?)–1512 Florence
1497: Claims to have discovered the coast of the Gulf of Mexico from the Bay of Campeche to part of the east coast of the U.S.A. Many authorities doubt the validity of his claims.
1499: Sailed with Ojeda in the service of Spain. Touched the Brazilian coast at 5° S and sailed northwest to the Amazon and a little way up the river.
1502: In the service of Portugal. Sailed from Europe to Rio de Janeiro Bay, and claimed to have reached 50° S and South Georgia.
1503: Claims to have sailed to Bahia in South America, but this is doubtful.

DA GAMA, VASCO
1460–1524 Portugal
1497–99: Sailed from Lisbon to Cape Verde and then went west (to avoid the currents in the Gulf of Guinea) to within 600 miles of the South American mainland. Touched the African coast again at St. Helena Bay, Mossel Bay, Natal, Mombasa, and Malindi. He was given a pilot to take him across the Arabian Sea to India, where he landed at the port of Calicut.
See maps on pages 63 and 64.
1502: From Portugal returned to Calicut, but this was a journey of plunder and destruction rather than one of exploration.

CABOT, JOHN
1450–98 Venice
1497: Sailed for the English. He set out from Bristol and went to Cape Breton Island, south Labrador (or Newfoundland).
1498: Rediscovered south Greenland. Sailed southward along the coast to Chesapeake Bay.

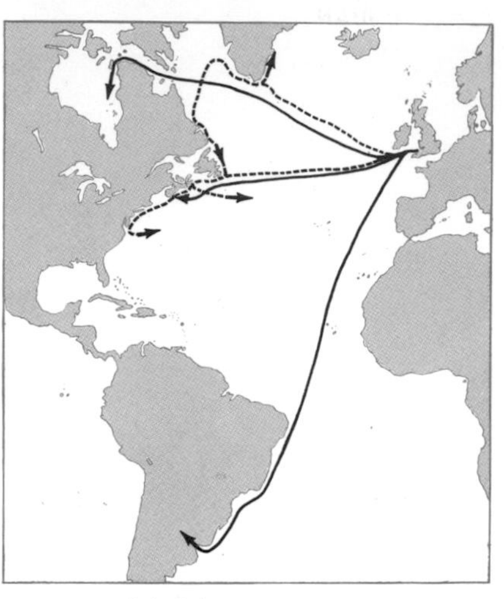

------- Cabot, J.
—— Cabot, S.

CABOT, SEBASTIAN
1476(?)–1557 England
1500: Sailed from Bristol to Nova Scotia.
1509: Sailed from Bristol, probably through Hudson Strait to Hudson Bay. A discontented crew forced his return. He was regarded as an authority on travel in high latitudes. *(In the service of Spain, 1512–48.)*
1526: He sailed to the South Atlantic in search of a route to the Spice Islands and the East; got as far as Río de la Plata and 500 miles up stream.

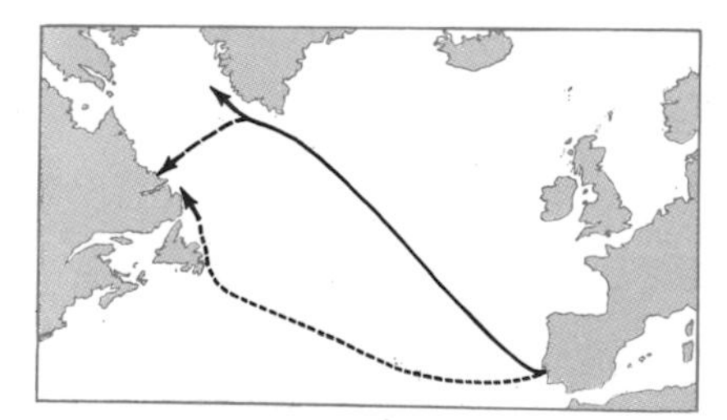

—— Corte-Real, G. and M.
– – – – Corte-Real, G.
------- Corte-Real, M.

CORTE-REAL, GASPAR
(?)1450–1501 Portugal
1500: Rediscovered Greenland.
1501: Sailed to Greenland, and to the North American coast (probably Labrador); did not return.

CORTE-REAL, MIGUEL
(?)–1502 Portugal
1501: Sailed with Gaspar as far as Greenland.
1502: Sailed to Newfoundland to search for his brother; never returned.
See map bottom of previous column.

CABRAL, PEDRO
1460–1526 Portugal
1500: Discovered Brazil on the way to India. Visited Calicut, but after riots he moved on to Cochin and to Cananor on the coast of Malabar.
See maps on pages 63 and 64.

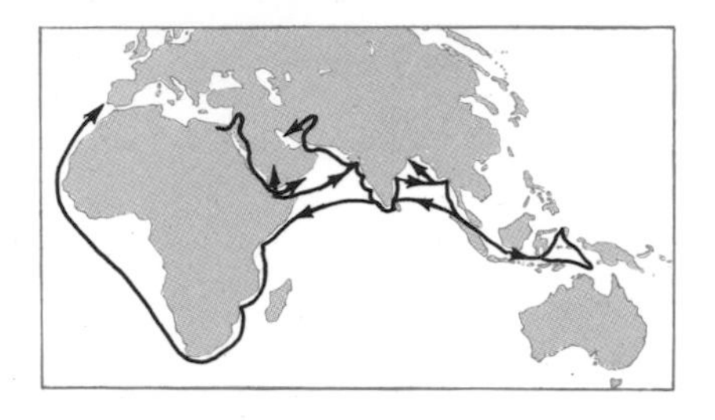

VARTHEMA, LUDOVICO DI
dates unknown Italy
1502–10: Left from Egypt, went to Damascus, then south to Medina and Mecca. From there to Aden and Diu by sea, then he went west to Hormuz by sea. He journeyed inland in Persia before returning to the Coromandel coast. He then went on to Ceylon, the East Indies including Java, and returned to Europe via the Cape of Good Hope.

MAGELLAN, FERDINAND
1480(?)–1521 Portugal
1505: Sailed with Sequira and Serrano. Went to Goa, Calicut, the Malacca coast, Malay Archipelago, Sumatra, and Ternate. Returned home in 1512.
1513: Fought against the Moors in Morocco.
1517: Renounced Portuguese citizenship after King Manuel had refused to finance an expedition to find a westward route to India.
1519: Set out on a voyage around the world for Spain. His first call was the Canary Islands; from there to Cape Verde Islands, Cape St. Augustine, Rio de Janeiro, Santa Cruz River, Tierra del Fuego, Philippines, where he was killed on the Island of Mactan.
See maps on page 81.

DE SOLÍS, JUAN DIAZ
1471–1516(?) Spain
1506: Sailed along the coast of Yucatán to Trujillo with Pinzón.
See map on page 73.
1516: Discovered the estuary of the Río de la Plata. Eaten by cannibals.

SEQUIRA, DIEGO LOPEZ DE
dates unknown Portugal
1509: Having sailed to Calicut with Magellan and Serrano, he crossed the Bay of Bengal to the Malacca coast and sailed around Sumatra.
See map on page 64.

SERRANO, FRANCISCO
dates unknown Portugal
1505: Sailed from Portugal to Calicut in the company of Magellan and Sequira.
1511: Went to north Java and the islands beyond, including Ternate. Stayed there for the rest of his life in the service of the native prince of Ternate.
See map on page 64.

BALBOA, VASCO NUÑEZ DE
1475–1517(?) Spain
1510: Was a stowaway on an expedition led by Encisco to San Sebastian, a settlement on the Isthmus of Panama; on finding the settlement ruined, they sailed on to Darien and founded a new settlement. Encisco was sent back to Spain, and Balboa became the expedition's leader.
1513: Made a land crossing of the Isthmus of Panama to St. Miguel Bay and Pearl Island. He was later arrested by Pizarro and then beheaded.
See maps on pages 73 and 93.

CORTÉZ, HERNANDO
1485–1547 Spain
1511: Sailed with Velasquez on an expedition to Cuba.
1518–21: Sailed from Cuba to Vera Cruz, then went inland between the mountains and descended to the plains of Thaxcala, with a detour to climb Popocatepetl. Went to Cholula and Mexico City in 1521. Went westward to the Pacific.
1524–26: From Mexico City he went through Tabasco to the town of Puerto Cortéz in Honduras; then he sailed to Trujillo.
1535–36: From the south coast of Mexico, he sailed part way up the Gulf of California.
See map on page 73.

DE SOTO, HERNANDO
1496(?)–1542 Spain
1519: Sailed to Darien with d'Avila.
1528: Went to Guatemala and then to Yucatán.
1530–35: Was with Pizarro in Peru.
1538: Sailed from Spain to Havana. Was made Governor of Cuba and Florida.
1539: Sailed from Cuba to Tampa, Apalachee Bay, went through Georgia into the Carolinas, then to the Alabama River and across to the Mississippi River. Went on to the Ozarks then down to the mouth of the Red River, where he died.
See map on page 73.

DE LEON, JUAN PONCE
1460–1521 Spain
1515: Sailed from Spain and touched the coasts of Florida and Cuba, but did not realize that Florida was part of the mainland.
See map on page 73.

PIZARRO, FRANCISCO
1471(?)–1541 Spain
1510: Sailed from Spain to Hispaniola and the Gulf of Uraba.
1513: He accompanied Balboa across the Isthmus of Panama.
1517: He arrested Balboa in Panama, and had him beheaded.
1524–27: From Panama he went to the river San Juan south to Tumbes and then back to Panama.
1528: He met Cortéz at Palos in Spain.
1531: He returned to Panama from Spain; sailed down the west coast of South America to the isle of Puna, inland to Tumbes, Caxamarca, and Cuzco.
1535: He founded the city of Lima.
See map on page 93.

DEL CANO, JUAN SEBASTIAN
(?)–1526 Spain
1519: Sailed with Magellan on his voyage around the world. After Magellan's death, he brought the expedition back to Spain.
See maps on page 81.

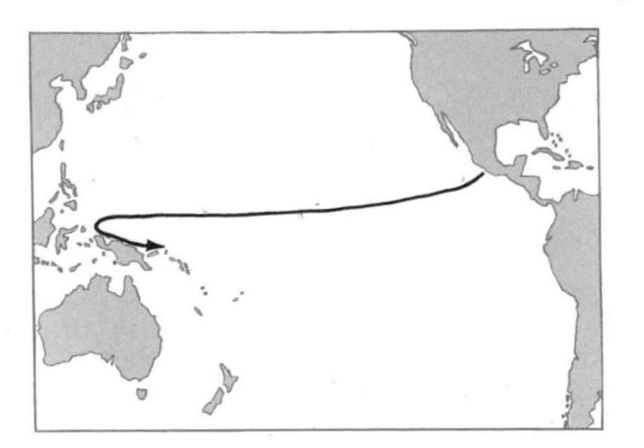

SAAVEDRA, ALVARO DE
(?)–1528(?) Spain
1527: Sailed from Mexico (under orders of Cortéz) across the Pacific to the Moluccas. Mentioned New Guinea in his writings. Died soon after setting out on return voyage.

DE VACA, CABEZA ALVAR NUÑEZ
1490–1559(?) Spain
1528: Traveled from Tampa Bay along the coast to Apalachee Bay, to the Islands of Misfortune off the coast of Texas. Crossed America from east to west. Reached the Colorado River in 1537.
See map on page 73.
1541: Sailed from Spain for Buenos Aires. At Santa Catherina Island he left the ships and marched overland to the Iguassu River, a tributary of the Paraná, and then went to Asunción. Traveled up the Paraguay to Xarayes and returned to be taken prisoner at Asunción. He was sent back to the coast and back to Spain after mutiny in 1545.

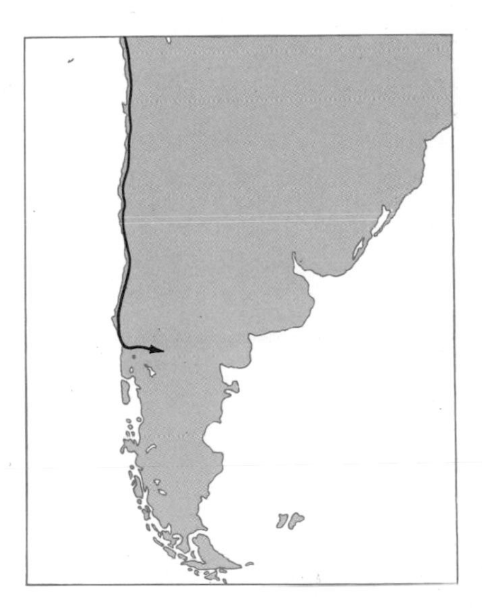

VALDÍVIA, PEDRO DE
1497(?)–1554 Spain
1530: Helped in the conquest of Venezuela.
1532: Accompanied Pizarro on his second Peru expedition.
1540: Went from Cuzco by the coast road (following Almagro's track) to Copiapo and Coquimbo; founded La Serena.
1541: Founded Santiago; brought in settlers and lived by farming.
1544: Sent ships south to Magellan's strait, and received good reports on the land to the south.
He founded the city of Valdívia.
Went north by sea to Lima and then inland to Cuzco.
Picked up reinforcements for his colony from Arequipa and Arica.
1552: Went east from Chile to the upper Negro River over the Andes.
Also see map on page 93.

PIZARRO, GONZALO
1505(?)–1548 Spain
1531: Accompanied Francisco Pizarro to Cuzco.
1539: Governor of Quito.
1540–43: Sent by his brother from Cuzco to Quito and into the Amazon Basin to the Napo River.
See map on page 93.

CARTIER, JACQUES
1491–1557 France
1534: Sailed from Saint-Malo to the northern end of the Strait of Belle Isle, then south along west coast of Newfoundland, across the Gulf of St. Lawrence to the northern end of Northumberland Strait. Returned via Gaspé Harbor and the Strait of Belle Isle.
1535–36: Sailed again to Newfoundland and through the Strait of Belle Isle, north of Anticosti Island, following the St. Lawrence to Quebec, the Charles River, and Montreal.
1541: Reached the Charles River but could not get up the St. Lawrence.
See map on page 109.

CORONADO, FRANCISCO DE
(?)1500–54 Spain
1535: Sailed to the New World.
1540–42: Explored large parts of the U.S.A. in the search of gold. Went to Quivira, near where the Arkansas and Kansas rivers approach each other. Members of his expedition made many journeys; on one they discovered the Grand Canyon.
See map on page 73.

ALMAGRO, DIEGO DE
(?)1475–1538 Spain
1535–37: Traveled from Cuzco through the Andes to north Chile, and reached as far south as 37° (Concepción); returned via the coast through the Atacama Desert.
See map on page 93.

QUESADA, GONZALO JIMENEZ DE
1499–1597 Spain
1535: Sailed from Spain via the Canary Islands to Santa Marta.
1536–39: From Santa Marta he went up the Magdalena River to Bogotá.
1569–71: During a search for El Dorado, he crossed the Andes to the Guaviare River and upper Orinoco.
See map on page 93.

MOSCOSO, LUIS DE
dates unknown Spain
1539–43: With De Soto on his trip from Tampa to the Red River. When De Soto died, Moscoso took charge. He went inland farther west, returned to the Red River mouth, and from there sailed down the Mississippi and along the coast of the Gulf to the Panuco River.
See map on page 73.

ULLOA, FRANCISCO DE
(?)–1540 Spain
1539: Sailed with two other boats up the Gulf of California and proved that lower California was not an island. Sailed up the west coast of the peninsula as far as Cedros Island.
See map on page 73.

XAVIER, FRANCIS
1506–52 Spain
1540–52: Set out from Europe, rounded the Cape to India. Went through the Strait of Malacca to the Spice Islands and to Ternate. He eventually landed in China on the coast of Kwangtung and sailed on to Japan. He again visited Malacca and Canton before he died.
See maps on pages 63 and 64.

PINTO, FERNANDO MENDEZ
1509–83 Portugal
1540–46: Sailed from Europe around the Cape to the Mekong River; went to Hainan Island, and then sailed on to Japan.
1549–51: Met Xavier in Japan. In 1558 he returned to Europe.
See map on page 64.

ORELLANA, FRANCISCO DE
1511–46 Spain
1541–43: Set out from Guayaquil with Gonzalo Pizarro, went to Quito and the Napo River. Was sent ahead down the Napo and sailed the Amazon to the sea. He was the first man to navigate the length of the Amazon to its outlet.
See map on page 93.

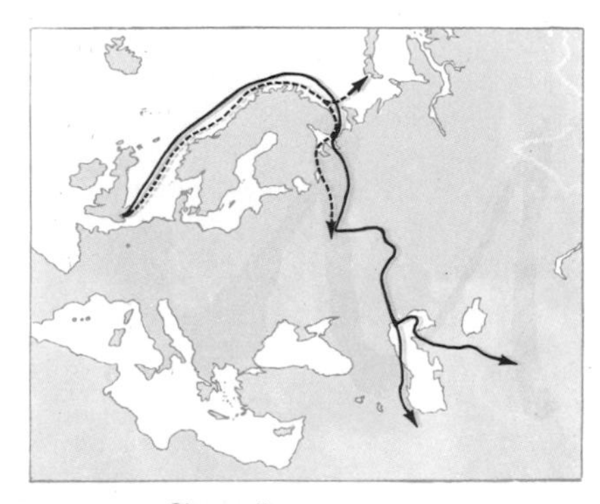

------------ Chancellor
———— Jenkinson

CHANCELLOR, RICHARD
(?)–1556 England
1553: Sailed from the Thames across the North Sea and up the coast of Norway to Novaya Zemlya. Followed the Kola Peninsula, crossed the White Sea and went to Moscow.
1555: Returned to Russia and won a monopoly of trade. During his return to England his ship went down and all hands were lost.
See map bottom of previous column.

JENKINSON, ANTHONY
(?)–1611 England
1557: After many years trading in the Levant, he went to Russia.
1558: Sent on a mission into Central Asia with letters from the Czar. He left Moscow, went down the Volga to Astrakhan, and sailed along the east coast of the Caspian, passed the Ural River and landed at Mangyshlak. Crossed the desert by camel to Urganj and then went up the Oxus and to Bukhara. Returned to Moscow by the same route.
1562: Sailed down the Volga to Astrakhan and crossed the Caspian to Derbent and then went on to Kazvin and back to Moscow.
See map bottom of previous column.

URSÚA, PEDRO DE
1526–61 Spain
1560: He left Lima and crossed the Andes to the Huallaga River. From there he went into the Amazon Basin, and was murdered by his own men in 1561 somewhere near the Amazon River. Aguirre became the leader.
See map on page 93.

AGUIRRE, LOPE DE
(?)1510–61 Spain
1561: Became the leader of Ursúa's expedition sometime after Ursúa was killed. His route to the Atlantic was probably down the Amazon to Manaus, up the Negro over to the Orinoco, and down to its mouth. From there he sailed round the northern coast to the region of Caracas and became a bandit.
See map on page 93.

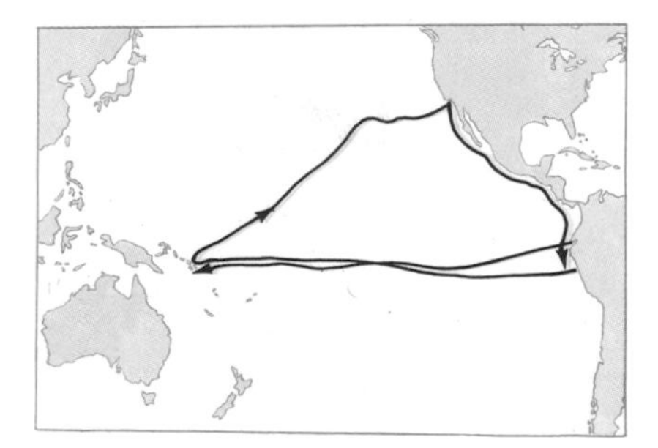

MENDAÑA, ALVARO DE
(?)–1595 Spain
1567: Sailed from Callao (port for Lima) to the Ellice Islands. Reached the Solomon Islands in 1568, then went on to the Marshall Islands. Sailed east across the Pacific and reached 30° N. He touched on the coast of California, then went down the coast to Lima.
1595: Left Peru again (with Quirós) and went to Lima, the Marquesas and Santa Cruz, where he died and Quirós, the pilot, took command.
See map bottom of previous column.

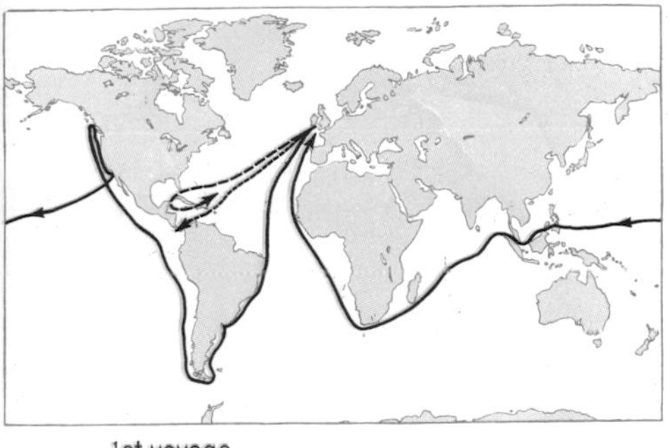

------ 1st voyage
.... 2nd voyage
—— 3rd voyage

DRAKE, SIR FRANCIS
1541(?)–96 England
1567: Sailed with John Hawkins on a pirate voyage to the Spanish territory in America.
1569: Went to the Caribbean again and climbed the mountains in Panama to have a look at the Pacific.
1577–80: Sailed to Brazil, to the Río de la Plata estuary, south to Patagonia, around Cape Horn into the Pacific. From there he went up the west coast of South America to Panama and as far north as Vancouver Island. When winter set in, he turned back and sheltered in San Francisco Bay. In 1579 he sailed for the Philippines, the Spice Islands, across the Indian Ocean, and around the Cape of Good Hope.

FROBISHER, SIR MARTIN
1535(?)–94 England
1576: Sailed to the Shetlands, South Greenland, Frobisher Bay, and Butchers Island, and back to Harwich.
1577: Went to the Orkneys, across to Greenland, and Baffin Island. He conducted coastal exploration and brought back a load of ore.
1578: Sailed again for the Canadian Arctic to find some "golden ore"; was blown into Hudson Strait during a storm.
See map on page 104.

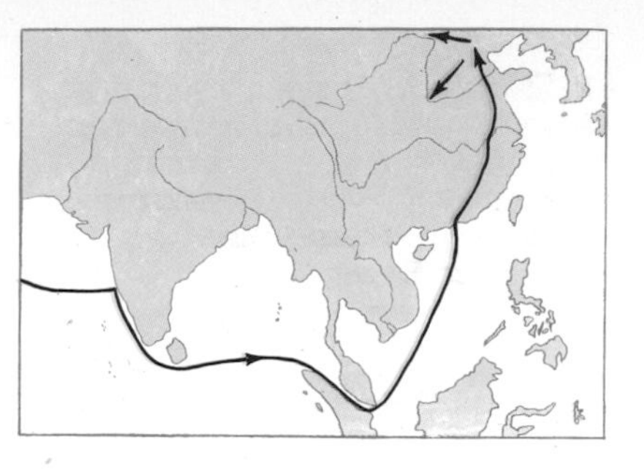

RICCI, MATTEO
1552–1610 Italy
1578: He stopped at Goa on his way to China.
1582: Reached Canton and crossed to Nanking on the Yangtze.
1598: Received by the Chinese court.
1601: Established himself at Peking and began a survey.
1603: As a Jesuit priest he made journeys into northern China from Peking.

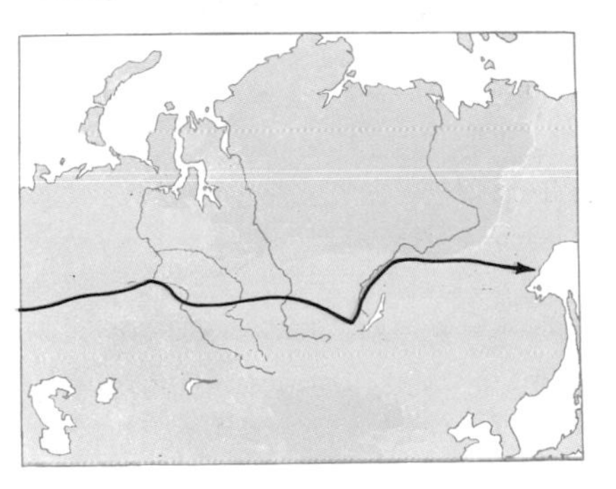

YERMAK
(?)–1585 Russia
1579: He fought in a battle at the Irtysh River against the Tartars. From 1580 on he pioneered the opening of Siberia, often following the rivers. His route is now followed by the trans-Siberian railway.

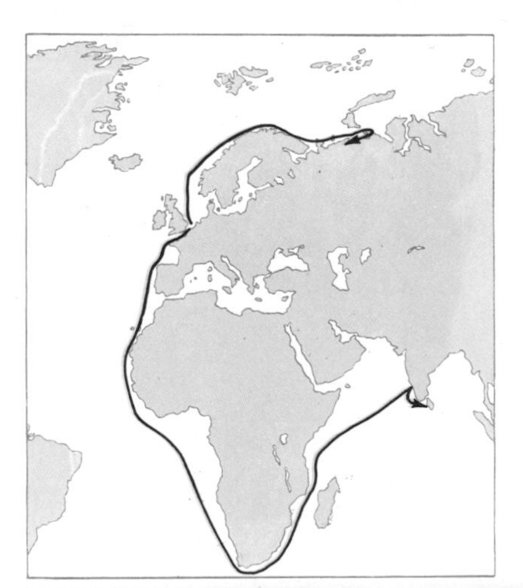

LINSCHOTEN, JAN HUYGHEN VAN
1563–1611 Holland
1583: From Holland he sailed around the Cape of Good Hope and visited Goa and south India. He returned to Holland after five years and gave a detailed report of Portuguese factories in southern India.
1594: With Barents, he sought a northeast passage. They got as far as Novaya Zemlya, Vaigach Island, then Linschoten sailed into the Kara Sea.
See map bottom of previous column.

RALEIGH, SIR WALTER
1552(?)–1618 England
1585–87: He led attempts to settle in Virginia.
1595: Sailed to the Orinoco delta and along the northern coast of South America.
1617: He made a second voyage to the Orinoco delta.
See map on page 93.

DAVIS, JOHN
1550(?)–1605 England
1585: Went to south Greenland, Gilbert Sound (now Godthaab), and Davis Strait.
1586: Made a second trip to Greenland, across to Cumberland Sound in Baffin Island, passed the entrance to Hudson Bay, and passed Hamilton Sound in Labrador, then went back to England.
1587: Went along the west coast of Greenland to Hope Sanderson (72°12′ N) and then turned west and southward because he could not get through to the north.
See map on page 104.
1591–93: Accompanied Cavendish in his search for a northwest passage. Discovered the Falkland Islands, near the tip of South America.
1601: He sailed to Table Bay, around the Cape of Good Hope to Madagascar, Chagos Archipelago, Nicobar Islands to the Moluccas, and then back to England. In 1605 he was killed fighting Japanese pirates in the East Indies.

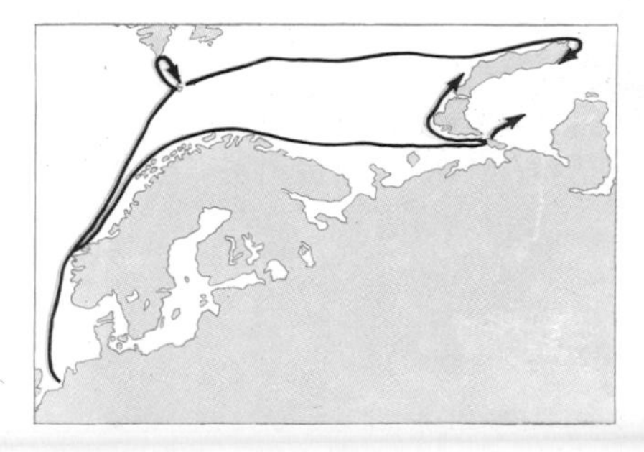

BARENTS, WILLEM
(?)–1597 Holland
1594: Sailed with Linschoten to Novaya Zemlya and up the west coast to the islands of Orange and then back to Vaigach Island; returned to Holland.
1595: He reached Vaigach Island and a little way into the Kara Sea.
1596–97: He discovered Bear Island and the larger Spitsbergen; after returning to Bear Island, he sailed on to Novaya Zemlya. He was forced to stay in the Arctic for the winter. Barents died when they were returning to Holland via the Kola Peninsula in open boats.
See map bottom of previous page.

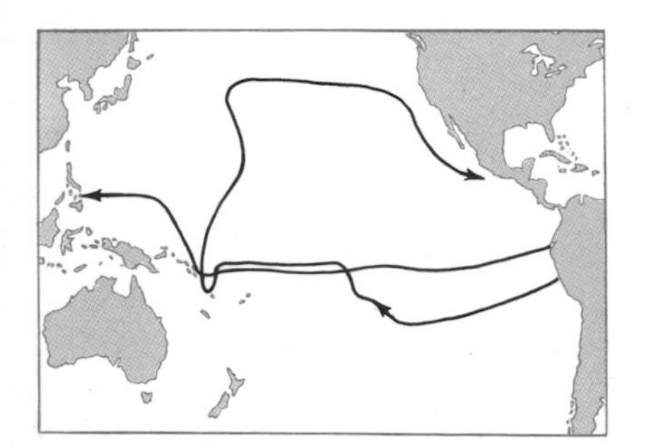

QUIRÓS, PEDRO FERNANDEZ DE
1565–1614 Spain
1595: Arrived in Peru and was made captain and chief pilot with Mendaña's second expedition. He sailed to the Marquesas and on to Santa Cruz where Mendaña died. The expedition continued on to Manila with Quirós as leader, but had many difficulties with Mendaña's widow.
1604: Left Spain again but was shipwrecked in the West Indies. Eventually got to Caracas and Lima.
1605: Sailed with Torres from Callao in Peru, reached the chain of islands to the east of Tahiti and went to the New Hebrides where he and Torres were accidentally separated. Quirós sailed on to Santa Cruz and then back to Acapulco.
1614: Set off from Spain for the New World, but died in Panama.

CHAMPLAIN, SAMUEL DE
1567–1635 France
Prior to 1603 he made a voyage to the West Indies and Mexico in the service of the king of Spain.
1603: He sailed from France via the Belle Isle Strait to the St. Lawrence, and went a little way up the Saguenay River.
1604–07: He reached Cape Breton Island, sailed along the coast of Nova Scotia into the Bay of Fundy, continued on down the coast to Cape Cod and on to Nantucket.
1608–09: Went to the St. Lawrence. Then south to Lake Champlain.
1611: Founded the Montreal settlement and discovered the Lachine Rapids.
1613: Went up the Ottawa River.
1615: With Brulé he went up the St. Lawrence and Ottawa River to Georgian Bay, overland to Lake Ontario, and Lake Oneida. Returned by the same route.
See map on page 109.

TORRES, LUIS VAEZ DE
dates unknown Spain
1605: Sailed with his friend Quirós as captain of the second ship. Left Callao and sailed to the New Hebrides where they were separated. He touched the northern end of the Great Barrier Reef and discovered the Torres Strait; he sailed on through the Moluccas to Manila where he wrote an account of the voyage.
See map on page 149.

HUDSON, HENRY
(?)–1611 England
1607: He sailed from England up the east coast of Greenland until his way was blocked by ice at 80°23′ N; he then turned to Spitsbergen.
1608: He searched for a northeast passage between Spitsbergen and Novaya Zemlya.
1609: In the service of the Dutch East India Company, he continued to search for a northeast passage. He sailed into the Barents Sea, then crossed the North Atlantic to Cape Cod, and went up the Hudson River almost to Troy.
1610: He reached Greenland, then sailed through Hudson Strait and into Hudson Bay and then south to James Bay, where he was lost. Bylot brought the ship back to England.
See map on page 104.

BRULÉ, ÉTIENNE
1592–1633(?) France
1608: He sailed to the New World with Champlain and became one of the first settlers in Quebec, where he remained for two years.
1610: He lived with the Algonquin Indians to learn their language.
1611–12: He lived with the Huron Indians, traveled with them and was probably the first white man to see Georgian Bay and Lake Huron.
1615: He went with Champlain to the St. Lawrence, Ottawa River, Georgian Bay, and Lake Ontario.
1615: He left Champlain and traveled with Indians across Lake Ontario, following a small stream to the Susquehanna, which led him to Chesapeake Bay.
1616: He returned to Lake Ontario and set off for the St. Lawrence but was captured by the Indians and tortured. He managed to escape and eventually reached the St. Lawrence.
1621: He traveled west to the shores of Lake Huron, passing French River and continuing along Manitoulin Island to the St. Mary River, Lake Superior, and possibly Duluth.
1633(?): He returned to his Indian friends at Toanche, but they killed and ate him.
See map on page 109.

JOURDAIN, JOHN
dates unknown England
1608: Went on an East India Company voyage to the Seychelles, Socotra, Aden, and inland in the Yemen. He journeyed in India the following year from Surat into the Indo-Gangetic Plain.
1612: Sailed from India to Sumatra, Malacca, Amboina and Ceram. He went home to England, then returned to the East Indies, and was killed.

BAFFIN, WILLIAM
1584–1622 England
1612: Voyage to Greenland.
1613: Voyage to Spitsbergen.
1614: Voyage to Spitsbergen.
1615: With Bylot as his captain, he explored Hudson Strait as far as Southampton Island.
1616: Went up the west coast of Greenland to Smith Sound and returned down the west coast of Baffin Bay, having visited Lancaster Sound. Although Baffin (as pilot) gets credit for these expeditions, Bylot was commander.
See map on page 104.
1620–22: He explored the Persian Gulf.

LE MAIRE, JACQUES
dates unknown Holland
See description of Schouten voyage, which follows.

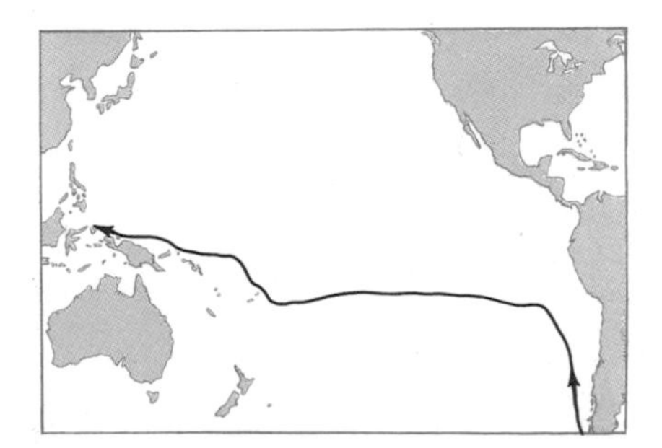

SCHOUTEN, WILLIAM
(?)1580–1625 Holland
1616: With Le Maire he sailed from Holland to discover a new route to the Indian Ocean. Discovering and rounding Cape Horn, they proved that Tierra del Fuego was not attached to a southern continent. Crossed the Pacific to Cocos Island, then turned north to the Fiji Islands and to Ternate, where the ships were confiscated by the Dutch who disbelieved the account of the voyage.
See map bottom of previous column.

ANDRADA, ANTONIO DE
dates unknown (?)
1624: Went from Agra in India through the Himalayas into Tibet; discovered one of the sources of the Ganges, also visited the upper Sutlej River.

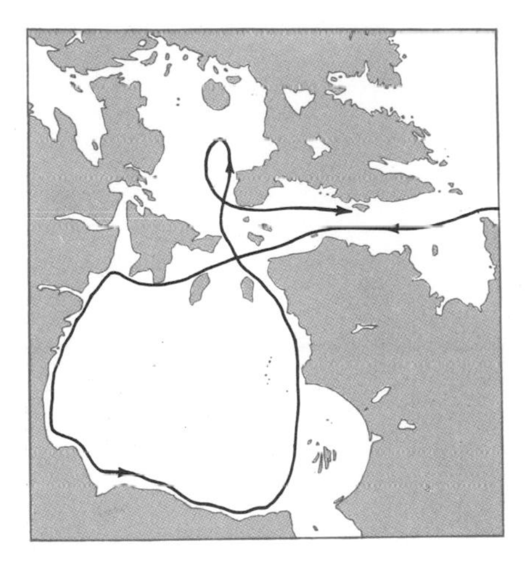

FOXE, LUKE
1586–1635 England
1631: He sailed from England to the Canadian Arctic, passing south of Southampton Island and around Hudson Bay. He went north into Foxe Basin, then back through Hudson Strait to England.

NICOLET, JEAN
1598–1642 France
1634: Seeking a way westward from the St. Lawrence, he reached Lake Huron and passed Manitoulin Island to Sault Ste. Marie; crossed northern end of Lake Michigan, into Green Bay and by the Fox River portage to Wisconsin and the upper Mississippi.
See map on page 109.

TEIXEIRA, PEDRO
(?)–1640 Portugal
1637: Went up the Amazon to Quito and back to Pará (modern Belém).
See map top of next column.

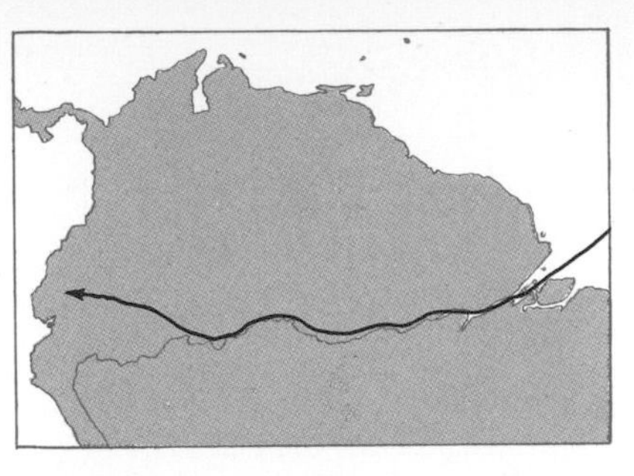

TASMAN, ABEL JANZOON
1603(?)–59 Holland
1642: He sailed from Batavia to Mauritius, went east and discovered Tasmania, and went on to discover New Zealand. He thought that Cook Strait was a gulf, so he coasted north to Three Kings Islands. He returned to Batavia via Tonga and New Guinea.
1644: He sailed along the northern coast of Australia and into the Gulf of Carpentaria. He also went north to the southeast part of Japan.
See map on page 149.

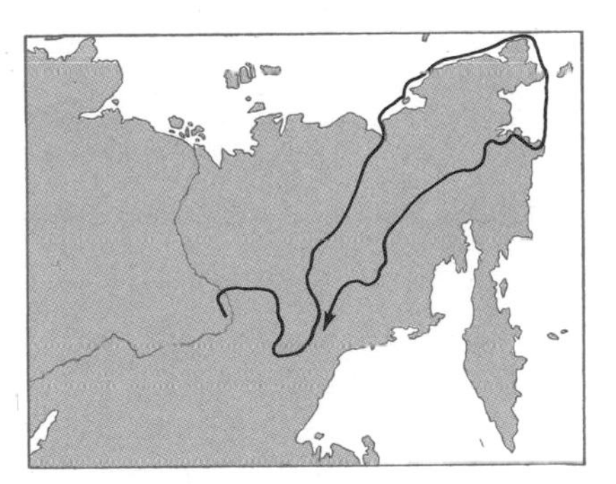

DEZHNEV
dates unknown Russia
1648: Went to the country of the Chukchees (near Yakutsk) in northeast Siberia. Sailed along the Kolyma River and along the Arctic coast to East Cape. The ship was wrecked but he traveled overland to the Anadyr River on to the Lena.

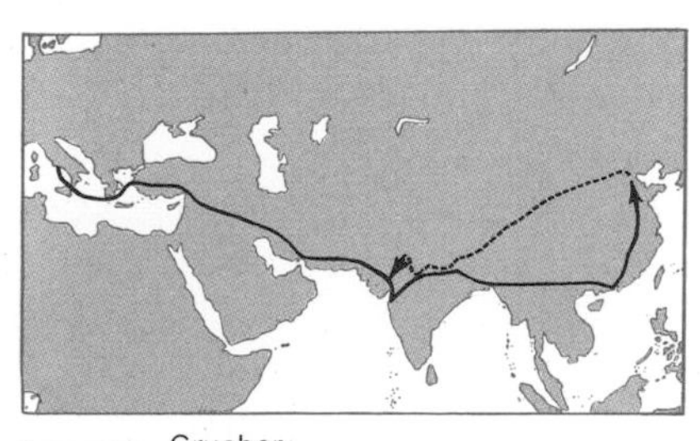

——— Grueber
------------ Grueber and D'Orville

D'ORVILLE, ALBERT
dates unknown Belgium
See journey of Grueber, which follows.

GRUEBER, JOHN
dates unknown Austria
1656: He left Rome and traveled by way of Hormuz overland to Surat (north of Bombay). He reached Macao in 1658 and went on to Peking.
1661: Joined by D'Orville, he left Peking and headed for Tibet, crossed the frontier near Koko Nor; went south to Lhasa, Nepal, and into India, where they visited Agra, Delhi, and Lahore. They went down the Indus to Tatta, through Makran, southern Persia, and Mesopotamia to Smyrna and then back to Rome.
See map bottom of previous column.

LA SALLE, RENÉ SIEUR DE
1643–87 France
1669–73: He visited the south shore of Lake Ontario, but found little interest when he saw the Niagara River. He crossed to Lake Erie, and went along the southern shore.
1678–82: From the St. Lawrence River he went with Hennepin to the Niagara River and discovered the famous falls. They sailed through the Great Lakes to the southern end of Lake Michigan. La Salle went overland to Lake Erie, returned to Lake Michigan, then went down the Mississippi.
1648–87: He sailed from France to the Gulf of Mexico, but missed the mouth of the Mississippi (which he was looking for) and landed at Matagorda Bay, Texas. He attempted exploration inland to the north but was unsuccessful, and he was assassinated by his own men.
Also see map on page 109.

HENNEPIN, LOUIS DE
1640–1701(?) Belgium
1678–79: With La Salle he arrived at the Niagara River and sailed to the south end of Lake Michigan. Hennepin went on to the Kankakee, a tributary of the Illinois, and visited the upper Mississippi.
See map on page 109.

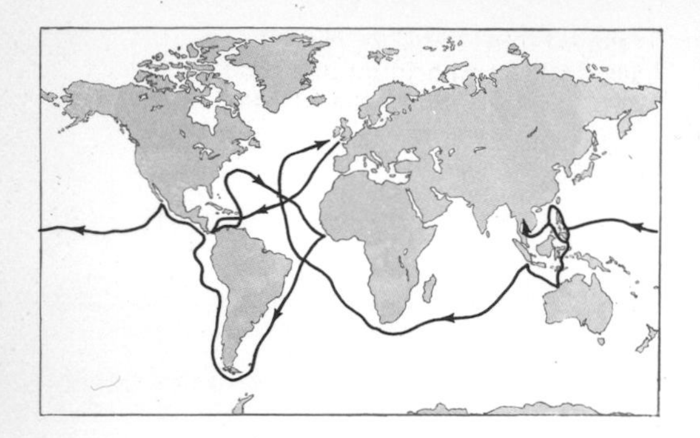

DAMPIER, WILLIAM
1652–1715 England
1679–91: He left England, criss-crossed the Atlantic three times (touching on the Spanish Main and Africa). He rounded Cape Horn, went as far north as lower California, then crossed the Pacific to the Philippines. He visited Cochin China, then sailed south, touching on the coast of Australia. He returned to England via Batavia and the Cape.
See map above.
1699–1700: He sailed via the Cape to the East Indies and explored the northwest coast of Australia from Shark Bay to Dampier's archipelago, and then sailed along the northern coast of New Guinea. On his way back to England he visited Ascension Island.
See map on page 149.

FRITZ, FATHER SAMUEL
1664–1724(?) Bohemia
1686–89: He traveled from Quito to the river Napo and down the Amazon to Pará.
1691–92: Went up the Amazon, up the Huallaga River, and over the Andes to Lima.
1693–1702: He returned to his mission in the Napo River area.
1704–13: Again with his mission he traveled in the upper Amazon Basin.
1714–24: He was with the Xeberos (now Jivaros) in the upper Amazon.

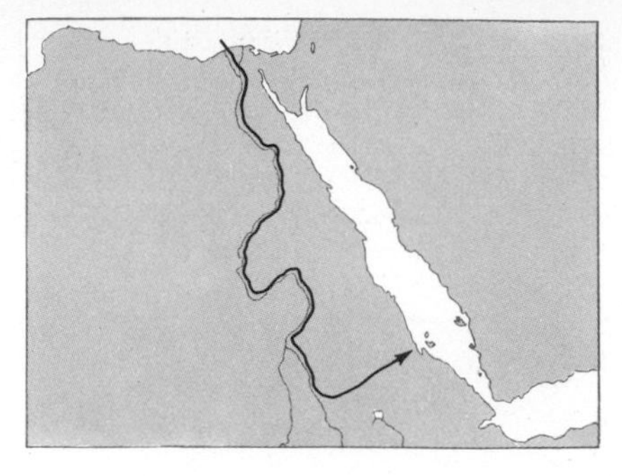

PONCET, DR. C.
dates unknown France
1699: With a party of missionaries, he went from Cairo to Dongola, Sennar, across the Blue Nile to Abyssinia and Gondar; returned to Europe from the port of Massawa.

LA VÉRENDRYE, SIEUR DE
(?)–1749 Canada
1717–28: Was a fur trader based on the St. Maurice River.
1728–32: He sailed along the northern shores of Lake Superior and crossed to Lake Nipigon. Here he was in charge of a trading post. He traveled west as far as the Lake of the Woods.
See map on page 109.
1732: Visited the Lake of the Woods and built Fort St. Charles on the shore. Although one son was killed by Indians and his nephew died of exposure, he continued on to the Red River, Lake Winnipeg, and the Assiniboine River.
1738: Went up the Assiniboine River, then across by Indian trail to Mandan villages on the Missouri, then north to the Saskatchewan as far as the forks.

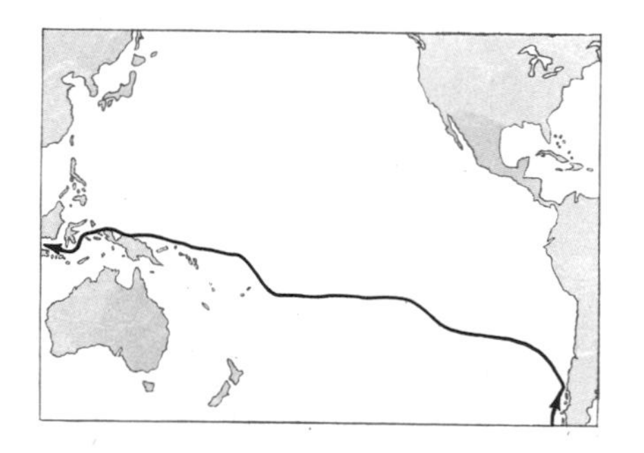

ROGGEVEEN, JACOB
dates unknown Holland
1721: Sailed from Holland via Cape Horn and landed on Easter Island. Sailed westward to the Low Archipelago, the Palliser, Society, and Samoa groups, reached New Britain and continued along the north coast of New Guinea to Batavia.

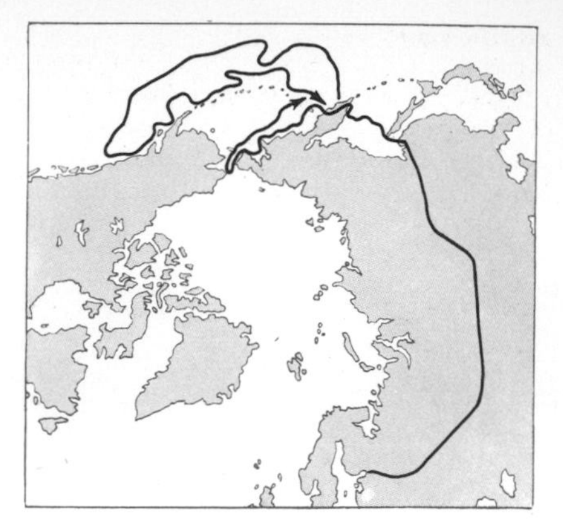

BERING, VITUS
1681–1741 Denmark
1724–30: Exploring in the service of Russia, he left St. Petersburg and traveled across Asia to Okhotsk; from there he went by sea to Kamchatka. From the east coast of the Kamchatka Peninsula, he sailed as far north as the East Cape. He concluded that Asia and America were not joined. He sailed into the Bering Strait, but failed to find land to the east.
1733–40: Preliminary work in eastern Siberia for his scientific expedition of 1740.
1740–41: He sailed from Petropavlovsk (on Kamchatka) to Kayak Island and across to the Alaskan coast and sighted Mt. St. Elias. On his return to Russia via the Aleutians, he died when he reached Bering Island.

LA CONDAMINE, CHARLES
1701–74 France
1736: Went on a scientific expedition to Peru (which then extended north to the Equator.)
1743: He left Quito for France, went down into the Amazon Basin to the Marañón River and down the Amazon as far as Manaus. Then he went part way up the Negro. He continued down the Amazon to Pará. He left for French Guiana and coasted the island of Marajó, passed northward to Guiana. Sailed from Paramaribo to Holland, and then to Paris.

ANSON, LORD
1697–1762 England
1740–44: During his voyage around the world, he called at the Chonos Archipelago, Chiloe Island, and the Juan Fernández Islands.

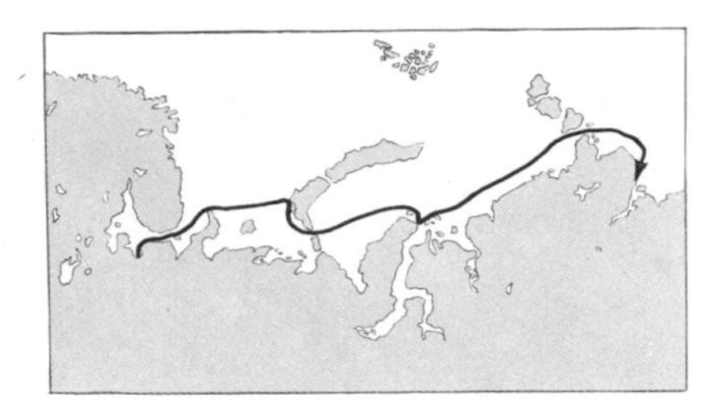

CHELYUSKIN
dates unknown Russia
1742: Sailed from the White Sea to Novaya Zemlya, estuary of the river Ob, and round north of Taimyr Peninsula, Asia's northern most point.

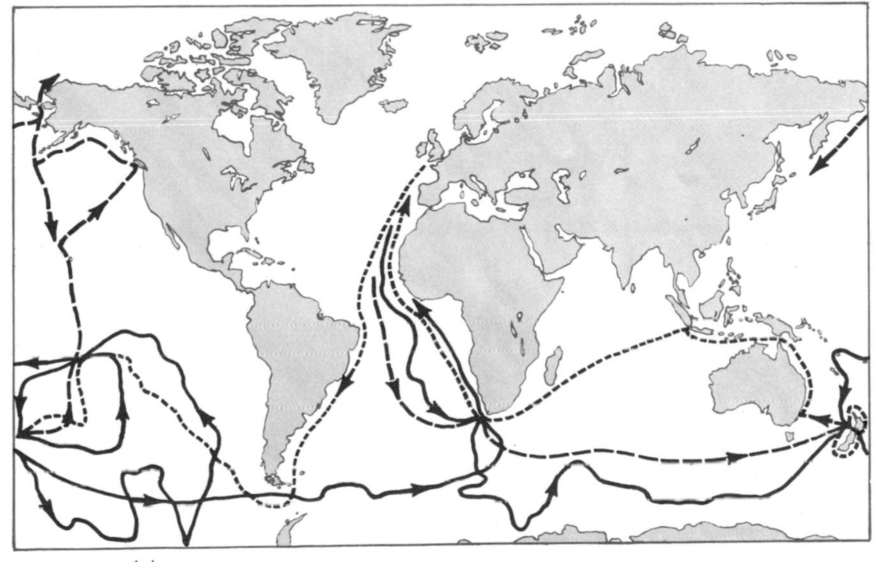

1st voyage
2nd voyage
3rd voyage

COOK, JAMES
1728–79 England
1759: Went with the Royal Navy to Canada and fought at Louisberg and Quebec. Surveyed the St. Lawrence.
1768–69: He rounded Cape Horn and sailed to Tahiti and the Society Islands. Sailed to 40° S. and then to New Zealand where he sailed northward along the east coast of North Island and down the west coast to Cook Strait. He explored the east coast of South Island and then sailed westward to Australia. Went north to the Endeavour River, through Torres Strait to Timor and along the south coast of Java, through the Strait of Sunda to Batavia, and back to England around the Cape.
1772–74: Sailed from England to the Cape and into Antarctic waters, to New Zealand. During his voyages in the South Pacific he visited Easter Island and Tahiti and crossed the Antarctic Circle. He finally sailed from New Zealand through Drake Strait, across the South Atlantic and back to England.
1776: He left England and went via the Cape of Good Hope to Kerguelen Island and New Zealand. He sailed to the Sandwich Islands (Hawaii) and along the coast of North America to Alaska. He went through the Bering Strait and sailed northeast until he was stopped by ice. Next he sailed southward along the Asian coast and returned to the Sandwich Islands, where he was killed.
Also see map on page 149.

NIEBUHR, KARSTEN
1733–1815 Denmark
1761–63: Dispatched by the king of Denmark to explore the fertile part of Arabia. Arrived at Jidda and went south along the coast to the Yemen and inland to San'a. Returned to the coast and went by sea to India. Returned to Europe.
See map on page 135.

BRUCE, JAMES
1730–94 Scotland
1768–73: Sailed to Egypt and up the Nile to Syene, crossed the desert to the Red Sea at Kosseir, sailed to Massawa, calling at ports on the Arabian coast on the way. He traveled inland from Massawa to Gondar, to the source of the Blue Nile. Traveled from the Blue Nile at Lake Tana to Khartoum and back to Egypt through the Nubian Desert and then down the Nile.
See map on page 164.

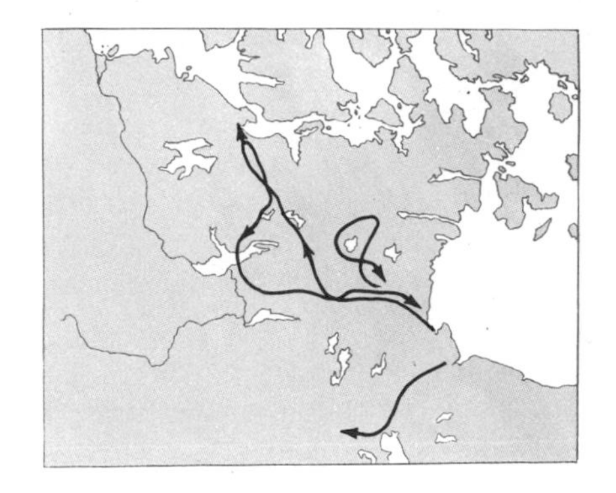

HEARNE, SAMUEL
1745–92 England
1770: He examined the west coast of Hudson Bay for the Hudson's Bay Company. He traveled inland from Churchill to the south of Chesterfield Inlet and to Dubawnt Lake.
1770–72: He traveled via Clinton Lake to the mouth of the Coppermine River and home via the Great Slave Lake.
1774: He established a post at Cumberland House on the lower Saskatchewan.

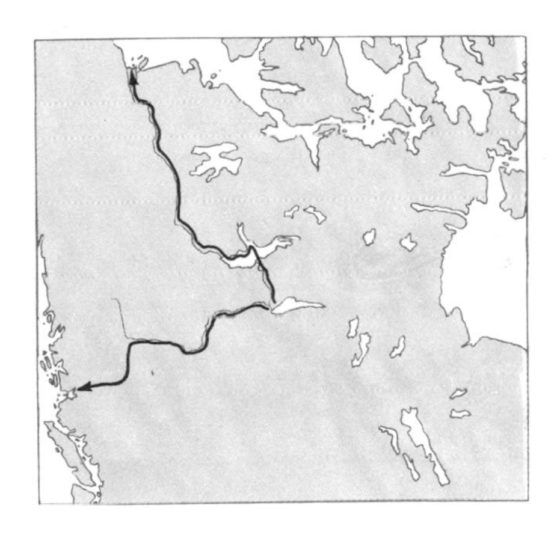

MACKENZIE, SIR ALEXANDER
1755(?)–1820 Scotland
1779: Arrived in Canada.
1785: Set off for Lake Athabaska.
1789: From Fort Chipewyan on Lake Athabaska, he went down the Slave River to the Great Slave Lake; then down the Mackenzie to its mouth.
1792–93: From Fort Chipewyan, he sailed west up the Peace River, followed the Parsnip stream in the Rocky Mountains, reached the Fraser River, and went down the Bella Coola River to the Pacific coast in Queen Charlotte Sound.

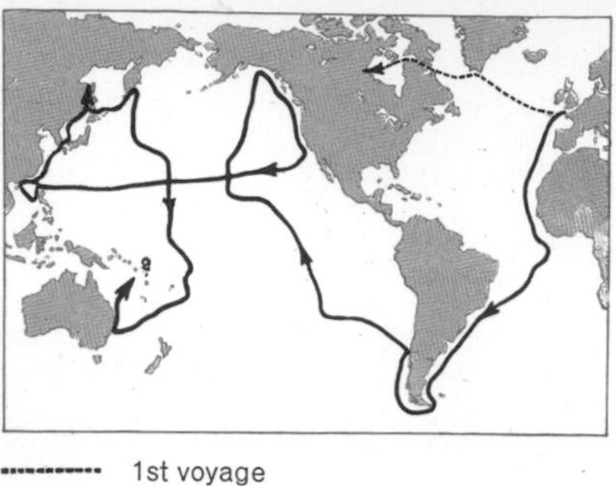

1st voyage
2nd voyage

LA PEROUSE, JEAN
1741–88 France
1781: He attacked the English in Hudson Bay.
1785: Sailed from Brest, rounded Cape Horn, and reached Easter Island; sailed northward to the Sandwich Islands and crossed to North America, where he sailed south to Monterey and then west to Macao in China and to the Philippines, through the Korean Strait and the Sea of Japan to the Gulf of Tartary. He proved that Sakhalin is an island. He went north through the islands to Kamchatka, sailed southward and reached Port Jackson in Australia. He left Botany Bay and was never heard of again.

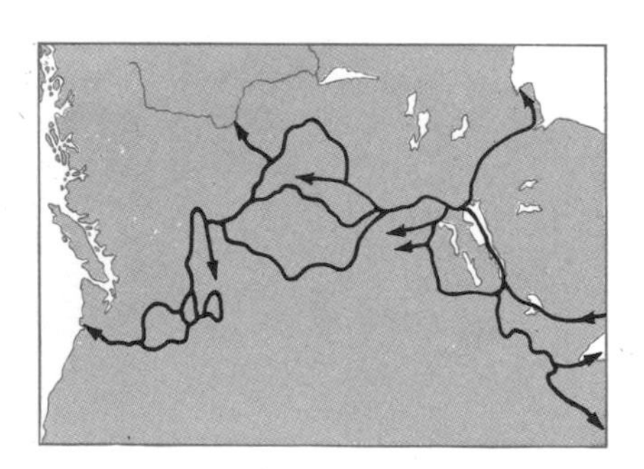

THOMPSON, DAVID
1770–1857 England
1785: He entered the service of Hudson's Bay Company.
1789–90: He worked as a surveyor, traveling along the Saskatchewan River to its mouth, then to the Hayes River.
1792–93: He worked on the Nelson River and parts of the Churchill River.
1793–97: Surveyed the territory between Cumberland House and York Factory.
1797–98: Entered the service of the Northwest Company; covered a wide territory from western Lake Superior to lakes Winnipeg and Winnipegosis, went along the Assiniboine River, Red River, the Missouri, to the source of the Mississippi and down to St. Louis.
1798: Went from Cumberland House to the Ile-à-la Crosse Lake and up the Beaver River.
1799: Went from Fort Saskatchewan to the Lesser Slave Lake and the Athabaska River.
1800: Surveyed the two branches of the Saskatchewan River and the Bow River.
1801–03: Discovered the headwaters of the Saskatchewan.
1807–11: He went from the North Saskatchewan River through the Kicking Horse Pass to the Columbia River and to Kootenay. Traveled widely in the regions of the upper Columbia River and went to the Pacific coast at Astoria.
1816–26: He surveyed for the U.S.-Canadian boundary from the St. Lawrence to the Lake of the Woods.

LACERDA, F. J. M. DE
(?)–1798 Portugal
1787: Explored the Cunene River.
1798: Traveled up the Zambezi, and crossed north to the Luangwa River, and died in Cazembe country between Lake Mweru and Lake Bangweulu.
See map on page 171.

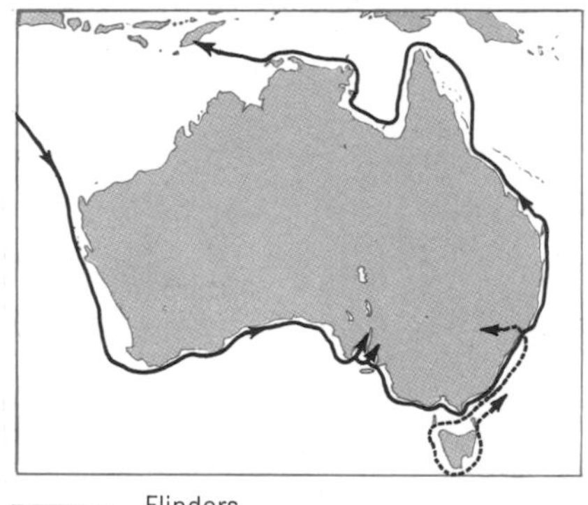

Flinders
Flinders and Bass

FLINDERS, MATTHEW
1774–1814 England
1795: Explored Botany Bay and the George River with Bass.
1798: With Bass, he went from Port Jackson along the coast between Australia and Tasmania, and then through Bass Strait and around Tasmania.
1801–02: From Batavia he reached the west Australian coast and examined the south coast between King George Sound and Cape Howe. He sailed into Spencer and St. Vincent gulfs, passing between Kangaroo Island and the mainland.
1803: He continued his coastal survey up the east coast and into the Gulf of Carpentaria. From there, after shipwreck, he finally reached Timor.

BASS, GEORGE
1763–1808(?) England
1795: With Flinders, he explored Botany Bay and George River to the south of Cook's survey.
1798: Still with Flinders, he sailed through Bass Strait, found King Island, and circumnavigated Tasmania.
See map in previous column.

PARK, MUNGO
1771–1806 Scotland
1795–97: Landed at the mouth of the Gambia and sailed 200 miles up river and then went by land to Medine and to the banks of the Senegal River. From here he crossed over to the upper Niger where it flowed east, then worked his way back to the coast.
1805–06: He traveled from the Gambia over to the Niger, down to Kabara near Timbuktu, and possibly the rapids at Bussa, where he was drowned.
See map on page 164.

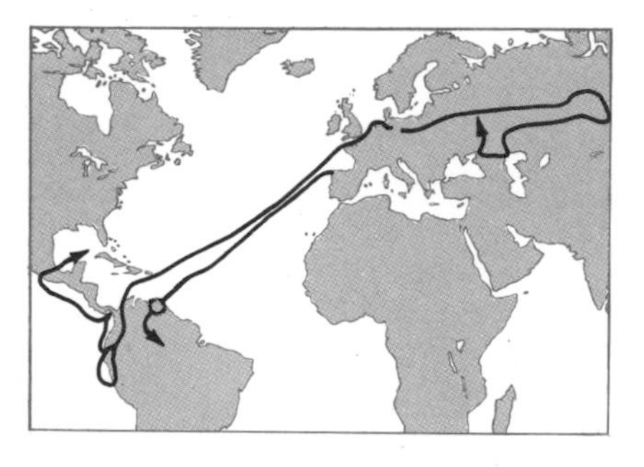

HUMBOLDT, BARON VON ALEXANDER
1769–1859 Germany
1799: Sailed from Europe to the mouth of the Orinoco, went up the river and proved that it was linked with the Amazon by a natural canal, now named the Casiquiare.
1800–01: Went to Cuba, crossed south to Cartagena, went up the Magdalena River, and visited Quito, Lima, and the sources of the Amazon.
1803: He continued in his travels, going to Acapulco on the west coast of Mexico, went to Mexico City, and then made excursions to Guanajuata, and Jalapa. He sailed home from Vera Cruz, calling at Philadelphia.
1829: Accompanied by Rose and Ehrenberg, he went to Moscow and then to Perm (Molotov). He visited Tobolsk, went to the Ob River, south to the Altai Mountains, returning to Moscow via Omsk, down the Volga to the shores of the Caspian, up the Don.

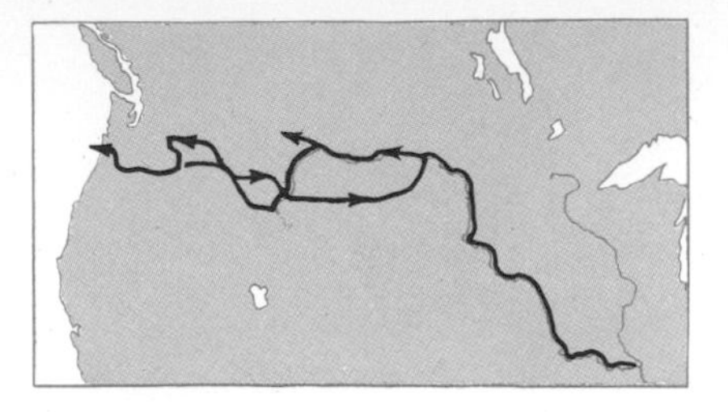

LEWIS, MERIWETHER
1774–1809 United States
See description of Clark's journey, which follows; and map above, which shows the Lewis and Clark route from St. Louis to the west coast and back to St. Louis.

CLARK, WILLIAM
1770–1838 United States
1804-06: With Lewis he went up the Missouri to the Mandan villages and to the foothills of the Rockies. From here they went up the tributary Maria's River and returned to the Missouri. They continued up the Missouri to its headwaters then crossed over the watershed to the Columbia River; went down the Columbia to its mouth. They returned by the Snake and Clearwater rivers and the Bitterroot Mountains to the head of the Jefferson River, then went down the Yellowstone River to the three forks of the Missouri and back to St. Louis.

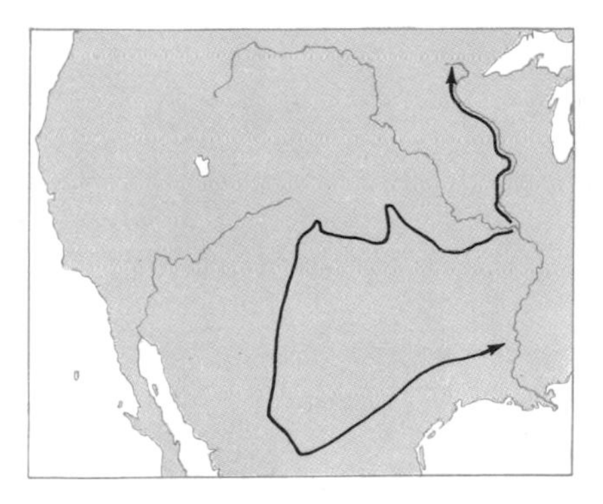

PIKE, ZEBULON
1779–1813 United States
1805: From St. Louis he went up the Mississippi to the falls of St. Antony and Lake Leech.
1806–07: From St. Louis on the Missouri he crossed to the Arkansas and followed it to its source. He discovered Pike's Peak, crossed into the valley of the Rio Grande. There he was taken prisoner by the Spanish and was taken down-river to El Paso and into Chihuahua. On being released, he returned east via Texas.

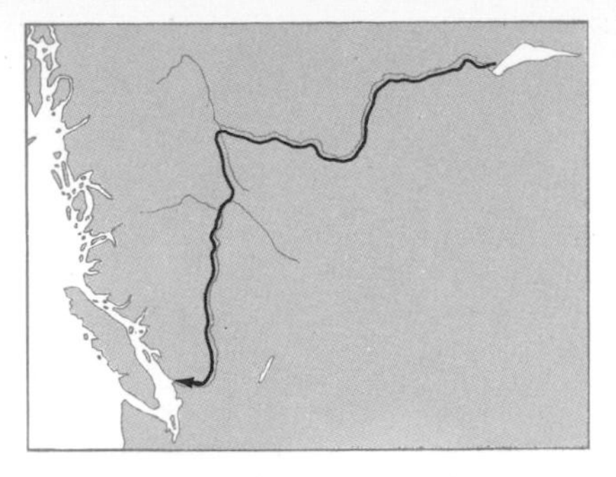

FRASER, SIMON
1776–1862 Canada
1805: He crossed the Rockies from Lake Athabaska; reached the junction of the Peace and Parsnip rivers.
1807: He went down the Fraser River, but did not quite reach the coast.

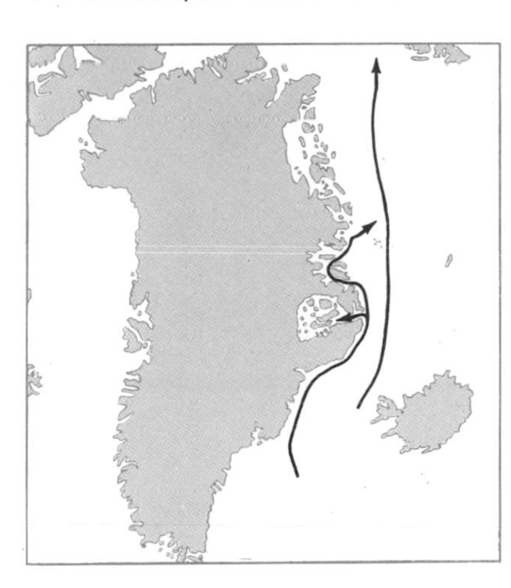

SCORESBY, WILLIAM
1760–1829 England
1806: Sailed up the eastern coast of Greenland to 81°30′ N. in the Spitsbergen area.
1818: Went with two ships to Spitsbergen to reach farther north.
1822: Charted 200 miles north of Scoresby Sound on the east coast of Greenland, from 64° N. to 75° N.

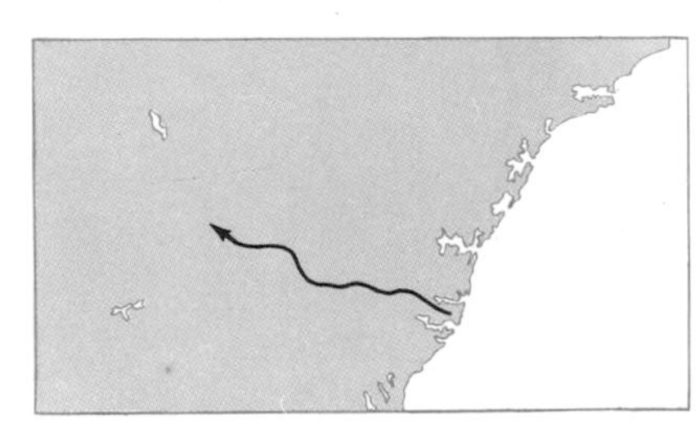

BLAXLAND, GREGORY
1778–1853 England
1810: He made two excursions up the Warragamba River west of Sydney.
1813: Crossed the Blue Mountains.
1815: Reached the site of Bathurst.

BURCKHARDT, JOHN LEWIS
1784–1812 Switzerland
1817: He visited the Holy Land and discovered the ruins of Petra.
1813–15: He left Cairo, went up the Nile, and crossed over to the port of Suakin on the Red Sea coast. He visited Jidda, Mecca and Medina.
See map on page 135.

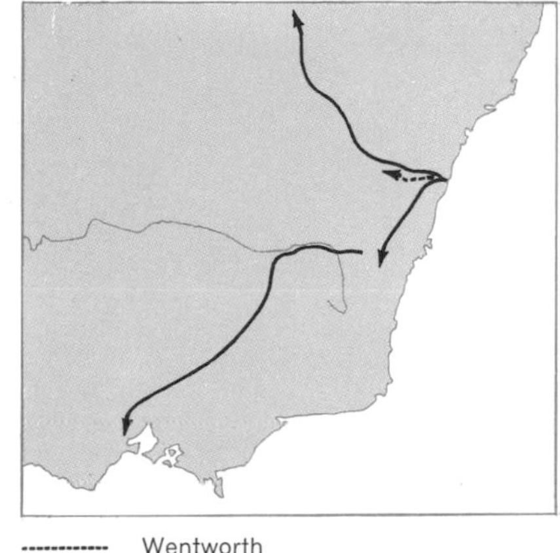

WENTWORTH, WILLIAM CHARLES
1793–1872 Australia
1813: From Sydney he found a way across Australia's Great Barrier Mountains with Blaxland.

HUME, HAMILTON
1797–1873 Australia
1814: Explored the Wingecarribee district near Sydney.
1818: He went south from Sydney to the Goulburn plains.
1822: Went to the Clyde River to Braidwood.
1824: From Lake George he went with Hovell over the upper Murrumbidgee. They discovered the Australian Alps, and reached Geelong.
1828: From Sydney he went with Sturt to the Macquarie River and north to the Castlereagh River.

CAILLIÉ, RENÉ
1799–1838 France
1816: Sailed for Senegal and spent some time traveling near St. Louis.
1824: He again visited Senegal.
1827–28: He landed in Sierra Leone and traveled eastward to the foot-hills of the Fouta Djallon and over to the upper Senegal and into the upper Niger. He started down the Niger to Djenné, Kabara (the port of Timbuktu), and Timbuktu. He crossed the Sahara to Morocco and reached Fès, then went to Tangier and back to France.
See map on page 164.

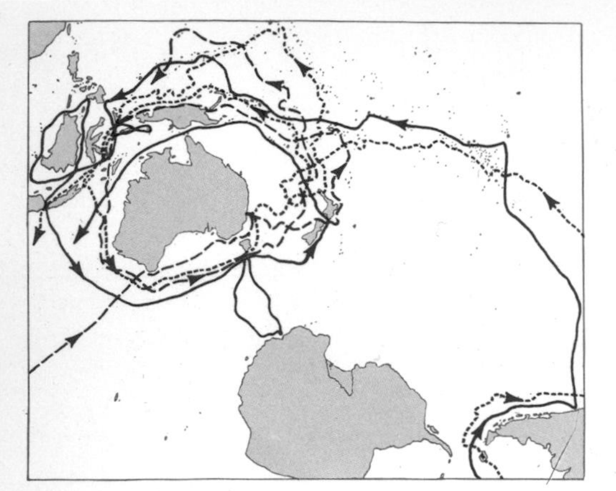

DUMONT D'URVILLE, JEAN
1780–1842 France
1822: He sailed with Duperrey to the Falkland Islands, went up the west coast of South America, then crossed the Pacific to New Ireland. He sailed to the Moluccas and around Australia, visiting southeastern Australia, New Zealand, the Carolines, and the East Indies.
1825–29: Sailed to the Pacific again, crossing the Indian Ocean to Tasmania and visiting Santa Cruz Island and the north coast of New Guinea. From here he again sailed around Australia.
1838–40: He sailed round Cape Horn to Batavia and Tasmania. Then he discovered Adélie Land in Antarctica.

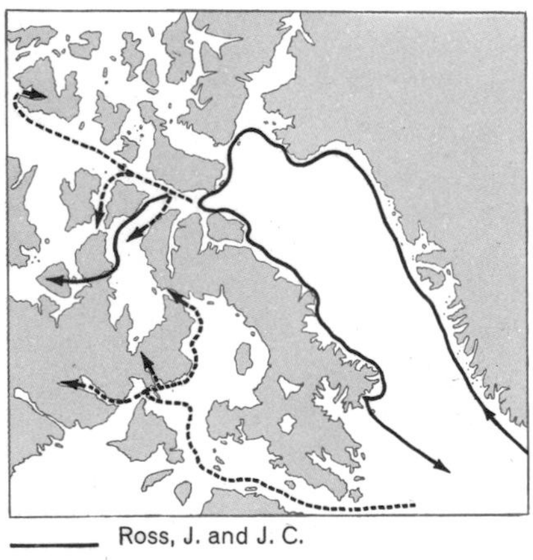

ROSS, SIR JOHN
1777–1856 Scotland
1818: Accompanied by his nephew, he sailed from England up Baffin Bay, touching Ellesmere Land and Devon Island. He went part way into Lancaster Sound, then went down the east coast of Baffin Island.
1829–33: Sailed again to the Canadian Arctic with his nephew, this time going through Lancaster Sound and Prince Regent Inlet to the Gulf of Boothia. They traveled overland across the Boothia Peninsula to King William Island.
1850–51: Sailed with his nephew to the Canadian Arctic in search of Franklin.

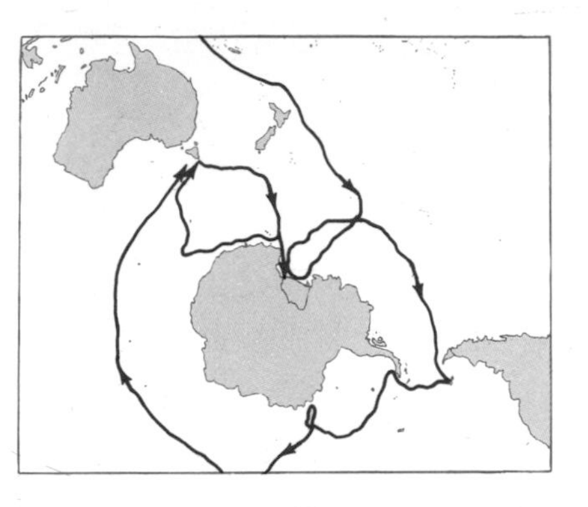

ROSS, SIR JAMES C.
1800–62 England
1818: With his uncle he sailed to Baffin Bay and Lancaster Sound.
1819–20: With Parry, he sailed through Lancaster Sound and Barrow Strait. They went westward along 630 miles of coast to Melville Island.
1821–23: Again with Parry, he explored northwest of Hudson Bay.
1824–25: Still with Parry, he went to Lancaster Sound but was shipwrecked.
1829–33: With his uncle, he reached King William Island.
1840–43: Sailed to the Antarctic and into the Ross Sea, discovering the volcanos Erebus and Terror. After cruising around the Ross Sea to 78°4' S., he set course for Tasmania, where he wintered. The second part of the voyage took him 1400 miles farther east to 78°9' S. The third part took him into the Weddell Sea area.
1848: Sailed to the Canadian Arctic in search of Franklin.

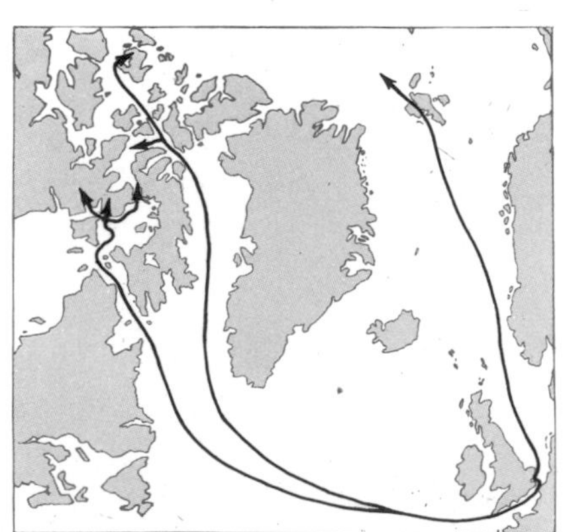

PARRY, LT. SIR WILLIAM EDWARD
1790–1855 England
1818: With John Ross and J. C. Ross, he sailed to Baffin Bay and Lancaster Sound.
1819–20: With J. C. Ross, he sailed through Lancaster Sound to Melville Island and reached 110° W.
1821–23: Again with J. C. Ross, he discovered Fury and Hecla Strait.
1824–25: Still with Ross, he went to Lancaster Sound, Prince Regent Inlet, but failed to get through.
1827: Tried to reach the North Pole from Spitsbergen, but failed.
See map bottom of previous column.

FRANKLIN, SIR JOHN
1786–1847 England
1818: Accompanied by Back, he made an attempt to get to the north of Spitsbergen.
1819–21: Accompanied by Back, he sailed into Hudson Bay and went overland to the Great Slave Lake and down the Coppermine River to the mouth, then westward for 500 miles to Cape Turnagain.
1825: Traveled down the Mackenzie to the mouth, then westward for 370 miles to Point Barrow; accompanied by Back.
1845–47: He sailed into Lancaster Sound and sailed south between Somerset Island and Prince of Wales Island. Somewhere in the region the ship was frozen in. The expedition tried to journey southward but all men perished.

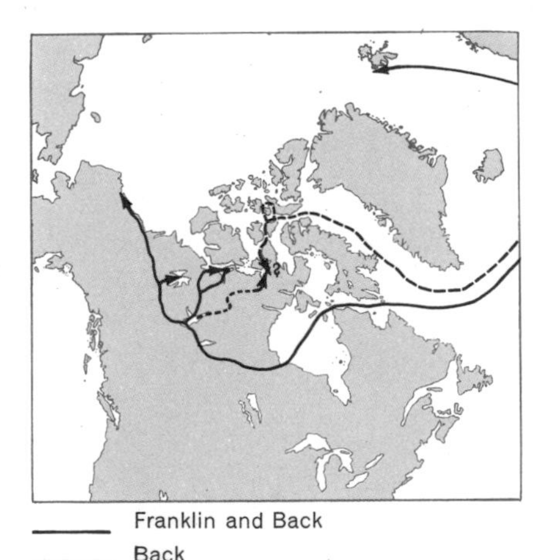

BACK, SIR GEORGE
1796–1878 England
1818: Sailed with Franklin to search for an ice-free passage north of Spitsbergen.
1819–21: With Franklin he made a land expedition across Canada: from York

Factory, to Great Slave Lake, Coppermine River, westward along the Arctic for 500 miles to Lake Turnagain.
1825: Still with Franklin, he started from New York and went to Great Slave Lake, then down the Mackenzie River, and visited the Great Bear Lake. He continued down the Mackenzie then went 370 miles west along the coast.
1833: He led a search expedition to look for Ross. He set out from the Great Slave Lake and went via the Great Fish River to its estuary (Back's River), to the coast and west to Cape Richardson.
1836: Was in Command of the *Terror* which was cought in the ice in Hudson Bay. He managed to free her and sail for England. He saved his ship, which was in a sinking condition, by running her aground on the Irish coast.

------------ Weddell, J.
———— Bellingshausen, F. von

WEDDELL, JAMES
1787–1834 England
1819–20: Sailed to the South Shetlands.
1822–23: Reached the South Orkneys; then went farther south to 74°15′ S., 34°16′ W.

BELLINGSHAUSEN, FABIAN VON
1779–1852 Estonia
1819–21: Sailed from Europe to Rio de Janeiro and south to South Georgia. He then sailed into the Antarctic and discovered Alexander I Island during his circumnavigation of Antarctica. During his voyage he crossed the Antarctic Circle at various places. Before returning to Europe, he stopped at Sydney.

CLAPPERTON, HUGH
1788–1827 Scotland
1822–25: With Denham, he tried to reach the Niger from Tripoli, crossed the Sahara to the region of Lake Chad, turned west but got only as far as Sokoto.
1825–27: With his servant Lander, he made another attempt to reach the Niger. He landed at Badagri near Lagos, crossed overland to Bussa on the Niger, and went to Kano and Sokoto, where he died.
See map on page 164.

DENHAM, DIXON
1786–1828 England
1822–25: With Clapperton, he crossed the Sahara to Bornu and saw Lake Chad; here he and Clapperton separated. He went on to the Shari River and explored a little to the south of Lake Chad before rejoining Clapperton and returning to Tripoli.
See map on page 164.

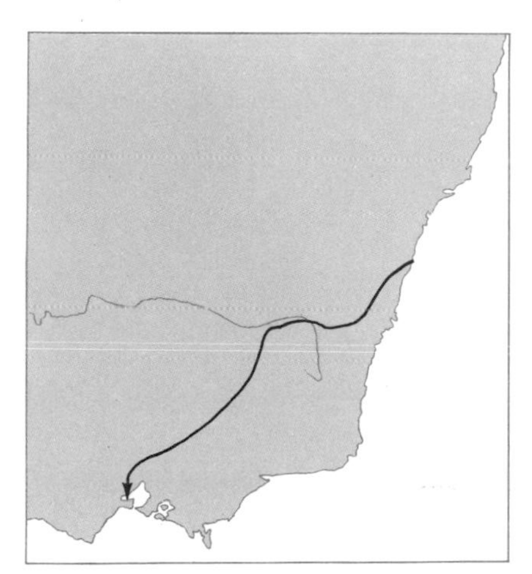

HOVELL, WILLIAM HILTON
1786–1875 England
1824: He went from Sidney to Lake George where he joined Hume. They went over the Murrumbidgee, across the Goulburn and Murray rivers to Port Phillip Bay.

LANDER, RICHARD LEMON
1804–34 England
1825–27: As Clapperton's servant he went from the West African coast to Bussa, Kano, and Sokoto, where Clapperton died.
1830: He again went from the West African coast (this time with his brother) inland to Bussa and then down the Niger to Brass at the mouth. He was forced to return to England by way of Rio de Janeiro since the only ship available was bound for South America.
See map on page 164.
1834: Died on one of his expeditions on the island of Fernando Po.

SMITH, JEDIDIAH
1798(?)–1831 United States
1826: He left Great Salt Lake for the southwest. He traveled down the

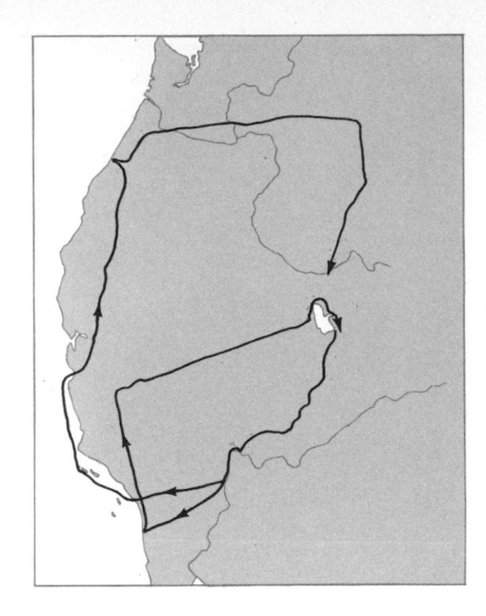

Virgin River to the Colorado then west to the coast to San Diego. Next he went north over the mountains to the San Joaquin River, then east through the Sonora Pass in the Sierra Nevada and across the desert back to Great Salt Lake.
1827: Set out again from Great Salt Lake to San Gabriel on the coast, then went by sea to Monterey. Went up the Sacramento River, over the Cascade Mountains to the Umpqua River, and down to the coast. Went down the Willamette to Fort Vancouver on the Colorado. Went to Spokane House and through the Flathead Pass to the Snake River.

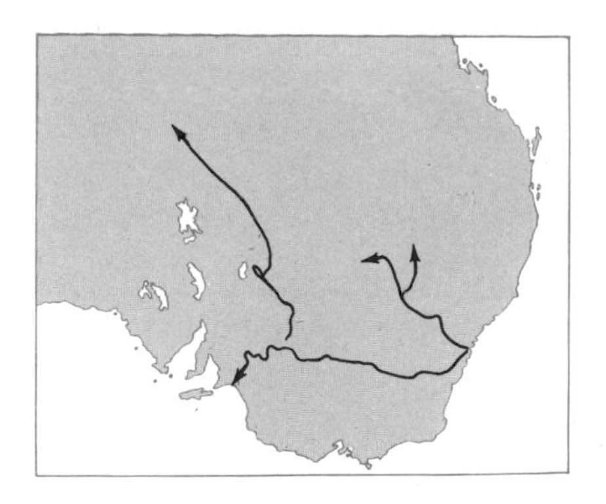

STURT, CHARLES
1795–1869 England
1827: Arrived at Sydney with his regiment to guard the convicts.
1828–29: From Sydney he crossed the Blue Mountains to the Macquarie River and went across to the Bogan River and down to the Darling, and then back to the Macquarie. From here he went to the Castlereagh River and to the Darling again.
1829: From Sydney he went to Lake

George, to the Murrumbidgee River and then by boat to its junction with the Murray and down to the sea at Encounter Bay. He returned up the Murray and back to Sydney.
1844: From Adelaide he went into the interior by the Murray and Darling rivers and then moved northwest across the Great Stony Desert. He crossed Coopers Creek and penetrated into the central Australian region.

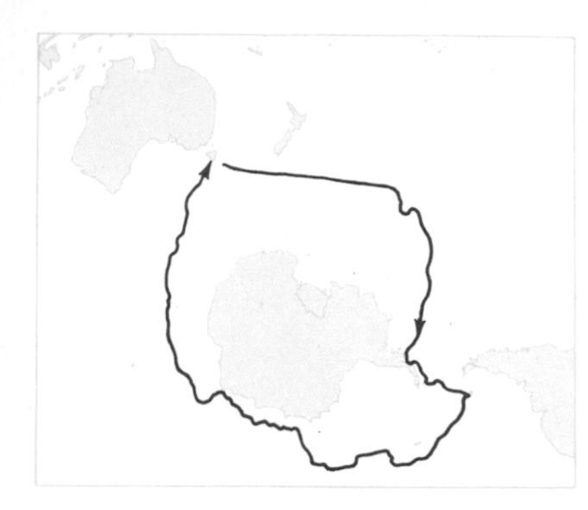

BISCOE, JOHN
(?)–1848 England
1831–32: Went from Tasmania and circumnavigated Antarctica, discovering Adelaide Island and Biscoe Island (off Graham Land), and touched the Antarctic Continent at Enderby Land.

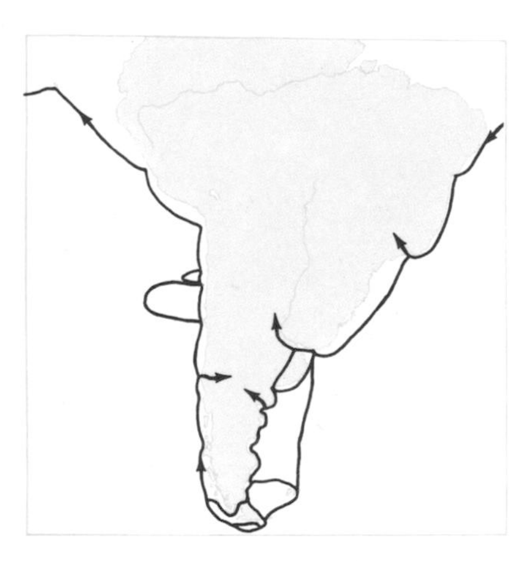

DARWIN, CHARLES
1809–82 England
1831: He sailed from England for South America; visited the islands of Rocas, Fernando de Noronha. He called at Bahia and Rio de Janeiro and then traveled a short distance inland. Next he went to the Río de la Plata and sailed down the coast, making extensive journeys inland up the Paraná and Colorado rivers and Buenos Aires to Bahia Blanca. He visited the Patagonian coast and the Falkland Islands, sailed through the Strait of Magellan and also around Cape Horn. He next sailed up the west coast as far as Lima, calling at various places and making one inland journey in Chile. He also visited the Galapagos Islands and returned home across the Pacific, thus completing a voyage around the world.

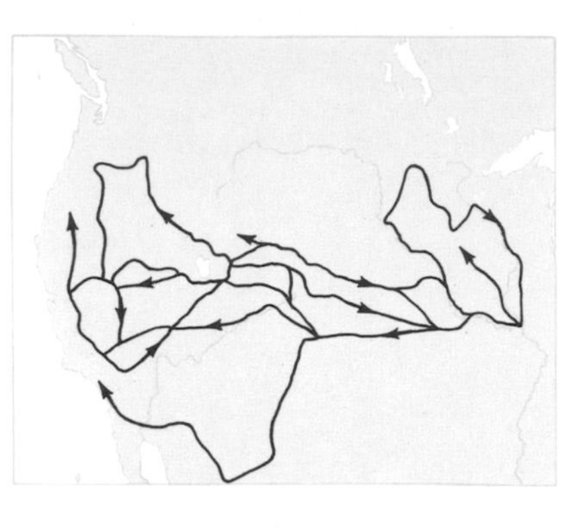

FRÉMONT, JOHN CHARLES
1813–90 United States
1838–40: With Nicollet, he surveyed the courses and land between the Mississippi and Missouri rivers.
1841: He made a survey of the Des Moines River.
1842: He explored the Kansas, North Platte, and Sweetwater rivers as far as South Pass, and he climbed Fremont Peak, which is the highest mountain in Wind River Mountains. He returned to Washington.
1843: Started from Kansas and went to Pike's Peak, Pueblo, Colorado, the Black Mountains, the Medicine Bow Mountains, the Sweetwater River, South Pass to Great Salt Lake. Next he went north to the Snake River and on to the Columbia River and Fort Vancouver. He returned around the Great Basin, crossing the Klamath and Carson rivers, the Sierras, the Sacramento Valley, the San Joaquin Valley, along the Spanish Trail to Santa Fé, and then on to Utah Lake, across to the headwaters of the Platte rivers and back to Pueblo.
1845: His party divided and crossed the Great Basin by two different trails. They rejoined at Walker Lake at the foot of the Sierra Nevada where they divided again. One party went by Sutter's Creek and the other by the south of the Sierra Nevada and met again at San Jose. Frémont's group went northward up the Sacramento and reached Klamath Lake, then turned west to explore the Cascade Range.
1848: He left Pueblo and went west across the Sangre de Cristo Mountains to the headwaters of the Rio Grande, and then went down-river to Toas and west to California.
1853: He left Kansas City, went over the Wasatch Mountains to Parawan and then turned southwest to the Sierra Nevada.

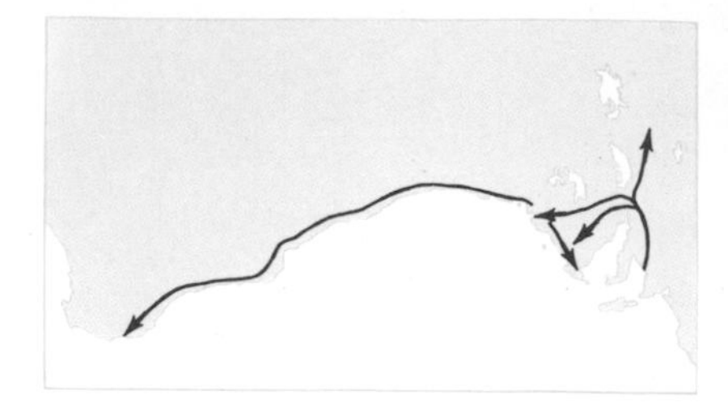

EYRE, EDWARD JOHN
1815–1901 England
1839: He started from his home which was 150 miles north of Adelaide, explored Flinders Range, climbed Mount Eyre and saw Lake Torrens.
Second journey: From Adelaide he went to Streaky Bay and crossed Lincoln's Peninsula (now Eyre Peninsula) from the west.
1840: He went to the Flinders Range as far as Mount Hopeless but turned back and explored to the west and beyond Streaky Bay; returned to Adelaide.
1841: After small excursions to the west he set out from Fowler's Bay and followed the south coast around the Great Australian Bight to Albany on the southwest coast.

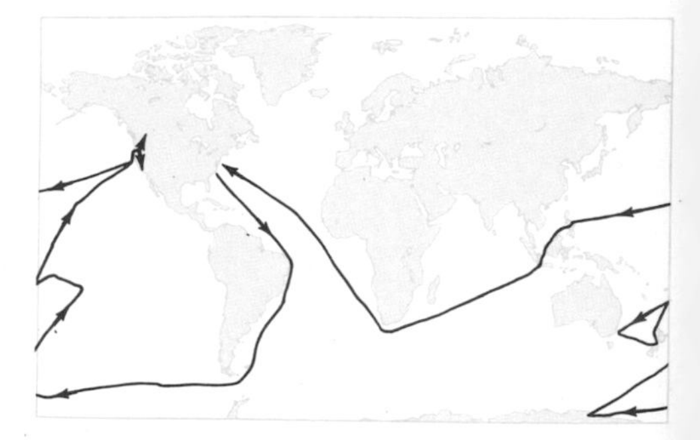

WILKES, CHARLES
1798–1877 United States
1839–41: Sailed from the east coast to the Antarctic and discovered Wilkes Land. On returning to the Pacific he surveyed the Paumotu group then visited Tahiti, the Samoas, Australia and New Zealand, Tonga Islands, Fiji, and the Sandwich Islands. He reached the Pacific coast of North America near the Columbia River and sent expeditions inland to survey the Columbia as far as Walla Walla and to explore

up the Willamette and over to the sources of the Sacramento, which he followed down to San Francisco. In the same year he sailed to Manila and returned to the United States by the Cape.

CROZIER, FRANCIS RAWDON MOIRA
1796(?)–1848 England
1840–43: He sailed with J. C. Ross to the Antarctic in the *Terror*.
See **ROSS** *entry.*
1845–47: He sailed with Franklin to the Canadian Arctic and perished along with the others.

LIVINGSTONE, DAVID
1813–73 Scotland
1841: Landed at Algoa Bay and traveled north over the veld to the Limpopo River.
1842: Explored to the northwest of the Drakensberg.
1849–51: After returning to England, he landed at the Cape and traveled north. Discovered Lake Ngami and reached the Zambezi River.
1852–54: Traveled up the Zambezi and west across the Bihé Plateau to Loanda on the coast. He returned to the Zambezi.
1854–56: Discovered Victoria Falls and traveled down the Zambezi to its mouth and to Quelimane.
1858–60: Returned up the Zambezi, came down-river, went up the Shire River and discovered Lake Nyasa.
1860–64: Explored the western side of Lake Nyasa; sailed from the mouth of the Zambezi to the Comoro Islands; back to Africa and up the Rovuma River.
1866–69: Explored from Lake Nyasa to Lake Mweru and north to Ujiji on Lake Tanganyika.
1869–73: Traveled from Ujiji to Nyangwe on the Congo, back to Lake Tanganyika, and south to Lake Bangweulu where he died.
See map on page 171.

HUC, ABBÉ
1813–60 France
1843–46: He arrived in China at Canton and traveled north to Peking. He left Peking disguised as a Lama, crossed the plains of Dolon Nor, the Hwang Ho and then went in a southwest direction to Koko Nor and Tsaidam. He continued on, crossed the upper reaches of the Yangtze, and reached Lhasa. On the return journey to Canton, he traveled east across the great rivers into the Red Basin and down the Yangtze.
See map on page 130.

BARTH, HEINRICH
1821–65 Germany
1844–46: He traveled overland from Tunis to Egypt and visited various countries of the Middle East.
1850: From Tripoli he went to Lake Chad and south to the Benue River, where it is joined by the Earo River. He went west to Yola, then east and returned to Lake Chad.
1852–55: From Lake Chad he went to Kano and Sokoto, Say on the Niger, and overland to Timbuktu. He returned down the Niger to Say and then west to Lake Chad; back across the desert through Murzuk to Tripoli, and back to England.
See map on page 164.

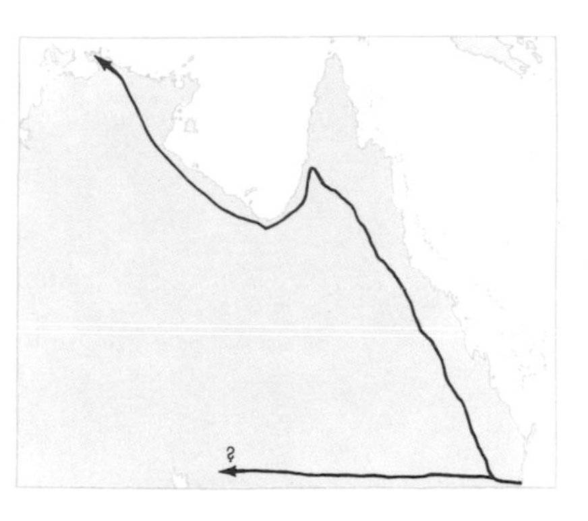

LEICHHARDT, DR. LUDWIG
1813–48 Germany
1844: He left Moreton Bay, went to the Condamine River and northeast to the Burdekin River, and down the Mitchell River to the Gulf of Carpentaria. He passed round the south of the Gulf to the extreme north of Arnhem Land.
1848: Set off from Moreton Bay to cross Australia from east to west.

GREGORY, SIR AUGUSTUS CHARLES
1819–1905 England
1846: From Perth he explored the Gascoyne River and country behind Shark Bay and northwest to latitude 27° S.
1855: He landed at Pearce Point and went up the Victoria River to Sturt's Creek, and followed a route similar to Leichhardt's in 1844, but in the opposite direction.
1857: He went to the Barcoo River, Strzelecki Creek, Lake Blanche, and Adelaide, thus completing two transcontinental journeys. (He also went on several journeys with his brother—F. T. Gregory—north of Perth.)

GREGORY, FRANCIS THOMAS
1821–88 England
1846: He explored Lake Moore northeast of Perth.
1857: He explored the Murchison River to Impey.
1858: He went to the Gascoyne Basin, Lyons River, and Mount Augustus.
1861: He started from Nichol Bay and went up the Fortescue River and followed its course as far as he could, then cut across to the Ashburton River. He returned to Nichol Bay and set off again inland to the Yule, Shaw, De Grey, Oakover rivers; went down the Oakover to the coast and back to Nichol Bay.
See map bottom of previous column.

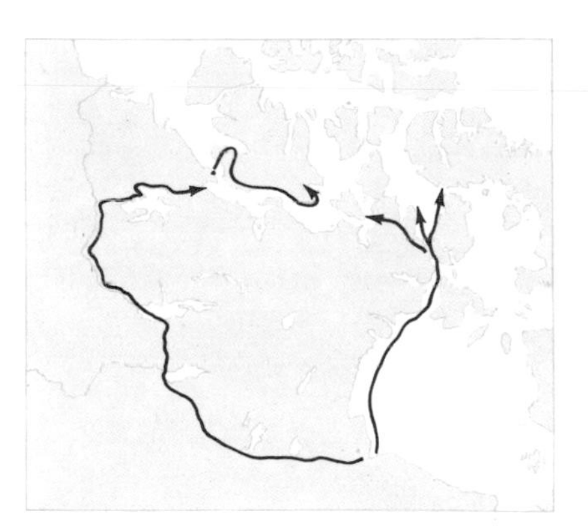

RAE, DR. JOHN
1813–93 Scotland
1846: In the service of Hudson's Bay Company, he went from Repulse Bay overland to Committee Bay.
1847: Went on a second journey to Committee Bay and explored both sides of the bay but did not quite reach Fury and Hecla Strait.
1851: On a search for Franklin, he went to the Coppermine River via the Great Slave Lake and Great Bear Lake, then on to Wollaston Land and east Victoria Island.
1854: He crossed Boothia Peninsula to the east coast of Kind William Island.

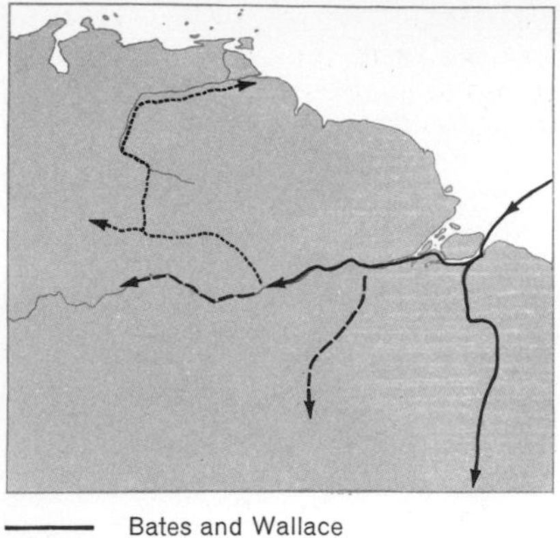

BATES, HENRY WALTER
1825–92 England
1848: With Wallace he went to Pará in South America and up the Tocantins River. Together they journeyed up the Amazon to Santarem, Obidos, and Manaus at the junction of the river Negro where they parted. Bates went on up river for about 400 miles before returning to Pará in 1852.
1857: He returned to Pará, went up to Santarem and up the Tapajóz River. After this journey he went up the Amazon to Ega, where he had been before.
1859: Sailed home to England after a journey of nearly two years.

WALLACE, ALFRED RUSSEL
1823–1913 England
1848: With Bates, he arrived at Pará. They went up the Tocantins River and up the Amazon to Manaus. From here Wallace continued up the Negro, explored up the Uaupes as far as the second cataract at Juaurite. He came down the Uaupes, continued up the Negro, crossed over to the Orinoco, went down the river and returned to England.
1854–60: He explored in the East Indies archipelago including New Guinea.

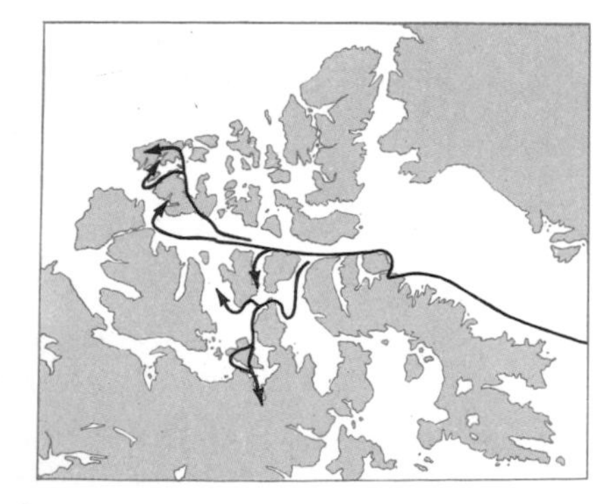

McCLINTOCK, SIR FRANCIS LEOPOLD
1819–1907 Ireland
1848: Went on a search expedition for Franklin from Baffin Bay with Sir James Ross.
1850: Went into the Canadian Arctic and visited Cornwallis Island and Melville Peninsula.
1852–53: He went around Melville Island, discovered and explored part of Prince Patrick Island. This voyage also was a search expedition for Franklin.
1857–59: Led an expedition to the Canadian Arctic, passing between Boothia Peninsula and King William Island, completing the discovery of the Prince of Wales Island. He found the message left by Franklin's expedition. He also explored McClintock Channel.
See map bottom of previous column.

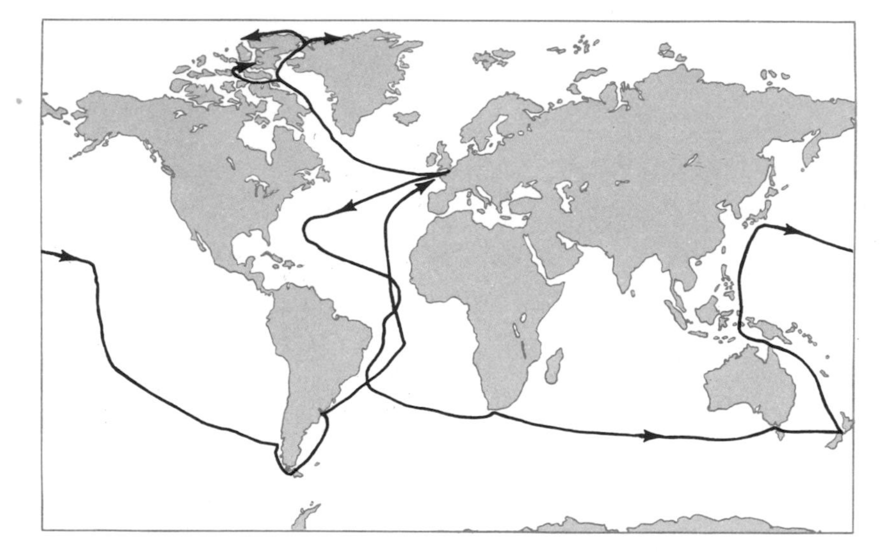

NARES, SIR GEORGE STRONG
1831–1915 England
1852: Sailed into the Canadian Arctic on one of the Franklin search expeditions. He went through Lancaster Sound and to the west and north of Devon Island.
1872–76: He was in command of the British Naval Expedition in the *Challenger*. He crossed the Atlantic three times and then went via Capetown to Melbourne, New Zealand, the East Indies, Japan, the Sandwich Islands, and Tahiti. He crossed to southern Chile, went through the Strait of Magellan to Montevideo, Ascension Island, and reached the Azores.
1876: He went into the Canadian Arctic through Smith Sound as far as 82° 27′ N. and discovered the Challenger Mountains.

BURTON, SIR RICHARD FRANCIS
1821–90 England
1853: He went to Arabia, visiting Medina and Mecca.
1854: Went from Aden across to Somaliland and traveled to Harrar with Speke.
1857–58: With Speke, he searched for the central African lakes. They left Zanzibar and traveled west to Lake Tanganykia at Ujiji: returned east to Tabora, where Burton and Speke separated.
1877: He visited the Holy Land.
(He also visited Fernando Po and Mount Cameroons.)
See maps on pages 135 and 171.

SPEKE, JOHN HANNING
1827–64 England
(Commissioned in the Indian Army and fought in the Punjab. Spent furloughs exploring in Tibet.)
1854: Went to Somaliland with Burton.
1857–58: Again with Burton, he went to East Africa. He left Burton at Tabora, went north and discovered Lake Victoria before returning to Zanzibar.
1860–63: With Grant, he went to East Africa again, inland to Lake Victoria, discovered Ripon Falls, and went along the Nile, but missed its entrance into Lake Albert.
See map on page 171.

NORDENSKJÖLD, BARON NILS ADOLF ERIK
1832–1901 Russia
(Settled in Sweden.)
1858: Went to Spitsbergen.
1861: Attempted to reach the North Pole by dog sledge from north Spitsbergen.

1864: Again visited Spitsbergen.
1868: Went to Spitsbergen and to 81°42′ N.
1870: Tried to cross Greenland from Disko Island off the west coast, but went only 30 miles before having to turn back.
1872: Reached Phipps Island in Spitsbergen.
1875: Made a preliminary trip to Novaya Zemlya in search of a northeast passage to the East.
1876: On his second attempt to find a northeast passage, he left Sweden and reached as far as the mouth of the Yenisei River.
1878–79: Discovered a northeast passage by sailing along the Arctic coast of Asia, through the Bering Strait to Japan; he returned to Scandinavia via the Indian Ocean and the Mediterranean through the recently opened Suez Canal.
1883: Went on his second expedition to Greenland and reached 75 miles inland from Aluatsivik Fiord, near Disko Island.
See map on page 178.

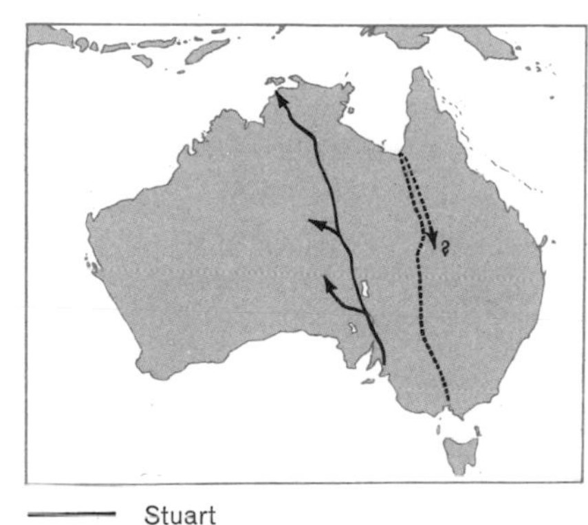

Stuart
Burke

STUART, JOHN McDOUALL
1815–66 Scotland
1844: He was with Sturt in Australia.
1858: Explored the area north of Lake Gairdner.
1860: Left Adelaide and skirted Lake Eyre to the west, reaching the MacDonnell Ranges, the Finke River, and the Stuart Range.
1861: He followed a similar route but got farther north before he was stopped by the dense bush near Ashburton Range.
1862: Went north from Adelaide and this time got through the bush, discovered the Daly River, and reached the northern coast.

BURKE, ROBERT O'HARA
1820–61 Ireland
1860: Burke and W. J. Wills were the first men to cross Australia from south to north. They went from Melbourne to Menindee on the Darling River, crossed Cooper's Creek, and reached the Flinders River to within sound of the sea. On the return journey they died somewhere between Cooper's Creek and Adelaide.

BAKER, SIR SAMUEL WHITE
1821–93 England
1861–64: He went up the Nile to Gondokoro where he met Speke (coming from Lake Victoria) and then continued south, discovering the outlet of the Nile at Lake Albert. Went round the lake by canoe and discovered the Murchison Falls; he returned to Gondokora and down the Nile to Khartoum.
See map on page 164.

RICHTHOFEN, FERDINAND, BARON VON
1833–1905 Germany
1867: Left Shanghai and went to Chinkiang, returned to Shanghai by a route south of the river.
1868: Traveled up the Yangtze as far as Hankow.
1868: Went from Chinkiang overland to the Shantung peninsula, crossed to Manchuria and returned to Peking. Went from Peking to Shanghai by sea.
1869: Went up the Yangtze for about 300 miles, returned to Shanghai.
1869: Went from Shanghai by sea to Canton, crossed China from south to north to Peking.
1870: Explored the area south of the mouth of the Yangtze.
1870: From Shanghai he traveled to Tientsin by sea, then by land to Peking. Next he traveled south and southwest to the Red Basin and down the Yangtze to Chinkiang.
See map on page 130.

ROHLFS, FRIEDRICH GERHARD
1831–96 Germany
1862: Went from Tangier to Fès and into the desert, attempting to reach Timbuktu, but failed.
1864: He crossed to Tripoli.
1865: From Tripoli to Murzuk, across the Sahara to Lake Chad, down the Benue River, then down the Niger.
1867–68: He was in Abyssinia.
1869: He skirted the north coast of Africa from Tripoli to Alexandria.
1874: He went on an expedition to Siwa in the Libyan Desert.
1878: He went from Tripoli to the Kufra oasis.
1880–81: He was again in Abyssinia, traveling from Massawa to the vicinity of the upper Blue Nile.
1885: German consul at Zanzibar.
See map on page 164.

SCHWEINFURTH, GEORG AUGUST
1836–1925 Germany
1863–66: He left Egypt and went across to the Red Sea coast, then down the coast and crossed to Khartoum through north Abyssinia.
1868–71: Sailed from Suez to Suakin and then went overland to Khartoum. Went up the Nile and crossed to the northern tributaries of the Congo; explored the area of the headwaters of the Ubangi; then went east toward Lake Albert.
See map on page 164.

STANLEY, SIR HENRY MORTON
1841 (?)–1904 United States
(Born in Wales and as a young boy sailed to New Orleans.)
1869: Went to Paris, Suez Canal, and to Zanzibar overland to Tabora and Ujiji on Lake Tanganyika. Here he found Livingstone, and they explored the northern end of the lake.
1874–75: Went from Zanzibar to Lake Victoria (circumnavigated it).
1875–76: Went from Lake Victoria to Lake Edward and to Lake Tanganyika.
1876–77: Went from Lake Tanganyika to the Lualaba River and down the Congo to its mouth.
1879–84: In the service of Belgium, he arrived at the Congo and went inland; discovered Lake Tumba, Lake Leopold II, and explored the middle tributaries of the Congo.
1888–89: He returned to the Congo and went up river, then went across to Lake Albert.
See map on page 171.

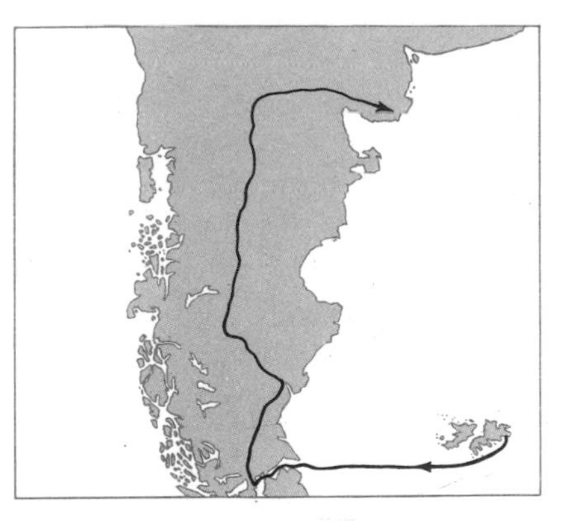

MUSTERS, GEORGE CHAWARTH
1841–79 England
1869–70: From the Falkland Islands he went to Punta Arenas (overlooking the Strait of Magellan), traveled north to the river Chico—following it nearly to its source—and continued through Patagonia parallel to the Andes, then to the coast at the river Negro mouth.

NACHTIGAL, GUSTAV
1834–85 Germany
1869–74: Went from Tripoli to Murzuk, then explored Tibesti, He crossed the Sahara to the Lake Chad region, then went eastward to Darfur. From here he continued to the Nile and returned to Cairo.
See map on page 164.

PRZHEVALSKY, NIKOLAI MIKHAILOVITCH
1839–88 Russia
1870–72: Went from Kyakhta to Urga and across the Gobi to Kalgan. He visited northeast Mongolia and went back to Kalgan. He also visited the Ordos country and then Peking. From Peking he set off westward, crossed the Hwang Ho and reached Koko Nor, Tsaidam, and the headwaters of the Yangtze. Returned by Koko Nor, Ala Shan, north across the Gobi to Urga.
1876–77: He left Kuldja, crossed the Tien Shan to the Tarim River and to Lob Nor, discovered the Altyn Tagh range, and returned to Kuldja.
1879: Went across the Dzungaria to Hami, over the Altyn Tagh and to east of Tsaidam, and south to within 170 miles of Lhasa. He then turned eastward, skirted the Hwang Ho, and crossed the Gobi to Kyakhta.
1883–85: Went from Urga, crossed the Gobi to Ala Shan, entered the upper valley of the Di Chu (Yangtze), and returned to explore the region of the source of the Hwang Ho south of Tsaidam. He turned north and recrossed the Altyn Tagh to Lob Nor, then turned westward along the southern edge of the Tarim Basin, crossed the Takla Makan Desert and the Tien Shan to Issyk Kul.
1888: He died at Karakol after setting out on his fifth journey.
See map on page 130.

MORENO, FRANCISCO
dates unknown (?)
1873–1902: Explored along the Argentine-Chile frontier, especially in Patagonia, from the river Negro southward, including the Lake Buenos Aires region.

CAMERON, VERNEY LOVETT
1844–94 England
1874: Crossed Africa from east to west. He set out from Zanzibar, crossed Lake Tanganyika, the Lukuga River, the watershed between the Congo and Zambezi, and reached Lobito on the coast of Angola.
See map on page 171.

DOUGHTY, CHARLES MONTAGU
1843–1926 England
1875–78: Went from England to the area east of the river Jordan, Damascus, then crossed the desert to Medain Salih, Taima, Haïl. From here he went east to Buraida before continuing to Mecca and then on to Jidda.
See map on page 135.

THOMSON, JOSEPH
1858–95 Scotland
1878: Set out from Dar-es-Salaam to Lake Nyasa, Lake Rukwa and to the Lukuga outlet on Lake Tanganyika, Ujiji. He tried to reach the Congo, but was unsuccessful, so he returned to the east coast via Tabora.
1881: Explored the Rovuma River.
1883: He set out for the Great Rift Valley, leaving Mombasa and visiting Lake Naivasha, Mount Kenya, and the northern shore of Lake Victoria. He returned by way of Mount Elgon, Lake Baringo, and a more easterly route. (He also journeyed in Algeria and Morocco; and in the service of the South Africa Company, he traveled extensively in southern Africa.)
See map on page 171.

PANDIT KRISHNA (A–K)
dates unknown India
1878–82: As a surveyor with the Indian government, he visited Lhasa and traveled north through Tibet to Koko Nor. He returned south by a more westerly route to the Di Chu (upper Yangtze). After going down-river for several miles, he crossed west to Lhasa.
See map on page 130.

JUNKER, WILHELM JOHANN
1840–92 Germany
1879–86: He left Khartoum, went up the White Nile to Malakal, crossed the Sudd region to the upper waters of the Ubangi River, where he explored the region of the Uele River. He returned to the White Nile, then went west of the river to Lake Albert, south to Lake Victoria, and to the east coast at Zanzibar.
See map on page 164.

DE LONG, GEORGE WASHINGTON
1844–81 United States
1879: He sailed north through the Bering Strait, and passed through the ice pack. The ship was frozen in, so the expedition set out on foot for the New Siberian Islands and eventually reached the north coast of Asia. De Long and some of his men died before help could reach them.
See map on page 178.

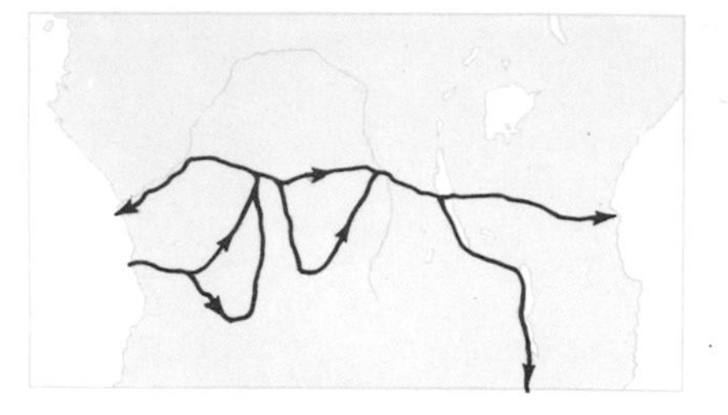

WISSMANN, VON H.
1853–1905 Germany
1880–83: He set out from Loanda on Africa's west coast, went to Malange, across to the Kasai River, and through the southern Congo Basin to Nyangwe on the Lualaba River. From here he went east to Lake Tanganyika, Ujiji, and through Tabora across to the east coast.
1884–85: He again went from Loanda to Malange, then turned northeast to the lower Kasai River and went down-river to the Congo, then down the Congo to its mouth.
1886: He went up the Congo and again explored the Kasai region, crossed over to Nyangwe and Lake Tanganyika. He turned south to Lake Nyasa, went down the Shire River and down the Zambezi to Quelimane.

NANSEN, FRIDTJOF
1861–1930 Norway
1882: Visited the east coast of Greenland.
1888: He was the first to cross southern Greenland from the east coast at 64°30′ N. to Godthaab.
1893–96: He sailed from Norway in the *Fram* to the vicinity of the New Siberian Islands, where he allowed himself to be deliberately frozen in. The ship drifted with the ice to 85°57′ N. Nansen left the ship near this point and tried to reach the North Pole by foot, but was forced back. He went to Franz Josef Land, where he wintered, then returned to the mainland.
See map on page 178.

PEARY, ROBERT, EDWIN
1856–1920 United States
1886: Went 120 miles inland in Greenland from the west coast at latitude 69°30′ N.
1891–97: Went to Inglefield Gulf in Smith Sound and then northeast overland to Independence Fiord, thus proving that Greenland is an island.
1893–95: He reached 83°N. from Independence Fiord.
1898–1901: He explored Grant Land (Ellesmere Land) and reached 83°37′N., the most northerly part of Greenland.
1902: He went from Repulse Bay to 84°17′ N., due north of Grant Land.
1905–06: From Grant Land he reached 87°6′ N.; he surveyed northern Ellesmere Land to Axel Heiberg Island.
1908–09: He finally reached the North Pole from the northern tip of Ellesmere Land.
See map on page 178.

YOUNGHUSBAND, SIR FRANCIS EDWARD
1863–1942 England
1886: After arriving in Peking he visited Manchuria.
1887: He set off westward from Peking to cross the Gobi Desert to Hami, Aksu and Kashgar at the western end of the Tarim Basin. He went south through the Karakoram Range to Srinager and on to Simla.
1888: He landed in Burma at Moulmein, went up the Salween River, across to the Mekong, and then west to Mandalay. This was while serving in the "Burmah War."
1889: He left Rawalpindi for Leh, traveled north through the Karakoram Pass to Yarkand. He returned via Gilgit to Rawalpindi, then went southwest to Quetta and Karachi.
1892–94: He explored the Kunar Valley and crossed to the upper Oxus.
1904: He went from Simla across the northern Ganges plain to Darjeeling, and then to Lhasa.
See map on page 130.

BINGER, LOUIS GUSTAV
dates unknown France
1887–89: He set out from the mouth of the Senegal and went through Bamako to the region south of the great bend of the Niger. He traced the watershed between the Niger and the Volta rivers, then went to Bingerville on the coast.
1892: He determinded the boundary between the Gold Coast and the Ivory Coast.
See map on page 164.
1892: Explored in the southern Sudan.

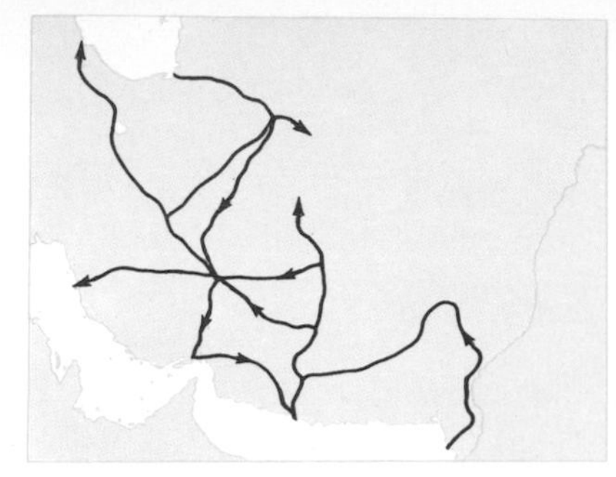

SYKES, SIR PERCY
1867–1945 England
1893: Went from the southeast shores of Caspian Sea to Asterabad, up the Atrak valley to Meshed, crossed Persia to Kerman, Shiraz, and Bushire on the coast of the Persian Gulf.
1893–94: He went from Chahrar on the south coast of Persia northward into Sarhad, climbed Koh-i-Taftan, returned through Kerman, Yezd, and Teheran to the Caspian Sea.
1894: From the Caspian Sea he went to Kashan, Yezd, and the country south of Kerman.
1897–1901: Explored in the country north of Bashakird from Bandar Abbas to Chahrar. He went into the Seistan region and then to the southwest of Kerman.
1902: Explored southeast of Kerman and then northeast to Meshed.
1906–10: Explored northeast between Meshed and Asterabad.
(As a surveyor during the first World War, he explored much of the territory between Baghdad, the Caspian Sea, and the Hindu Kush.)

HEDIN, SVEN ANDERS
1865–1952 Sweden
1891: He visited Bukhara, then Samarkand, and went through Andijan to Kashgar. He crossed north over the Tien Shan to Issyk Kul, then turned west to Tashkent and Samarkand.
1894–97: He reached Tashkent, Kashgar, and traveled extensively in the Pamirs and the Tarim Basin. He visited Kurla in the northeast and Khotan and Keriya in the south. He crossed the Kunlun Shan to Koko Nor, went over the Ordos to Kalgan, then north across the Gobi.
1899–1902: He again traveled widely in the Tarim Basin, this time particularly in the Lob Nor area. He crossed southward over the Plateau of Tibet before turning westward (just north of the Brahmaputra River) to Leh, then went north over the Karakoram to Yarkand and Kashgar.
1906: On this journey he explored on the Plateau of Tibet, the upper Brahmaputra, and finally crossed the Indo-Gangetic plain.
1908: He was again north of the Himalayas, traveling in Tibet and in the Karakoram.
1928–33: He was with a Sino-Swedish expedition which traveled overland from Shanghai to Peking, then across the Gobi Desert to Turfan. He visited many towns in the Tarim Basin, including Kurla, Kashgar, Khotan, and he explored extensively the area to the north of Lob Nor. He finally went from Urumchi through the Dzungaria to Russia.
1933–35: He was road prospecting for the Chinese government. He left Peking and traveled across the Gobi to Urumchi, went on to Ansi (which is north of the Nan Shan), then west to Lob Nor. Finally he traveled east through Langchow and Sian to Chinkiang, Shanghai, then north to Peking and into Russia.
See map on page 130.

LARSEN, C. A.
dates unknown Norway
1893: He discovered Oscar II Land on Graham Land.
1902–03: Explored part of Weddell Sea with Nordenskjöld (Otto).
See map on page 186.

STEIN, SIR AUREL
1862–1943 Hungary
1900: He traveled from Srinager to Gilgit, went west to the Hindu Kush and Pamirs. He then crossed east to Khotan in the Tarim Basin and Keriya. Finally he turned west again to Kashgar and Samarkand.
1906–08: He left the northern Punjab again for the Hindu Kush and Pamirs region, then went on to Keriya in the southern Tarim Basin. This time he crossed the basin northward to Kurla and Turfan. He explored the Lob Nor and Charchan areas to the Nan Shan.
1913: He traveled to Srinager, Gilgit, and north through the Karakoram to Kashgar. From here he went along the northern fringe of the Tarim Basin to Kurla, south to Lob Nor and Charchan, and again east to the Nan Shan. From here he crossed the western end of the Gobi Desert to Urumchi, eventually returning to Kashgar.
1915: He traveled from Kashgar through the Pamirs and the Hindu Kush into Afghanistan.
See map on page 130.

SCOTT, ROBERT FALCON
1868–1912 England
1901–04: Made an expedition to the Antarctic (with Shackleton and Wilson), landed at Cape Adare, discovered King Edward VII Land, and proved that Mount Erebus and Mount Terror were on an island (Ross Island). He also proved that McMurdo "Bay" was a strait. The three men sledged inland to 82°17′ S., and Scott made a journey onto the high continental plateau.
1910–13: He led an expedition to McMurdo Sound with Wilson, making his famous journey to the pole by way of the Beardmore Glacier. Scott died in 1912, but the expedition carried on.
See map on page 186.

WILSON, DR. EDWARD ADRIAN
1872–1912 England
1901–04: Was with Scott and Shackleton in the Antarctic.
1912: Reached the South Pole with Scott and died. (See **SCOTT**).
See map on page 186.

SHACKLETON, ERNEST HENRY
1874–1922 England
1901–04: With Scott's expedition he coasted the Ross Barrier and discovered Kind Edward VII Land. From the south of Ross Island, he sledged overland to 82°17′ S.
1907–09: With Mawson he landed at Cape Royds on Ross Island in McMurdo Sound. He climbed a long way up Mount Erebus and then made an attempt to reach the Pole by way of the Beardmore Glacier. He reached 88°23′ S.—113 miles from the Pole.
1914–17: He planned to cross Antarctica from the Weddell Sea, but the ship was crushed by ice and sank. Marooned on the ice, the party eventually reached Elephant Island near the north tip of Graham Land. He then made his famous voyage in an open boat to South Georgia. Landing on the uninhabited side, he was forced to cross the difficult, mountainous island. With help, he returned to Elephant Island and rescued the rest of his party.
See map on page 186.
1921: On setting out for Enderby Land, he died in South Georgia.

NORDENSKJÖLD, OTTO
1869–1928 Sweden
1902–03: He sailed with Larsen to the South Shetlands, Louis Philippe Land, and the western part of the Weddell Sea.
See map on page 186.

DRYGALSKI, DR. ERICH VON
1865–1950 Germany
1901–03: He sailed from Kiel with the German Antarctic Expedition to Kerguelen and Heard islands, then south to the Antarctic Continent. He discovered Kaiser Wilhelm II Land and Mount Gauss.
See map on page 186.

AMUNDSEN, ROALD
1872–1928 Norway
1903–06: On an expedition to the Canadian Arctic he reached Beechey Island, Boothia Peninsula, and Peel Sound. He sailed east and south of King William Island, where his ship was stuck in the ice. He went overland to the Yukon then returned to the ship, which had been freed. He sailed through McClintock Strait and out of the Arctic via the Bering Strait and reached San Francisco. On this voyage he discovered a northwest passage to the East.
1911–13: On an expedition to the Antarctic he reached the Bay of Whales, and traveled over the Ross Barrier and became the first man to reach the South Pole.
1918–20: He sailed through the northeast passage to the East.
1921: He attempted to repeat Nansen's drift and reach the North Pole by aircraft, but he managed to get only as far as 87°43′ N.
1925–26: He flew with Ellsworth in a dirigible from Spitsbergen and over the Pole to Point Barrow.
1928: He died while trying to rescue General Nobile, who was attempting to repeat Amundsen's 1925 flight.
See maps on pages 178 and 186.

FILCHNER, WILHELM
1877–1957 Germany
1905: Explored the upper Hwang Ho and the country south to Szechwan. He visited Shensi, Shansi, and the area between Langchow and Kansu.
1912: Made an expedition to the Weddell Sea, discovered Luitpold Land.
See map on page 186.

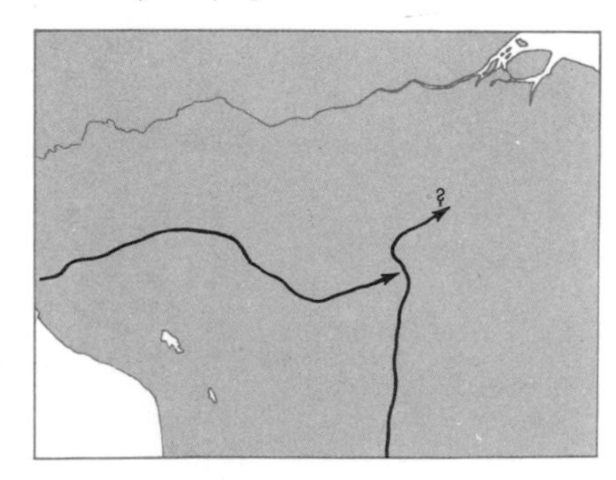

FAWCETT, COL. P. H.
(?)–1925(?) England
1906: Explored in the region of the boundary of Bolivia and Brazil, the Verde River, and the Mato Grosso.
1913: He went to Cuyaba (near the headwaters of the Paraguay River) and explored the Mato Grosso and the Xingu River area.
1925: Lost without trace in Mato Grosso or Xingu area.
See map bottom of previous column.

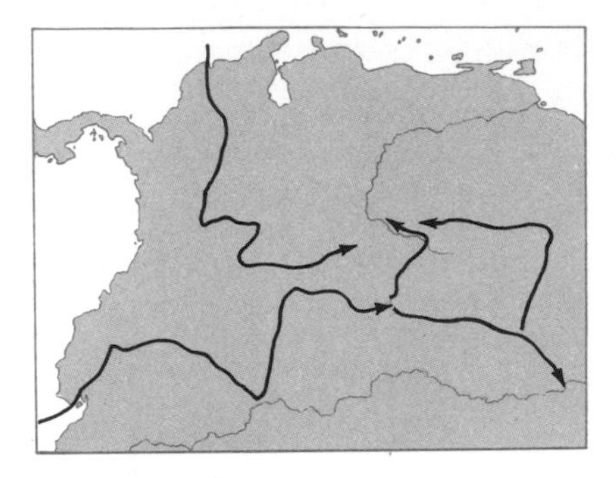

RICE, DR. HAMILTON
1875–1956 United States
1907: Went from Quito across the Andes then down the Napo River to the Amazon. He crossed to the river Uaupés and explored it to its junction with the Río Negro.
1912–13: He went from Cartagena to Bogotá, then over the Andes to the Ariari River, and explored the Icana and part of the Inirida rivers (upper tributaries of the Orinoco).
1917: He completed a survey of the Río Negro to Manaus.
1919–20: He surveyed up the Río Negro from the Uaupés River to the Casiquiare and upper Orinoco rivers. (First use of wireless and airplane.)
1924–25: He surveyed on the river Branco, the Uraricoera River, and across to the upper Orinoco by the Serra Parima.

MAWSON, SIR DOUGLAS
1882–1958 England
(Went to Australia when a boy.)
1907–09: Went to the Ross Barrier and to the south magnetic pole with the Shackleton expedition.
1911–14: Explored the area between Kaiser Wilhelm II Land and Victoria Land in the Antarctic. He discovered George V and Queen Mary Lands.
1929–31: During his third expedition to the Antarctic he discovered MacRobertson Land, and sailed along the edge of the continent for several hundred miles.
See map on page 186.

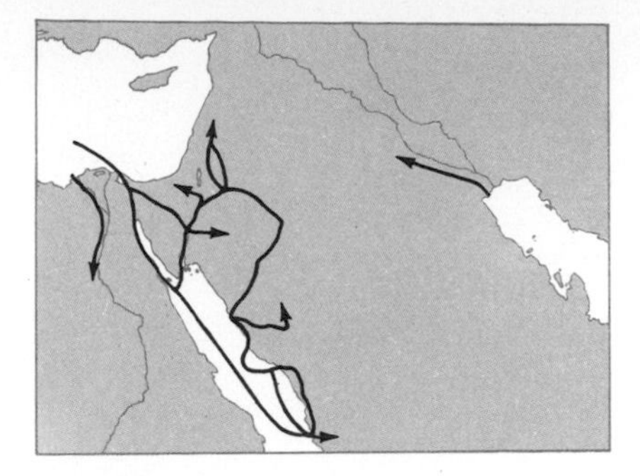

LAWRENCE, THOMAS EDWARD
1888–1935 England
1910: Toured Syria on foot.
1911: Traveled up the Euphrates.
1913–14: Surveyed in north Sinai Peninsula.
1915: Traveled up the Nile to Asyut.
1916: Visited Jidda, Medina, and Nefud region.
1926: Served with the R.A.F. on the Northwest Frontier in India.

BELL, GERTRUDE
1868–1926 England
1913–14: She went to Damascus; traveled east of the railway line running from Damascus to Hasan, then went east to Haïl, northeast to the Euphrates, to Baghdad, and returned by Palmyra to Dasmacus.
See map on page 135.

STEFANSSON, VILHJALMUR
1879–1952 United States
1908–12: He went to the Mackenzie River and worked from the Horton River to Coronation Gulf, Victoria Island, and west to Point Barrow.
1913–18: Went on a Canadian Arctic expedition, through the Bering Strait, Beaufort Sea, sailed to Prince Patrick Island, discovered an island to the north; he also visited Wrangel Island.
See map on page 178.
1924: He visited the Macdonnell Ranges in central Australia.

PHILBY, HARRY ST. JOHN
1885– England
(Born in Ceylon of British parents.)
1917: Went from Baghdad to the Persian Gulf, to Hofuf, Riyadh, visited the ruins of Dariyan, crossed by the Sagta Pass and followed the Pilgrim route to Mecca. From Jidda he went to Bombay and Basra before returning to Arabia.
1918: He went from the head of the Persian Gulf to Riyadh and south into the Rub' al Khali to Sulaiyil in the Wadi Dawasir.
1920–22: Went from Amman in Jordan to Jauf and Karbala near the Euphrates.
1931–32: Went from Hofuf south across the Jafura Desert and through the Rub' al Khali to the Dawasir Oasis.
1936: Traveled in southwest Arabia between Mecca and the Hadhramaut to Mukalla.
See map on page 135.

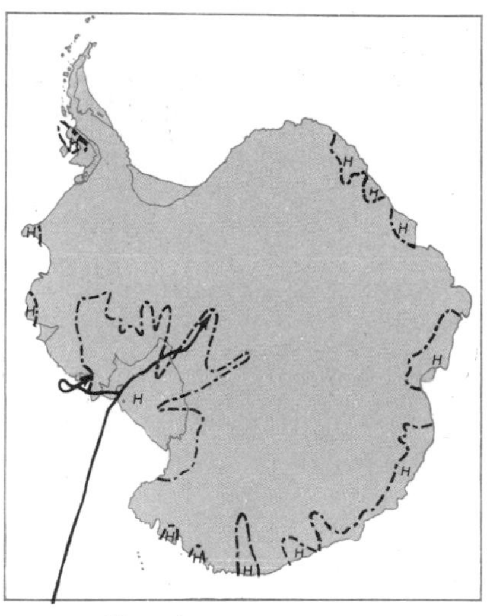

Air routes
Area of Operation High Jump

BYRD, RICHARD E.
1888–1957 United States
1926: Made a flight from Spitsbergen to the North Pole and returned to Spitsbergen.
1929: Set up a base in the Antarctic at Little America near the Bay of Whales. He examined Marie Byrd Land to the east of the Ross Barrier and made a sledge journey south to Queen Maud range. Made a flight to the pole and back.
1933: Visited Little America and explored to the south for about 120 miles.
1938–41: He surveyed inland from Little America, and made flights including one to Adelaide Island (off Graham Land).
1947–48: In command of Operation High Jump.

THOMAS, BERTRAM
1892–1950 England
1928–29: Landed to the south of Ras al Had (eastern tip of Arabian Peninsula). He traveled southwest along the coast to Dhufar and Salala and struck north into Rub' al Khali.
1930–31: Landed at Salala and traveled north across the Rub'al Khali to Qatar peninsula.
See map on page 135.

WATKINS, GINO
1907–1932 England
1928: Went to Hamilton Inlet in Labrador and explored the Hamilton River.
1930–31: Led an expedition to Greenland and went 250 miles inland from Angmagssalik; also went to Mount Forel and around the southern tip of Greenland in an open boat to Julianehaab.
1932: Drowned in Kayak accident near Angmagssalik.
See map on page 178.

FUCHS, SIR VIVIAN
1908– England
1929: Went with the "Cambridge East Greenland Expedition" as geologist.
1930: Went on a Cambridge expedition to the East African lakes.
1931: Went on an archeaological expedition to East Africa.
1933: Explored Lake Rudolf in the Rift Valley.
1937: Went to Lake Rukwa in East Africa.
1942: Went to West Africa.
1947–50: Leader of the Falkland Islands Dependencies Survey in Antarctica.
1950: Director of the Falkland Island Dependencies Survey.
1955–58: Leader of Commonwealth Trans-Antarctic Expedition; he crossed the continent from the Weddell Sea to the Ross Sea. (As director of F.I.D.S., he is still doing work in the Antarctic.)
See maps on pages 178 and 186.

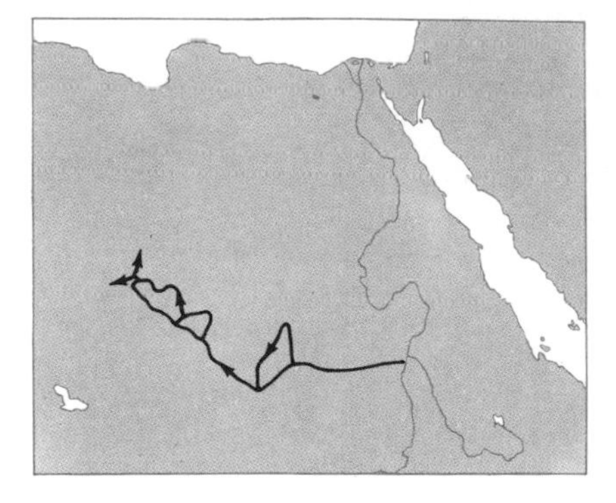

THESIGER, WILFRED PATRICK
1910– England
1930: Went on a mission to Abyssinia and explored the Awash River.
1934: Explored the Awash region and Aussa region to the north.
1935-39: In the Sudan Political Service, he explored from Khartoum west to the Darfur mountain region and northwest to Tibesti.
See map here.

1939–45: During World War II he served in Ethiopa, Syria, and North African campaigns.
1945–46: Explored in south Arabia from Salala, to the northeast in the "Empty Quarter" and north of the Hadhramaut to Mukalla. He also visited Jidda and worked in the Hajaz Mountains.
1946–47: Explored from Salala north to the "Empty Quarter" and southwest to Mukalla. He then returned to the Hajaz region.
1947–48: He traveled from Mukalla to Sulaiyil, then crossed north of the Rub' al Khali to the coast at the mouth of the Persian Gulf.
1948–50: Explored extensively in the Oman, using Buraimi as his headquarters.
See map on page 135.

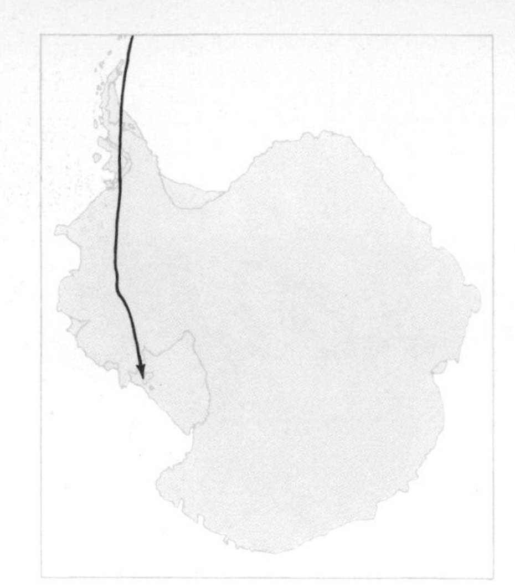

Ellsworth flight

ELLSWORTH, LINCOLN
1880–1951 United States
1935: Flew from Dundee Island near Graham Land to the Bay of Whales near Little America. He was the first man to cross the continent, although he accomplished it by air.
1939: He made flights to the interior of Antarctica, east of the Ross Sea.

HILLARY, SIR EDMUND
1919– New Zealand
1953: Was the first man to climb Mount Everest.
1957–58: Leader of the New Zealand party in the Commonwealth Trans-Antarctic Expedition. He traveled from the Scott Base on the Ross Barrier to the South Pole.
See map on page 186.

Spheres of Exploration

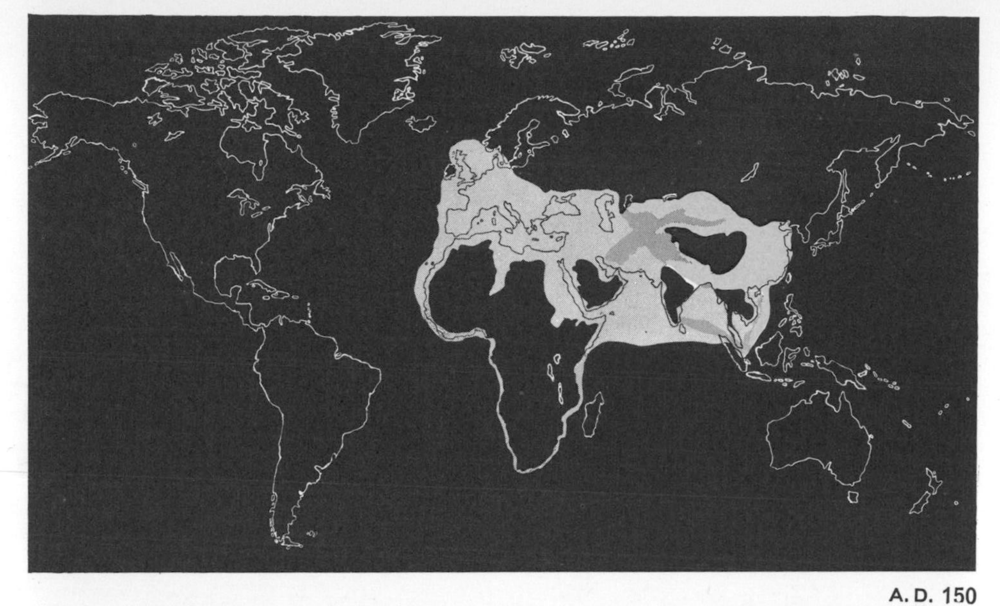

A. D. 150

These three diagrams amplify the large summary maps appearing on pages 40-41, 60-61, and 84-85.

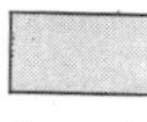

Area known to the West

Area known to the East

Area known to the Islamic world

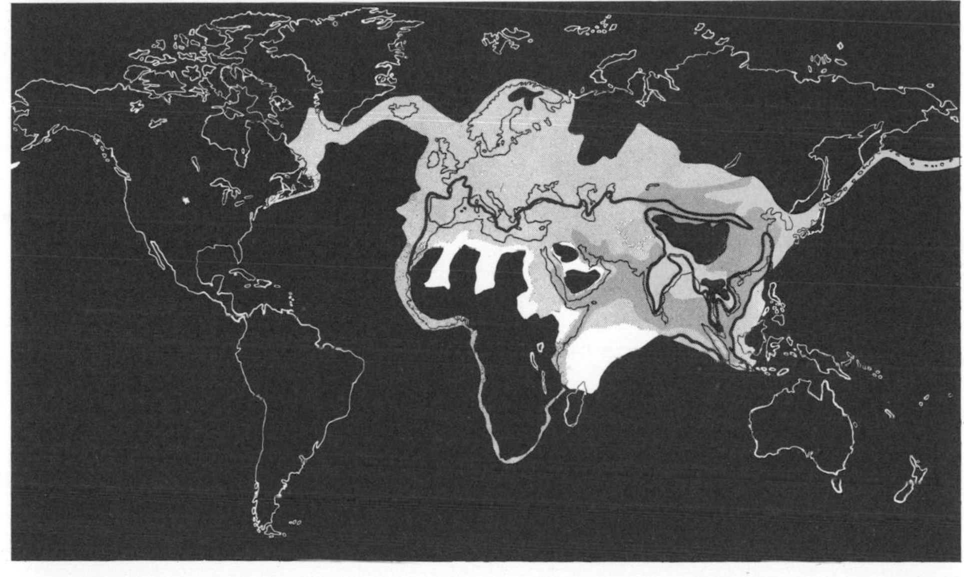

A. D. 1420

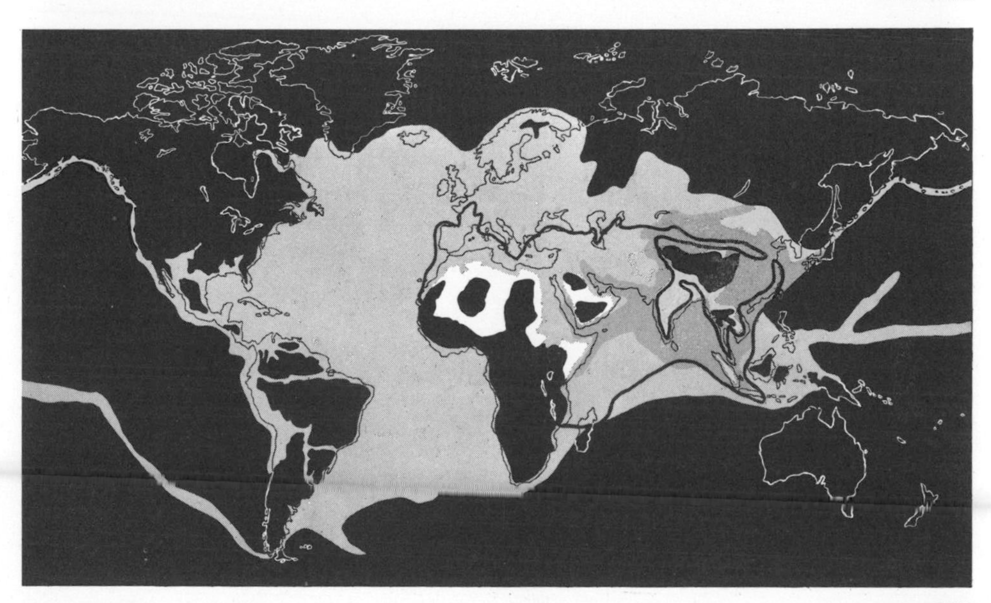

A. D. 1550

The 24 maps on the following two pages show the extent of exploration of the world's six major land masses from the year 1700 to 1900.

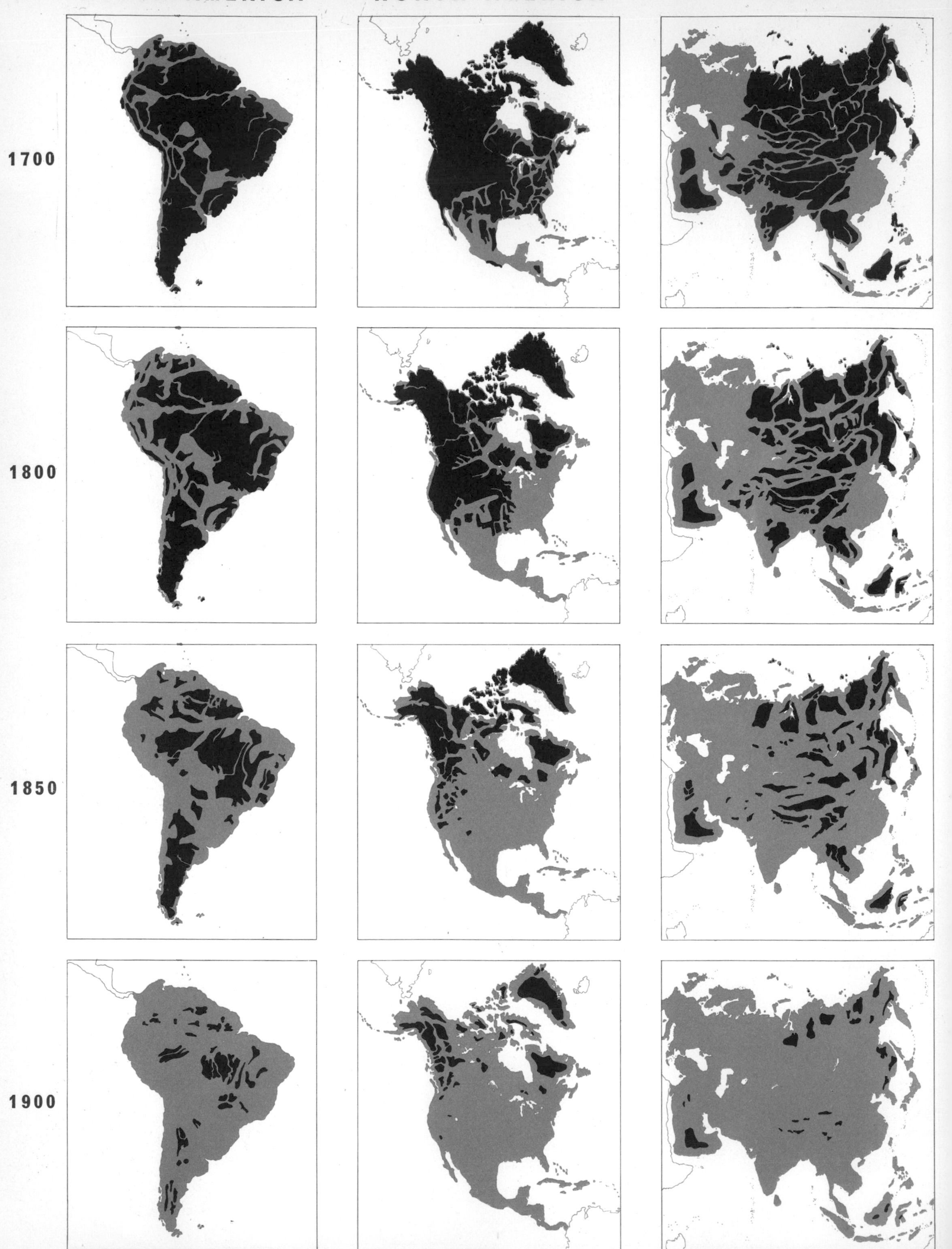
SOUTH AMERICA
NORTH AMERICA
ASIA
1700
1800
1850
1900

AUSTRALIA

ANTARCTICA

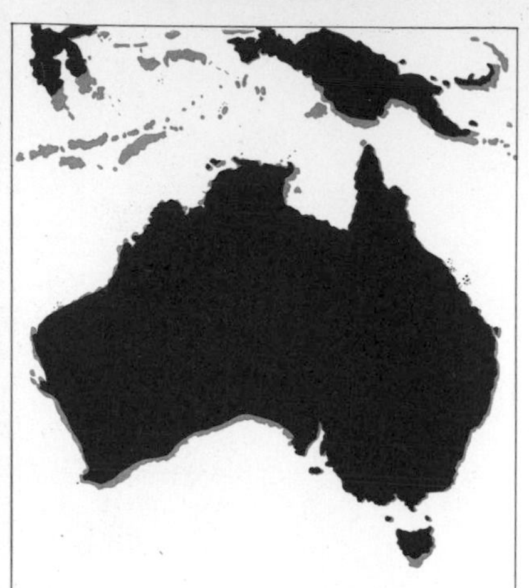

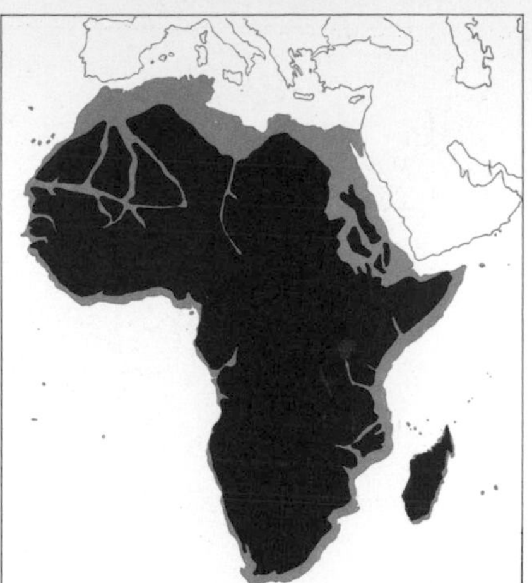

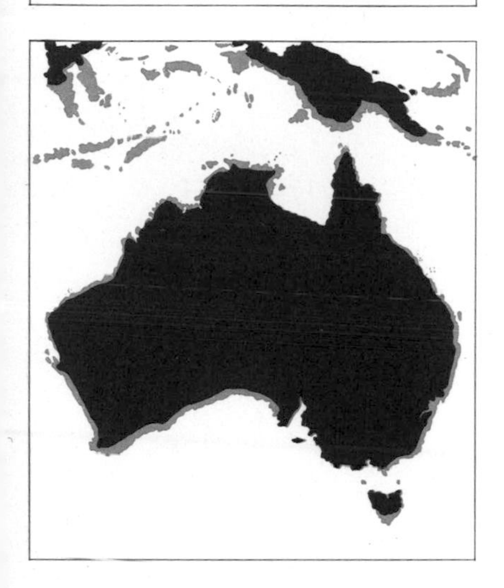

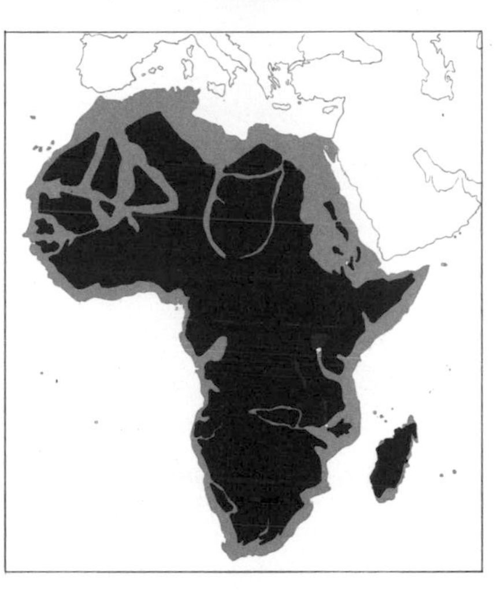

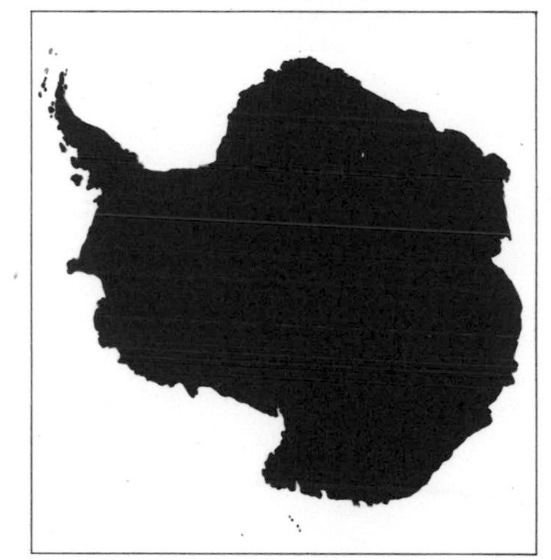

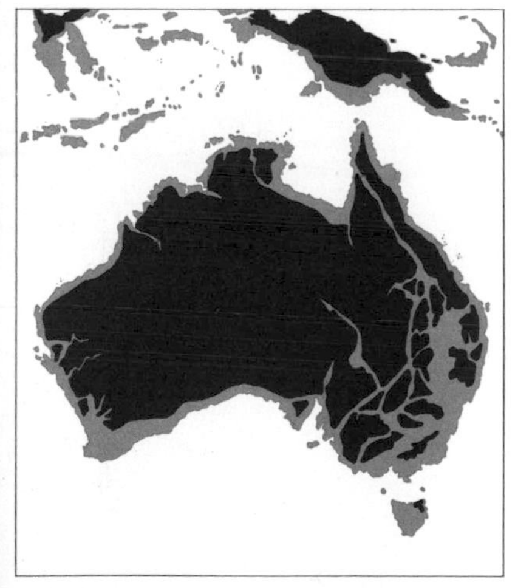

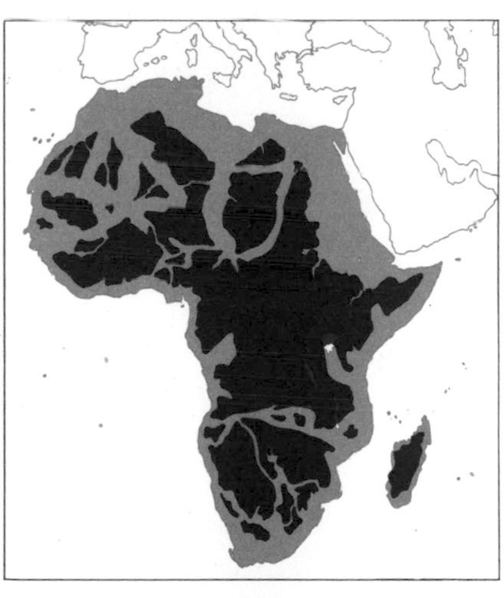

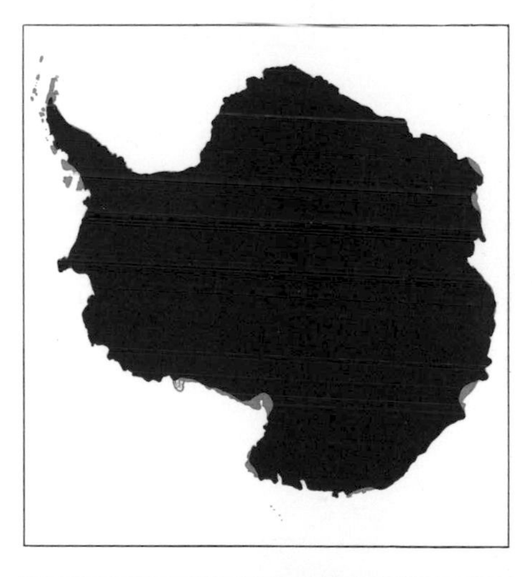

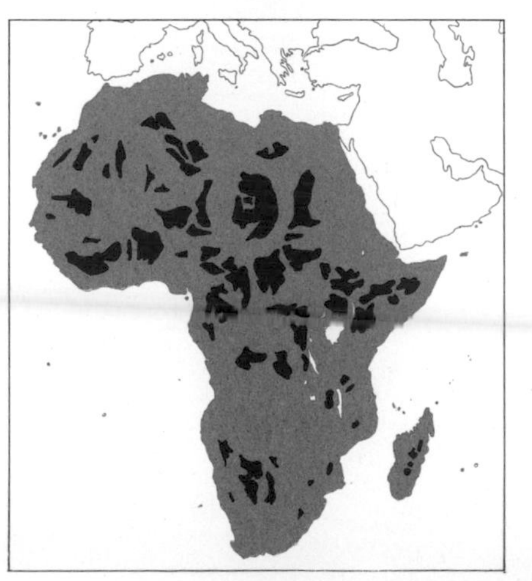

Illustration credits

9 GEOGRAPHICAL PROJECTS LTD.
10 Archers *after Obermaier*
12 Paleolithic hand axe, photograph *British Museum (Natural History)*
12 Wounded bison *after Breuil*
13 Diagram GEOGRAPHICAL PROJECTS LTD.
14 Woman gathering honey *after Obermaier*
14 Storage jar "*Digging up Jericho,*" *by Kathleen Kenyon; published by Ernest Benn*
15 Neolithic hafted axe, photograph *British Museum (Natural History)*
16 Fleeing stags and trout "*Art in the Ice Age,*" *by Johannes Maringer and Hans-George Bandi;*
published by Holbein Publishing Co., Ltd., Basel
16 Neolithic hut *as above*
17 Early Bronze Age plowing scene *Courtesy Prof. J. G. D. Clark*
17 Woman spinning *Archives Photographiques, Paris*
18 Egyptian boat, painting PETER SULLIVAN *Courtesy Science Museum, London*
19 Cuneiform tablet, photograph MICHAEL HOLFORD *British Museum*
19 Babylonian war chariots (from the Standard of Ur), photograph ADPRINT *British Museum*
20 War chariot, photograph PERRET *Musée de l'Homme, Paris*
20 Neolithic model of hut "*Prehistoric Art,*" *published by Spring Books, London*
21 Mesopotamian river boat *British Museum*
22 GEOGRAPHICAL PROJECTS LTD.
23 Sumerian warriors (from the Stele of the Vultures), photograph *Mansell*
24 Cultivation of corn, photograph *Mansell*
24 Servant carrying hares, photograph *Mansell*
25 Boat of Queen Hatshepsut (from a bas-relief at Deir-el-Bahri)
26 Palace of Knossos, photograph JOHN FRENCH
26 Fresco of bullfighting, painting PETER SULLIVAN *(after "L'Art de la Crête," by Zervos; published by Editions Cahiers d'Art)*
27 Goddess of the Serpents, photograph MICHAEL HOLFORD *("L'Art de la Crête," by Zervos; published by Editions Cahiers d'Art)*
28 Minoan prince *as above*
29 GEOGRAPHICAL PROJECTS LTD.
30 Phoenician armed galley, photograph *Mansell*
31 Shell "Murex Trunculus," "*History of Phoenicia,*" *by Rawlinson; published by Longmans Green and Co., Ltd.*
32 Archers of guard of King of Persia (from a 5th century B. C. frieze at Persepolis)
32 Boar hunter (from Scythian belt buckle), "*The Scythians,*" *by Tamara Talbot Rice, Ancient Peoples and Places Series; published by Thames and Hudson*
33 Pancake ice, photograph PONTING *Paul Popper*
34 Darius, photograph *Mansell*
35 Greek merchant galley *British Museum*
36 Alexander the Great, photograph *Mansell*
37 GEOGRAPHICAL PROJECTS LTD.
37 Horseman of Alexander the Great (from the Sarcophogus at Sidon), photograph *Mansell*
38 Roman aquaduct, photograph *Mansell*

38 Peutinger table, photograph MICHAEL HOLFORD *British Museum*
39 Trajan column, photograph *Mansell*
40 Ptolemy map, photograph *British Museum*
41 GEOGRAPHICAL PROJECTS LTD.
42 GEOGRAPHICAL PROJECTS LTD.
43 Great Wall of China, photograph *Paul Popper*
44 Early Chinese travelers, photograph *Radio Times Hulton Picture Library*
45 Mongol horsemen, painting PETER SULLIVAN *"Chinese Painting," by Peter Swann; published by Zwemmer; and Courtesy of Victoria and Albert Museum, London*
46 St. Brendan (from an ancient manuscript)
47 Viking ship (from a 9th-century tombstone) *Courtesy Kungl. Vitterhetsakadamien, Stockholm*
48 Hvalso church Greenland *Courtesy Danish Ministry of Foreign Affairs*
48 Gokstad ship, photograph *Mansell*
49 GEOGRAPHICAL PROJECTS LTD.
50 Idrisi world map *Bibliothèque Nationale, Paris*
51 Arab boat *Bibliothèque Nationale, Paris*
52 Arab caravan (from a 13th-century ms. of school of Baghdad), photograph *Bibliothèque Nationale, Paris*
53 Arab boat *Bibliothèque Nationale, Paris*
53 Central Asian nomads *"Astley's Voyages and Travels"; published in London, 1745*
54 Rubruquis *Courtesy Master and Fellows of Corpus Christi College, Cambridge*
55 GEOGRAPHICAL PROJECTS LTD.
56 Polo Brothers with caravan (trom the Catalan Atlas of 1375), *Courtesy "Geographical Magazine"*
57 Gifts for the Khan *"Les Livres Graun Caam," Bodleian Library, Oxford*
58 Marco Polo *Radio Times Hulton Picture Library*
59 Palace of Cambaluc (from Fra Mauro World Map, 1459), *British Museum*
60 GEOGRAPHICAL PROJECTS LTD.
63 Map of west African coast (from the Chart of Ginea Portugalexe, c. 1490) *British Museum*
63 GEOGRAPHICAL PROJECTS LTD.
64 GEOGRAPHICAL PROJECTS LTD.
65 Henry the Navigator, photopraph *Bibliothèque Nationale, Paris*
65 Ships rounding Cape (from the "Atlas of Guillaume le Testu," 1556) photograph *Bibliothèque Nationale, Paris*
66 Vasco da Gama, photograph MICHAEL HOLFORD *Bibliothèque Nationale, Lisbon*
67 Indian boats *"Astley's Voyages and Travels"; published in London, 1745*
68 Hormuz *Bibliothèque Nationale, Paris*
69 Japanese screen, photograph J-A LAVAUD *Musée Guimet*
70 Christopher Columbus (old print)
71 Cod fishing in Newfoundland (from a map of America by N. le Fer, 1698), *Histoire de la Découverte de la Terre; Larousse*
71 GEOGRAPHICAL PROJECTS LTD.
73 GEOGRAPHICAL PROJECTS LTD.
74 The Indians of Brazil (old print)

75 Cortéz arriving in Mexico (from the Codex Azcatitlan) *Bibliothèque Nationale, Paris*
75 Francisco Pizarro (old print)
76 Amazon rain forest in Surinam, photograph NICHOLAS GUPPY
77 GEOGRAPHICAL PROJECTS LTD.
78 Mexican drawing (from the Codex Kingsborough), photograph MICHAEL HOLFORD *British Museum*
79 Map of South America, by Diego Gutierrez, *1562 British Museum*
80 Ferdinand Magellan (old print)
80 Magellan's ship "Victoria" *Radio Times Hulton Picture Library*
80 Pigafetta drawing (from his diary of Magellan's Voyage) *Bibliothèque Nationale, Paris*
81 GEOGRAPHICAL PROJECTS LTD.
82 Juan de la Cosa World Map, 1496, *British Museum*
83 Mercator World Map *National Maritime Museum, Greenwich*
84 GEOGRAPHICAL PROJECTS LTD.
86 GEOGRAPHICAL PROJECTS LTD.
88 Peruvian head "*Art in Ancient Peru," by H. Ubbelohde-Doering; published by Ernst Wasmuth*
88 Inca doorway, photograph *Paul Popper*
89 Trujillo Bay, photograph MICHAEL HOLFORD *Courtesy Victoria and Albert Museum, London*
90 Portuguese landing in Brazil, photograph MICHAEL HOLFORD *British Museum*
91 Buccaneer (from a map of America by N. le Fer, 1698), *photograph "Histoire de la Découverte de la Terre"; Larousse*
92 Sir Walter Raleigh (old print)
93 GEOGRAPHICAL PROJECTS LTD.
94 Humboldt in South America (from the "Atlas des Regiones Equinoxiales, 1800") *Courtesy British Museum (National History)*
95 Natives of Tierra del Fuego (old print)
96 Darwin's ship "Beagle" *Courtesy Sir Charles Darwin, and the Royal Geographical Society*
97 Page from Bates' diary, photograph MICHAEL HOLFORD *Courtesy British Museum (Natural History)*
99 GEOGRAPHICAL PROJECTS LTD.
100 GEOGRAPHICAL PROJECTS LTD.
101 Eskimos, photograph *Bulletin and Scotts Pictorial*
102 History of the Mixtecs (from the Codex Selden) *Bodleian Library, Oxford*
103 Cree Indians in a tent, photograph MICHAEL HOLFORD *"Journey to the North Polar Sea 1819–22"; by Sir John Franklin*
103 Indians in canoes (old print)
104 GEOGRAPHICAL PROJECTS LTD.
104 Frobisher in a kayak *Radio Times Hulton Picture Library*
105 Cartier arriving in Canada, painting PETER SULLIVAN (adapted from the Vallard Map); *Courtesy Public Archives of Canada*
106 Sir Martin Frobisher, painting CORNELIUS KETEL, photograph *Bodleian Library, Oxford*
107 Woodcut map, photograph MICHAEL HOLFORD *British Museum*
107 Map of Baffin's voyage, 1615, photograph *British Museum*

108 Niagara Falls "*Nouvelle découverte d'un très grand pays... entre le Nouveau Mexique et la Mer Glaciale*"; *published in Utrecht, 1597*
109 GEOGRAPHICAL PROJECTS LTD.
110 GEOGRAPHICAL PROJECTS LTD.
110 Tobacco smokers, "*Histoire de la Découverte de la Terre*"; *Larousse*
111 The Mackenzie Stone *Courtesy Public Archives of Canada*
112 Crossing the rapids *Courtesy Hudson's Bay Company*
113 The Rocky Mountains, photograph MICHAEL HOLFORD *Currier & Ives lithograph*
114 Lewis and Clark (woodcuts from *Diary of Patrick Gass*)
115 Emigrants leaving Liverpool "*Illustrated London News,*" *July, 1856*
117 GEOGRAPHICAL PROJECTS LTD.
118 GEOGRAPHICAL PROJECTS LTD.
120 Hsüan-tsang, painting PETER SULLIVAN *Courtesy Mansell*
121 Chinese travelers *Courtesy Dorothy Woodman*
122 Painting of giraffe on silk *Ralph M. Chait Collection*
122 Chinese navigation chart "*Science and Civilization in China,*" *by Joseph Needham, with collaboration of Wang Ling; Cambridge University Press, 1959*
123 Map of west China *as above*
124 St. Francis Xavier (old print)
124 Moscow (old print)
125 Indian cotton wall hanging, photograph MICHAEL HOLFORD *Courtesy Victoria and Albert Museum, London*
126 Canton (old print)
127 De Veer's woodcuts "*Relation des Trois Voyages des Bateaux Hollandais et Zelandais au Nord de la Norvège, Muscovie Russie et Tartarie, 1598*
128 Bering map, photograph MICHAEL HOLFORD *British Museum*
129 Matteo Ricci (old print)
130 GEOGRAPHICAL PROJECTS LTD.
132 Bridge in Tibet, photograph *Paul Popper*
133 Lhasa, photograph FRANCIS YOUNGHUSBAND *Courtesy Royal Geographical Society*
134 The Takhtrawan, photograph MICHAEL HOLFORD
135 GEOGRAPHICAL PROJECTS LTD.
136 Arabs of the Yemen "*Description de l'Arabie,*" *by M. Niebuhr; published at Copenhagen by N. Möller*
137 The Empty Quarter, photograph WILFRED THESIGER
138 Diagram GEOGRAPHICAL PROJECTS LTD.
139 GEOGRAPHICAL PROJECTS LTD.
140 GEOGRAPHICAL PROJECTS LTD.
142 Polynesians in canoes *Radio Times Hulton Picture Library*
143 GEOGRAPHICAL PROJECTS LTD.
144 Map of "Terra Australis," photograph MICHAEL HOLFORD *British Museum*
145 Map of Pacific islands drawn by Hack in 1669, photograph MICHAEL HOLFORD *British Museum*
146 Dutch Fleet (from Gerrit's map of the South Seas), photograph *Bibliothèque Nationale, Paris*
147 Tasman sketch *British Museum*
148 Hobart, photograph MICHAEL HOLFORD *Victoria and Albert Museum, London*
149 GEOGRAPHICAL PROJECTS LTD.

150 Mr. Banks receiving visitors "*Voyage to the Pacific, 1776*," *by James Cook*
151 Captain James Cook (old print)
151 Kangaroos (old print)
152 Captain Stirling's exploring party, photograph MICHAEL HOLFORD *Victoria and Albert Museum, London*
153 The depot Glen "*Narrative of an Expedition into Central Australia*," *by Capt. Charles Sturt; published by F. & W. Boone*
154 Early settlers in Australia "*Illustrated London News*," *1851*
155 Warburton's expedition "*Journey Across Australia*," *by Col. P. E. Warburton*
157 GEOGRAPHICAL PROJECTS LTD.
158 GEOGRAPHICAL PROJECTS LTD.
160 The Mountains of the Moon, photograph J. DE HEINZELIN *Institut des Parcs Nationaux du Congo Belge, Brussels*
161 Stowage of slaves "*The Cries of Africa to the Inhabitants of Europe*," *by Thomas Clarkson, M. A.; published by Anti-Slavery Society*
161 Figure of slave *Bibliothèque Nationale, Paris*
162 African ivory carving, photograph *British Museum*
163 Prester John (from the "Atlas of Diogo Homem," 1558)
163 James Bruce "*Travels to Discover the Source of the Nile, 1768–73*"
165 GEOGRAPHICAL PROJECTS LTD.
166 Minutes of African Association meeting *Courtesy University Library, Cambridge*
167 Mungo Park crossing the Black River "*Travels in the Interior Districts of Africa*," *by Mungo Park*
168 The Sahara, photograph EMIL SCHULTHESS
169 Sultan of Begharmi "*Travels in North and Central Africa, by Major Denham, Capt. Clapham, and Dr. Oudney; published by John Murray*
169 Speke's arrival at Unyoro "*The Albert Nyanza*," *by Sir Samuel White Baker; published by Macmillan*
170 Crossing the Niger "*Travels in Central Africa*," *by F. Barth*
171 GEOGRAPHICAL PROJECTS LTD.
172 Livingstone crossing the Makata River "*How I found Livingstone*," *by H. M. Stanley, 1872*
173 The Victoria Falls, photograph EMIL SCHULTHESS
174 Stanley at the Albert Nyanza "*In darkest Africa*," *by H. M. Stanley; published by Low*
175 Campbell in Madagascar (old print)
177 GEOGRAPHICAL PROJECTS LTD.
178 GEOGRAPHICAL PROJECTS LTD.
180 Sperm whale, *Mansell*
180 Ross meets Eskimos, photograph MICHAEL HOLFORD
181 Parry's ships, photograph MICHAEL HOLFORD
182 Franklin landing (old print)
183 Franklin search poster, photograph MICHAEL HOLFORD *Courtesy Royal Geographical Society*
183 Roll call on the "Alert," lithograph by E. L. MOSS *Courtesy National Maritime Museum, Greenwich*
184 Nansen sketch *Radio Times Hulton Picture Library*
185 Icescape, near North Greenland, photograph *Polar Photos*
185 *New York Times*

186 GEOGRAPHICAL PROJECTS LTD.
187 View of ice islands (old print) *"Second Voyage to the South Seas," by Capt. J. Cook*
188 Adélie penguins, photograph PONTING *Paul Popper*
189 A gale in the pack ice, painting by E. DAVIS photograph MICHAEL HOLFORD *Courtesy National Maritime Museum, Greenwich*
189 "Endurance" in ice, photograph HURLEY *Royal Geographical Society*
190 The "Terra Nova," photograph PONTING *Paul Popper*
191 Scott's party, watercolor DR. E. A. WILSON *"South Polar Times" No. 3*
192 Diver *"The Silent World," film by Jean Jacques Cousteau*
193 Alexander in diving bell *Courtesy Bibliothèque de Burgoyne*
194 Bathyscaphe "Trieste," photograph *Reuter*
194 Echo-sounder *National Institute of Oceanography, England*
195 Pumasillo west face *"The Puma's Claw," by Simon Clark; published by Hutchinson and Co., Ltd.*
196 Atomic submarine "Skate" *U.S.I.S.*
197 Fuchs' party, surveyors *Copyright Trans-Antarctic Expedition*
197 Tractor train *U.S.I.S.*
198 Group of archers *"Art in the Ice Age," by Johannes Maringer and Hans-Georg Bandi; published by Holbein Publishing Co., Ltd., Basel*
199 Part of the Milky Way *Courtesy University of Chicago Press*
200 Balloon *Mansell*
201 First flight *Radio Times Hulton Picture Library*
202 Diagram of space GORDON CRAMP
203 Mercury space capsule being assembled *U.S.I.S.*
203 Diagram of rocket principle HARRIET COLE
203 Mercury space capsule being fired *U.S.I.S.*
204 Diagram of rocket GORDON CRAMP
204 Paddlewheel satellite *U.S.I.S.*
205 Rocket landing on moon, painting PETER SULLIVAN *Courtesy American Bosch Arma Corporation; original painting by Frank L. Tinsley*
206 Chinese junks, photograph *Paul Popper*
207 Roman ship *Mansell*
208 Seal of Ipswich *Courtesy National Maritime Museum, Greenwich*
208 Shell and bamboo chart *Courtesy Science Museum, London*
209 Chinese compass *Courtesy National Maritime Museum, Greenwich*
209 Crown compass *Courtesy National Maritime Museum, Greenwich*
209 Cross staff *Courtesy National Maritime Museum, Greenwich*
210 Astrolabe *Courtesy National Maritime Museum, Greenwich*
210 Sextant *Courtesy National Maritime Museum, Greenwich*
210 Chronometer *Courtesy National Maritime Museum, Greenwich*
211 Portolano chart *Courtesy National Maritime Museum, Greenwich*
endpapers: GEOGRAPHICAL PROJECTS LTD.

Books about explorers and exploration

GENERAL

Ancient Explorers, M. Cary and E. H. Warmington (Methuen)

Crusades, The, Harold Lamb (Doubleday)

Earth Conquerors, Lives and Achievements of the Great Explorers, J. L. Mitchell (Doubleday)

Eyes of Discovery, The, John Bakeless (Lippincott)

Global Atlas, The, Frank Debenham (Golden)

Great Adventures and Explorations, V. Stefansson (Dial)

Great Moments in Exploration, Marion Lansing (Doubleday)

Hakluyt's Collection of the Early Voyages, Travels, and Discoveries of the English Nation, Richard Hakluyt (R. H. Evans). This comprehensive work has been published in several editions of varying numbers of volumes. A more compact edition is entitled:

The Principal Navigations, Voyages, Traffiques & Discoveries of the English Nation, edited by John Masefield (E. P. Dutton) (Publications of the Hakluyt Society, London, deal exclusively with explorers and exploration.)

Hannibal: One Man Against Rome, Harold Lamb (Doubleday)

Histoire de la Découverte de la Terre, Ch. de la Roncière (Larousse)

Histoire Universelle des Explorations, (4 vols.) (Nouvelle Librairie de France)

History of Exploration from the Earliest Times to the Present Day, The, Sir Percy Sykes (George Routledge)

History of Geographical Discovery and Exploration, The, J. N. L. Baker (Houghton Mifflin)

Mainsprings of Civilization, Ellsworth Huntington (John Wiley)

March of the Muscovy, The, Harold Lamb (Doubleday)

Masterworks of Travel and Exploration, edited by Richard D. Mallery (Doubleday)

Nature is Your Guide, Harold Gatty (Barrie)

On the Trail of Ancient Man, Roy Chapman Andrews (Putnam's)

Prehistory of European Society, The, V. Gordon Childe (Pelican)

Prince Henry the Navigator: The Hero of Portugal and of Modern Discovery, 1394-1460 A.D., C. Raymond Beazley (Putnam's)

Sir Walter Raleigh: That Damned Upstart, Donald Barr Chidsey (John Day)

Six Great Explorers, David Divine (Hamish Hamilton)

Travel and Travellers of the Middle Ages, edited by Arthur Percival Newton (Knopf)

Travels and Researches of Alexander von Humboldt, The, Alexander von Humboldt, edited by W. Macgillivray (Harper)

Unrolling the Map, Leonard Outhwaite (Constable)

Untold Story of Exploration, Lowell Thomas (Doubleday)

World is Round, The, Frank Debenham (Rathbone)

SOUTH AMERICA

Conquest of New Granada, The, Sir Clements Markham (Elder) (The Quesada Story)

Discovery of the Amazon, According to the Account of Friar Gaspar de Carvajal and Other Documents, José Toribio Medina, translated by Bertram T. Lee, edited by H. C. Heaton (American Geographical Society Special Publication No. 17) (Material on Orellana)

Discovery of the Large and Bewtiful Empire of Guiana, The, Sir Walter Raleigh, edited by V. T. Harlow (Argonaut Press)

Hernando de Soto: Together with an Account of One of His Captains, Goncalo Silvestre, R. B. Cunninghame Graham (Dial)

History of the Conquest of Peru, William H. Prescott (Harper)

Incas and other Men, George Woodcock (Faber and Faber)

Incredible Pizarro: Conqueror of Peru, Frank Shay (Mohawk)

Narrative of Travels on the Amazon and Rio Negro, Alfred R. A. Wallace (Macmillan, London)

Naturalist on the Amazons, W. H. Bates (Everyman's Library)

Odyssey of Cabeza de Vaca, The, Morris Bishop (Century)

Pedro deValdívia: Conqueror of Chile, R. B. Cunninghame Graham (Heinemann)

Realm of the Incas, Victor W. Von Hagen (Mentor)

Voyage of the "Beagle," Charles Darwin (Everyman's Library)

NORTH AMERICA

Cartier to Frontenac: Geographical Discovery in the Interior of North America 1534–1700, Justin Winsor (Houghton, Mifflin)

Discovery of Canada, The, Lawrence J. Burpee (Graphic)

Explorers of North America, 1492–1806, J. B. Brebner (Anchor)

First Across the Continent, Noah Brooks (Scribner's) (An account of the Lewis and Clark Expedition)

Frémont: The West's Greatest Adventurer, Allan Nevins (Harper)

Hernando de Soto: Together With an Account of One of His Captains, Gonçalo Silvestre, R. B. Cunninghame Graham (Dial)

History of the Expedition Under the Command of Captains Lewis & Clark, Meriwether Lewis and William Clark (Allerton)

New Found World: How North America Was Discovered and Explored, Harold Lamb (Doubleday)

Journey of Alvar Nuñez de Vaca, and His Companions from Florida to the Pacific, 1528–1536, The, translated by Fanny Bandelier, edited by Ad. F. Bandelier (Allerton)

La Salle and the Discovery of the Great West, Francis Parkman (Little, Brown)

Life of Sir Martin Frobisher, The, William McFee (Harper)

Memoirs of My Life, John Charles Frémont (Belford, Clarke)

Pioneer America: Its First 3 Centuries, Carl Drepperd (Doubleday)

Search for the Western Sea, The: The Story of the Exploration of North-western America, Lawrence J. Burpee (Alston Rivers)

Spanish Conquest in America, The, Sir Arthur Helps (John W. Parker)

Spanish Explorers in the Southern United States 1528-1543, edited by F. W. Hodge and T. H. Lewis (Barnes and Noble)

Struggle for a Continent, The, Francis Parkman, edited by Pelham Edgar (Little, Brown)

Voyages from Montreal Through the Continent of North America to the Frozen and Pacific Oceans in 1789 and 1793, Alexander Mackenzie (the Radisson Society)

Voyages of Jacques Cartier, The, Jacques Cartier, translated by H. P. Biggar (F. A. Acland)

Voyages of Samuel de Champlain, 1604–1618, Samuel de Champlain, edited by W. L. Grant (Barnes and Noble)

Westward Crossings, The, Jeanette Mirsky (Allan Wingate)

NORTH AMERICA—CENTRAL AMERICA

Ancient Maya, The, S. G. Morley (Oxford)

Aztecs of Mexico, The, G. C. Vaillant (Pelican)

History of the Conquest of Mexico, William H. Prescott (Harper)

Memoirs... Containing a True and Full Account of the Discovery and Conquest of Mexico and New Spain, Bernal Diaz, translated by John Ingram Lockhart (J. Hatchard)

ASIA

Alexander of Macedon, Harold Lamb (Doubleday)

Bering's Voyages, An Account of the Efforts of the Russians to Determine the Relation of Asia and America, F. A. Golder (the American Geographical Society)

Conquest of Central Asia, The, A Narrative of the Exploration of the Central Asiatic Expedition in Mongolia and China, 1921–1930, Roy Chapman Andrews (the American Museum of Natural History)

Conquest of Tibet, A, Sven Hedin, translated by Julius Lincoln (Dutton)

Desert Road to Turkestan, The, Owen Lattimore (Methuen)

Epic of Mount Everest, The, Sir Francis Younghusband (Longmans, Green)

From Kulja, Across the Tian Shan to Lob-Nor, Prejevalsky, translated by E. Delmar Morgan (Sampson Low)

Genghis Khan: Emperor of All Men, Harold Lamb (Doubleday)

Huc and Gabet: Travels in Tartary, Thibet, and China, Abbé (Evariste Régis) Huc, edited by P. Pelliot (G. Routledge)

Ibn Batuta: Travels in Asia and Africa, 1325–1354, translated by H. A. R. Gibb (George Routledge)

Innermost Asia, Sir Aurel Stein (Clarendon)

Journey of William of Rubruck to the Eastern Parts of the World, The, 1253–55, as Narrated by Himself, with Two Accounts of the Early Journey of John of Pain de Carpini, translated by W. Woodville Rockhill (The Hakluyt Society, London)

Long Old Road in China, The, Langdon Warner (Doubleday)

My Life as an Explorer, Sven Hedin (Doubleday)

N. Mongolia, Prejevalsky, translated by E. Delmar Morgan (Sampson Low)

Origins of Oriental Civilization, The, Walter A. Fairservis, Jr. (Mentor)

Suleiman the Magnificent, Harold Lamb (Doubleday)

Through Asia, Sven Hedin (Harper)

Travels of Marco Polo, The, translated by R. E. Latham (Penguin) (There are many editions of Marco Polo's travels.)

ASIA—NEAR EAST

Arabian Sands, Wilfred Thesiger (Longmans)

Birth of Civilization in the Near East, The, Henri Frankfort (Anchor)

Burton: Arabian Nights Adventurer, Fairfax Downey (Scribner's)

Life of Captain Sir Rich'd F. Burton, The, Isabel Burton (Chapman & Hall)

Passages from Arabia Deserta, Charles M. Doughty (Penguin)

They Wrote on Clay, Edward Chiera (Phoenix)

AUSTRALIA

Ancient Voyagers in the Pacific, Andrew Sharp (Polynesian Society)

Dampier's Voyages, William Dampier (E. Grant Richards)

Early Explorers in Australia, Ida Lee (Methuen)

History of Australian Exploration, E. Favenc (Turner, Henderson)

Journey Across the Western Interior of Australia, Col. P. E. Warburton (Sampson Low)

Two Expeditions into the Interior of Southern Australia, Charles Sturt (Smith, Elder)

AFRICA

Albert N'Yanza, Great Basin of the Nile, and Explorations of the Nile Sources, The, Sir Samuel Baker (Lippincott)

Culture of Ancient Egypt, The, John A. Wilson (Phoenix)

David Livingstone, George Seaver (Lutterworth)

How I Found Livingstone, Henry M. Stanley (Scribner, Armstrong)

Ibn Battuta: Travels in Asia and Africa, 1325–1354, translated by H. A. R. Gibb (George Routledge)

In Darkest Africa, Henry M. Stanley (Scribner's)

Journal of an Expedition to Explore the Course and Termination of the Niger, Richard and John Lander (Harper)

Last Journals of David Livingstone in Central Africa, The, David Livingstone, edited by Rev. Horace Waller (Harper)

Life and Travels of Mungo Park, The, Mungo Park (Harper)

Nyasaland: Land of the Lake, Frank Debenham (HMSO)

Prehistory of Southern Africa, The, J. Desmond Clark (Pelican)

Suleiman the Magnificent, Harold Lamb (Doubleday)

Way to Ilala, The, Frank Debenham (Longmans)

ARCTIC

Arctic Journeys, Edward Shackleton (Hodder and Stoughton)

Ends of the Earth and **An Explorer Comes Home,** Roy Chapman Andrews (Doubleday)

Farthest North, Fridtjof Nansen (Harper)

First Flight Across the Polar Sea, The, Roald Amundsen and Lincoln Ellsworth (Hutchinson)

Friendly Arctic, The, Vilhjalmur Stefansson (Macmillan, New York)

Great North, The, Felice Bellotti (Andre Deutsch)

Handbook of Polar Discoveries, A. W. Greely (T. Fisher Unwin)

High Arctic, Mike Banks (J. M. Dent)

Journey from Prince of Wales's Fort in Hudson's Bay to the Northern Ocean, A, Samuel Hearne (Publications of the Champlain Society, Vol. 6, 1911)

Nansen the Explorer, Edward Shackleton (H. F. & G. Witherby)

North Pole, The, Robert E. Peary (Frederick A. Stokes)

North West Passage, The, Roald Amundsen (Archibald Constable)

Three Voyages of William Barents to the Arctic Regions, The, Gerrit de Veer, edited by Lt. Koolemans Beynen (the Hakluyt Society)

To the North! Jeannette Mirsky (Viking)

Two Against the Ice, Ejnar Mikkelsen (Rupert Hart-Davis)

Voyage of the Vega Round Asia and Europe, The, A. E. Nordenskjöld, translated by Alexander Leslie (Macmillan, London)

White Road, The, L. P. Kirwan (Hollis & Carter)

ANTARCTIC

Antarctica, Frank Debenham (John Murray)

Crossing of the Antarctic, The, Sir Vivian Fuchs and Sir Edmund Hillary (Cassell)

Endurance, Alfred Lansing (McGraw-Hill)

Handbook of Polar Discoveries, A. W. Greely (T. Fisher Unwin)

Little America, Richard E. Byrd (Putnam's)

Lonely South, The, André Migot (Rupert Hart-Davis)

Quest for a Continent, Walter Sullivan (Secker & Warburg)

Race for the Pole, John Edward Weems (Holt)

Scott's Last Expedition, Captain R. F. Scott (Smith Elder)

Shackleton, Margery and James Fisher (Barrie)

Siege of the South Pole, The, Hugh R. Mill (Frederick A. Stokes)

South, Sir Ernest Shackleton (Heinemann)

South of the Sun, Russell Owen (John Day)

Voyage of Discovery and Research in the Southern and Antarctic Regions, During the Years 1839–43, A, Sir James Clark Ross (J. Murray)

White Road, The, L. P. Kirwan (Hollis & Carter)

Work of the Byrd Antarctic Expedition 1928–1930, The, W. J. G. Joerg (the American Geographical Society)

Worst Journey in the World, The, Apsley Cherry-Garrard (Penguin)

SEA AND SHIPS

Ancient Voyages in the Pacific, Andrew Sharp (Pelican)

Age of Fighting Sail, The, C. S. Forester (Doubleday)

Balboa of Darien: Discoverer of the Pacific, K. Romoli (Doubleday)

Book of Old Ships, The, Henry B. Culver (Doubleday)

Exploring the Deep Pacific, Helen Raitt (Staples)

Golden Adventures of Balboa, Arthur Strawn (John Lane)

Golden Book of the Dutch Navigators, The, Hendrik Willem van Loon (Century)

Great Iron Ship, The, James Dugan (Hamish Hamilton)

Great Norwegian Expeditions, Richter and Ruser Larsen (Dreyers Forlag)

Half Mile Down, William Beebe (Harcourt Brace)

History of Marine Navigation, A, Per Collindet (Batsford)

In Balloon & Bathyscaphe, Auguste Piccard (Cassell)

Kon Tiki Expedition, The, Thor Heyerdahl (George Allen and Unwin)

Life and Voyages of Christopher Columbus, The, Washington Irving (Putnam's)

Magellan, Arthur Sturges Hildebrand (Harcourt, Brace)

Magellan's Voyage Around the World, Antonio Pigafetta, translated by James Alexander Robertson (A. H. Clark)

Man Explores the Sea, James Dugan (Pelican)

Modern Adventurers Under the Sea, Patrick Pringle (Harrap)

Sir Francis Drake, Christopher Lloyd (Faber and Faber)

Three Famous Voyages of Captain James Cook Round the World, The, James Cook (Everyman's Library)

Two Thousand Fathoms Down, Georges Houot and Pierre Willm (Hamish Hamilton and Rupert Hart-Davis)

Vikings, The, Johannes Brondsted (Pelican)

Vikings of the Sunrise, Peter H. Buck (Lippincott)

Vinland Voyages, The, Matthias Thördarson (the American Geographical Society Research Series No. 18)

Voyage Round the World, J. F. G. de la Pérouse (Lackington, Allen)

General index

Map index

The relief colouring for the back endpaper is explained by the key on page 142.

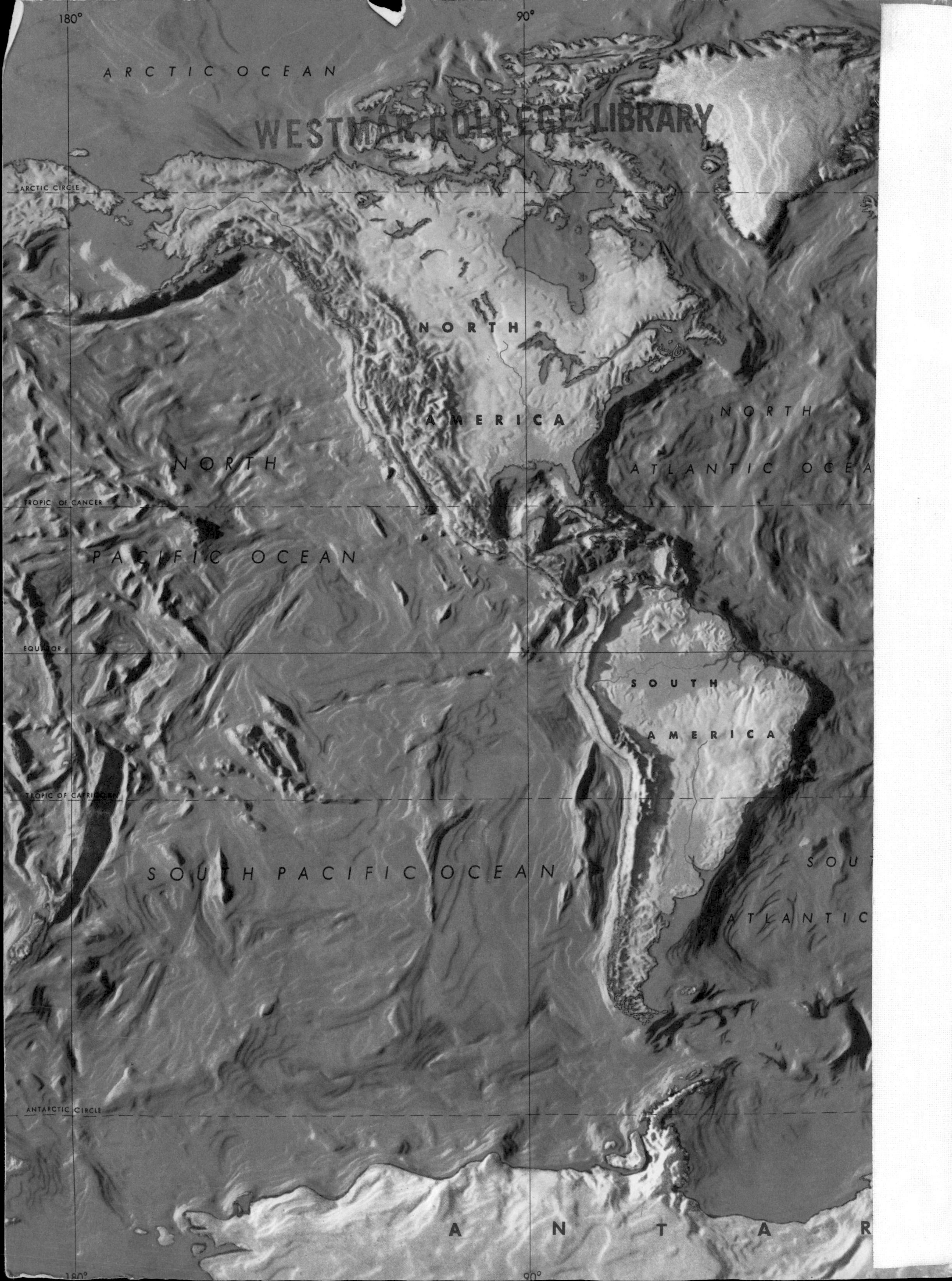
180°
90°
ARCTIC OCEAN
ARCTIC CIRCLE
NORTH AMERICA
NORTH
ATLANTIC OCEA
NORTH
PACIFIC OCEAN
TROPIC OF CANCER
EQUATOR
SOUTH AMERICA
TROPIC OF CAPRICORN
SOUTH PACIFIC OCEAN
SOUT
ATLANTIC
ANTARCTIC CIRCLE
ANTAR
180°
90°